The Politics of Progressive Education

The Politics of
Progressive Education

The Odenwaldschule in Nazi Germany

Dennis Shirley

Harvard University Press
Cambridge, Massachusetts   London, England   1992

Copyright © 1992 by the President and Fellows
   of Harvard College
All rights reserved
Printed in the United States of America
10 9 8 7 6 5 4 3 2 1

This book is printed on acid-free paper, and its binding
materials have been chosen for strength and durability.

Library of Congress Cataloging-in-Publication Data

Shirley, Dennis, 1955–
   The politics of progressive education: the Odenwaldschule in
Nazi Germany / Dennis Shirley.
      p.   cm.
   Includes bibliographical references and index.
   ISBN 0-674-68759-0
   1. Odenwaldschule—History.   2. Progressive education—
Germany—History.   3. Geheeb, Paul.   I. Title.
LF3195.02S54   1992
370'.943—dc20   91-25462
                                                        CIP

To my parents,
Margaret Jane and Edward Lynn Shirley

Contents

Part III: Consequences

Illustrations

Following page 133

1   Paul and Edith Geheeb, 1909.

2   Max Cassirer, October 1928.

3   Werner Meyer, 1930.

4   Heinrich Sachs and Paul Geheeb, 1930.

5   Paul Geheeb and *Kameraden* during a meeting of the *Wartekonferenz.*

6   Air bath exercises at the Odenwaldschule.

7   Storm troopers in the Odenwaldschule in March 1933.

8   Gender-segregated marches through the countryside.

9   The Gemeinschaft der Odenwaldschule prepares for sporting events in July 1935.

10   Paul Geheeb with students at the Ecole d'Humanité in the postwar period.

Figures 1–4, 7, and 10 are from the Ecole d'Humanité Archives.

Figures 5, 6, 8, and 9 are from the Odenwaldschule Archives.

Acknowledgments

My first thanks go to Natalie and Armin Lüthi-Peterson, the directors of the Ecole d'Humanité. They have unflaggingly supported my work in education with their friendship and counsel for more than a decade. Thanks are likewise due to Margot Schiller of the Ecole, who has taken on the immense task of organizing Paul and Edith Geheeb's literary materials, and Larry and Evi Matson, who graciously allowed me to turn their living room into my private office while I was working on the first drafts of the book at the Ecole. I would also like to thank Ruth Cohn, Sarah Hudspith, Alain Richard, and Frédéric and Fränzi Bächtold-Barth of the Ecole for their friendship and support during the many years I have been working on this project.

I am deeply indebted to Uta and Stephen Forstat of the Odenwaldschule for their hospitality and assistance during my many visits to Oberhambach. Without their constant engagement in my work it would have been impossible to progress so rapidly in my research. Dagny Wasmund, Henner Müller-Holz, and the former director of the Odenwaldschule, Gerold Becker, deserve my warmest thanks for the many lively and rewarding conversations which enriched my thinking about the history of the school.

I owe a special note of thanks to the alumni and former teachers of the Odenwaldschule who shared much of their lives with me in interviews and correspondence. Esra Steinitz, Elisabeth Sachs, Marina Jakimow, Walter Büchler, Theodor Scharmann, Henry Cassirer, and Martin Wagenschein told me about many of their experiences in the school, including those that were not pleasant to recall or easy to discuss.

I wish to thank Patricia Albjerg Graham, Joel Perlmann, and Richard Hunt for their many close readings of an early version of the manuscript. Wolfgang Edelstein, Jane and Reinhard Bendix, Heinz-Elmar Tenorth, Jürgen Helmchen, and Martin Näf all gave valuable comments on this work at different stages of its development.

I could never have written this book without financial support, and wish to acknowledge the generous funding I have received from the German Academic Exchange Service, the Chancellor's Fellowship of the Alexander von Humboldt Foundation, and the President's Fund at Rice University. I am particularly grateful for substantial publication subsidies from the Humboldt Foundation and Rice University.

I am also grateful to the following organizations, which kindly granted me permission to quote from or reproduce materials: Ecole d'Humanité Archives, for quotations from the correspondence of Paul and Edith Geheeb and others, and for photographs; Odenwaldschule Archives, for quotations and photographs; and Klett Verlag, for extensive quotations from Paul Geheeb's *Briefe*. The map was created by Raimund Zimmerman of the Historical Institute of the University of the Saarland.

Finally, my deepest thanks go to my wife, Shelley Cochran, whom I met a decade ago at the Ecole d'Humanité when we were both beginning teachers. Her continual readiness to read, edit, and discuss my writing has been a joy, and she has surrounded my work with an atmosphere of love and happiness.

The Politics of Progressive Education

Locations of the Ecole d'Humanité in Switzerland (1934–1946)

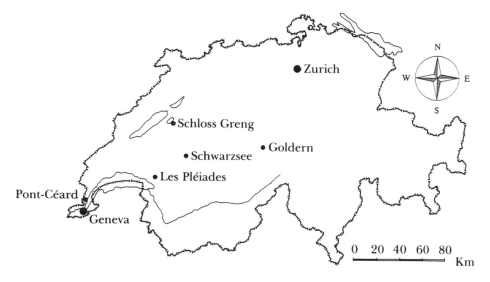

Introduction

In the late afternoon on 7 March 1933 a dozen Nazi storm troopers climbed into three cars in the small southwestern German village of Heppenheim. Armed with carbines and exhilarated by their party's recent electoral victory, the men drove through vineyards, apple orchards, farms, and pastures, toward a hilltop adorned with elegant houses that faced south toward Heidelberg. Their destination was a small boarding school called the "Odenwaldschule," which was viewed by unfriendly local observers as a "communist Jew school." The leader of the storm troopers, Werner Goerendt, who had been active in Nazi politics for five years, had suffered two brain concussions at the hands of left-wing opponents, and was eager to exact revenge on a highly visible and vulnerable scapegoat.

The Odenwaldschule was populated by close to two hundred teachers and students and was one of the crown jewels of the international progressive education movement in 1933. For twenty-three years its founder and director, Paul Geheeb, had labored to create a school community based on tolerance for people from different backgrounds with diverse perspectives. Before starting the Odenwaldschule in 1910, Geheeb had been active in the German women's movement, and he had translated his values into practice by making the Odenwaldschule the first fully coeducational boarding school in Germany. The school had almost been shut down by the government during the First World War because of Geheeb's pacifism and his refusal to celebrate patriotic events such as the Kaiser's birthday, but a timely intervention by a friendly archduke ensured its survival. In the 1920s the Odenwaldschule—with no grades, no grade levels, and a prevailing spirit and practice of freedom—prospered and became a mecca for school reformers from around the world.

The great prestige of the Odenwaldschule among liberal admirers only increased local Nazis' resentment of the school, and the Nazi seizure of power gave these locals a long-awaited chance to act. The storm troopers veered off the paved road, sped across the brook at the entrance to the Odenwaldschule, and drove up the curving hill to stop in front of the main building, Goethe Haus. The troopers jumped from their cars, drew their weapons, pointed them at students and teachers, and swiftly seized control of the main campus. Goerendt and five others burst into Paul Geheeb's office in Humboldt Haus, ransacked his possessions, and confiscated left-wing literature.

The storm troopers then ordered the entire student body and teaching faculty into the auditorium in Plato Haus. With Goerendt presiding, they demanded that those who supported communism identify themselves and turn over any political literature they possessed. Pale and speechless, Paul Geheeb sat with his students in the auditorium. When no one stepped forward, some of the storm troopers identified students they had seen agitating in the 5 March elections, searched their rooms, and indeed found a small number of communist brochures. The Nazis then ordered students to bring them all of the communist literature on campus. The students fanned out and brought back the books they thought the Nazis wanted. After a stay of more than two hours, the storm troopers departed, carrying off copies of Marx's *Capital,* travel books about Russia, literature on coeducation, chemistry books with suspiciously red covers, and a Sanskrit dictionary—which they mistook for Hebrew.

Emboldened by their successful search and their newfound powers, the storm troopers returned four days later with a company of fifty men. This time they beat up two Jewish teachers, arrested one of them, and undertook a comprehensive search of the school on their own. Students helped each other to hide or destroy literature they thought the Nazis would confiscate, and the school was filled with the sound of flushing toilets as potentially incriminating papers disappeared.

Appalled by the spontaneous nature of the Nazi raids and alarmed about the security of his students and teachers, Paul Geheeb subsequently began organizing public and surreptitious strategies to contest the escalating Nazi control of the school. He wrote letters to the press and to the government to protest the raids, and he urged foreign school reformers to direct letters to the German government asking it to protect the school. While publicly carrying out a campaign to preserve the Odenwaldschule, Geheeb also made plans to emigrate should the Nazis begin systematically to destroy the school.

This scenario—bold Nazi strikes designed to cow opponents and the bewildered response of frightened citizens—was enacted thousands of times in Germany in March 1933. The Nazis intervened in all aspects of civil society, from churches to unions to sports clubs to schools. Yet the developments in the Odenwaldschule were unique. When the Nazis seized power that March, they typically struck first at the groups they perceived as their major enemies: communists, social democrats, trade unionists, and Jews. The first raid on the Odenwaldschule happened *before* the Nazis in Hesse hit such obvious targets as the Hessian Social Democratic Party headquarters and the local offices of the Social Democratic newspaper, and even before they had fully secured power by taking control of the Hessian Ministry of the Interior or ousting the Social Democratic President of Hesse. Why did storm troopers attack a small progressive boarding school so early and with such vehemence? What kinds of reforms would they foist upon the school? How would the educators in that school, and the director, Paul Geheeb, respond to their incursions?[1]

This book is a description and analysis of Paul Geheeb's leadership of the Odenwaldschule in the period following the Nazi seizure of power. To understand the original purpose and character of the school, I first present highlights of Paul Geheeb's youth, survey his early pedagogical apprenticeships, and review his founding of the Odenwaldschule in 1910. I then trace the evolution of the school in the last years of the Second Empire and throughout the Weimar Republic, covering its major pedagogical principles, curricular innovations, and structural changes.

The Nazi seizure of power marked a major hiatus in the history of the Odenwaldschule. From March 1933 to March 1934—the first year of Nazi rule—Geheeb and his colleagues made decisions which set the course of their lives for the next twelve years. In this time Geheeb moved from an initial effort to establish a *modus vivendi* with the Nazis to opposition to their transformation of the Odenwaldschule. The Nazis took many of the Odenwaldschule's key features—student self-government, egalitarian relationships between the sexes, common participation in school events regardless of ethnic or religious background, an overarching ethos of reverence for life—and either destroyed or radically transformed them. By December 1933 Geheeb was convinced that any hope of carrying out truly humanistic education would be impossible under the Nazis. He issued letters to all of his faculty provisionally dismissing them from their work as of March 1934.

Yet the rush of events proved to be more complex than Geheeb had anticipated. Two of his closest colleagues, Heinrich Sachs and Werner

Meyer, felt that Geheeb's principled opposition to the Nazis was understandable, but that he had unwittingly abandoned the Odenwaldschule precisely when it most needed to be preserved. When Geheeb emigrated from Germany in March 1934, Sachs and Meyer reconstituted the school as the "Gemeinschaft der Odenwaldschule," going much further than Geheeb to accommodate Nazi reforms. Meanwhile, Geheeb continued his work in Switzerland and founded a new school, the "Ecole d'Humanité." Both schools were beset with constant crises, but in spite of the obstacles to their survival they persisted through the end of the Third Reich in 1945.

This volume describes and analyzes the conflict between Geheeb and the Nazis, the splintering of the Odenwaldschule in 1934, and the subsequent destinies of the Gemeinschaft der Odenwaldschule and the Ecole d'Humanité. Such a study is important for several reasons. First, there is the intrinsic human interest of the story itself, which appeals not only to the specialist in the history of education or Nazi Germany but also to the lay reader. Paul Geheeb's efforts to found a school based on progressive principles in the unlikely setting of Imperial Germany, the struggles and successes of the school in the Weimar Republic, the rapid Nazi transformation of the Odenwaldschule, Geheeb's odyssey through five Swiss cantons in twelve years, the development of the Ecole d'Humanité as a haven for refugee children, and finally Geheeb's emotional conflict with Sachs after the war—all of this makes for compelling and dramatic history, full of unexpected developments and friction between ethical norms, personal decision making, and political power.

Second, a study of Geheeb and the Odenwaldschule enables us to answer many historical and pedagogical questions of enduring interest. In what way was the Odenwaldschule a part of the international "progressive education" or "new education" movement, and how did it relate to the indigenous German analogue known as "reform pedagogy?" How did the Nazis organize their educational policies in relation to the Odenwaldschule, and in what manner did Paul Geheeb respond to their interventions? To what degree was Geheeb's opposition to the Nazi reforms purely defensive and a matter of preserving the school's autonomy, and to what extent was he motivated by political and ethical objections? Can one generalize about other schools on the basis of a case study of Paul Geheeb and the Odenwaldschule?

This volume will play a role in strengthening an emergent approach to education in the Nazi period. Until recently, two paradigms dominated the history of education in the Third Reich. The first was based on top-down analyses of Nazi reforms and examined the kinds of pedagogical, curricular, and structural changes the Nazis made in schools. Historians assembled anthologies of Nazi decrees, interpreted Nazi school curricula, and examined the most ferociously pro-Nazi schools. The historical landscape was more or less vacant, however, when it came to exploring the *subjective responses* of educators to Nazi reforms. Were German teachers, on the whole, passionately pro-Nazi, apathetic, or critical of the regime? Were certain groups of teachers—for example, elementary, secondary, or university-level faculty—more susceptible to Nazism than others? How did religion, ethnicity, class, and gender influence loyalty or nonconformity? By not asking such questions, historians flattened out the diversity of the German population, and the manner in which individuals and groups either expedited or impeded Nazi reforms went untouched.[2]

The second paradigm focused more on intellectual history. Several monographs described the theories of reactionary intellectuals from the Second Empire or Weimar Republic, and attempted to show how they created an atmosphere conducive to the rise of national socialism. Others examined Nazi theorists of education, and tried to show their affinities to or their ruptures with other German intellectual traditions. Just as with the first paradigm, however, works in this approach generally evaded questions pertaining to popular receptions of either pre-Nazi reactionary thinkers or Nazi theorists of education. It was left to speculation as to how much weight could credibly be placed on such theoretical influences.[3]

Although both of these paradigms had problematic aspects—particularly related to agency and the subjective motivations of educators in the Third Reich—they accomplished a great deal in clarifying our understanding of intellectual antecedents of Nazism and the exact Nazi strategy for transforming schools to saturate them with a pro-Nazi spirit. The studies of Nazi school reform opened up interesting issues touching on the internal divisions of Nazism that made the regime more "polycratic" than "totalitarian" in nature, whatever the aspirations and boasts of the Nazi Party. By demarcating the increasingly virulent Nazi interventions in schools during the Third Reich, such analyses mapped out the manner in which the regime sought to penetrate and appropriate German schools for its own purposes. By investigating the intellectual precursors of national socialism and explicitly National Socialist theorists of education, scholars identified prevailing themes in the cultural climate of Germany in the first third of the century and their appropriation by official ideologists in the

Nazi regime. Yet it is striking that neither paradigm addresses that which is essential from the point of view of social history—namely, how educators *responded* to Nazi reforms at the moment when the reforms were imposed on their particular schools. Only since the mid-1980s have we begun to investigate the residual agency possessed by teachers in the Third Reich, and to ask which factors led them to support, disengage from, or oppose the regime.

The approach to this book did not develop in a vacuum. I have profited from the work of a small group of historians—Martin Broszat, Ian Kershaw, and Detlev Peukert—who have explored differentiated approaches to Nazi society which gauged the exact boundaries of popular enthusiasm for, apathy toward, and criticism of the Nazi regime. By transforming our approach to German society in the Third Reich to move beyond strict dichotomies of either unconditional support for national socialism or adamant resistance, these historians have enabled us to explore the vast intermediate terrain of conformism, resignation, dissent, intermittent refusals, and systematic forms of opposition which never developed into explicitly political challenges to the Nazi state. They have further enabled us to see the way in which individuals could be supportive of some aspects of the Nazi regime—such as the economic reforms which benefited the middle class or the recovery of the Saar in the prewar years—but critical of others, such as Nazi support for euthanasia or the conduct of German foreign policy during the Second World War.[4]

In the history of education in particular, an explosion of studies in recent years has analyzed the nature of popular responses to Nazi school policies. Case studies of individual teachers, schools in urban centers such as Berlin and Hamburg, rural schools, Catholic schools, and émigré reform pedagogical schools, show that the popular reaction was more contingent on specific policies and uneven in its overall development than one might suspect. Yet even in these studies one often misses a sense of the exact incidents and interpretations which led educators to shift from accommodationism to opposition.[5]

This study is based on the conviction that one of the most important things we can learn from the Nazi era involves questions pertaining to the way in which popular acceptance of fascist regimes—which is not identical with approval—is either won or lost. By placing the emphasis on the intentional and incremental character of Paul Geheeb's development from compliance to opposition, one can discover the manner in which the new Nazi school reforms—pedagogical, curricular, and political—catalyzed Geheeb's alienation from the regime, his determination to close the Odenwaldschule, and his decision to leave Germany. Such a minutely investigated case study—the most comprehensive to date of one school director's response to Nazi changes in education in his school—can then allow us to ask broader questions about education and national socialism. One upshot of the inquiry, for example, will be to contribute to current debates on the degree to which German reform educators either supported or opposed Nazi interventions in education.

Paul Geheeb is generally recognized as one of the best German practitioners and representatives of "new education," a romantic movement in education which swept Western Europe and the United States in the last decade of the nineteenth and the first third of the twentieth century. The new school movement, which was developed with different emphases as "progressive education" in the United States and England, *"education nouvelle"* in France, and "reform pedagogy" in Germany, introduced bold reforms which continue to provoke controversy today. Those reforms included far-reaching student self-government, flexible curricula programs, hands-on approaches to learning, and a deemphasis on competition and rivalry between students as expressed in grades and awards. The "new education" movement in general has received much attention by historians, yet most studies have been curiously parochial and have only focused on researchers' home countries. As a result, even those readers of English who are well versed in the history of American progressive education are unlikely to have heard of Paul Geheeb and the Odenwaldschule, let alone to have pondered the consequences of Nazi reforms in the school during the Third Reich.[6]

Oddly enough, the situation has hardly been better for readers of German. While such readers could gain access to a biography of Geheeb and a history of the Odenwaldschule, these studies told us almost nothing about Paul Geheeb's exact motivations in contesting the Nazi transformation of his school. There are a number of reasons for this. First, the only histories of Paul Geheeb and the Odenwaldschule were compiled by Walter Schäfer, who was a director of the school in the 1960s. Schäfer's work was largely uncritical of Geheeb and the school's past, and he may have been hesitant to probe too deeply into the Nazi period for fear of evoking controversy among the alumni. Second, most of the primary documents for this book are stored in Paul Geheeb's old office at the Ecole d'Humanité, and at the time I conducted my research the material was largely unorganized. Until her death in April 1982, Edith Geheeb exercised a discretionary control over the primary documents. Since then the Ecole's directors have handled the material, and their ties to Paul and Edith Geheeb

have led them to maintain strict control over access to the primary
documents. In fact, it is highly unlikely that I would have had access
to the papers upon which the book is based had I not been a teacher
at the Ecole from 1980 to 1983.

The primary documents at the Ecole d'Humanité throw a tremendous new light on Geheeb's opposition to Nazi school reform in the
Odenwaldschule, and I was thrilled to find papers which explain incidents hitherto oblique or altogether unknown to historians. These
include the precise minutes of Geheeb's combative faculty meetings
with Nazi teachers in the Odenwaldschule in the autumn of 1933;
Geheeb's fine, penciled notes, which he passed to his deaf friend
Adolphe Ferrière as part of their "conversations" during Geheeb's visits to Switzerland in 1933 and 1934; and Geheeb's exhaustive correspondence to family members, government officials, and educational
colleagues. From these papers, with the selective incorporation of
documents from primarily German public archives, I was able to
reconstruct in detail the exact kinds of deliberations, confusions, and
arguments Geheeb encountered as he desperately fought against Nazi
reforms.

This volume aspires to be neither a biography of Paul Geheeb nor
a history of the Odenwaldschule, although it contains elements of
both. It is, rather, an effort to use the first year of crisis following the
Nazi seizure of power as a medium for investigating Geheeb's
responses to Nazi incursions in the Odenwaldschule. To enhance the
intelligibility of those responses I have drawn freely upon Geheeb's
biography, the institutional history of the Odenwaldschule, and the
social history of German education. I have also explored the complex
and unresolved consequences of Geheeb's decisions, to show that
decisions made in 1933 have had a lasting impact on the school and
its alumni—an impact which continues today.

Although I intend for this book to have sufficient intellectual rigor
to make for a compelling narrative and a solid contribution to history,
on the deepest level I have written it to repay a debt. I loved teaching
at the Ecole d'Humanité, and found the humanistic, individualized
approach to education practiced there to be a refreshing corrective to
my own schooling. I was distressed to find, however, that little work
had been done on the history of the Ecole. The school was in danger
of losing a sense of its origins.

This deficiency became particularly poignant in the fall of 1981,
when a small cluster of students, expressing their enthusiasm for
punk music, began sporting swastikas on their coats and scrawling
them on the school's walls. In any school the presence of swastikas

could and should create problems; in a school founded by anti-Nazi émigrés it was impossible to belittle or ignore such symbols. As part of a concerned group of teachers and students, I met with Edith Geheeb—who was then ninety-six years old—and listened to her talk about the complex origins and the intense personal drama which lay behind the founding of the Ecole. As twilight settled over the northern flank of the Alps, Edith dazzled us with her smooth blend of German and English and her incisive memory. She moved easily from anecdote to explanation to further illuminating anecdotes, unraveling the circumstances and decisions which led her to migrate with her husband out of Germany almost a half a century earlier. Eventually our group prepared an evening assembly on the meaning of the swastika, and we recapitulated what Edith had told us to the assembled students and teachers of the school. The swastikas disappeared—not because we ordered students to remove them but because the students were moved by Edith's experience and understood that swastikas carried more meaning than the simple shock value they had ascribed to them. The following April Edith passed away, and a major chapter in the history of the Ecole closed.

After Edith's death I resolved to write the history of the transition from the Odenwaldschule to the Ecole d'Humanité. The research has been richly rewarding, and not only on an intellectual level. Through studying the Geheebs' educational work, I have been exposed to and appropriated the basis of what I hold to be the most enduring merits of their practice of education for my own work as an educator. If I have achieved my goal in this book, the reader will encounter a pedagogical *Weltanschauung* through Paul Geheeb that resonates with a subtle but profound balance of individual self-realization, tolerance for others' differences, and a humanistically construed practice of social responsibility. To contribute to that project, and to ensure its continuity, has been the largest motivating force and raison d'être of the book at hand.

_____ part I

Origins

chapter 1

Paul Geheeb's Youth and Educational Apprenticeships, 1870–1909

Few towns in Germany in 1870 were more idyllic than tiny Geisa, located in the heart of the Second Empire and home to some fifteen hundred souls. A traveler to Geisa in the year of German unification would have found an intimate community of well-tempered citizens living in neat and simple houses, comfortably acclimated to the surrounding countryside of lush meadows and the undulating green mountains of the Rhön valley. The spires of the Catholic and Protestant churches dominated the city's architecture, and a spacious synagogue accommodated the religious needs of Geisa's unusually large Jewish population. An open market stood in the center of town, and customers easily wandered from its vegetable and fruit stands to the village apothecary, owned and managed by Adalbert and Adolphine Geheeb.

Into this harmonious setting Paul Geheeb was born on 10 October 1870. Paul's family was ancient stock in Geisa; his great-grandfather had been a deacon in the Protestant church, and his grandfather had begun the apothecary in 1845 and managed it until it was destroyed by a fire in 1858. Paul's grandfather died in 1859, but his grandmother was determined that their only son, Adalbert, resume her husband's trade. Through unceasing labor, Minna Geheeb made sure that the apothecary was slowly rebuilt and stocked with all of the medicines necessary to revitalize the family business. Had she consulted Adalbert, however, she might have spared herself the effort. Adalbert's father had taught him both the Latin and German names of all of the plants in the Rhön by the time Adalbert was fourteen years old. Under his father's tutelage, Adalbert developed a wealth of knowledge about botany in general and a passion for the study of moss in particular. First as an adolescent and later as an adult, Adalbert often left Geisa for long excursions through the Rhön to gather moss, study its properties, and publish his findings in scientific journals. Given his interests in research, Adalbert found his daily work in the apothecary to be a burden rather than a joy. To enable her husband to carry on his research, Adolphine became proficient in managing the apothecary and adept at filling even the most complex prescriptions.

Paul was the second son born to Adalbert and Adolphine, and his birth was followed by that of two brothers and a younger sister. Adalbert and Adolphine were dedicated parents. Adalbert inculcated a love of nature in his children; Paul was only eight years old when he signed one of his first Christmas thank-you letters to his grandfather with the sobriquet "Paul Geheeb, natural scientist." Paul's mother, Adolphine, on the other hand, loved great literature, and she shared her enthusiasm for the writings of Johann Wolfgang Goethe and Wilhelm von Humboldt with her son. In his boyhood, Paul idealized her as a "noble, divine being" who possessed "unusual spiritual and emotional depth." Weekly chamber concerts at the Geheebs', in which the Catholic priest, the Protestant minister and the rabbi of Geisa visited to play music with Paul's parents, increased the cultured atmosphere of the home and instilled in the children an early appreciation of different religions.[1]

Paul Geheeb's childhood was blessed by his mother's enthusiasm for poetry and art, his father's tutoring in botany, his untroubled relationship with his siblings, and the family's frequent outings into the splendid forests surrounding Geisa. "Nowhere were we so happy," he enthused, "as when we could go to the woods and see the birds, rabbits, deer, and foxes, and marvel at the splendor of the flowers, the foliage, and the trees."[2]

When he was twelve years old, Paul moved to the nearby city of Fulda to live with his grandparents on his mother's side and to study at the *Gymnasium*. While he was in Fulda the peaceful life he had known at Geisa disintegrated. His younger sister, Anna, learned that her father was pursuing a romantic liaison with Emmy Bélart, an old friend of Adalbert's who had often accompanied the family on their excursions. Adalbert became increasingly brazen about his adultery, and indulged his passions at home even when Adolphine and the children were in other rooms. Adolphine was bitterly disappointed with her husband, and found herself battling not only to keep the household intact and the apothecary functioning but also against increasingly painful physical ailments. When she sought treatment for her discomfort, she learned that she was suffering from cancer of the abdomen. After a long period of protracted pain she died on 15 November 1884.

Paul Geheeb was fourteen years old when the news of his mother's death arrived in Fulda. He experienced her death as "the greatest catastrophe of my life," and almost two years later wrote to his maternal grandmother,

> Unfortunately you can't imagine what shadows, what a curse 15 November 1884 has thrown over me and my entire life. It has robbed me forever of the possibility to feel at peace and happy, and the pain, which one had hoped time would heal, only grows greater.

Paul abandoned his early fascination with botany, which he associated with his father, and became increasingly preoccupied with theology and ethics. In particular, he turned to Christ's life and preachings for support, which gave him an "irrepressible drive to help people." Yet his depression persisted in spite of his new religious interests.[3]

Adalbert Geheeb was unabashed in his indifference to Adolphine's death. He began plans for his marriage to Emmy just two weeks after Adolphine passed away, and the two were married five months later. Adolphine's side of the family bitterly reproached Adalbert for his liaison with Emmy, and Paul heard all of their criticisms while staying with them in Fulda. Although Paul had loved his mother dearly, he did not hold his father's rapid remarriage against him, and wrote to his grandmother, "I can never agree that this was an immoral act." To weaken the influence of Adolphine's family on Paul, Adalbert moved him out of his maternal grandmother's home in August 1886. Paul moved to a guest house in Eisenach, to study at his father's alma mater, the local *Gymnasium*. He graduated with the *Abitur* diploma in the spring of 1889.[4]

Paul Geheeb then served a year of compulsory military service in Giessen, where he "was surrounded by brutality and cruelty," and "completely lost the ability to think of anything with any depth." To mitigate the stupefying effects of his army service he joined a fraternal organization called the *Allgemeiner Deutscher Burschenbund*. Paul enjoyed the collegiality of the *Burschenbund*, but it failed to satisfy his deeper yearnings. As soon as Paul finished his term of duty, he moved to Berlin to enter university studies in the fall of 1890. He was thrilled with the stimulation and diversity of German's capital city. "To be able to study there is an indescribable joy," he wrote. "Perhaps I will stay there permanently."[5]

The excitement of Berlin led Paul to break off his association with the *Burschenbund,* which had helped him while in the army but now appeared to him to be a pleasant but ultimately meaningless exercise in group conformity. Complaining that the group "lacks any absolute (that is, ethical) value" he insisted that "I am, however, accustomed to judge everything according to its ethical meaning." Using that criterion, Geheeb found that the *Burschenbund* had little to say, for it was primarily committed to taking care of its own; it was "simply its own purpose." While Geheeb was not able to explain precisely which measure he used to gauge "ethical meaning" at this point, he made it clear that he was in search of a tenable foundation for morality which would help him to direct the course of his everyday life. Maintaining his membership in the *Burschenbund,* he felt, would only distract him from this higher purpose.[6]

Rather than immerse himself in his course work, Paul Geheeb turned to the tumult of Berlin as an important part of his education. He discovered a metropolis filled by the most diverse kinds of political and cultural reformers, all endeavoring in one way or another to respond to the complex mixture of industrialization and modernization which animated German society in the 1890s. He attended rallies held by the Social Democrats, heard lectures given by feminist leaders, participated in temperance society meetings, and learned of religious reformers' efforts to combine Christianity with socialism. He explored the full spectrum of left-wing politics, found himself in sympathy with many of the reformers' goals, and decided to play a role himself in creating social change.

Of all of the social movements which enlivened German society in the 1890s, Paul Geheeb found himself most committed to feminism. The women's movement was quite small at the time, but perhaps because of his mother's experience, Geheeb was responsive to feminists' criticisms of the sexual double standard, their insistence on improved working conditions for women, and their demand for the franchise. On his own initiative, Geheeb began reading journals and literature addressing the topic of women's emancipation, including Margaret Fuller's *Woman in the Nineteenth Century* and August Bebel's *Woman and Socialism.* He was particularly impressed by Minna Cauer, one of the leaders of the radical wing of the German women's movement, and following one of her public addresses he wrote her to express his enthusiasm for her ideas. Frau Cauer responded appreciatively, and Geheeb soon was helping her with her political agitation on an almost daily basis.[7]

Minna Cauer quickly educated Geheeb about the major issues facing the women's movement, and she also enabled him to win an insid-

er's view of political activism in Berlin. The two heard the Social Democratic leader August Bebel on many occasions, and Geheeb was
impressed with Bebel's enthusiastic following among the working
class. Among middle class reformers, Cauer and Geheeb befriended
Moritz von Egidy, a former army officer who had undergone a religious conversion, become a pacifist, and sought to apply Christian
ethics to social problems. Geheeb also provided supportive work for
temperance associations, the Society for Ethical Culture, the Union
for Opposition to Anti-Semitism, and progressive student unions.[8]

The friendship with Minna Cauer was crucial for Paul Geheeb in
many respects. She not only inspired him through her political activism, but she also enabled him to regain his psychological equilibrium
for the first time since his mother's death. Cauer was twenty-nine
years older than Geheeb, and he found in her a mother figure. He
wrote to her,

> Consider that I once lived in a completely intimate and wonderful rela-
> tionship with my mother. Everyone thought I was her favorite child and
> believed we were inseparable. That I should continue to live when she
> was no more—I couldn't even consider this possibility.
>
> And then, really, I didn't "live" any more after my mother died. Slowly
> I dragged myself through the years, with death my only thought . . .
> Then came a happier period, which indeed was often rich with joys. But
> my being was always driven by a dissatisfied confusion and quest for a
> happiness I once had. I felt myself pulled first toward this woman and
> then toward that one, but none of them reached that ideal woman which
> my soul envisioned, and therefore each joy brought bitter disappoint-
> ment. Thus I stumbled for seven years.
>
> In *you* I have finally found peace.
>
> What I sensed in the first hour that I came to know you has been
> confirmed ever since on a daily basis: that *you* are the mother for whom
> I have searched for years, often filled with confused pain, and always
> with deepest longing.
>
> What I am saying to you here I ask you please not to take as a hallu-
> cination but as that which it is—as a summary of the history of my inner
> life! Then you will see, then you must see, how endlessly happy you
> make me.

The transference from his own mother to Frau Cauer was so strong
that Paul soon opened his many letters to her with "My dear mother"
as the salutation.[9]

In spite of Geheeb's fondness for Minna Cauer and Berlin, he left
the capital city in the summer of 1892 to continue his academic studies at the University of Jena. At Jena, he would be able to maintain

more regular contact with his family and particularly with his younger sister Anna, who suffered greatly under her new stepmother. Jena also was the contemporary center of liberal theology in Germany and as such offered a promising location for Geheeb's religious studies. Finally, Jena was closer to nature, which provided Geheeb with solace and rejuvenation.[10]

Geheeb's move to Jena proved to be of major importance to him in awakening his interest in education. A religious studies and philosophy seminar taught by Richard Adalbert Lipsius, a prominent theologian, sparked Geheeb's interest. As part of Lipsius's organization of the seminar, each student had to prepare a presentation on one of the philosophers covered in the syllabus. Lipsius assigned Geheeb the responsibility of covering Hegel, and Geheeb worked on assembling his commentary with a fellow student named Hermann Lietz, who had the task of presenting Fichte. Although Geheeb enjoyed his study of Hegel, his reading of Fichte was a powerful revelation, which opened him to the specifically pedagogical dimension of classical German idealism and awakened his interest in contemporary school reform.[11]

The key text which captured Geheeb's imagination was Fichte's *Addresses to the German Nation.* Delivered in 1807 and 1808 when Berlin was occupied by Napoleon's troops, Fichte's lectures linked a voluntaristic social philosophy to the challenge of reconstruction in a Germany united and freed from French tutelage. Fichte had been impressed by the work of Heinrich Pestalozzi in Switzerland, who had established rural boarding schools for poor children and attempted to develop a theory and practice of teaching which focused more on the development of the child's entire personality than upon the acquisition of information. Referring to Pestalozzi's example, Fichte appealed to Germans to establish thousands of similar schools in which young people could learn to integrate their own needs with those of their communities and to fight for moral principles. Fichte attacked what he saw as the corrupting aspects of the metropolis and the constricting influences of the family, and he shared the nature romanticism which Pestalozzi had acquired from his own mentor, Jean-Jacques Rousseau. Fichte argued that it was imperative for young people to grow up in close contact with the land, to remove themselves from the narcissistic aspects of commercial society, and to develop idealistic attitudes which would uplift not only Germany but all of Europe to the highest levels of moral conduct. In a passage which Geheeb would later cite as an inspiration for his own work,

Fichte insisted that single-sex schools were unhealthy and that boarding schools should be fully coeducational.

Fichte's program for educational reform was in many ways vague and self-contradictory. His *Addresses* were more of a philosophical tract than a concrete agenda for school reform, and many passages in them were shrouded in the nebulous language of German idealism, which allowed for many different and mutually exclusive readings of Fichte's major concerns. These ambiguities were later to have fateful consequences for Geheeb's educational work and his cooperation with Lietz. Regardless of these problems, however, Fichte's enthusiastic description of rural boarding schools inculcating children with robust idealism and attending to all facets of their personal development greatly impressed Geheeb. The fact that Fichte had taught at the University of Jena must have heightened Geheeb's receptivity to his message.[12]

With Fichte as the point of entry, Geheeb began exploring the philosophical and pedagogical conceptions of a whole range of German idealists. He immersed himself in the writings of Immanuel Kant, Friedrich Schiller, Wilhelm von Humboldt, and Johann Wolfgang Goethe, studying their writings on the nature and purposes of a broadly defined humanistic education. Geheeb was particularly struck by the philosophy of education transmitted by Goethe in a twin set of novels, *Wilhelm Meisters Lehrjahre* and the more ambitious and enigmatic *Wilhelm Meisters Wanderjahre*. Both books together form a comprehensive *Bildungsroman*, or educational novel, in which Goethe described the complex development of an individual who appropriated, discarded, and synthesized different parts of his experience as he gradually matured and realized the deepest levels of his personality.

In one famous passage of the *Wanderjahre*, Wilhelm Meister encountered a "pedagogical province" set in a beautiful and isolated rural setting. Basing his description on an actual school founded by a disciple of Pestalozzi in Switzerland, Goethe envisioned the pedagogical province as a community where the boundaries between school, work, and art collapsed and were transformed into a harmonious educational utopia. The province inculcated each child with reverence for the diverse forms of life and a sense for the significance of his own position in the ongoing development and prosperity of his community. Through an ethic of care and a comprehensive education which attended to children's affective as well as cognitive needs, educators in the province enabled individual development and social responsibilities to reach a complementary synthesis in which the tensions between the two were brought into a rich spiritual harmony.[13]

Geheeb was greatly taken by Goethe's depiction of the pedagogical province and the philosophy of education which stood behind *Wilhelm Meister*. Through his studies of the German idealists, and of Fichte and Goethe in particular, Geheeb discovered the power and resilience of the concept of *Bildung*, one of the cornerstones of the idealist legacy. A notoriously ambiguous term, *Bildung* was used by late eighteenth- and early nineteenth-century idealists to denote a whole range of capabilities and attitudes. It conveyed at once a prestigous social standing, the possession of the *Abitur* won at the end of studies in the *Gymnasium*, familiarity with the culture of antiquity, and a romantic idealization of individual self-realization. In Geheeb's reading, this latter definition was the most important, and in his hands *Bildung* became a means of validating the rights of the individual over and against the demands of an artificially constructed modern society. Idealistic by inclination, Geheeb set Fichte's boarding schools and Goethe's pedagogical province against the German schools of his day, and found the latter sorely wanting.[14]

On the one hand, Geheeb's emergent criticism of German public schools was misplaced. Throughout the nineteenth century, many educators considered Germany to have the finest public school system of any country in the world. Germany passed some of the earliest compulsory education laws in the West, and secondary school and university reforms implemented by Wilhelm von Humboldt during his tenure as Minister of Education in Prussia created a rigorous academic curriculum which emphasized the learning of ancient languages and history. Nineteenth-century German schools became sites of pilgrimage by foreign school reformers, who marveled at classes with clear and sequential instruction, professionally trained teachers with thorough competence in their subject areas, and diligent, obedient students. The high standards set by the schools, and the state's willingness to invest in superlative teacher education programs, were credited by many with creating the scientific and technical expertise that fueled Germany's economic take-off in the last quarter of the century.[15]

Yet Paul Geheeb was scarcely alone in finding fault with German education in the 1890s, in spite of the system's achievements. On the contrary, the schools were under constant attack at this time. Educational modernizers wanted to drop the emphasis on ancient languages and history from the *Gymnasium* curriculum and instead emphasize modern languages, the sciences, and mathematics; feminists demanded the end to prohibitions on women entering the universities, and called for higher-quality instruction and curricula in girls' schools; iconoclastic cultural critics such as Friedrich Nietzsche, Paul de Lagarde, and Julius Langbehn claimed that the school system was destroying individual creativity for the sake of a spiritually impoverished utilitarianism; and Social Democrats argued that the organization of schools was rigged to serve the interests of the most conservative sectors of the bourgeoisie and the aristocracy.[16]

Paul Geheeb's reflections on education were stimulated by these varied criticisms of German schooling, but they did not provide the point of departure for his increasing commitment to education. According to Geheeb, it was while Lietz and he were attending Lipsius's seminar in 1892 and encountering the pedagogical theories of German idealists in general and Fichte in particular that the two young men decided to start experimental schools. The practical obstacles to their project were formidable, but Lietz and Geheeb were both young and there was a lively agitation in Germany for bold new kinds of schools. The likelihood that state ministries of education would not share their educational ideals did not deflect Lietz or Geheeb, for the boom in German industrial development created a middle-class constituency with sufficient disposable income to support a private boarding school with innovative structures. Yet the path to the implementation of a new school could not be direct. Before any kind of a school could be started, Lietz and Geheeb would have to complete their academic work and acquire practical teaching experience.[17]

In the spring of 1893 Paul Geheeb received his first degree, in theology, and he subsequently gave a sermon at the Schillerkirche in Jena. In his sermon, Geheeb repudiated literal readings of Christ's healing of the diseased and in the process offended much of the congregation. The sermon was the first and only one that he gave in his life and appears to have closed off whatever tendencies he may have had for pursuing a career in the clergy.

In May 1893 Geheeb began working as a teacher at an experimental private school for children with nervous ailments. The school was directed by Johannes Trüper and was located at Sophienhöhe on the outskirts of Jena. After a brief internship there he joined Hermann Lietz on the faculty of the Laboratory School at the University of Jena. Under the leadership of Wilhelm Rein, a prominent philosopher of education, the Laboratory School at Jena was one of the most daring pedagogical institutions in Germany in the 1890s. Rein encouraged his student teachers to develop close personal relationships with their students rather than the distant and authoritarian ties which were predominant at the time, and he sought to develop the learner's whole personality rather than to emphasize strictly cognitive study. As part of an effort to use a variety of pedagogical styles and curricular resources to teach young people, student teachers in the Laboratory School took their pupils on hikes, worked in gardens with them, and brought them to concerts. The students came from working-class neighborhoods and appear to have been tremendously receptive to the spirit and practice of the school.[18]

As the Laboratory School became justly famous as one of the most innovative schools in Europe, it attracted a number of international visitors who were interested in appropriating elements of its pedagogical style. In 1893 a British educator, Cecil Reddie, observed some of its classes and quickly struck up a friendship with Lietz. Lietz learned that Reddie was the director of a new school in Britain called "Abbotsholme," which was experimenting with innovations similar to those used in the Laboratory School. After Reddie returned to Britain, he wrote to Rein to ask him to recommend teachers for Abbotsholme, and Rein recommended Lietz for a position. Soon thereafter Lietz was heading to Derbyshire in the Midlands to work at Abbotsholme for one year.

Lietz's internship at Abbotsholme was to have far-reaching consequences. Like the Laboratory School in Jena, Abbotsholme was a bold innovation in school reform for its time, and it became the prototype for a movement of over seventy similar schools throughout Europe and the United States in the first third of the twentieth century. Reddie led Abbotsholme with the goal of appropriating all that was best in a traditional British public school—that is, a private, all-male boarding school—while discarding its many petty cruelties, its prudery, and its separation of curriculum content from the life of the child. Stimulated by Rein's work at Jena, yet an independent educator in his own right, Reddie aimed to reconstruct education with new practices which prefigured much that was to blossom later in the progressive education movement. In the place of rote memorization, Reddie encouraged learning by doing; in the place of Victorian circumspection, he frankly educated young boys about sex; in the place of the traditional school curriculum which fragmented knowledge into different disciplines, Reddie strove to develop the latent interdependence of all forms of inquiry and explanation. He constantly took his pupils out of the classroom and engaged them in hands-on projects involving carpentry, masonry, gardening, and animal husbandry. Topping off the heady atmosphere was Reddie's charismatic and even demagogic joy in berating the narrowness of much traditional education and in trumpeting the dawning of a new age in school reform.[19]

Lietz was thrilled with the innovations at Abbotsholme and soon became intimate friends with Reddie. The two were natural allies. Not only did they share similar interests in pedagogy, but Reddie had taken a doctorate in chemistry at the University of Göttingen and was fluent in German. His studies had focused on the natural sciences, but he had also read philosophy, and coincidentally, had been impressed with Fichte. According to Geheeb, "One can say that Lietz first met with the realization of Fichte's pedagogy in England. And that made a tremendous impression on him."[20]

With Reddie's support, Lietz determined to lay the groundwork for "new schools"—which were understood to be private boarding schools with the innovative pedagogies practiced in Abbotsholme—in Germany. Lietz wrote a narrative of his experiences and mailed the drafts of his manuscript to Geheeb, who edited it for publication. According to Lietz, pathbreaking schools similar to Abbotsholme were needed in his homeland to provide models of change for the public school system, and he planned to start them. By 1898 Lietz had accumulated sufficient capital from philanthropists to open his first school at a small estate called "Pulvermühle" near Ilsenburg in the Harz mountains of Saxony. Lietz called the school a *"Landerziehungsheim"*—an ugly neologism which translates literally as a "country educational home." In spite of its awkward title, Lietz's dedication and the impressive energy he devoted to his pupils helped the new school rapidly acquire more applicants than it could house. To accommodate additional students, Lietz opened a second school in 1901 at Haubinda near Hildburghausen in Thuringia, and by 1902 over 150 students were attending his schools.[21]

Lietz's *Landerziehungsheime* were heavily indebted to his prior experience in the Laboratory School and Abbotsholme. Lietz encouraged his students to undertake a wide range of activities in nature, to devote themselves to the social skills acquired by working with their peers on group projects, and to make a continual effort to integrate intellectual and applied kinds of knowledge. Whereas German public school teachers maintained only formal relationships with their students, Lietz took his students on bike trips and hikes with him as part of an effort to experience closeness through joint efforts; whereas public school teachers tended to stress the acquisition of facts, Lietz emphasized the social character of learning and the importance of forging connections between school knowledge and life in a community. Students worked in gardens, built walls, built houses, and tended animals—not as extracurricular activities, but as the heart of the school's curriculum. Following Reddie's example, Lietz unapologetically dominated his schools with his frenetic idealism, relentless companionship with young people, unquestioning self-sacrifice, and an unwavering, almost megalomaniacal conviction of his growing importance as the initiator of a successful school reform.

While Lietz was successfully starting his first *Landerziehungsheime*, Geheeb was continuing his university studies, stopping only when he had a full twenty semesters behind him. He never received a doctorate, electing to give the 300 marks he needed to cover the costs for his exams to a recovering alcoholic with a large family, whom he assisted as part of his work in the temperance movement. He did write a thesis on "Spinoza's Concept of God and Its Influence on the Thinkers of the Classical Period" to enable him to teach at the *Gymnasium*. Although no evidence can be found that Geheeb placed much emphasis on the thesis, the title alone suggests his interest in the pantheistic humanism espoused by Spinoza and its reception by idealists such as Goethe. Dissatisfied with his purely intellectual training, and intrigued by Lietz's efforts to combine intellectual and manual skills, Geheeb then spent a half year learning carpentry and bookbinding in Jena.[22]

Unlike Lietz's, Geheeb's first teaching experiences were fraught with difficulties. After completing his university studies, Geheeb followed Wilhelm Rein's suggestion that he work at a new sanatorium for children recovering from illnesses on the North Sea island of Föhr. To his dismay, he found himself caring for close to sixty children on a full-time basis. He promptly exhausted himself and left his position after only a year and a half to recover in Stuttgart.

Eager to assist his friend and confident of his talents, Lietz invited Geheeb to work at Haubinda. Geheeb joined Lietz's faculty as a teacher in 1902, and with Lietz's encouragement visited Abbotsholme briefly as a biology teacher. As Lietz was increasingly busy with plans to start a third school, he appointed Geheeb director of Haubinda in 1904.

Compared to Geheeb's previous pedagogical efforts, his work at Haubinda was a triumph. His students were enthusiastic, he enjoyed his work, and he anticipated that he would spend the rest of his life leading Haubinda and cooperating with Lietz. Under Geheeb's leadership Haubinda expanded to accommodate 130 students. Geheeb did experience some differences with parents, for he conducted the religious services at Haubinda in a broad and undogmatic manner that offended those who wanted their children to receive a more orthodox religious education. As for Lietz, he now spent most of his time founding a new *Landerziehungsheim* at Schloss Bieberstein near Fulda—a site to which Geheeb had directed him as ideal for a third school. Just as the cooperation between Geheeb and Lietz was reaching its zenith, however, they found themselves engaged in a series of conflicts.[23]

The disputes between Lietz and Geheeb originated in a mixture of personal, political and pedagogical issues. As long as the two men kept their attention on the utopian visions of Fichte's *Addresses* or Goethe's "pedagogical province," the ambiguous and inclusive language of German idealism masked their differences. As they moved from theory to practice, however, Geheeb confronted numerous problems, not only with the formal structure of Lietz's *Landerziehungsheime*, but also with Lietz's overall pedagogical style. These problems could be ignored in the short run out of tact or timidity but Geheeb found it impossible to avoid them when they constantly resurfaced in his daily educational work.

Much of Geheeb's social activism in Berlin and Jena in the 1890s had brought him in contact with liberal humanistic circles, which had awakened him to the injustices afflicting women and the working class. Whatever impact Geheeb may have had upon Lietz with his ideas, that impact appears to have been shattered by Reddie, who exerted a far more conservative and nationalistic influence on Lietz. Like Reddie, Lietz became misogynistic, which must have grated against Geheeb's feminism. When it came to criticizing the authoritarianism of traditional schools, Reddie and Lietz were brilliant, but they replaced older forms of arbitrary authority with equally capricious ones of their own, brooking no protest from student or teacher alike. Both Reddie and Lietz moved from an early interest in socialism to nationalism. Reddie's enthusiasm for Germany provoked his intense hatred of Britain during the First World War, and his insistence on preaching Teutonic nationalism essentially destroyed Abbotsholme. In addition to these political differences, personal and pedagogical styles became sources of conflict over time: Lietz was constantly leading and exhorting his students, whereas Geheeb preferred to elicit students' perspectives to enable them to develop their own thinking from within.[24]

The latent differences became manifest in a series of rapidly escalating, overlapping crises which touched virtually all aspects of school life at Haubinda. Lietz alienated Geheeb and other liberals on his faculty when he attempted to censor the modern foreign literature that Geheeb and a colleague, Gustav Wyneken, had introduced in Haubinda, on the grounds that it was un-German and immoral. Lietz found nothing immoral, however, in taking out a subscription to an anti-Semitic newspaper, Theodor Fritsch's *Der Hammer*, for circulation in Haubinda's library—an act which angered not only Jewish teachers and students but also their liberal allies such as Geheeb.

Geheeb and Lietz also clashed regarding appropriate manners of recruiting students and faculty. Geheeb protested against a brochure issued by Lietz advertising his schools in 1904 with a clause stating that "Jews will only be admitted as exceptions." Lietz's response was to tape paper over the offending sentence, which any curious reader could flip up to read the anti-Semitic statement. In addition, Geheeb felt that some of the pupils at Haubinda desperately needed women on the school's faculty, but Lietz resisted his efforts to employ them. In terms of pedagogical atmosphere, Geheeb enjoyed informal contact with his students, and offered them the informal "Du" rather than the polite "Sie," which offended Lietz's sense of propriety. Geheeb also used assemblies of the entire school, which Lietz had inaugurated, to allow far higher levels of student self-government than Lietz found appropriate. When Haubinda appeared to be facing fiscal problems in the spring of 1906, Lietz accused Geheeb of mismanaging the school's funds and announced his intent to demote Geheeb to the status of a teacher.[25]

There probably was some truth to Lietz's claim of fiscal impropriety, for Geheeb exhibited a lifelong pattern of accepting scholarship students into his schools with little reservation and assuming that the money would be found to cover their expenses. Yet Lietz himself appears to have had a lackadaisical attitude toward economic obligations, and even his most devoted followers generally recognized that Lietz was using the economic argument to punish a colleague whose approach to education was markedly more liberal than Lietz found appropriate. His demotion of Geheeb prompted many of the most talented faculty and students at Haubinda to join Geheeb in leaving Haubinda to start a new school. The atmosphere at Haubinda was so tense at this point that the liberal Duke of Sachsen-Meiningen, who admired Geheeb, sent a gendarme to guard him as he packed his belongings and departed.[26]

Geheeb's next move was to open a *"Freie Schulgemeinde"* ("Free School Community") at Wickersdorf, which lay about forty kilometers northeast of Haubinda, on 1 September 1906. Eager to assist Geheeb, the Duke of Sachsen-Meiningen had given him a portion of a country estate upon which to build the new school. Responding to recruiting efforts by Geheeb and Wyneken, thirty-three students defected from the Lietz schools at Ilsendorf, Haubinda, and Schloss Bieberstein and followed them to Wickersdorf. Many of their liberal teachers came with them.[27]

The teachers who started Wickersdorf derived important structural principles from Lietz's schools but modified school life to grant their students more liberties. The *Schulgemeinde,* an open assembly in which faculty and students discussed problems in school life and attempted to hammer out solutions, was a marked departure from practices in the Lietz schools. In addition to this aspect of self-government, Geheeb pushed to make Wickersdorf the first coeducational boarding school in Germany, apparently recalling Fichte's emphasis on coeducation in his *Addresses to the German Nation.* Boys and girls lived in separate houses, and boys vastly outnumbered the girls, but in general the two sexes associated with each other freely in all aspects of school life.[28]

The significance of the coeducational character of Wickersdorf was profound. At the outset of the twentieth century, single-sex secondary schools were an immutable fact of life in Germany, with the few exceptions made either in isolated rural areas or in relatively progressive states in the southwest. To suggest within this context that boys and girls could live and learn together in a boarding school setting was to breach an entrenched cultural taboo which insisted on strict segregation of the sexes.

Wickersdorf quickly became famous as a pioneering institution of pedagogical reform in Imperial Germany. Geheeb soon renewed his contacts with the women's movement. One of Minna Cauer's closest allies and a leader of feminism's radical wing, Lily Braun, sent her son Otto to the school. In their public addresses feminist leaders Clara Zetkin, Lily Braun, and Hedwig Dohm expressed enthusiasm for the new school and the example it offered for educational reform.[29]

Geheeb was now gaining increased visibility as a school reformer. By opposing Lietz, Geheeb won respect as a courageous educator with personal integrity, and many liberal parents appreciated the intimate relationships he cultivated with young people and the tolerant *Weltanschauung* he propagated through his pedagogical work. By making a clean break with Lietz and by daring to start a coeducational boarding school, Geheeb indicated that he was willing to take the risk to institutionalize his own values and that his earlier political work in the women's movement would continue through the medium of school

reform. His risks appeared to be paying off. Enrollments at Wickersdorf almost doubled in the first year and a half, with sixty-five students enrolled by March 1908.[30]

In spite of the promising character of Wickersdorf, Geheeb's manner of leading the school once again provoked conflict. His long
friendship with Lietz had been of great importance to him in spite of
their arguments and he now suffered from depression. Seeking a respite to collect himself, Geheeb promoted his old ally from the Lietz
schools, Gustav Wyneken, to share the leadership of Wickersdorf.
This proved to be a major blunder, for Wyneken was an ambitious
and argumentative figure whose cooperation with Geheeb quickly
turned into opposition. Whereas Geheeb was content to make Wickersdorf a showcase for the accelerating movement for educational
reform in Germany, Wyneken had grander aspirations; he wanted to
make Wickersdorf the educational wing of the German youth movement, an inchoate, largely middle-class phenomenon of urban youth
who rebelled against the philistinism of bourgeois society and tried to
develop an autonomous culture of their own. When Geheeb refused
to incorporate the movement into Wickersdorf's mission, Wyneken
launched into bitter criticisms of his colleague—at points during the
Schulgemeinde meetings—which left Geheeb stunned and speechless.
Wyneken rapidly outmaneuvered Geheeb, won the students and faculty at Wickersdorf over to his side, and after only a year and a half
of tumult Geheeb resigned from his position as director. On 6 February 1909 he left the small Thuringian village to recover in a sanatorium managed by a friend in Stuttgart.[31]

It was now seventeen years since Geheeb had resolved with Lietz to
start a new school founded on Fichte's *Addresses to the German Nation*.
Unlike Lietz, Geheeb now had little to show for all of his years of
study and labor. Geheeb had failed to hold a steady teaching job for
more than a few years, had been removed as the director of a *Landerziehungsheim,* and was forced to leave his newly founded *Freie Schulgemeinde* at Wickersdorf. "I live from catastrophe to catastrophe," he
lamented.[32]

The continuation of Paul Geheeb's work as an educator now came
through a personal liaison. When his work at Haubinda had started
to crumble, making Geheeb desperate for support, he had married an
old friend, Helene Merck. The marriage did not withstand the debacle at Wickersdorf and the two separated. While at Wickersdorf, however, Geheeb hired a young teacher named Edith Cassirer. Edith came
from a prominent social background. She was the only daughter of

Berlin magnate Max Cassirer, who owned a cellulose factory in Silesia and a lumber business in Berlin. The Cassirers were one of the most prominent German Jewish families. Edith's cousins included Bruno Cassirer, a well-known publisher, and Paul Cassirer, who owned one of Berlin's avant-garde art galleries; other cousins who later gained fame included Ernst Cassirer, the philosopher and intellectual historian, and Kurt Goldstein, the Gestalt psychologist.

In spite of the lively atmosphere at the Cassirers' home, Edith Cassirer detested her life in Berlin. Her mother was protective and eager to match her up with a prospective husband, but many of Edith's suitors were financially motivated and she felt manipulated by her mother's organization of a constant stream of fortune hunters. Seeking to develop her own interests and talents, Edith studied to be a kindergarten teacher at the Pestalozzi-Froebel Haus, a teacher education school founded and led by politically and pedagogically progressive women who developed new modes of teaching and community outreach which prefigured later innovations of the settlement house movement. Unfortunately for Edith, her parents strongly disapproved of her work in the school, and they probably shared the nineteenth-century prejudice that only women who were unable to find marriage partners entered teaching. Edith's parents prevented her from graduating from the Pestalozzi-Froebel Haus by insisting that she accompany them on vacation to Italy at the time of examinations.

Undaunted, Edith returned with them to Berlin and then volunteered to work with children under the supervision of Hedwig Heyl and Anna von Gierke, two activists in the education of working-class youth. She proved to be a gifted teacher who won over throngs of vivacious and unruly urban youngsters through a careful balance of tact, forcefulness, and creativity. Once again over her parents' objections, Edith then became active in the women's movement in Berlin, and she worked closely with Alice Salomon, the founder of the first settlement houses in Germany. Yet in spite of all of these achievements, Edith still lived with her parents when she was twenty-two years old and felt suffocated by their incessant control over her everyday life.[33]

It was in this context that Cassirer first heard of the new *Freie Schulgemeinde* at Wickersdorf. She quickly decided that its experimental spirit might be just what she needed to win some distance from her parents' constraints, and she applied for a teaching position. Alice Salomon attempted to dissuade Edith, for she knew that Edith's parents would view Paul Geheeb with suspicion because of his reputation as a pedagogical *enfant terrible*. Salomon's fears proved accurate. Edith mentioned her plans to her father while dancing with him at a formal party at their home, and Max Cassirer flew into a rage, publicly threatening to disown her. After several days of reflection, however, he agreed to accompany his daughter to Wickersdorf on a preliminary journey to judge the matter for himself.[34]

To prepare Paul Geheeb for the visit by the Cassirers, Alice Salomon wrote him a lengthy letter explaining the importance of the trip for Edith and requesting that he handle the matter tactfully:

> Edith Cassirer is twenty-two years old and the only daughter of very wealthy parents, who live in a wonderful home. As a result of her independent disposition, she has been opposed to luxury and superficiality ever since she was small. As a result, she has fought constantly with her parents, who don't want to understand that she doesn't want to be like them. Ever since she was fourteen she has been active in social work and she received a good teacher's education at the Pestalozzi-Froebel Haus. She loves children and plants and knows how to lead. She has taken a horde of fifty roughneck boys who had been fighting with knives and brought them under control. She will definitely be able to handle the tasks you will place upon her—precisely because they are *tasks* and are located in the beautiful countryside . . .
>
> I don't know if you can imagine how much a rich girl can suffer in the culture I've described. For me the situation is simply that I would like for once to be able to place my dearest child, whom I love with all my heart, in a healthy environment. You save so many children's souls. Help me to save the little soul of this adult before it is decimated.
>
> I know that it sounds as though I want to place a new burden upon you and I know that you need to hire someone who can really help you in your work. But her energy and her unique pedagogical and maternal talents will definitely be a help as soon as she is settled with you. For now, just help her to be able to come to you. You don't need to worry that she is too spoiled. I've traveled with her and know that she knows how to take care of herself. She only needs a *healthy* atmosphere.
>
> You will find the father to be a clever man who simply finds his daughter's notions about leaving her beautiful home and parents to be crazy. You might be able to find the right way to win him over to your work. He is actually quite interested in unusual things and people. It is simply that he can't grasp or tolerate the idea that *his* own daughter is unusual.[35]

Edith and Max Cassirer left Berlin before sunrise and arrived in Wickersdorf to find Paul Geheeb just as he was concluding a small conference with some of the school's teachers. The director looked as eccentric as Alice Salomon had warned. He wore a full dark beard, a plain shirt open at the collar, a rugged blue jacket and knickers, and sandals on his bare feet. After a brief introduction, Geheeb and the

Cassirers set off to survey the school's grounds. As they trudged through wet February snow, Max Cassirer couldn't resist quipping, "You really do have practical shoes—the water runs in through the front and shoots right out the back!" To Edith's delight, however, her father was able to see the positive aspects of Wickersdorf. The new school struck him as an interesting experiment which his daughter should be able to explore if she felt a calling for that line of work.

Edith Cassirer was hired at Wickersdorf in the spring of 1908. At that time the school was already polarized into separate camps which supported either Geheeb or Wyneken, and the first question posed to Edith by teachers when she arrived was whether she supported the "Wyneken party" or the "Geheeb party." She declined to take a position and strove to maintain her independence as she adapted to her new home.

As Paul Geheeb's support within the school dwindled, he cast about for allies. When Alice Salomon came to visit Edith, he told her that he wished to marry Edith. "Well, have you talked to Edith about it?" wondered Alice. "No," he replied, "I haven't dared, but I just wanted to ask you how we can arrange it." "Listen," said Alice. "I can't judge things from your perspective, and I certainly can't ask Edith about it. If I did I would completely destroy her independence here, and she wouldn't know where she should live and work. I'm going to leave here very troubled, but I won't tell Edith about this."

Shortly thereafter, Edith led a group of students on a hike. She became lost in the woods, found herself circling again and again to the same spot, and was in despair as the last light of day faded into night.

> And finally it was ten o'clock, and we came up to a tree, and from the tree we heard an ominous "Schuschuschuschuuu, schuschuschu-schuuu!" I was terrified and the children gathered all around, and suddenly something huge jumped down from the tree. It was Paulus! He had waited and was very worried about us. He then led us in triumph to a hotel where we had dinner. And that was the point when the romance began, during that hike.

Paul Geheeb courted Edith continually in the weeks following the hike and won her consent to marriage. When Geheeb left Wickersdorf in April 1909 and entered the sanatorium, his attachment to Edith Cassirer was one of his few supports after his second failed attempt at school leadership.[36]

Edith's parents were appalled when they learned of Edith's plans. Paul Geheeb was unemployed, owed numerous debts, and appeared to be utterly incompetent in his profession. He was thirty-nine years old, whereas she was only twenty-four. His first marriage had failed. As if these flaws were not enough, Geheeb appeared to lack any sense of tact or decorum. When he traveled to Berlin to ask Max Cassirer for his daughter's hand in marriage, he could come up with no more convincing reply to Cassirer's inquiries regarding his fiscal solvency than to say, "You're a wealthy man. You've supported your daughter until now, and I haven't thought about it." When Cassirer told Geheeb that he had spoken with the lawyer who represented Helene Merck during the divorce proceedings and inquired as to whether Geheeb was marrying Edith for economic reasons, Geheeb announced, "Herr Cassirer, I'm not marrying your daughter," and walked out on him. Such volatile conduct gave the Cassirers all the proof they needed to believe that Edith was in danger of marrying an iconoclast with minimal prospects for a secure—let alone prosperous—future. The prospect of intermarriage with a gentile was never an issue, for the Cassirers were fully assimilated and Edith had been baptized as a Protestant.[37]

Throughout the summer of 1909 Paul and Edith fought separate battles. Paul traveled throughout Germany and sought to renew his work by attempting yet again to start a school in which he could realize his pedagogical ideals; Edith sought to persuade her family that their impressions of Paul were wrong and their love was genuine. The couple maintained a steady flow of correspondence to keep each other informed of developments.

Although traumatized by his experiences in Haubinda and Wickersdorf, Paul Geheeb remained convinced that he could make a major contribution to school reform. In spite of his failures, Geheeb had impressed many parents with his ability to educate their children, and some were clearly saddened by his departures from Haubinda and Wickersdorf. In addition, Geheeb's work at the two schools had brought him into contact with other educational reformers who were ready to assist him in starting a new school.

Paul Geheeb spent the summer of 1909 traveling in Germany. He met with officials concerned with school policy in different German states, visited potential sites for a new school, and sought out sympathetic benefactors who might be able to help him with funding. The search was a difficult one because he wanted to develop the coeducational part of his work beyond the level achieved in Wickersdorf and most officials were skeptical about coeducation. Geheeb now wanted to begin a school which would not have only boys, as in the

Lietz schools, nor boys and girls in separate houses, as in Wickersdorf. He wished to open the first "new school" in Europe which would have a comprehensive coeducation in which boys and girls could live in the same houses in adjacent rooms.[38]

Geheeb's first inquiries, to Bavarian officials, were frustrating. Unfortunately, his brother Reinhold worked on a Munich magazine called *Simplizissimus* which was frequently critical of the government, and the conservative educational officials said, "With one Geheeb in Bavaria we already have more than enough!" Geheeb then pursued an offer from school officials in the Duchy of Saxony to take over an experimental school to be established in the planned city of Hellerau on the outskirts of Dresden. Geheeb rejected the plan when he found that many of the officials in the Ministry of Culture supported an ideological line on school reform associated with Ferdinand Avenarius's journal *Der Kunstwart*. Geheeb supported the philosophy of education espoused in the *Kunstwart* and himself contributed to it on occasion, but he had no desire to align himself with another reformer's ideology, a move which could provoke another clash such as he had experienced with Lietz and Wyneken.[39]

After exploring additional possibilities throughout Germany, Geheeb found that only Sachsen-Meiningen, Saxony, Oldenburg and the Grand Duchy of Hesse responded positively to his inquiries. He decided to target his energies on Hesse. The small Duchy had made some modest experiments with coeducation in the public schools, and the proximity of large cities such as Frankfurt, Heidelberg, and Mannheim provided a potentially rich population of students. In August 1909 Geheeb rented a hotel room in Darmstadt, drew up a forty-page proposal for a school to be established in the Odenwald between Darmstadt and Heidelberg, and submitted it to school officials in the Ministry of the Interior.[40]

Geheeb opened his proposal by stating his intent to start a boarding school which would serve the children of parents who were not able to dedicate themselves sufficiently to the education of their children in light of their social obligations or personal difficulties. The new school would rectify the shortcomings of the Lietz schools and Wickersdorf and represent "a model school which would attract the attention of the widest possible circles insofar as it will seek to apply and justify the most progressive pedagogical theories in practice." Reviewing his previous educational work, Geheeb stated that Lietz's *Landerziehungsheime* had made a major contribution to educational practice in Germany. The Lietz Schools integrated the learning of academic subject matters with hands-on activities, collegiality in community, and robust self-reliance. Valuable as these achievements were, one nonetheless needed to make a "distinction between permanently valuable achievements on the one hand and weaknesses and questionable sides on the other." Geheeb held that while Lietz had correctly followed one of his philosophical mentors, Fichte, in starting boarding schools in the countryside and encouraging vigorous contact with nature for his students, Lietz himself lacked a spiritual appreciation of nature and tended to perceive it as an obstacle to be overcome in almost militaristic terms. Further, Lietz's schools excluded girls, which inevitably made the educational atmosphere of his homes one-sided and prepared students poorly for their future contacts with members of the opposite sex. Wickersdorf had overcome this deficiency, but had a separate problem; it was so far away from any city that it was almost impossible for its students to enjoy the cultural benefits of the metropolis. A school in the Odenwald forest situated in the center of a triangle shaped by Heidelberg, Mannheim and Frankfurt, on the other hand, could extend the cultural diversity of the city to children. Geheeb refrained from mentioning the profound personal and pedagogical conflicts he had with Lietz and Wyneken.

About one-third of Geheeb's manuscript was dedicated to a defense of coeducation. According to Geheeb, coeducation was central to any education of value because it introduced children to the reality of human differentiation and taught them to be comfortable with and to thrive in relationship to such differentiation. Geheeb rejected the idea that coeducational schools should disregard the differences between boys and girls:

> To prevent all misunderstandings, we explicitly state that we recognize and honor the differences between the sexes and take it to be our task to raise the boy as masculine and the girl as feminine as possible. Nothing appears to us more absurd than efforts which attempt to avoid sexual differences.

From his perspective, rather, a humanistic education would teach children to acknowledge and appreciate their differences, not only those between the sexes, but those in all domains of human development:

> We ask above all: what is greater and more important between boys on the one hand and girls on the other, that which they share or that which is different? And regarding their differences, are there more differences between boys and girls or between boys and boys? From sexual differentiation we derive nothing more than the pedagogical challenge of individuation for education and instruction.

For Geheeb, coeducation was not so much an issue in its own right as a ramification of a larger issue, one which involved deep-seated cul-

tural attitudes which repressed and segregated those who were different rather than engaging with and learning from those differences. Single-sex education was a "monstrosity, a crime against the
wisdom of nature," not because it socialized boys and girls to different
roles, but because it did not allow boys and girls to develop their own
individual identities through free and equal exchange with one
another.[41]

To help legitimize his arguments for coeducation Geheeb quoted
passages from prestigious advocates such as Fichte and Marianne
Weber, and referred to successful experiments with it in the United
States, Britain, and Sweden. None of the passages he selected suggested that boys and girls might have developed their differences
exclusively from processes of socialization; Geheeb believed rather
that there were fundamental, naturally endowed characterological
differences between the sexes. In this regard, Geheeb shared the
assumptions of most "first-wave" feminists, who based their arguments for the emancipation of women on women's perceived differences from men rather than on men's and women's fundamental
equality. Rather than approach those differences as problematic,
Geheeb sought to make the centerpiece of his educational project the
diffusion of a worldview which would honor differences and use them
as points of reference for one's personal self-realization.[42]

While Paul Geheeb labored to lay the groundwork for the new school,
Edith Cassirer stayed in Berlin and attempted to work out a reconciliation with her parents. Edith's efforts were complicated by her recognition that "in and of itself my father hadn't done anything wrong.
He just wanted to take care of me, but he didn't know that he was
dealing with such a rascal." Edith fully understood her father's criticisms of Paul, and while it is clear that she loved her fiancé, she was
aware of his flaws. She wrote Paul and confronted him with the immaturity of much of his conduct, referring to his rash decision to marry
Helene Merck when his professional life was in turmoil, the lack of
foresight he showed in raising Wyneken to the status of co-director of
Wickersdorf, his weak and vacillating response to Wyneken's effort to
expel him from Wickersdorf, and his nonchalant reaction to Max Cassirer's concerns for Edith's future well-being. In the meantime, however, Edith found little solace with her family.

A breakthrough occurred on September 13, when Dr. Ludwig
Nagel of the Hessian Ministry of the Interior accepted Paul Geheeb's
proposal to start a coeducational boarding school in the Odenwald.
The approval by Hesse may have indicated to Edith's parents that
Paul Geheeb, whatever his oddities, might have some redeeming

value. After many tears and much familial turmoil, Edith persuaded them that a reconciliation and a renewal of the engagement should occur. In spite of her parents' qualms, Paul Geheeb and Edith Cassirer married on 18 October 1909. Immediately after the ceremony, Max Cassirer took his daughter aside and told her, "It is completely clear, Edith, that you won't stay with this man. But when you do leave, please come to us."[43]

Paul and Edith settled in Darmstadt after their wedding. To Edith's disappointment, Paul paid almost no attention to her, but continued working relentlessly on his plans for the new school. Geheeb traveled throughout the Duchy of Hesse and to Frankfurt, the closest metropolis, searching for benefactors to help fund the new school. When he found a beautiful location in the village of Oberhambach near the Bergstrasse, which connected Frankfurt with Heidelberg, Max Cassirer responded to his daughter's request that he come and visit the proposed site. Cassirer traveled to Darmstadt, persuaded himself that the project might be successful, and volunteered to underwrite the school. According to Paul Geheeb, he was "very embarassed" by Cassirer's generosity; on the other hand, his frank remarks regarding fiscal dependency in his previous discussions with Cassirer showed that Geheeb was not exactly averse to financial backing from his father-in-law. From Cassirer's point of view, as much as he mistrusted Geheeb, it was impossible that his daughter and son-in-law should publicly solicit support from philanthropists in metropolitan areas like Frankfurt when his own affluence was well known. Cassirer subsequently purchased an old inn called the "Lindenstein" in Oberhambach, which would serve as the school's first building, and went with his daughter and son-in-law to meet a local architect to design and construct new houses for the rest of the school.

After so many years of challenge and defeat, Paul Geheeb was thrilled with the plans for the new school, which struck him as a "fairy-tale" resolution to his personal and professional difficulties. Unlike Lietz, who had to battle with the most primitive conditions to build up his schools, Geheeb was to help conceptualize and then to receive with minimum effort a row of majestic buildings nestled in a winding valley with a beautiful overview of the landscape stretching south to Heidelberg. Paul and Edith Geheeb decided to open the new school in April 1910, and they called it the "Odenwaldschule," after the nearby Odenwald forest.[44]

chapter 2

The Odenwaldschule, 1910–1930

The Geheebs faced a tremendous amount of work to open the Oden-waldschule on schedule. The Lindenstein required major structural repairs to make the building safe and comfortable for children. The school needed talented teachers who would be willing not only to instruct the students but also to live with them on an almost continuous basis. The Geheebs had to find parents who would entrust their children to them and pay the tuition and boarding costs. In addition to these challenges, it was not yet clear what kind of a schedule should be created for the new school, and how Paul Geheeb would actually establish the experimental program he described in his proposal to the Hessian Ministry of the Interior.

With Max Cassirer's assistance, the physical repairs were assured of a quick and professional solution. Cassirer hired workers to strip out all of the parts of the Lindenstein that required replacement, install new materials and equipment, and improve all aspects of the building to render it inhabitable and comfortable. Central heating and gas lighting were put in the Lindenstein at a combined cost of 37,000 marks. Edith hired personnel to staff the kitchen and to assist with maintenance, and she oversaw all of the detail work as the last arrangements were made and the final curtains were hung. She continued to witness the mandarin-like indifference of her husband to practical matters. Noting that an expensive new piano had been unloaded by movers outside the Lindenstein and that a storm was approaching, she asked Paul where it should be placed. "Hmm, we'll have to think about that," he responded, and retired for his midday nap. Only Edith's initiative in corralling some workers to bring the piano in and place it in an appropriate room saved it from ruin in the ensuing downpour.[1]

Instead of dealing with the physical arrangement of the school, Paul Geheeb dedicated himself to recruiting excellent teachers and a first crop of students. His major discovery for the faculty was Otto Erdmann, a mathematics instructor in the *Realgymnasium* in Darmstadt. Erdmann was a charismatic instructor who participated in the prewar youth movement. When not teaching at the *Realgymnasium*, Erdmann used his leisure time to lead his students on hikes and to sing with them, using the musical bible of the youth groups, the *Zupfgeigenhansl*. As late as 5 March the Geheebs had no students enrolled for their spring semester, and Erdmann endeavored to solve the problem by recommending the school to his *Realgymnasium* admirers. He traveled with six of them on the train from Darmstadt to Heppenheim as the construction was underway and hiked with them up the gently sloping path to Oberhambach. "I had told them a great deal about the new school in the Odenwald," he recalled, "and I couldn't answer all of their questions. But now it was really like a dream as we climbed up the valley. A school? Here, among the blossoming cherry trees? Improbable, unbelievable!" The students were fascinated with Erdmann's description of Geheeb, which Erdmann embellished by describing Geheeb's colorful appearance, his ambitious plans for creating a new kind of school, and the prospect of novel freedoms for the students. When the school finally opened on 10 April, fourteen students had enrolled, and the majority of them had been recommended by Erdmann.

Only one of the first group of students was female—an inauspicious beginning for a school dedicated to coeducation. Rather than coming from avant-garde or pedagogically inclined families, most of the students were scions of Prussian nobles stationed at a garrison in Darmstadt. As they arrived, Edith found herself in a "completely bizarre milieu," as these aristocratic children acclimated themselves to the liberal atmosphere she tried to establish with her bohemian husband.[2]

For Paul Geheeb, however, the social standing of the children was unimportant. Before April 1910 he had never had the opportunity to establish a school with as many liberties and as much fiscal security as he now enjoyed. Geheeb's voice trembled as he rose to give an official welcome to the new children. With careful deliberation, Geheeb began his remarks by quoting a favorite verse from Goethe's "Prooemion," and then delivered his address:

> Dear colleagues and children—we stand at the beginning of an immense task. In the last months many hands have been active here, working to build us a home which will allow us to live well between the mountains

and the blossoming meadows of the Odenwald. But that has simply been the superficial beginning. We stand confronted with our work. It has to do with building something which, just as heaven is higher than our earth, should reach higher than this house. However beautiful our home should be, it can only serve as a replication of eternal values. For if anything serves eternal values, it must be an association of similar human beings who form a spiritual community which conscientiously cares for the culture of the soul—a living community in which each member is carried by the love of the others and is lifted higher, toward true service to God.

Geheeb told the students that the splendor of the Odenwald did not provide an adequate justification for the new school. Nor, he contended, was the new school legitimated by the fact that some unfortunate children might find a home there when no other was available to them.

The purpose of our establishment lies much more in our firm belief that it is possible to create here what school should be, but chooses not to be in the public schools. a place where children can learn to work and to develop their humanity.

Yet this project of developing one's "humanity"—as yet unspecified— would entail serious self-discipline:

Whoever has come here with the expectation that the work of learning is going to be made more comfortable will certainly be disappointed. No, we don't want to make it more comfortable. We want to make it more difficult by setting higher goals and making greater demands on your insight, your initiative, your energy, and your intellectual desires. Of course, we will make things somewhat easier by not narrowing down or suppressing the creative powers residing in you. Rather, we shall try to bring about their freer development and a more powerful sense of strength with the hope of making you independent so that you need us less and less . . . Do you believe that you have come to the land of freedom? Yes, you have, if you understand how to use your freedom.

Finally, it was imperative that the new students learn to love their new community:

Youth is a holy time and of fundamental importance for one's entire life. But what good is it if your time is holy to us but not to you? I trust, however, that you will love our school, the community of your comrades and your older friends who live and work here on your behalf. It can't be indifferent to you whether our school prospers or whether the goal of a community filled with life and work is reached or not. We form a community in which the rights and duties are distributed equally among the old and the young. The condition of our house, paths, and garden is up to each of you just as much as to me; each of us is partially responsible.

Paul Geheeb was later to state that he really had no program when the Odenwaldschule opened and that the members of the small school community simply began to live with one another. "I was only anxious," he claimed, "to make sure that no customs or arrangements from traditional schools or boarding schools slipped in which would have no sense or necessity for us." Yet already in his welcoming remarks Geheeb set a tone for the Odenwaldschule. The opening citation from Goethe and the religious language of his appeal transmitted Geheeb's background in German idealism, which he subsequently brought up when disciplining children, corresponding with parents, and securing the relationship of the school to the Hessian Ministry of Culture. The emphasis on freedom and the oppositional stance toward the culture of public schools signaled Geheeb's endeavor to ensure that the Odenwaldschule would not be a private school which simply replicated the structure of public schools with better curricula and more talented teachers. Rather, Geheeb conveyed to the students that those who were bold and reflective could win an unparalleled sense of personal liberty in the school, which they could test through their concrete participation in the community. Through the value that Geheeb placed on the communitarian character of the Odenwaldschule, and the sense of shared responsibilities he hoped would be carried by teachers and students, he expressed his intent that students replace an institutional approach with a more familial one. Finally, by bringing up the importance of love for the community, Geheeb demonstrated that he was willing to venture into the more vulnerable and intimate dimensions of human personality and to hope that these would play an enlivening and uplifting role in the Odenwaldschule.[3]

Paul Geheeb borrowed heavily from his prior experiences at Haubinda and Wickersdorf in establishing the new structures in the Odenwaldschule. As in each of those schools, the new children who came to the Odenwaldschule were placed in pedagogical "families"— small groups of students headed by one or two teachers—as their primary site of orientation to the school. At Wickersdorf, Geheeb and Wyneken dropped the labels of "students" and "teachers" and replaced these with *Kameraden* ("comrades") and *Mitarbeiter* ("coworkers") respectively. Geheeb continued to use these titles in the Odenwaldschule. While today the term *"Kamerad"* evokes recollec-

tions of militarism stemming from the Third Reich, at the turn of the
century it had a more supple, less problematic connotation. Geheeb
hoped that the new expressions would facilitate greater collegiality in
the Odenwaldschule and mark a clear rupture with public school customs.

The Odenwaldschule also continued the *Schulgemeinde* structure
which Geheeb and Wyneken had inaugurated in Wickersdorf. The
Schulgemeinde was a biweekly forum in which all of the members of
the community, *Kameraden* and *Mitarbeiter,* assembled to discuss practical problems of school life and to seek their solutions. The topics
addressed in the meetings concerned both practical concerns, such as
maintaining cleanliness and discipline in the school, and major organizational issues, such as proposals to reformulate the course schedule. The *Schulgemeinde* was thoroughly democratic, and many new
Kameraden were astonished to find that "in the *Schulgemeinde* a nine-
year old has exactly the same vote as Paul Geheeb." Each session was
led by a *Kamerad* elected by his or her peers and the *Mitarbeiter.* If
some *Kameraden* violated commonly agreed-upon principles of the
school, the members of the *Schulgemeinde* could decide to take away
their votes until they improved their behavior.

Religious and cultural practices from Haubinda and Wickersdorf
were also integrated into the Odenwaldschule. Following Reddie's
example at Abbotsholme, Lietz introduced in the *Landerziehungsheime*
religious *Kapelle,* which were based primarily on readings from scrip-
ture. Unlike Reddie and Lietz, Geheeb used these meetings—which
he preferred to call *"Andachten,"* or "meditations"—to read from
poetry, short stories, or any resources which conveyed a broadly
humanistic *Weltanschauung. Andachten* were presented every Sunday
evening in the Odenwaldschule; each week, Geheeb, a group of *Mitarbeiter,* or even some enterprising *Kameraden* read selections from a text
or shared an issue of personal meaning. Geheeb drew much of his
material from the short stories of Leo Tolstoy or Selma Lagerlöf, and
the reading of the stories was often either introduced or concluded
when a few *Kameraden* and *Mitarbeiter* played a short piece of music
from a classical composer.[4]

Geheeb took four other practices directly from the Lietz schools.
Each morning began with "air baths," or exercises done outside in the
nude by students. These exercises reflected *Zeitgeist* currents in the
youth movement and back-to-nature "life reform" movements, which
criticized modern society for increasingly separating individuals from
contact with nature. Girls and boys did their exercises in different
areas in open terrain in the woods behind the school. The second

practice was that of hikes in the countryside, which often took as long as a week or ten days. Paul Geheeb hoped that *Kameraden* would use the hikes to learn to appreciate the beauty of nature, to experience something of their own latent strengths and resources, and to assist one another in a setting in which responsibility to one's group really mattered.

A third practice taken over from the Lietz schools involved the reading of quotations to students once a day before a mealtime. Quotations typically were taken from the works of the classical idealists, such as Goethe or Fichte, but they also came from the writings of late nineteenth-century cultural critics such as Friedrich Nietzsche or Paul de Lagarde. On occasion, Geheeb read aloud from a newspaper article, frequently from a feminist source such as Helene Lange's journal *Die Frau* or Minna Cauer's *Die Frauenbewegung*. Whatever the source, the purpose of the reading was to stimulate the students to reflect for a moment about the deeper issues and purposes of life before settling in to their meals. Finally, conferences for only the *Mitarbeiter* appear to have been an important decision-making forum. Allegedly, *Mitarbeiter* conferences existed only to discuss students' psychosocial and intellectual development in order to prepare reports for parents. Some *Kameraden*, however, held that the *Mitarbeiter* used conferences to deliberate on school policy issues raised in the *Schulgemeinden*.[5]

Considering all the rituals which Paul Geheeb took from his work at Haubinda and Wickersdorf, one might wonder whether there was anything new in the Odenwaldschule at all. The greatest break with the other schools lay in the expanded coeducational dimension of the Odenwaldschule, with teenage boys and girls rooming next to one another in all of the houses in the school. *Within* the Odenwaldschule coeducation was scarcely an issue; it was taken for granted that young people of different sexes could assume the responsibility of living together without rampant promiscuity. Once an atmosphere was established in which the students understood that respect for others regardless of sex was indeed the ruling principle at the school, coeducation appears to have been a false problem, which preoccupied the local Catholic priest and visiting adults more than the *Kameraden* and *Mitarbeiter* of the school.[6]

The second major structural innovation at the Odenwaldschule concerned the organization of classes. The course system in the school underwent several modifications in its first few years. The Geheebs and their *Mitarbeiter* rejected the system of grade levels which stratified children by age and ability in the German public schools and which had been preserved in the Lietz schools and Wickersdorf. Grade levels were believed to neglect the individual differences among students and to produce resentful outsiders when students failed to master a subject and had to repeat a year. In addition, the Geheebs were anxious to avoid anything approaching a standardized curriculum which compelled students to learn material at the same pace and in the same manner. Instead of grade levels, the Odenwaldschule set up *Kursgemeinschaften* or "course communities" for students generally over ten years old, which met for two hours each day to learn subjects in a concentrated fashion. While students generally were clustered with those of their same age level, there was nothing unusual in a course made up of students spread out over several years. Students were responsible for selecting their areas of study, pursuing them diligently, and evaluating their own work in cooperation with their instructors.[7]

Otto Erdmann played a major role in developing the new course system in the Odenwaldschule. In consultation with Geheeb and through the deliberative medium of the *Schulgemeinde,* the community decided to establish two *Kursgemeinschaften* for the individual *Kamerad* each day. In the mornings *Kameraden* studied two academic subjects, such as mathematics, the sciences or the humanities. In the afternoons the *Kameraden* were to balance their academic learning with independent activities in the arts and crafts. The *Mitarbeiter* and *Kameraden* quickly found, however, that many *Kameraden* did not know how to use their afternoons productively. According to Edith, "they were bored and threw stones at houses and windows and picked fights ... it wasn't terrible, just unproductive." The *Mitarbeiter* responded by introducing a third period in which *Kameraden* took courses in music, art, or handicrafts, also for two hours. These afternoon courses, like the morning courses, changed on a monthly basis, anticipating and encouraging the cultivation of students' talents and areas of interest.[8]

Grades were never used as a means of motivating students to learn in the Odenwaldschule. Grades, it was held, taught students to focus on the extrinsic results of learning rather than its intrinsic rewards; they also socialized students to be competitive rather than cooperative in their approach to education. In lieu of grades, *Mitarbeiter* wrote individual reports on the achievements of *Kameraden* in their courses. In their reports the *Mitarbeiter* described not only the intellectual gains of their students but also commented upon students' independence, collegiality, and creativity. To ensure that the *Kameraden* learned to evaluate and improve on their own work, *Kameraden* also wrote reports about their own learning and their progress in mastering different subjects.

The presentation and evaluation of learning also had a public dimension in the Odenwaldschule. At the end of each month the entire school gathered for a *Kursschlussschulgemeinde* to present and hear reports about what had been accomplished in the separate courses. Rather than simply giving a dry report on their curricula, *Kameraden* performed scenes from plays studied in their literature courses, used maps and props to explain historical incidents, and showed the results of experiments conducted in chemistry classes. As a consequence, *Kameraden* practiced peer teaching, learned to acquire confidence in the value of their learning, and "at the end of every four weeks a complete overview of all of the real work done in the school is achieved by all of its members." This meeting celebrated the completion of a month's work and helped to evaluate the *modus operandi* of the course system, correct difficulties, and organize the course offerings for the coming month.[9]

In this organization of learning the Odenwaldschule was one of the pioneering progressive schools in Germany and the first school within the *Landerziehungsheim* movement which radically restructured its approach to curricula. Lietz and Wyneken, for all of their innovations, remained traditionalists when it came to the instruction of individual courses. Only the Odenwaldschule among the *Landerziehungsheime* took the initiative to establish a course plan which brought together the individual students' freedom of curricula choice, community interaction regarding the formation of course groups, and critical reflection by the entire school of its progress in monthly assemblies. The stability of the overall structure allowed for flexibility in its implementation, so that students could exercise their freedom well within supple parameters.

All of the key practices of the Odenwaldschule—coeducation, the course system, the family system, the *Schulgemeinden, Andachten,* hikes, and air baths—were introduced and became part of the structure of the school within the first four years. Some of the practices, such as coeducation, provided the very foundation of the school, whereas other components, such as the course system, required experimentation and reorganization before the *Mitarbeiter* and *Kameraden* settled on the final arrangement. In the majority of instances Paul Geheeb played a restrained leadership role, preferring to see the entire community deliberate on issues and come to its own solutions. After a

Schulgemeinde meeting in 1911, one *Mitarbeiter* wrote about Geheeb's interest in students' experiences:

> [Geheeb] . . . asks the children about the advantages and disadvantages with the morning courses. He observes that with this arrangement one could work for months or even for a half year without getting to a certain subject. The children are satisfied with the organization of the mornings. They should then express whether they have made progress and whether they need to reproach themselves or their teachers. One student thinks that there isn't enough independent work, because right now everyone is working together too much. One sees how also among the students the thoughts are becoming directed toward individualized instruction.

Geheeb played a strong role in influencing the development of the *Schulgemeinde* meetings, but he also valued its democratic character seriously enough to refrain from forcing through his own opinion. As Otto Erdmann noted,

> You ask: in the *Schulgemeinde* did one essentially follow Paul Geheeb? I can remember that sometimes there was a vigorous opposition against the leadership and against Paul Geheeb personally. When he was voted against, he subordinated himself to the majority vote. But in general his ideas and ideals gave the direction.[10]

Yet what exactly were Paul Geheeb's ideas? Paul Geheeb was hesitant about articulating anything as codified as a philosophy of education. "Intellectual reflection has always played a minor role in my life," he said. "Only after we had been living together for months and even years did the theoretical elements follow." Yet Geheeb did develop certain principles which made up the *sine qua non* of a romantic and idealistic philosophy of education. From his point of view, the Odenwaldschule was just one "expression of a century-and-a-half-old cultural movement which originated with Goethe and Fichte." For Geheeb, this movement

> created an interpretation of education which understands education less as the process of the older person who influences, leads, and instructs than as the developmental process in every person which stretches from birth to death and in which unconscious and then gradually conscious relationships develop. Through this interaction every individual recognizes himself in relationship to his environment, with people and things, nature and culture, and either integrates the received impressions of the educational material fruitfully to develop his or her own individuality or rejects them.

This educational doctrine does not begin with a philosophical description of cultural goods and their intrinsic value as educational material for youth, nor with a list of educational goals that should be imposed on the child from without, nor with a chapter about discipline and a system of punishment, nor with considerations about how the educator should develop authority in relation to the child by taking him by the hand and transmitting as much knowledge to him as possible. The child is our point of departure, and in the foreground of our interest stands our study of the inexhaustible richness of childhood strengths and characteristics and the infinite richness of individuals.[11]

Geheeb's philosophy of education took its point of departure from the needs and orientation of the individual child. In the popular phrase of German reform pedagogues, it was a pedagogy *"vom Kinde aus,"* "from the child's point of view." For Geheeb, all of education and indeed all of social life was to sustain and further the process of psychological individuation, which in turn should enrich the social and cultural life of any given community. Geheeb often quoted the Greek poet Pindar's saying, "Become who thou art!" For Geheeb, Pindar's dictum encouraged students to resist external coercions and to realize their latent strengths. In Geheeb's *Weltanschauung*, the Pindar quote

> contains for us the highest maxim of human development as well as the essence of pedagogical wisdom. It says essentially the same thing as development toward autonomy . . . All of life and of experience, everything which people call "happiness" or "unhappiness," all of destiny and the sufferings and occasional joys which the gods grant humanity—even work, professions, friendship, marriage, and all of the closer and broader relationships in human communities such as the family, neighborhood, and state—all are only instruments to enable the individual to realize himself. Become an individual, become that individual who in the entire world only you, irreplaceably and uniquely you, can become through the development of your latent and fundamental personality![12]

According to Geheeb, an educational commitment to the principle of individuation within a school community would have multiple consequences not only on the structural arrangements of a school but also on the overall learning atmosphere. Rather than concentrating on learning various facts which would be useful for a later professional life, a school which would follow this principle to its full extent would shift its emphasis towards a more process-oriented and individualized approach to learning. Geheeb wrote,

> If we really follow the imperative to "Become who thou art!" then self-cultivation *(Bildung)* is neither a collection of cultural goods nor an object

which we can own, but a being and a becoming. This formation of individuality, which develops according to its own inner laws, stands in continual interaction with nature and the cultural products of the individual's environment, which it sometimes accepts and sometimes transforms, but which never reaches a conclusion. Whereas the dominant school system is most concerned with the quantitative learning of children and understands learning almost exclusively in intellectual terms, the organization of a true educational workshop for children must consider their individual differentiation.

Geheeb saw this "individual differentiation" as the most remarkable feature of human existence:

Of all wonders, the greatest wonder is the sheerly inexhaustible, and in the strictest sense infinite, fact of creation. Every day nature propagates masses of spores and not one of the creatures which develop from them is exactly the same as another; of the thousands of infants which daily emerge from mothers' wombs, not one is exactly the same as another.

Geheeb continually referred to "the infinite richness of unique individuals" and urged others to "view with Goethean eyes the endless abundance of individuals and to find delight in the diversity of individual forms."[13]

Geheeb held that the greatest damage inflicted by German public schools on children lay in the schools' tendency to level individual differences and to compel children to conform to group norms. He believed that authoritarian relationships between teachers and students, repetitious drills which allowed few opportunities for individual expression, and enforced competition between students for intellectual knowledge suppressed children's own motivations to learn. When educators experienced difficulties with their pupils in trying to impose learning goals upon them, Geheeb stated that it "only serves the 'educators' right, for God does not wish to destroy the infinite richness of unique individuals through the viewpoints of a herd of degenerates with narrow-minded programs."[14]

Yet how was one to live with others in a school community if all of its members were continually pursuing their self-realization without respect for their peers and teachers? Geheeb quoted Goethe, with a dictum which he placed on the frontispiece of brochures advertising the Odenwaldschule:

Healthy children bring much with them. Nature has given them everything they need to persevere; it is our duty to develop this and often they develop it better on their own. But there is one thing which no one brings with them to the world, and is nonetheless that on which all else depends: reverence!

For Geheeb, reverence entailed responsibility, which was another core principle of his educational philosophy. Geheeb did not equate "education to autonomy" with egocentrism. Autonomy referred not just to self-determination, but also to "the responsibility of everyone for themselves and for the collectivity." "Have you ever tried to examine the development of pedagogical ideas," he wrote to a friend, "from the viewpoint that individualism and social responsibility are comparable to two foci of an ellipse, as twin locomotives which dominate all human and cultural developments?"[15]

In terms of translating this tension between individuation and social responsibility into school practice, Geheeb sought to create an educational atmosphere which would bring the two "foci of an ellipse" into a dynamic balance.

> An organic community dedicated to its youth with the purpose of furthering the development of autonomy in all areas has a definite character with regard to its organization and its social life. All of the arrangements in the community, and above all in its prevailing spirit, aim toward developing in each child as early as possible a strong sense of responsibility for himself, for his comrades, and for the entire life of the community.

The task of educators within this community would be to establish the external structures which would further individuation and social responsibility. Geheeb asked,

> What can we do to help these characteristics and strengths to unfold optimally within the totality of the harmonious personality? How can we avoid every temptation to constrict and miseducate? How must the environment of the child be arranged so that the need of every child for order and discipline is just as satisfied as his needs for spontaneity, activity, and free movement?[16]

To answer these questions, Geheeb turned to reform educator Georg Kerschensteiner's "fundamental axiom of education." Kerschensteiner was a personal friend of Geheeb's whom he had met at Haubinda and had tried to help Geheeb start his new school in Bavaria after the Wickersdorf debacle. According to Kerschensteiner's "fundamental axiom," "the education of the individual is only facilitated through those cultural products whose spiritual structure corresponds either entirely or partly to his individual psyche." A community which wished to further this process of individuation would place a wide range of "cultural products" within reach of children. Concretely, this meant workshops for learning handicrafts; proximity to woods for exploring nature; facilities for music and painting for artistic expression; and whatever other settings and activities the school community could acquire to stimulate children's overall development. Ideally, the combination of academic and artistic courses in the Odenwaldschule would enable students to develop their individuality in line with the spirit of Kerschensteiner's axiom.[17]

These "cultural products" would be not only inanimate objects, but also the most different kinds of people. Geheeb wanted the Odenwaldschule to attract a wide range of people with different characteristics and from diverse backgrounds. Coeducation was one part of this general appreciation of differences and the conviction that individual self-realization could only occur in settings with the most multifarious kinds of people and materials.

Although Paul Geheeb recognized that theory plays a role in the organization and success of any school, he downplayed the importance of his own ideas in the Odenwaldschule. He liked to call the Odenwaldschule a *"Lebensgemeinschaft,"* or "community of life," which in ideal terms would be marked by an equal sense of involvement and responsibility by all of its members. To ensure the success of such a *Lebensgemeinschaft,* it was imperative that the director refrain from constantly intervening in the school with his own principles. In line with this romantic emphasis on community, Geheeb's philosophy of education remained purposefully untotalized and full of unresolved ambiguities. The value placed on community consensus and an open-minded, nonsystemic approach to education made the Odenwaldschule remarkably malleable, so that the exact organization of the school—the structure of the *Schulgemeinde,* the relationship between the morning academic courses and the more practical afternoon courses, the content of the *Andachten*—continually changed on the basis of shifting community priorities. Principles emphasizing reverence for life, individual self-realization, and responsibility to the community played a role in these developments, but their exact institutional manifestations were not sacrosanct.

The humanism and tolerance conveyed in Paul Geheeb's pedagogical *Weltanschauung* had immediate benefits in terms of recruiting students to the Odenwaldschule. The school expanded rapidly in its first few years, enrolling sixty-eight students on a full-time basis by 1914. To accommodate the rise in enrollments, Max Cassirer poured capital into the school. He built four new houses which could accommodate

a total of eighty *Kameraden,* with apartments included for the *Mitarbeiter* with families. Paul Geheeb had already renamed the Lindenstein in honor of Goethe; the new houses were named after Fichte,
Herder, Schiller, and Wilhelm von Humboldt, who became, in
Geheeb's idealistic cosmology, the "heroes" of the Odenwaldschule.
To further honor the "heroes," the Odenwaldschule began celebrating their birthdays by performing their plays, reading their poetry or
essays, and enjoying a full day of festivities.

The outbreak of the First World War in August 1914 marked a
major hiatus in the history of the school, not only because of the scope
of the event in general but also because of the proximity of the school
to France. Unlike most Germans, Paul Geheeb was appalled by the
outbreak of the war; he told Edith, "I don't care who wins as long as
the murdering stops." According to Edith, once the war began in earnest the school "completely collapsed." Among the *Mitarbeiter,* almost
all of the men either enlisted in the military or were drafted, and
many women departed to join the Red Cross. Student enrollments
dropped, supplies of fuel and food were strictly rationed, and the
army stationed a company of soldiers in the new houses.

The First World War almost caused the termination of the Odenwaldschule at one point, when police intercepted a letter from a *Mitarbeiter* who was enthusiastic about the spirit of pacifism in the school.
The teacher wrote about how the school celebrated neither German
victories or the Kaiser's birthday, how the victims of the war on all
sides were mourned, and how Paul Geheeb hated the war and
described it as "mass murder." Only the intervention of Ernst Ludwig,
the liberal Archduke of Hesse, prevented the school from being summarily closed.[18]

Once the war was over and the Weimar Republic had been established, the Odenwaldschule entered the period of its greatest prosperity and fame. The democratic motif in the *Schulgemeinden* no
longer was an implicit challenge to the monarchy of the Second
Empire but rather appeared to be a progressive prefiguration of the
republican sentiments in the Weimar constitution. Similarly, Geheeb's
emphasis on coeducation seemed in spirit to foreshadow Weimar's
codification of women's rights by expanding the franchise to include
women. Finally, government officials in the Weimar Republic were far
more sympathetic than their predecessors to the spirit of schools like
the Odenwaldschule.

Profound transitions occurred not only at the level of the German
state in the postwar period, but also in education. In the prewar years

there were a number of fledgling school reform movements, which battered away at the rigidity and conservatism of the public school system. These movements grew in response to the travails of industrialization and modernization, and a wave of talented reformers focused attention on the character of German schools and the kinds of values they inculcated in young people. They found much to criticize. Reformers sympathetic to the spirit of progressive ideas in "new education" complained that curricula were decided in advance by faculty with no consultation from students; course work was exhausting and highly competitive; students felt anonymous and hostile toward their teachers. Conservative reformers, on the other hand, lamented the decline in classical studies in the *Gymnasium,* and warned against the materialism, mechanization, and dehumanization which they identified as consequences of industrial capitalism. A new breed of popular literature condemned the rigidity and authoritarian character of public schools, including Hermann Hesse's *Beneath the Wheel,* Frank Wedekind's "Spring Awakening," and Heinrich Mann's *Professor Unrat.*[19]

Impatient with the pace of reform and eager to pioneer new theories of curriculum and instruction, German educators swiftly produced a dizzying array of initiatives. These ranged from ambitious art education projects, to new kinds of industrial and vocational training, to popular "folk colleges" (where working-class adults continued their educations on evenings and weekends), to the movement of *Landerziehungsheime* initiated by Lietz. Many of the new undertakings emerged in complete isolation from one another, and intense rivalries between reformers marred many of their attempts to develop a mutually rewarding exchange of their experiences. By the time of the Weimar Republic a broadly based movement of "new education" or "reform pedagogy," which sought to transform schools root and branch, had gained a firm foothold in German society.

Like foreign reformers in the progressive education movement, German educators developed "activity schools" and "work schools," which linked cognitive learning with hands-on activities. They sought to dissolve the institutional barriers which separated schools from the surrounding communities, and they took students on week-long hikes in nature in the hope that adventure-based experiences would educate in a more profound manner than classroom recitations. They tried to rethink the overall structure of schools to accommodate the diverse needs and interests of their individual students, and they redesigned the shape of their classrooms and even their doors and windows in the belief that every part of a classroom setting deserved serious consideration. An eclectic, combative, and messianic group, German reform educators developed bold new theories of education, publicized their efforts to win adherents, and debated their positions within a burgeoning number of journals. They won increasing acceptance in German society in the Weimar Republic, and even made considerable headway in reforming the practice of education in the public schools.[20]

The Odenwaldschule reflected one small part of the increasing success and visibility of reform pedagogy in the Weimar Republic. The student body declined during the First World War but rose to 110 in 1919 and climbed steadily throughout the 1920s to reach 190 *Kameraden* in 1930. To accommodate the new students, three additional houses were built and were named "Plato Haus," "Pestalozzi Haus," and "Cassirer Haus."[21]

The female student population of the Odenwaldschule generally fluctuated between thirty and forty percent. This proportion fell short of the optimal fifty percent one might wish to claim for a school practicing full coeducation. Rumors about sexual promiscuity in the school appear to have been common in the villages surrounding the Odenwaldschule, but the reality within the school appears to have been much more tepid. If there were problems related to sexuality, the Geheebs handled them in a discreet fashion.

The Odenwaldschule attracted a diverse student body, but it did not reflect the overall distribution of ethnic and religious groups in Germany. In particular, the school attracted an unusually high number of Jews and a low number of Catholics. In the late Second Empire and Weimar Republic the number of Jews in Germany never surpassed one percent of the population. Catholics made up thirty-six percent of the population in 1910 and thirty-two percent in 1925. In the Odenwaldschule, however, the Jewish population fluctuated between fifteen and twenty-seven percent after the first two years of the school; the Catholic population, on the other hand, was sometimes wholly absent and never reached more than ten percent.[22]

Although initially striking, these figures are not discordant with general findings concerning the location of Jews and Catholics in the German educational system. Jews as a group tended to place a high value on education and had a higher per capita income than other religious groups. They were more likely to be urban dwellers and sympathetic to social movements that were considered modern, such as feminism and its educational correlate, coeducation. Many Jews came to the school from the comparatively large and prosperous Jewish population in nearby Frankfurt; those from farther afield were often attracted by the Cassirers' word-of-mouth advertising in Berlin. Jews were likely to be conducive to the liberal and tolerant *Weltanschauung* elaborated by Geheeb, which complemented assimilationist aspirations. The general knowledge that Max Cassirer provided the capital which got the school started and that Edith Geheeb was his daughter must have attracted Jews who wanted to give their children quality educations and avoid the anti-Semitic incidents which occurred at the Lietz schools.

Catholics, on the other hand, were concentrated in agricultural occupations and in small towns. Their income was the lowest of German religious groups, and their embeddedness in rural enclaves led them to be critical of avant-garde theories and institutional innovations. According to one alumnus, the local Catholic priest "was the greatest enemy of the school, for coeducation was immoral and it was taken for granted that farmers' children wouldn't be allowed to go to this school." Geheeb's theories about the equal value of all religions must have been threatening to parents who believed that their religion existed on a plane of truth superior to that of other creeds.[23]

As one would expect, the largest religious grouping in the school was Protestant. This group may have been attracted by knowing that Geheeb had studied Protestant theology, and that whatever pantheistic beliefs he might espouse, he was culturally anchored in Protestantism. Furthermore, both the Grand Duchy of Hesse in Imperial Germany and its Weimar successor, the Free Hessian State, were predominantly Protestant.

Tuition costs at the Odenwaldschule were high and *de facto* excluded students from working-class and many middle-class families. A scholarship fund was established in the waning years of the Weimar Republic which enabled students with lower family incomes to come to the school. Even with such a fund, however, the expense of the school placed a serious limitation on the idealization of diversity in Geheeb's philosophy of education. In many years, the tuition receipts were not sufficient to cover the costs of running the school. When this was the case, Max Cassirer wrote a check and restored the balance.[24]

After the peculiar dominance of Prussian aristocrats in the Odenwaldschule in its first years the school increasingly attracted children who came from prominent families of the liberal intelligentsia. Novelist Thomas Mann's son Klaus, playwright Frank Wedekind's daughter Pamela, the religious socialist Emil Fuchs' children Gerhard and Christel, youth-movement painter Fidus's daughter Drude, and *Welt-*

bühne editor Carl von Ossietzsky's daughter Rosalinde all attended the Odenwaldschule. Many students came because they experienced difficulties in public schools or because of familial problems in their homes. Sonja Latk was only seven years old when she came to the Odenwaldschule from a broken home with parents who had "neither space nor time for her," and the school appeared to have a disproportionately high number of students from such backgrounds. Others had parents from liberal backgrounds who were suspicious of nationalistic elements in the public schools and wanted their children to receive an education which stressed intercultural tolerance and international reconciliation. Emil Fuchs sent his son Gerhard to the Odenwaldschule because Gerhard, who had suffered from asthma attacks since he was four years old, was continually getting into fights at school. In the conservative *Gymnasium* at Eisenach, Gerhard had defended a Jewish pupil whom nationalist pupils had bullied, and those students subsequently tormented Gerhard. His father decided that he could not justify to himself continuing to send his son to the school under these circumstances. Some students came because of recent traumas which necessitated their removal to a friendlier environment. Paul Krantz, the son of a café musician in Berlin, was sent to the Odenwaldschule after being dismissed on charges of assisting a homicide in a "student murder trial" which was exploited by the sensationalist media. Students who came from these troubling circumstances were particularly grateful for the humanistic and protective atmosphere of the Odenwaldschule.[25]

Paul Geheeb's attitude to student enrollment appeared to be one of openness to whoever was interested regardless of ideology or personal circumstances. He was delighted when shortly after the First World War he received inquiries on the same day from the son of a murdered German communist, Kurt Eisner, and from a child of the nobility. "I was so pleased that people in the different camps understood my work," he said, referring to the principle of tolerance toward those with different values.[26]

Along with a differentiated student body came a staff of *Mitarbeiter* with varied backgrounds. Werner Meyer, a former student of Karl Jaspers at the University of Heidelberg, gave immensely popular history classes and directed plays. Martin Wagenschein developed an innovative pedagogy of "exemplary learning" and coordinated the school's course plan. Heinrich Sachs was an art teacher who quickly internalized the atmosphere of the Odenwaldschule, gave himself the nickname of "Erasmus," and became one of Geheeb's closest friends. Alwine von Keller was the favorite teacher of many students and was very influential in the school. She first came to the Odenwaldschule in 1916 after founding an artistic society with the youth-movement painter Fidus and the novelist Gertrude Prellwitz. Fidus and von Keller sent their children to the Odenwaldschule, and Prellwitz wrote a novel about one of them which was popular in the German youth movement.[27]

While not every *Mitarbeiter* claimed to be a pedagogical luminary, the Odenwaldschule attracted an unusually high ratio of bright and committed young teachers. Otto Friedrich Bullnow, a famous philosopher and historian of education, taught in the school, as did Heinrich Jacoby, a prominent music educator, and Peter Suhrkamp, who later became one of West Germany's major publishers. Martin Buber, who lived in nearby Heppenheim, often visited the school, spoke with faculty and *Kameraden*, and made himself available for individual consultation with students. Finally, "helping guests" came to the school and gave classes for several weeks in exchange for room and board. *Kameraden* and *Mitarbeiter* alike continually received fresh impulses from visitors interested in educational issues, and the combination of talent and pedagogical experimentation made the Odenwaldschule one of the most stimulating school settings in Germany.[28]

Regretfully, the relationship between the two leading *Mitarbeiter* of the school, Paul and Edith Geheeb, appears to have been unhappy for many of their years at the Odenwaldschule. After they moved out of Darmstadt the two never really lived together, but occupied separate apartments on different floors, first in Goethe Haus and then in Humboldt Haus. Agaath Hamaker-Willink, a visiting teacher, commented in her journal,

> I never see them as a married couple. No looks, no gestures . . . Edith is the most alone of all of us . . . I always see her alone. Paulus has in her his most loyal *Mitarbeiter*, but does she have more in Paulus than an ideal and a tremendous amount of work?

The phrase "most loyal *Mitarbeiter*," captured the asymmetry in the relationship between Paul and Edith. The stationery of the Odenwaldschule listed only Paul as the director, and even Edith constantly described the Odenwaldschule as *his* school, in spite of the fact that the property was actually owned by her father. The term *"Mitarbeiter"* is ambiguous, for it casts Edith as both a colleague and an employee of Geheeb. Finally, the adjective "loyal," with its associations of unquestioning obedience, suggests a clear-cut deference of Edith to Paul. Paul Geheeb's feminism seemed real enough in both his philos-

ophy of education and the coeducational structure of the Odenwaldschule, but it found meager realization in his private married life.[29]

This asymmetry was also played out in more intimate areas. In 1920
Paul Geheeb had an affair with Lili Schäfer, the widowed sister of
Max Weber. The relationship was broken off by Paul, and the dis-
traught Lili committed suicide. Her four children were then taken in
by Max and Marianne Weber and subsequently received much of
their education in the Odenwaldschule. In later years both Paul and
Edith were to explore extramarital romantic liaisons, but in spite of
their problems they retained a strong attachment to one another and
none of their other relationships was strong enough to shake the marriage.[30]

After his initial generous funding, Max Cassirer continued to play
an active role in the development of the Odenwaldschule. He regularly visited the school and showed a strong interest not only in funding and the improvement of the physical plant but also in the development of individual *Kameraden*. Although Cassirer and Geheeb had
serious differences at the outset of their relationship, Cassirer grew
increasingly impressed with Geheeb's pedagogical achievements,
and Geheeb's affection for and gratitude to his father-in-law was
immense. "You're not an educator by profession," Geheeb wrote to
Cassirer in an open letter in the school journal,

> but a man who is filled with such resilient love for others, and who con-
> stantly strives to understand the development of each individual with
> such overpowering generosity as you, becomes the finest educator, alto-
> gether unconsciously and unintentionally . . . Without you our commu-
> nity of children could neither have existed nor developed so happily.

While Cassirer appreciated Geheeb's compliments, there was always
something troubling for him about the Odenwaldschule, perhaps
because he sensed the difficulties between Paul and Edith. He
referred to the Odenwaldschule as his "problem child," and sadly
commented, "One always loves one's problem child the most."[31]

Whatever difficulties the Geheebs may have encountered with one
another on a personal level, their problems appear to have caused few
difficulties for the *Kameraden*. The overwhelming impression given by
the children who passed through the Odenwaldschule is one of profound gratitude. The students' enthusiasm derived from many different sources. The flexible course system, which allowed students to
develop their own areas of inquiry while working in small groups,
gave students a chance to pursue the topics which most interested

them in a manner which appears to have been highly successful. "The entire form of instruction was based on free will and independence, and not on compulsion or external pressure," alumnus Dankwart Rüstow recalled. "We didn't learn because we had to, or to show off to others, but because of our joy and interest in the subject." For many *Kameraden*, the freedom extended to students to develop and refine their knowledge in different areas of inquiry stood in marked contrast to the more teacher-centered pedagogies practiced in traditional schools. Reingart Ahrem came to the Odenwaldschule from a school in which he had been marched through a rigid academic curriculum that in no way enabled him to formulate his own questions. He was thrilled to find himself in a setting in which teachers actually asked him what he was most interested in learning about. "In the Oden-waldschule we were *allowed* to learn," he observed, "and that was a great part of its tremendous success."[32]

The *Kameraden* were also enthusiastic about the *Schulgemeinde* and the earnestness with which student self-government was practiced in the Odenwaldschule. *Schulgemeinden* were devoted to every conceivable topic, including relatively trivial concerns, such as joint decisions on the best way to keep the school grounds clean or to organize hiking trips, to fundamental issues of school organization, such as proposals from students on ways to improve the course schedule or the monthly *Kursschlussschulgemeinde* meetings. In extraordinary circumstances, a *Schulgemeinde* meeting could take hours. Toward the end of the First World War, for example, when there was a terrible shortage of food in the school, a lengthy *Schulgemeinde* was held when it was discovered that a piece of bread had been stolen. Although one could hardly be surprised that such an incident occurred in a school with almost one hundred children, it became the centerpiece for a *Schulgemeinde* in which the fundamental issue was not to find and punish the culprit but to make it clear to everyone that theft in such difficult times could destroy the cohesiveness and spirit of the entire school community.

Just as *Kameraden* were pleased with the freedom and flexibility of the course system, they also were thrilled with the spirit of open discussion and decision making with real consequences in the *Schulgemeinde* meetings. Marlisbeth Niederhöffer-Trusen noted that

Free speech, freedom of opinion, freedom of religion—we took all of that for granted, because in the *Schulgemeinde* everyone could say what he thought, and we listened to anyone without rejecting him right away, and really responded. When a decision was made, one had the satisfying feeling that it wasn't ordered from above but that we all really found it to be good and necessary.

The *Schulgemeinden* trained students in democratic skills involving problem solving, group leadership, the shaping of consensus, and voting. Even shy students often became involved. After her first two years in the Odenwaldschule, a withdrawn *Kameradin* named Dodo Kroner was delighted when Paul Geheeb nominated her to be the leader of the *Schulgemeinde*. "This girl is so reserved," he said, "we must give her a chance to take on a position, so that she will really develop!" "I found that just incredible," Kroner later recalled, "because it was enormously important for me to take on some real responsibility." Although the younger students rarely took on leadership roles, they were honored to feel included in the school's deliberations. "I think it's beautiful," twelve-year-old Gideon Strauss wrote, "that the young and old *Kameraden* have equal rights, and that the older ones respect what the little ones say, even when it doesn't make sense."[33]

Given Geheeb's emphasis on tolerance of and appreciation for individual differences, it is perhaps not surprising that coeducation, rather than being a major issue, was rarely addressed in the actual day-to-day life of the school. One *Kameradin* recalled that

> We lived in the individual "families" with a teacher or a married couple, as if we were a family with boys and girls of all ages mixed together. And we weren't handled any differently in this situation than siblings are usually handled. Nobody thought anything about it if you sat in your room with a boy or went for a walk together or even took off for the whole day. One didn't have to do it secretly, but it happened just as naturally as if he were your brother, and it was exactly that which made it so unproblematic and spontaneous.

In terms of course enrollments, Paul Geheeb noted that boys rarely signed up for the afternoon courses in cooking and girls showed little interest in the courses where they could learn to make keys and locks. He did not appear disturbed by the gender imbalance, however; from his perspective, the main point was that individuals of each sex were encouraged to develop their personalities in manners they found appropriate.[34]

Much of the enthusiasm for the Odenwaldschule appears to have come not so much from the structural arrangements as from Paul Geheeb's gentle manner of directing the school. One *Kamerad* described it as "leadership in the sense of oriental wisdom: action through inaction," a second as "active passivity," and a third elaborated:

> I never again met anyone who could believe in such a brave and uncompromising way. And the strange thing was that he actually did nothing.

At least, one never or only rarely ever noticed it. All of the ideas about the way we lived together came from him. He didn't intervene in the mechanism, but floated above it like God above the creation.

Klaus Mann wrote in his autobiography,

This humanistic educator—yes, Paul Geheeb was one, if I ever knew one!—did not believe in the "leadership principle." He believed much more that the democratic method was the most appropriate one to obtain and sustain the necessary balance between freedom and discipline. The Odenwaldschule was a republic in which power emanated from the people, that is, from the young people. The headmaster was satisfied with the role of a fatherly adviser, mediator, and representative. The students were called *"Kameraden"* and formed a parliament which made all of the decisions for the important questions of the community. The student assembly, or *"Schulgemeinde,"* which met at regular intervals, determined the laws and hierarchy of the institution. It could punish and even banish asocial elements. It had the right to modify and abolish rules established by the headmaster.

That there once could be such a school in Germany! Nationalism and racist madness never stopped poisoning the public life of the Reich. Here, however, in an oasis of culture, tolerance ruled.[35]

For many *Kameraden,* the compassionate atmosphere of the Oden-waldschule allowed them for the first time to discover and accept their own uniqueness and to find ways to put it to good purpose. They described their school as a "paradise for children," and a "paradise of freedom," where "Paulus tenderly taught us the essence of freedom." *Kamerad* Walter Matuschke found the spirit of the Odenwaldschule to be "incredibly new, indeed revolutionary":

The freedom which prevailed here was the greatest surprise for me. The self-government of the students in the *Schulgemeinden* and the many offices which students controlled were also surprising. That there were no report cards and therefore no failures, that boys and girls lived in rooms directly next to each other! All of this was unheard of.

When one *Kamerad,* Friedel Hellmund, wanted to test Geheeb to see whether he could really do what he wanted, he refused to attend math class. Geheeb's response was to tell Friedel that he could well understand how a young man could tire of a routine and that he probably knew best when he wished to return to work. Observing that Geheeb understood his situation, Friedel subsequently returned to class. Other *Kameraden* had similar experiences.[36]

Much of Geheeb's success lay in the emotional warmth he established with his students—the affective components of his life and work. Sometimes Geheeb expressed his fondness for his students

60   *Origins*

through a simple gesture of kindness, as when he noticed a withdrawn student in the school and made sure that he visited with the child to put him or her at ease. *Kameradin* Ruth Blundon, who at first felt badly dislocated in the Odenwaldschule, felt that he invested tremendous energy in her. She appreciated many quiet hours in his study, "a green warm room, in which Paulus moved noiselessly in his light sandals," and in which he read to her from some of his favorite passages by Hölderlin and Nietzsche. She praised his "infinite tolerance, his supreme confidence in us, even when we were odd, absurd, and immature," and felt that

> It is in the Odenwaldschule that I learned that the individual has a right to be different; that there is not a one and only "role" which each and every woman or man, parent or child is called upon to play; that to be deviant is not necessarily bad, but may be good, that it may be a challenge, a misfortune, and a blessing at the same time.

Most commonly, the importance of love in the school was an unspoken phenomenon; on occasion, however, Geheeb articulated its significance for the school at *Schulgemeinden*. *Kameradin* Lilla Fuchs was present at one such meeting, and wrote down her impressions:

> Herr Geheeb said to us that the theme for the new school year [was] "We want to learn to love," with "love" in the real sense of the word: to feel my way into another person, so that his interests are mine, and I really try to understand all of him. We Germans often hold that great knowledge is more important than anything else, but a heart full of love has a thousand times more value. A loving look is so comforting, and one understands it better than any lecture. Even the great thinker Schopenhauer placed a golden heart above all.

Even when not stated explicitly, however, the students felt Geheeb's warmth and interest in their well-being. By integrating affective education into the Odenwaldschule, Geheeb won the admiration of numerous *Kameraden,* who were glad for a respite from the strictly cognitive emphasis of traditional schools.[37]

While many of the *Kameraden* who attended the Odenwaldschule thrived in its carefully cultivated milieu, there were limits to Paul Geheeb's tolerance of destructive behavior. When students overstepped the boundaries of liberties extended by the Odenwaldschule, Geheeb firmly cut them out of the community by expelling them from the school. In such instances, Geheeb revealed an otherwise concealed and aggressive side to his personality. One *Kamerad* disappeared from the campus and it was not discovered until days later that he was in Darmstadt; Geheeb wrote the parents and suggested that arresting him would be appropriate. Other students used an outbreak of scarlet fever in the school to persuade their parents to send them home early for vacation; Geheeb resented the implication that he was imprudent and wrote the parents that their children should not return if they could not place more trust in the school. Geheeb charged one *Kamerad* who transgressed the principles of the school with "betrayal," and referred to the example of Gandhi's nonviolent activism in India. "I fear, my dear young man," he fumed, "that you'll never be ready to go to jail for a great idea."

On other occasions Geheeb pulled his idealistic mentors into the fray, and aphorisms from Goethe and Wilhelm von Humboldt popped up in letters in which he admonished students and even parents for disrupting the internal tranquility of the Odenwaldschule. Geheeb criticized one mother who had trouble separating from her son and did not allow him to acclimate to the Odenwaldschule by urging her to "act egotistically for a while, and to dedicate all of your time and energy to think about your own life and development." He then followed with one of his favorite quotes from Humboldt: "The first law of all morality is to educate yourself; the second is to influence others, through who you are." Even in his reprimands, however, his gentle spirit often prevailed. After expelling a *Kamerad* from the Odenwaldschule, he wrote him, "What sense does it make for you to ask for forgiveness? What else can I do, but not stop loving you and wishing you all of the best?"[38]

Although Geheeb's leadership style emphasized respect for individual interests and eccentricities, some *Kameraden* occasionally experienced that tolerance negatively as indifference. One young *Kameradin*, Elisabeth Johnson, was terribly unhappy in the Odenwaldschule for two years, and she felt that neither Paul nor Edith Geheeb noticed her plight or tried to help her. Friedburg Rüstow was bullied by a cohort of girls who cut off handfuls of her hair; when she went to Geheeb for assistance, he simply placed her hair in a box, told her it would be fine there, and never reprimanded the girls. Friedburg's brother, Dankwart, was only able to gain relief from a tormenter by thrashing him soundly after lunch with a huge cluster of *Kameraden* watching and no adult intervention.[39]

Many of the conflicts in the Odenwaldschule appear to have resulted from violations of the high level of trust Geheeb and the *Mitarbeiter* placed in the *Kameraden*—violations such as stealing, drinking alcohol, committing petty acts of vandalism, or otherwise undermining the principle of responsibility that Geheeb emphasized. Occasionally, however, conflicts arose over sensitive topics such as religion.

During the First World War, a Jewish *Mitarbeiter,* Margarete Moses, wished to read aloud for the Sunday *Andacht* from Hasidic texts recently translated into German by Martin Buber. Paul Geheeb was delighted with her initiative, and she succeeded in awakening the enthusiasm of the many Jewish students in the school for their religious heritage. Some of the Jewish students subsequently returned home for the holidays and reproached their parents for not sharing more of their Judaism with them. Their assimilated parents were upset by their children's new attitudes, however, and Paul Geheeb began receiving complaints. Bowing to the pressure, Geheeb explained the situation to Moses and asked her to be more subdued with her enthusiasm for Hasidism.

Geheeb showed a more emotional side on religious issues in his response to an article in the student newspaper in 1927. A new *Kamerad,* Ernst Zinn, had come to the Odenwaldschule from a strict Christian background and had found religious education in the Odenwaldschule in general and in the *Andachten* in particular to be far too muted. Zinn charged that in the Odenwaldschule "there is no religious life, either in the community or among individuals." Geheeb wrote a sharp response to Zinn and claimed that

> The Odenwaldschule has never wanted to be a denominational community, nor has it ever wanted to represent an interdenominational hodgepodge, but rather it has always been concerned with developing and caring for a supradenominational religiosity. Taking the point of departure from the conviction that . . . all people (yes, really all people: Jews, Christians, Hottentots, etc.!) are "God's children" and, as with a proper father, are equally close to his heart . . . We have found it to be our noblest and holiest task to develop and to emphasize this binding and original religiosity, which transcends all denominational and cultural differences and which is common to all people as belonging to this "childhood to God."

Geheeb's reaction revealed his fundamental refusal to accommodate intolerance on issues of religious and moral development. Geheeb was often silent on many issues of school policy, for he believed that the efforts made by *Kameraden* to solve problems without his intervention were among the most important learning experiences offered in the Odenwaldschule. When Geheeb felt that students were denigrating others with different creeds, however, he did not hesitate to come forward with a forceful articulation of his own perspective. He concluded his article by referring to "the fantasy of our own cult" in the Odenwaldschule. Separate from mainstream religions, this "cult" would respect individuals' theological convictions and develop school practices which would encompass the full range of religious expressions. According to Geheeb, such a cult "has always surfaced before our eyes like a distant and intangible dream which would correspond to the values and supradenominational character of our religious community."[40]

Geheeb's interest in establishing a "cult" was reflected in his eccentric appearance. He avoided conventional masculine attire such as suits and ties and continued to sport the short knickerbockers popular in the youth movement at the turn of the century. As the decades passed, Geheeb's long mottled beard turned white, offsetting his bold black eyebrows and lending him an even more prophetic facade. In addition to his unusual appearance, Geheeb allowed others to call him "Paulus," which in German is usually used only to identify Christ's disciple Paul. The acceptance of the name "Paulus" represents a subtle double maneuver, for it conveys both closeness—a first-name relationship between students and the director of a school—and superiority—because of the hagiographic association with the biblical Paul. Geheeb combined both meanings to his advantage in the day-to-day business of leading the Odenwaldschule. Through name and countenance, Paul Geheeb represented himself as a singular phenomenon, an eclectic embodiment of an educational philosophy based on individuation and difference.

While the vast majority of Paul Geheeb's work from 1910 to 1930 was dedicated to the internal development of the Odenwaldschule, the school did not exist in a vacuum. The Odenwaldschule had to regulate its relationship with its neighbors in the Bergstrasse region and with government authorities at the Ministry of Culture in Darmstadt. Geheeb also entered two educational organizations with markedly different constituencies and aims. These affiliations and relationships influenced the internal life of the school.

The Odenwaldschule experienced ambivalent relationships with its immediate neighbors, the farmers of the Hambacher Valley and the villagers of the nearby small town of Heppenheim. The farmers in the Hambacher Valley were invited to festivals and other special events in the school and some gained employment by assisting with maintenance. Because of the mutual reliance entailed in life in a small rural setting, most contacts had a face-to-face personal character. Many relationships between villagers and residents of the Odenwaldschule were friendly. On the other hand, the unusual character of the Odenwaldschule in a conservative rural setting also attracted negative attention. Morning exercises in the nude, coeducation, the high tuition of the school, the antagonism of the local Catholic church, feminism, and the fact that the school was owned by a prosperous Jew from Berlin fueled an undercurrent of resentment and stereotyping. Alumnus Richard Erdoes complained,

> The rumor that I came from that ungodly, subversive institution, the Odenwaldschule, where depraved children of both sexes cavorted stark naked in the woods, where four-letter words went unpunished, where pupils were taught to pick edible mushrooms instead of geometry, preceded me wherever I went.

Paul Geheeb attempted to mitigate such rumors by inviting individuals who held such prejudices to visit the school themselves. He served critics generous servings of coffee and a local specialty, plum pie, and hoped that those who saw the school for themselves would revise their judgments. Try as he might, however, Geheeb was never able to change completely the reputation of the Odenwaldschule as a "communist Jew school."[41]

Relationships with the Ministry of Culture in Darmstadt were likewise ambivalent. On the one hand, the Ministry had proved daring enough to provide a home for the first fully coeducational boarding school in Germany, and for this Geheeb always expressed gratitude. The Ministry assisted the school in awarding the *Abitur* for the completion of studies, although *Kameraden* could not take their examinations in the school under the supervision of their own *Mitarbeiter* until 1931. On the other hand, Geheeb experienced friction with the Ministry about his refusal to celebrate the Kaiser's birthday or German war victories and was also criticized for the secular spirit of religious instruction in the school. These criticisms disappeared with the collapse of Imperial Germany, however, and Geheeb enjoyed fruitful relations with the Ministry in the Weimar Republic.

In terms of associational affiliations, the first pedagogical group Geheeb joined was the New Education Fellowship, the international umbrella group of progressive educators founded in Calais in 1921. Geheeb was a passionate supporter of the NEF, with which he identified not only in terms of progressive approaches to teaching and learning but also with regard to social reconstruction and cross-cultural understanding. The NEF was a crucial vehicle for his coming into contact with prominent educational reformers, such as Beatrice Ensor, Helen Parkhurst, and Rabindranath Tagore, all of whom visited the Odenwaldschule in the 1920s.

Geheeb's work with the NEF was important not only on an organizational level but also as a means of cultivating personal friendships with educators outside of Germany. One example was Adolphe Ferrière, who was one of the greatest organizers and synthesizers of continental progressive education. Ferrière had first contacted Geheeb while Geheeb was at Wickersdorf to gather information about coeducation in "new schools." The two educators subsequently met repeatedly at NEF conferences. Ferrière was a tireless missionary for educational reform who was on the faculty of the Institut Jean-Jacques Rousseau in Geneva, taught at the University of Geneva, edited the NEF journal *Pour l'Ere Nouvelle,* and headed the NEF section for French, Spanish, and Portuguese speakers. Ferrière had helped Elisabeth Huguenin, a Swiss colleague, write a book on the Odenwaldschule, and he sent his own son Claude to the school. In Ferrière, Geheeb found one of his closest friends and an important link to the "Geneva school" of educators at the Institut Jean-Jacques Rousseau. Ferrière also brought Geheeb into contact with religiously minded writers and reformers such as Romain Rolland and Albert Schweitzer.

Geheeb's friendship with Ferrière enabled a constant exchange between German and French variants of progressive education. Ferrière often recommended *Mitarbeiter* to Geheeb, and Geheeb proofread translations of Ferrière's work from French to German. Geheeb first visited Ferrière at his home in Switzerland in 1926 and their friendship blossomed thereafter, with the two often hiking together, discussing educational themes, and with Geheeb reporting on these experiences in the student newspaper, *Der neue Waldkauz.*[42]

Geheeb also enjoyed fruitful contacts with Anglo-American school reformers. He idolized Beatrice Ensor, the British president of the NEF, and after visiting her school at Frensham Heights he created an exchange program between students there and in the Odenwaldschule. Among American progressive educators, he was enchanted by Marietta Johnson, the founder of the Fairhope School in Alabama, which he thought was "the one school in North America most similar to the Odenwaldschule." To reach out to English-speaking audiences, he published articles on the Odenwaldschule in *Progressive Education* and *The New Era in Home and School,* the journals of American and British progressive educators respectively. His experiences with foreign progressive educators in the NEF were so positive that he claimed that "I can probably say that there is nothing in the world other than the Odenwaldschule which is so fulfilling and important for me as the New Education Fellowship."[43]

Geheeb was less enthusiastic about the second educational organization with which he affiliated, the Association of German *Landerzie-*

hungsheime and Free *Schulgemeinden*. This organization was founded in October 1924 at a special assembly in the Odenwaldschule as part of an effort to establish an ongoing medium for debate and exchange among the more than a dozen "new schools" which had been founded since Lietz's first successes at the turn of the century. Lietz had died in 1919, and Wyneken had been driven out of Wickersdorf after engaging in homosexual activities with students, so Geheeb's old enemies were no longer a challenge to him.

Geheeb hoped that the association would serve as a forum for exchanging innovative practices and intensifying pedagogical commitment in *Landerziehungsheimen*. In reality, however, he found its meetings banal and his colleagues mundane:

> These meetings are among the worst experiences of my life, and I cannot think back on them without a sense of shame at having belonged to this society for so many years. We never discussed the great problems of humanistic education in our meetings but only superficial and in particular financial questions.

While the association proved disappointing, Geheeb's encounters with other German *Landerziehungsheime* were nonetheless important in compelling him to recognize how different the Odenwaldschule had become from its sister schools. Geheeb noted that although the schools had beautiful rural settings and all of the conditions for daring pedagogical projects, they reproduced the most anachronistic teachings styles and failed to transmit any sense of idealism to young people. After visiting the *Landerziehungsheim* at Schondorf, Geheeb wrote to Ferrière,

> If the Odenwaldschule among all of the free schools in Germany stands on the extreme left wing, then the Schondorfer *Landerziehungsheim* certainly represents the most extreme point of the right wing ... It was interesting to compare the differences between the people there and those with me. Among the young and old there are undifferentiated, simple, nice, docile people, who do their duties without any problems. Here by us there is an atmosphere always full of problems, the children are vastly different and interesting due to their complicated and difficult personalities (and to a large extent their unusual talents).

Geheeb was completely opposed to the "strictly nationalistic and reactionary spirit in all cultural affairs" at Schondorf. He nonetheless remained a full-fledged member of the Association of German *Landerziehungsheime,* apparently hoping that the conservative schools would return to what he saw as their original task of pedagogical innovation and social transformation.[44]

By 1930 the Odenwaldschule could point to numerous successes and anticipate the celebration of two decades of productive and creative work. The school had initiated the first thoroughly coeducational boarding school in Germany; it had attracted international attention for its innovative course plan and far-reaching student self-government; it had fused diverse elements of German idealism, fin-de-siècle feminism, and modern educational reform to create an exciting and unique learning environment. The Odenwaldschule was hailed by prominent German educators as "the most comprehensive and daring experimental school in Germany and perhaps in all of Europe," and two visiting American scholars found that "coeducation is real in the Odenwaldschule, to a degree approximated by scarcely half a dozen other schools in the world." When Adolphe Ferrière conducted a survey of "new schools" in England, France, Belgium, and Germany in 1920 to measure the degree of their willingness to explore progressive reforms such as coeducation, student self-government, and student-centered instruction, only the Odenwaldschule received the highest possible score. The traumas Paul Geheeb had endured at Haubinda and Wickersdorf over two decades earlier disappeared in the wake of his triumph in Oberhambach, and his tenacity in undertaking one last attempt to start a school of his own had been bountifully repaid.[45]

In spite of its successes, there were serious criticisms of the school in its first twenty years. One of the most important of these concerned its exclusivity as an expensive private school, which belied the democratic principles of the *Schulgemeinde* and the universalistic claims Geheeb advanced on behalf of the school. The diversity of the Odenwaldschule was limited by strict class boundaries, and while there were many children in the school who had parents with left-wing values, they were overwhelmingly drawn from the middle-class and upper-class intelligentsia. This class exclusivity gave the Odenwaldschule a highly unrepresentative character in terms of the larger German population. Klaus Mann wrote, "One discussed the poor who lived outside with the same compassionate alienation which the decadent characters of *The Magic Mountain* had for those down in the flatlands."[46]

Another problem in the school appeared to lie in the area of academic achievement. Almost all of the *Kameraden* who desired to were able to graduate from the Odenwaldschule with the *Abitur*, which permitted them to attend universities. In retrospect, however, many students wished that they had been placed under more pressure to take certain courses and to learn habits of academic discipline that the Odenwaldschule not only neglected but sometimes even denigrated. Albert Weber-Schäfer left the Odenwaldschule with only a minimal knowledge of mathematics; Arthur Venn wished that he had studied Latin with more discipline and consistency; Ovene Jessen, Inge Badenhausen, and Gertrud Hoffman all found that their fellow students at the university knew more than them. Alumni also generally found that they were completely unprepared for the more mundane aspects of university studies, such as "cramming"; Hilde Cupey found herself learning for the first time at the university how to absorb massive amounts of information and to express her knowledge in an examination format. On the other hand, these same students found that their individual initiative, overall method of study, and ability to interpret complex problems were much more developed than those of their university peers.

A third criticism of the school was that Geheeb's definition of autonomy was overwhelming. One Dutch student teacher wrote, "One has to discover, do, and organize everything here oneself. We lack a director, who could give help and leadership." The same student teacher noted that Geheeb's quotes from the classics were often inaudible because he mumbled into his beard and that the idealistic philosophy of the school was belied by the haggard faces of *Mitarbeiter* who worked without respite in the relentlessly demanding context of a boarding school. It is interesting to note, however, that this same teaching intern learned to practice her own autonomy in the school, and wrote that

> the children are raised from the first day on in this fashion, but when one is twenty-eight years old and suddenly immersed in it after one has always had a "leader" it almost takes one's breath away. Once you get your breath back, you breathe more easily and can truly unfold and reach a much higher level.

This facilitation of independence was precisely the goal which Geheeb desired for *Kameraden* and *Mitarbeiter* alike.[47]

Finally, a fourth criticism of the Odenwaldschule was that it was "too idealistic." The Odenwaldschule secluded young people from pressing social problems, which was sensible when children were young but irresponsible when older adolescents needed to prepare for the duties of citizenship. Although efforts were made over the years to pay due regard to citizenship education, this was usually

defined primarily with reference to participation in the Odenwaldschule and rarely extended beyond the idyllic setting of Oberhambach. Alumnus Felix von Mendelssohn complained,

> It's beautiful and good to preach about Goethe, Hölderlin, "Humanitas,"
> and "reverence for life," and to quote wise sayings from the corner of
> the dining room. But one shouldn't forget in the process to explain to
> the children that one is dealing with praiseworthy but also highly sub-
> jective idealizations and embellishments of life. These can enhance our
> appreciation for life and ease our contacts with other people, but they
> often aren't enough to lead a good marriage, educate children, or make
> reasonable political decisions.

At its worst, Mendelssohn argued, "one floated in the clouds," and,
instead of confronting the many problems of German society,
adopted an escapist attitude toward the outside world.[48]
Not all of the students found the Odenwaldschule so apolitical.
Alumnus Theodor Scharmann recalled encounters in which Geheeb
made it clear that he remained true to the reformist political perspectives he had held as far back as the 1890s. According to Scharmann,
Geheeb was upset on one occasion when he found that a periodical,
Das Andere Deutschland, kept disappearing from the school's library.
This journal—"the other Germany"—was a major forum for a broad
representation of left-wing sentiment in the Weimar Republic. "You
know exactly that this 'other Germany' is also my Germany," Geheeb
told Scharmann. "Make sure that it no longer disappears." Scharmann conceded that Geheeb's political views were often muted, but
elaborated,

> It would have contradicted his gentle and personalized pedagogy to urge
> systematically that a student take up political reflections when doing so
> didn't derive from the individual's needs. Where he found this need for
> political orientation and clarification, he encouraged it—in the sense of
> the "other Germany!"

In general, Geheeb's political sentiments reflected his religious background. He thus felt closest to, and referred his students most frequently to, examples of spiritually inspired reformers, such as Leo
Tolstoy, Rabindranath Tagore, Mahatma Gandhi, and Romain Rolland.[49]
Whatever criticisms were made of the Odenwaldschule at the close
of its first two decades, even its detractors had to concede that the
school had engendered a major new example of school reform which

suggested new pathways for mainstream educational practices. From the vantage point of today the reforms in the Odenwaldschule may seem insignificant, representing at best a peculiar Teutonic offshoot of the progressive education movement. From a historical perspective, however, the Odenwaldschule was one of the few schools in Germany in particular and Europe in general to take the progressive program to its furthest limits. The school explored the real problems and promises of student self-government, student-centered curricula, coeducation in the fullest sense of the term, informal relationships between teachers and students, and the integration of academic and applied kinds of learning. Even today few school reformers dare to follow the kinds of reforms implemented in the Odenwaldschule, preferring to adhere to the safer and more traditional forms of teacher-centered, hierarchical, and curriculum-oriented learning institutions.

The innovative practices in the Odenwaldschule were particularly noteworthy given their social context. In a country with weak democratic traditions, the Odenwaldschule empowered children to exercise democracy on a daily basis; in a country marked by political polarization, the Odenwaldschule not only tolerated but thrived on individual differences; in a country which had hitherto had a largely authoritarian and hierarchical school system, the *Mitarbeiter* and *Kameraden* of the Odenwaldschule attempted to redefine authority, reconstruct hierarchy, and establish learning communities based on students' interests. Given the problematic aspects of many features of mainstream German society, the remoteness of the Odenwaldschule from those problems may not have been merely escapist, but may have enabled a more autonomous and creative school culture to come into being than would otherwise have been possible.

After Geheeb's failures at Haubinda and Wickersdorf, the Odenwaldschule was nothing less than a triumph. Given the problems he had experienced in those two schools—which sent him to a sanatorium to recover—it would have been easy for Geheeb to abandon pedagogical experimentation altogether. Instead, he remained true to his vision of a bold and successful alternative school and persisted in his dream of creating it in practice. Geheeb expanded upon his work in the previous schools by inventing a creative course schedule, institutionalizing coeducation in the most far-reaching sense of the term, and striking out on bold new paths in student self-governance. Whatever its preoccupations with its own problems, the Odenwaldschule reached out beyond its borders to prefigure sexual equality through a philosophy of women's emancipation and coeducation, youthful self-governance through *Schulgemeinde* meetings, and international solidarity through pacifism and work in the NEF. Combined with the multiple instances of communitarian self-determination and Geheeb's gentle but firm manner of leading the school, these practices shaped a lively and self-critical school community which largely realized Geheeb's ambitious project proposal submitted to the Hessian Ministry of the Interior in 1909. The Odenwaldschule would not rest secure on these achievements, however, and would be tested with fundamentally new challenges as it prepared to enter its third decade.

Outer Dangers and Inner Reforms, 1930–1932

In April 1930 the Odenwaldschule was preparing to mark its twentieth anniversary. Many alumni and *Mitarbeiter* had been looking forward to this event for years and were anticipating a festive reunion of old friends and colleagues. Rather than celebrate the anniversary in April, the group planning the event decided to synchronize the celebration with Paul Geheeb's sixtieth birthday in October. As a special gift to her husband, Edith began asking Paulus's many friends to mail her hand-written greetings for her husband, which she wanted to arrange in a special volume and present to him on his birthday.

In most institutions, the celebration of an anniversary is a relatively straightforward event in which leading individuals are honored and their achievements acclaimed. As the momentum began developing for the twentieth anniversary of the Odenwaldschule, however, a complex political and pedagogical issue emerged and increasingly occupied the students and teachers. With characteristic panache, Paul Geheeb decided to set the school's anniversary and his birthdate in the background, and to transform the festivities into a conference to address the key issues animating *Kameraden, Mitarbeiter,* and alumni.

The origins of the controversy went back to a public lecture Paul Geheeb had given in Darmstadt the previous year. Entitled "New Education," the speech was printed in the student journal of the Odenwaldschule, *Der neue Waldkauz,* in December 1929. In the paper, Geheeb presented his philosophy of education in a stylistically refined and elegant address which articulated his idealistic premises. He explained his interpretation of the importance of individuation and interdependence in the context of a school community, upheld the importance of coeducation for the psychological and social maturation of children, and confidently proclaimed the enduring merits of tolerant pedagogical *Weltanschauungen.*[1]

For years, many of Geheeb's students had listened to his idealistic interpretations of education with scarcely a murmur of serious criticism. By the time his lecture was circulated to *Kameraden,* alumni, and parents in early 1930, however, that acquiesence was gone, and the cause of its disappearance came not from the realm of ideas but from the escalating sense of economic and political crisis in Germany. The Weimar Republic had never been a strong government, and the relative stability it enjoyed from 1924 to 1929 rapidly disintegrated at the decade's end. The New York stock market crash on 24 October 1929 led to drastic cut-backs on the short-term credits which previously had helped sustain the German economy. Unemployment soared, and the National Socialist party, led by Adolf Hitler, appeared to be winning more and more followers. Many Germans were desperately seeking effective responses to the crises. These unsettling new realities provoked the first serious and public challenge to Geheeb's ideas since the inception of the school.

Ironically, the leader of the counteroffensive was one of Geheeb's favorite alumni, Gerhard Fuchs. Fuchs's father, Emil, was one of Germany's leading religious socialists, and Gerhard inherited his father's rigorous sense of social responsibility. When Paul Geheeb composed his final report for Gerhard prior to his graduation in 1928, he extended unreserved praise to his pupil. "Gerhard's contributions were always exemplary," he wrote. "In critical situations he was often the conscience of our *Schulgemeinde.* Comradery, social sensitivity, and continual readiness to help are developed in Gerhard to the highest degree." Fuchs had been elected the leader of the *Schulgemeinde* on several occasions, had written articles in the student newspaper, and appears to have been one of the *Kameraden* who most comprehended the purpose and potential of the Odenwaldschule.[2]

On leaving the Odenwaldschule, however, Fuchs was startled to find that his education in Geheeb's "pedagogical province" left him poorly equipped to understand the many problems of German society in the late Weimar Republic. In an open letter to the student newspaper, Fuchs stated that this inability was not peculiar to him but appeared to be a common problem for many alumni. Only by adapting to the outside world and slowly developing one's own position in it could one come to any kind of intellectual clarity about the origins of the problems in Germany society and devise successful strategies for addressing them. From Fuchs's perspective, the contemporary crisis was a direct outgrowth of the failures of capitalism and would be resolved through "the growing proletarian class, which is trying to create a new form of social organization." Rather than assist this process, the Odenwaldschule, which enjoyed a "relatively secure financial basis," was obsessed with the world of classical idealism, which only translated indirectly into political awareness. According to Fuchs, the school was completely "cut off from the cultural, social, political realities of the present, untroubled by the objective results of an older cultural tradition." Although Fuchs conceded that he had learned a tremendous amount in the Odenwaldschule, he demanded that the school revoke its political escapism and take a stance in relationship to the current crisis.[3]

Fuchs's article sparked a lively debate in the pages of *Der neue Waldkauz* and among the students, faculty, and alumni of the Odenwaldschule. Walter Solmitz, another alumnus of the school, responded to Fuchs's article in the next issue of the *Waldkauz*. Solmitz claimed that the very fact that Fuchs used the student newspaper to pose such critical questions to the school proved that the school was indeed in touch with political issues. According to Solmitz, the critical edge in Fuchs's essay was a manifestation of the best Odenwaldschule tradition of pluralism and liberalism. *Mitarbeiter* Werner Meyer also responded to Fuchs's article, claiming that the Odenwaldschule dealt with political issues in its history classes, in its guest lecturers, and through its continual contacts with alumni who shared their political concerns with the school. Even as readers of Fuchs's article were discussing his perspective and defending the Odenwaldschule, however, outside events appeared to underscore the urgency of Fuchs's concerns. In September the Nazis won their first major electoral victories and became the second largest political party in the Reichstag.[4]

When the twentieth anniversary meeting finally began in early October, over 150 alumni made the journey to Oberhambach. On the evening prior to the first discussions, Paul Geheeb welcomed the guests and thanked them for coming. He asked the visitors not to dwell upon the past at the reunion but to focus upon the tasks of the Odenwaldschule in the current historical context. In a concession to Fuchs, Geheeb agreed that the Odenwaldschule was isolated from the events transpiring in Germany:

> Even in the years in which Germany has suffered more than it has in centuries our school has felt no economic emergency. Perhaps we have had it too easy . . . A small being, we have not shown ourselves to be mature enough to take on the tasks which demanding times place before us.

For Geheeb, however, the correct response did not lie in the domain of explictly political reflection or action. He opposed Fuchs's suggestion that the idealistic heritage and the emphasis on it in the Odenwaldschule were in need of fundamental reconceptualization. From Geheeb's perspective, the "heroes" whose names adorned the houses of the Odenwaldschule were more than adequate to address Fuchs's concerns:

> After a twenty-year existence we are just beginning to take seriously the mission which Fichte assigned to us: to develop the central idea of our school—the idea of personal responsibility—and to form flexible forms of community life in a fruitful fashion so that our school will be shaped into an educational workshop in Goethe's sense. With our view directed toward the future, we join together in these days as friends and members of the Odenwaldschule. We want to hear about the experiences of our alumni, and we want to struggle with one another for clarity about the tasks of our time and fruitful paths for the development of work and of life.[5]

The following morning began with an introduction by Alwine von Keller. According to Keller, the decision to plan three days of discussions about the Odenwaldschule's position in contemporary Germany arose as a result of the call from former *Kameraden* to heighten the school's political awareness. Fuchs's essay in *Der neue Waldkauz* provided the "point of departure for discussion, because here a burning question is directed to the school by former *Kameraden*." Urging the festival participants to cultivate a "free-spirited critical love" toward the Odenwaldschule, von Keller called upon those present to investigate the relationship between the role of humanistic ideals in the Odenwaldschule and the transition of *Kameraden* from the school to their work or university studies after leaving the Odenwaldschule. The conference agenda focused on problems relating to society, politics, international issues, and relationships between the sexes.[6]

After von Keller's introduction, Gerhard Fuchs gave a public address in which he attempted to redefine and sharpen the points raised in his composition in *Der neue Waldkauz*. According to Fuchs, the *Kameraden* and *Mitarbeiter* of the Odenwaldschule lived in an almost hermetically sealed environment in which they enjoyed the refined milieu of German classicism without perceiving either the elitist character of many of their privileges or the social forces in the Weimar Republic which were fighting to increase the access of all social strata to Germany's classical heritage. Fuchs rejected Meyer's claim that the Odenwaldschule was doing enough for political education by discussing political issues in history classes or by inviting guests who were politically active to speak. Without an experiential component, Fuchs held, political education was superficial, and this experiential aspect was missing at the Odenwaldschule:

> In the Odenwaldschule one can only interpret that which is important in today's social and professional life theoretically and through observation, but not through experience. That strikes me as the most important point. For theoretical observation can only communicate a certain position, and therein lies the danger of dogma. Only experience can lead to an autonomous and independent position that allows one to realize what is important in education.

Fuchs held that if experiential education in regard to political issues were brought into the Odenwaldschule, *Kameraden* would be compelled to recognize the necessity of political change in Germany. Yet experiential education would not be enough; one also had to give students the intellectual skills to analyze complex social issues such as unemployment and nationalism. These *Kameraden* should then fulfill the task assigned to them by Martin Buber, who had stated that "the Odenwaldschule must send out shock troops who would attempt to realize for the entire society what is realized here on a small scale." For Fuchs, this entailed recognizing that the classical ideals of the late eighteenth and early nineteenth centuries had become political ideas in the twentieth. In the context of the late Weimar Republic, Fuchs believed that these ideas had to be socialistic.[7]

Although much of Paul Geheeb's work was under attack at the twentieth anniversary assembly, Geheeb declined to take up a defensive attitude. He listened attentively to Fuchs's concerns and to the animated debate among alumni, *Mitarbeiter,* and *Kameraden.* During the breaks between the workshops he solicited the perspectives of his former students on the issues Fuchs raised. He was chatting with Erich Ernst Noth when he overheard Alwine von Keller state that "the uniform of the Nazis had to be respected, for some of the pupils wore it and did not thereby indicate disloyalty to the school." "At this point," Noth recalled,

> even the overtolerant Paul Geheeb protested. This decisive friend of peace and apostle of reconciliation amongst peoples would never have wanted to educate one of his own pupils to be a Nazi. That one of his own could even have put on this uniform must have seemed to him not only betrayal, but precisely proof of his own failure.

Shortly afterwards, Geheeb ran into Theodor Scharmann in front of Humboldt Haus. An Indian *Mitarbeiter,* V. N. Sharma, had delivered a laudatory speech to Geheeb at the conference, saying "Sahib! In the shadow of your tree many animals find shelter!" and Geheeb was curious to know what Scharmann thought of the address. "He was certainly right," Scharmann responded, "but Paulus, too many animals find shelter beneath your tree—including Nazis!" As Scharmann later remembered, "He looked at me for a moment, and I knew this tortured look, which simultaneously was so full of understanding. He then went on his way. I had once again acted tactlessly."[8]

The October conference persuaded Geheeb that something needed to be done to revitalize the Odenwaldschule and to reassert the element of social responsibility that he had always believed to be a cornerstone of his philosophy of education. At one of the later sessions, Geheeb said that he had often been plagued by the elite character of the school and its overrepresentation of children from socially privileged backgrounds. "I admit I've lived with a very bad conscience here for many years," he said. "In most cases the *Kameraden* are too spoiled." Yet regardless of its students' class backgrounds, the Odenwaldschule itself had to accept some responsibility for Fuchs's challenge. "We can't honestly say we do everything possible to educate socially aware people," Geheeb conceded.[9]

Largely as a result of the October conference, the school began a "political work group" to increase political awareness among *Kameraden*. At one meeting of this group Geheeb urged the *Kameraden* to understand the gravity of the political situation in Germany: "It can suddenly happen that we all might be forced most suddenly to make clear decisions," he said. "We must not be unprepared for this." While it was important that the students learn to think independently and hear many different interpretations of political events,

> there are naturally certain things that are unacceptable for us. Therein one can see that we also have a "position," for example, in regard to living together with different peoples. If a speaker wanted to convince us of the necessity and perhaps even the blessings of a new war, I would forbid him to speak. Someone else who would show us the way to peace among peoples I would gladly allow to speak.

Geheeb now defined clear limits to his previous romantic descriptions of "the infinite richness of individuals."[10]

Following the October anniversary Geheeb began informal meetings with older *Kameraden* every Monday night to discuss reforms which would address the issues raised by Fuchs and other alumni. Geheeb appeared interested in initiating changes which would go to the heart of the grievances without surrendering the idealistic philosophy of the Odenwaldschule.

As part of the effort to gather new ideas about restructuring the Odenwaldschule, the Geheebs visited the "Free School and Work Community of Leztlingen," a school led by Bernhard Uffrecht. At Letzlingen students not only practiced full self-government, but they also ran the school's electrical and maintenance facilities and undertook all of the school's bookkeeping. Geheeb considered Letzlingen to be the closest German approximation of A. S. Neill's Summerhill in Britain and decided to appropriate many of its more experimental features for the Odenwaldschule.[11]

By March 1931 Geheeb believed he had achieved clarity about the major sources of problems in the Odenwaldschule. He brought a new proposal to the *Schulgemeinde* on 18 March, one which he hoped would address concerns raised in the October conference and force the *Kameraden* to take on higher levels of social responsibility. Geheeb opened his address to the *Schulgemeinde* by referring to the diverse calls for change in the school:

> Since last autumn many initiatives have become more and more overt here in the *Schulgemeinden* and in project groups, especially from the more mature *Kameraden*, and these have become more and more intense in the last months . . . The great and heavy responsibility that each member of our community carries has become more and more apparent to each of our most mature *Kameraden* as well as to many of the younger ones. Many anticipate reforms.[12]

Geheeb then proposed a major reform to be instituted in the Odenwaldschule following the Easter vacation. According to Geheeb, the old "family system" of the Odenwaldschule was antiquated. Under this system all *Kameraden* lived in pedagogical "families," in which *Mitarbeiter* oversaw their everyday lives and their social and psychological development. The disadvantage of this system, according to Geheeb, was that *Kameraden* could slough off their responsibilities for the well-being of the school community onto the *Mitarbeiter*. Further, families could form "in-groups," in which *Kameraden* identified themselves with their immediate families but not with the Odenwaldschule at large.

Geheeb proposed that it was time for the Odenwaldschule to dissolve its "family system" and to introduce a new system in which the *Kameraden* would carry more responsibility for all aspects of school life. Under this arrangement all *Mitarbeiter* would move to Plato Haus and the *Kameraden* would occupy the other houses by themselves, with the exception of the kindergarten in Pestalozzi Haus. In each of the other houses five of the most mature *Kameraden* would take over the position of *"Warte"* or "wardens." These *Warte* would be responsible for ensuring that all of the everyday tasks of the *Kameraden* in their house ran smoothly and for coordinating the organization of their house communities *(Hausgemeinschaften)* with those of the rest of the school. One *Wart* would be responsible for cleanliness in each house, another would oversee the academic schedules of the *Kameraden*, a third would organize students' trips to and from the school between semesters, a fourth would take care of hygiene, and a fifth would handle students' pocket money.[13]

Geheeb hoped that this new *Wartesystem* would impel the students in the school to develop self-reliance without the continual guidance of the *Mitarbeiter:* "It can't be emphasized strongly enough that this new arrangement should serve the highest goal of stimulating the sense of responsibility and cooperation among the *Kameraden* to the highest possible degree." He was hopeful that this reform would carry the ethos of responsibility of the Odenwaldschule to its full realization: "We believe that with this arrangement we will reach the highest point of what is currently possible among free schools today."[14]

Far from being delighted with Geheeb's proposal for a *Wartesystem*, many students in the *Schulgemeinde* were appalled by the suggested reform. Students who were preparing for their graduation were not eager to sacrifice their leisure time to administer monetary or cleaning responsibilities. Others worried that *Kameraden* who needed a guiding hand would be disoriented without a stable adult presence to fall back upon. Regardless of these reservations, Geheeb pushed the reform through the meeting. Geheeb felt that the *Kameraden* had to learn to take on more responsibility and to transcend their personal concerns to grasp their interdependence and reliance upon the broader school community. In undertaking this action, which in many ways undercut Geheeb's previous emphasis on institutions such as the *Schulgemeinde*, Geheeb attempted not only to address the criticisms of the Odenwaldschule raised at the twentieth anniversary meeting but also to break through an impasse regarding student self-government which had surfaced as early as 1927.[15]

Many of the articles in the student newspaper in 1931 and 1932 concern interpretations by *Kameraden* of the new *Wartesystem*. From these articles it appears that the *Kameraden* experienced tremendous difficulties in carrying the responsibilities entailed in the new arrangements. Yet it is also clear that they experienced the new system as a challenge which they tried very hard to support. One student wrote that

> The *Kameraden* have not yet found a good solution to the question of responsibility for themselves. But I was amazed at how often *Kameraden* reflect upon whether they can do it or not. The new organization hasn't worked completely everywhere. The adults often have to become involved.

Another student who had taken on the role of *Wart* found that the greatest challenge of the new system was that it required him to live out his ideals in his relationships with his peers:

> The personal example of the individual is that which exercises a fundamental influence on others, not his ideal premises and theories. Seen from this perspective, the entire problem is actually a question of self-discipline for the individual . . . I believe, therefore, that one can hold only the *Warte* themselves responsible for everything which goes wrong, for they haven't shown the others a better way. In other words, they haven't changed their own lives in order to bring about a decisive change in the other *Kameraden* . . . The path of personal self-discipline is more difficult and takes longer. But it is the only way. Here one must act, and not preach activity.[16]

While the articles in *Der neue Waldkauz* impress the reader with their idealism and open confession of difficulties in implementing the new system, these articles were nonetheless reviewed by a *Mitarbeiter,* Werner Meyer, and it may be that more critical pieces were barred from publication. In this respect a document by Heinz Schlee entitled "Concerning Student Self-Government in the Odenwaldschule" casts a different light on the *Wartesystem.* Schlee visited the Odenwaldschule in the spring of 1931 as part of his field studies in teacher education. There can be no question that his interpretation was subjected to editorial control by a Mitarbeiter.[17]

Schlee had been active in the German youth movements of the Weimar Republic and was interested in affinities between student self-government in the Odenwaldschule and in the autonomous youth organizations with which he was familiar. While Schlee saw similarities between youth groups such as the *Wandervogel* and the *Wartesystem* in the Odenwaldschule, he was convinced that the work of the *Warte* in the school was "actually much more difficult." Youth movement leaders directed self-selected and enthusiastic groups, but *Warte* often had to work with indifferent if not hostile peers. Schlee was concerned that the *Warte* would rapidly be exhausted by their responsibilities:

"In this Sisyphean task people (and especially young people) are quickly destroyed."

Not only did the *Warte* in the Odenwaldschule have critical peers to work with, according to Schlee, but they also lacked opportunities to recuperate from the strains of their responsibilities. The youth movement leader had the chance to regenerate between hikes and other activities, but the *Wart* "never has a break; he is always responsible for the daily activities." Schlee detected a schism between Geheeb's rhetoric about the importance of the entire Odenwaldschule community and the reality of the individual in the *Wartesystem:* "There are actually many in this school which so professes the importance of community who are left hanging and feel abandoned and unhappy." Schlee contended that the individual *Kamerad* was probably better off under the earlier family system, for then each *Kamerad* could establish contact more easily with a supportive *Mitarbeiter.* Under the *Wartesystem,* however, the *Mitarbeiter* were all segregated in Plato Haus and the new student had to "take the initiative himself to approach a *Mitarbeiter.*"[18]

Kameraden certainly had troubles with the *Wartesystem.* Many experienced it as a "pure overburden" and a "great mistake" which did not result in great pedagogical triumphs but in "dissolution" and "pure chaos." Edith Geheeb later commented that in spite of the rhetoric about student responsibility, her husband had actually sabotaged it in the school when he reserved for himself the privilege of appointing the *Warte.* "Don't ask me how he determined the mature *Kameraden!*" she said.[19]

In spite of the criticisms of the *Wartesystem,* all accounts agree that it challenged the *Kameraden* of the Odenwaldschule to increase their responsibility both for themselves and for their school. On the other hand, one can question whether these purely formal and internal reforms adequately responded to the criticisms raised by Fuchs and his colleagues at the twentieth-anniversary festival. Ironically, the reforms entailed in the *Wartesystem* fixated the attention of the *Kameraden* and the *Mitarbeiter* on the internal developments of the school more than ever. Fuchs's criticism, however, focused not on the autonomous organization of the Odenwaldschule but on the nearly complete rupture between the culture of the school and the external political circumstances which rendered Germany more and more vulnerable to fascism. In spite of the bold character of the *Wartesystem* reforms, the *political* problem which Fuchs identified was transformed into a debate on internal *pedagogical* arrangements. Unintentionally, Geheeb's reforms confirmed Fuchs's contention that the Odenwaldschule failed to address the political crisis of the Weimar Republic.

Yet it remained to be seen whether the *Wartesystem* might play a positive role in warding off the kinds of external interventions which
Geheeb had intuited might form a threatening part of the school's
future.

Geheeb traveled to Switzerland to visit Adolphe Ferrière in late July
1931 and suffered a ruptured hernia there on 11 August. He was
then hospitalized in the Clinique La Prairie in the small town of Clar-
ens, from which he sent a letter to the opening *Schulgemeinde* of the
autumn session. In the letter, Geheeb commented on both the political situation in Germany and the internal reforms in the Odenwaldschule:

> The political situation in Germany and in the world in general seems
> terribly serious. The worst aspect appears to me to be the fact that, in
> Germany, neither in governmental circles nor in any political party is
> there a truly great statesman at work who could take on the enormous
> tasks of our time—a really great man, a statesman not in the form of a
> Bismarck but in the spirit of Romain Rolland. Although the world is
> filled with mistrust and fanatical preparations for war, there are also bril-
> liant and productive forces everywhere at work. Tagore and Gandhi's
> message of nonviolent reconciliation and cultural cooperation is finding
> a powerful resonance in America and in Europe. Never before in history
> have the nations so strongly realized that they should come together as
> *"humanity."*
>   We are prepared and braced for everything. Not in the same sense as
> is the rabble of the metropolis, which loses itself in dance and alcohol,
> and screams *"après nous le déluge."* Rather, being braced for everything
> means for us: in the consciousness of the highest development of
> humanity to stand up against all that may come against us with victorious
> superiority. The more grave the times, the more threatened our exis-
> tence, the more bravely we will pull together all of our strengths to fulfill
> our tasks within our community to their highest perfection. Each one of
> us will confront the terrible seriousness of our time, both in our school
> and outside of it, with heroic determination. The more we are complete
> and secure with our project, the more we will be able to represent and
> defend it against every act of violence with a good conscience and there-
> fore with more success and victory.
>   The tasks that our community imposes on us every day are to be
> grasped directly. Our school is in the midst of a critical transitional pro-
> cess from the old inherited family system to the responsibility of the
> *Kameraden* for themselves in an institutional arrangement. In the months
> between Easter and summer vacation we could only begin; this autumn
> we must focus all of our efforts on building up the new organization and
> on bringing to every *Kamerad*—even the smallest—the consciousness that

the house *Wart* is there to show the younger *Kameraden* a role model of
how to lead one's daily life and how to engage oneself for the community, so that one can eventually become a house *Wart* oneself . . . The
new organization of the Odenwaldschule has been described on many
sides as "daring." No greater praise and no stronger encouragement
could be given it. It is always daring to live according to an idea, but life
is truly worth living only for those who know how to live for and with a
great idea.

Geheeb reflected a pattern in German politics when he suggested that
the resolution to his country's problems lay in the presence of a strong
leader, rather than in increased popular participation in democratic
institutions. He appealed to students' idealism in supporting the new
Wartesystem and confronting the political crisis in Germany, but he
failed to offer explicit support for parliamentary democracy or to
articulate a serious analysis of the crisis. Some students may have
sensed a connection between the pedagogical reform in the Odenwaldschule and the political context in Germany, but whatever relationship Geheeb might have perceived between strengthening the
Wartesystem and addressing the impending collapse of democracy
remained oblique.[20]

After Geheeb's return from Switzerland he discovered that for the
first time he had to deal with a significant emergence of Nazi sympathies among *Kameraden*. A small cohort was led informally by Heinrich Barth, a student from Hamburg. Barth made anti-Semitic
remarks to Jewish students, gathered political propaganda from the
local Nazi Party in Heppenheim and diffused it in Oberhambach, and
loudly refused to travel in the same train compartment with Jews.
Geheeb was appalled by the spirit of this group, and wrote to Barth's
mother,

> We owe it to Heinrich's constantly repeated, utterly tactless, and un-
> ashamed remarks that we now have had to live in the Odenwaldschule
> with anti-Semitic insults, ugly obscenities, swastikas scrawled on doors
> and walls, and a significant destruction of our earlier beautiful and
> peaceful cooperation between those of different races and religious
> beliefs . . . Heinrich's crude narrow-mindedness is working like a poison
> on the previously so lovely and fraternal spirit of our community . . . I
> have exercised prudence in dealing with him, but not without pangs of
> anxiety about how long I must expose our Jewish children and our com-
> munity to his provocations and obscenities.

Geheeb urged Frau Barth and her husband to shelter their son from
National Socialist influences at home and to dissuade him from con-

tinuing his political agitation in the school. To counteract the influence of Barth and his group, a new course on Jewish culture and history was organized and taught in the summer of 1932; Geheeb visited the course to indicate his support for the subject.[21]

Given the tense political climate, it is not surprising that fights occasionally erupted. In one instance, an American *Kamerad*, McGregor Gray, had a running dispute with "a Jewish boy whose father had been decorated in WWI" and "who was, incongruously, a Nazi, convinced that his father's heroism balanced his Semitic heritage." When it came to blows between the two boys over politics, a *Mitarbeiter* intervened and ordered Gray to his room. Gray's roommate took the matter before the house community which was headed by five *Warte*. Gray was "released and became a hero of the anti-Nazi resistance" in the school.[22]

In times of political crisis educators are tempted to politicize school life to address pressing issues. This tendency was present in the Odenwaldschule, largely through Fuch's intervention, but it did not succeed in redirecting the focus of the school. For many *Kameraden* and *Mitarbeiter* in the school, politics was a peripheral concern, and they found themselves fully absorbed in their classes, interpersonal relationships, and recreational activities. The first overt and massive political interventions in the school would be made by National Socialists, who would demonstrate none of Geheeb's concerns for student autonomy, coeducation, or idealistic self-cultivation.

part II

The Transformation of the Odenwaldschule

chapter 4

A Storm Trooper's Revenge: January–March, 1933

As the Odenwaldschule concentrated on the reforms entailed in the *Wartesystem,* the outer dangers which Fuchs had identified became more and more critical. Massive unemployment continued unabated; economic elites failed to establish a cohesive power bloc which secured political liberties; three chancellors were appointed in as many years; Nazi agitation increased in intensity and in popular success. In spite of the threatening climate, many Germans were unable to rouse much anxiety about the potentially radical character of Nazi reforms. When Paul Geheeb wrote to Edith in the winter of 1932 and urged her to gather all of her strength for the upcoming conflicts he feared would overtake the Odenwaldschule, she thought to herself, "He really is a crazy guy. Now he is thinking that if Hitler or God knows who should take power that they won't have anything better to do than to worry about our school, yet that won't interest them at all."

When the mainstream parties appeared incapable of breaking the back of the depression or forming stable alliances, Reich President Paul Hindenburg turned to the Nazis. On 30 January 1933 Hindenburg appointed Adolf Hitler chancellor of the republic. The constitutional liberties of the left-wing opposition were curtailed, but emergency clauses in the Weimar constitution gave these infringements an appearance of legality. The strongest supporters of the consititution, the Social Democrats, decided to wait for a clear violation before calling a general strike.[1]

Observing the increasing sense of political crisis, the *Kameraden* in the Odenwaldschule sought to clarify the relationship of the school to the new government. They addressed their concerns to the school's *Mitarbeiter* in a *Schulgemeinde* meeting. Werner Meyer, the history instructor, attempted to allay their anxieties and explained that the change of chancellorship in January was entirely legal. At that point Paulus jumped up from his seat and contradicted him. "We don't want to falsify history here," he asserted. Geheeb felt that, given the current crisis in Germany, it was a bad time to quibble over the letter of the law. "This is a gang of criminals which has seized power and they haven't done it legally," he told the *Kameraden*. "You should learn to make accurate judgments."[2]

On 27 February 1933 the Reichstag building was set afire, and Hitler used the arson as an excuse to suspend constitutional rights of free speech and due process. The Nazis used his emergency decree "for the protection of the people and the state" to arrest and terrorize their opponents. They focused primarily on communists, but also threatened all of those whom they described as *Volksfeinde*—"enemies of the people"—which included Jews, Social Democrats, pacifists, and feminists. Although the Nazis struck terror into many working-class neighborhoods, many middle-class Germans supported them, particularly in their repression of the communists. On 5 March the Nazis received forty-four percent of the popular vote in Reichstag elections. This gave them a majority in coalition with the German National People's Party.

Hitler's decree of 28 February empowered the Reich government to "assume full powers in any federal state whose government proved unable or unwilling to restore public order and security." In the aftermath of the 5 March elections, local Nazi SA (*Sturmabteilung*) and SS (*Schutzstaffel*) paramilitary units undertook numerous raids against political opponents throughout Germany. Instead of suppressing these spontaneous raids, Minister of the Interior Wilhelm Frick used the ensuing unrest as a pretext to replace locally elected governments—which were said to be incapable of responding effectively to the chaos—with hand-selected Nazi police commissars. These commisars promptly united their police with the local SA and SS and continued the repression of Nazi opponents with renewed intensity. The transition from local democratically based control of the police to control by the Nazis represented "the decisive revolutionary act of National Socialism" and secured for the Nazis total control of local state governments.[3]

The Nazis quickly seized power in Hesse, the home state of the Odenwaldschule. Wilhelm Leuschner was Hessian Minister of the Interior at the time of the Nazi takeover. Leuschner was a strong Social Democrat, and he had placed many Social Democrats in leading positions in the Hessian police force. Leuschner had taken firm action against Nazi violations of law in Hesse, and the Nazis were eager to remove him from power. When Frick claimed that the local Hessian situation was out of control on 6 March, he placed the Hessian police under his jurisdiction and appointed Nazi Heinrich Müller to take charge of them. Müller immediately ordered the dismissal of numerous policemen with Social Democratic loyalties who had been hired by Leuschner. They were replaced with Nazis who intimidated and arrested their political opponents.[4]

In the political chaos of the time, the first attacks of SA, SS, and police were directed not only against overt political enemies. Major interventions were also directed against individuals who had committed personal transgressions against Nazis or their allies. Motives of personal revenge often fused with those of political conflict.

The Odenwaldschule initially became caught up in the political turmoil of March 1933 in Germany for reasons which had little connection with pedagogy or the specific educational *Weltanschauung* of the school. Rather, a personal intrigue of employee versus employer, gentile versus Jew, provided the backdrop for the first major Nazi interventions in the school following the March elections. The origin of the conflict occurred not in Hesse but in Max Cassirer's cellulose factory in Silesia. Remote as that setting was to Oberhambach, differences which had originated there more than fifteen years earlier were to have direct repercussions on the first National Socialist interventions in the Odenwaldschule.[5]

From 1905 to 1917, Clemens Goerendt was the manager of Cassirer's factory in Silesia, Tillgener and Co. According to Cassirer, Goerendt left the firm in 1917 of his own free will. Cassirer was surprised when he learned several years later that Goerendt was suing him to receive a retirement pension. Goerendt's contract contained no provision for a pension; furthermore Goerendt had received an income of 37,000 Reichsmark in his last year of work, enough to situate him in the higher income ranks of Germany's technical intelligentsia. In court Goerendt's suit was dismissed as legally unfounded. Cassirer nonetheless subsequently paid Goerendt 200 RM a month until Goerendt's death in 1930, although under no legal compulsion to do so.

Although Clemens Goerendt and his wife Paula both sent Cassirer expressions of appreciation for his assistance in the years following the court case, it appears that they privately despised Cassirer. In Goerendt's version of his departure from Tillgener and Co., he was pressured to leave his work so that Cassirer would be under no obligation to pay Goerendt a pension. In times of financial stability, Goerendt's story might have been forgotten as a grudge more worth

abandoning than sustaining, but Germany in the early 1920s was in
both political and economic crisis. The inflation of 1923 devastated
the Goerendt family savings. Goerendt subsequently worked for several years in a firm in Königsberg in East Prussia. His family then
moved to Heppenheim, a small city eight kilometers west of the
Odenwaldschule, where they lived in "relative comfort."[6]

Goerendt's son Werner joined his father's personal hatred of Max
Cassirer with a fanatical support of national socialism. Werner
Goerendt joined the Nazi party in 1928 when he was nineteen years
old. Although nominally a student, Goerendt devoted almost all of
his energies to organizing the party in South Hesse. He became the
district leader for the party as well as a leader of the SA. Goerendt
became a target for anti-Nazi activists, who on two separate occasions
attacked him, giving him concussions each time and back problems
which were to plague him for years. Long before the Nazis took
power Goerendt boasted publicly that as soon as his party seized state
control he would lead a raid against the Odenwaldschule.[7]

Whether Clemens Goerendt was fired or pressured to leave his
work by Cassirer remains a historical mystery, but it hardly matters.
If Goerendt was fired, then his son's resentment of Cassirer was chan-
neled through the Nazis in their raids of the Odenwaldschule. If he
was not fired, then Cassirer was a scapegoat for a decision which he
later regretted. In either case, Cassirer's Jewish background made
him vulnerable to attacks by the Nazis.

One can easily imagine the young Werner Goerendt's impressions
of the Odenwaldschule in the beginning of 1933. Paul Geheeb's pacifism and emphasis on intercultural awareness, coeducation based on
the principle of equality between the sexes, and democratic principles
extended to young children—all sponsored by a Jew whom the young
Goerendt thought had ruined his father—must have seemed a pure
incarnation of all of the internationalist and liberal principles most
detested by the Nazis. The open vulnerability of a rural school with
pacifist principles made the Odenwaldschule easy to raid without risk-
ing counterattack—unlike the communists and other left-wing opponents whose street fights had so injured Goerendt.[8]

The first raids on the Odenwaldschule were initiated, coordinated,
and led by Werner Goerendt. On 7 March Goerendt led a group of
approximately a dozen of the SA in a first search of the Odenwaldschule. At around 4:00 in the afternoon they drove in three cars up
to the school, occupied the entrances to its buildings, and called all of
the *Kameraden* and *Mitarbeiter* into the assembly hall. The Nazis justi-

fied their raid by claiming that it was their duty to confiscate communist literature. They claimed that they had seen students from the Odenwaldschule wearing communist buttons and distributing party propaganda in Heppenheim. Paul Geheeb's protests that the Odenwaldschule was protected by the government and the Hessian Ministry of Culture were scorned by the Nazis, who told Geheeb that the old Ministry from the Weimar Republic had been deposed and a new Ministry was forming under Nazi leadership. They told the assembled *Mitarbeiter* and *Kameraden* that everything would change in the Odenwaldschule now that the Nazis controlled state power.[9]

As the first step in changing the Odenwaldschule, Goerendt and his colleagues announced that they would confiscate all of the communist literature in the school. They then asked that students who supported the communists identify themselves and turn in their literature. No students responded. One of the Nazis then claimed that he recognized one of the students, and a search of her room indeed revealed communist literature. Several of her companions then turned over similar information and the Nazis conducted a search of the school which lasted two hours.

Geheeb was deeply alarmed at this first search of the Odenwaldschule. Apparently, the Odenwaldschule was high on the local Nazis' list of enemies, for the search of the school occurred on the same day and even prior to the Nazi occupation of far more obvious political targets such as the Hessian Social Democratic Party headquarters, the local offices of the Social Democratic newspaper, the Hessian Ministry of the Interior, and the apartment of Hessian President Adelung. The Nazis had pointed firearms at *Mitarbeiter* and *Kameraden,* and while there had been no violence, Geheeb was afraid that a similar raid could recur at any point, with far more tragic consequences. To prevent future raids he wrote immediately to the Hessian Ministry of Culture in Darmstadt to request an official investigation of the Odenwaldschule. He hoped that if he could gather some support both from old Ministry officials and from incoming Nazi officials, he could preempt another spontaneous raid by Goerendt and the SA.[10]

The Nazi intervention in the Odenwaldschule was publicized in the national press. The *Frankfurter Zeitung,* one of Germany's major newspapers, published an article on 10 March covering Nazi interventions in Hesse and stating that

> According to reliable sources, house searches for literature and weapons led only to isolated findings. Extensive printed materials and insignias of the Communist party were confiscated in Paul Geheeb's famous Odenwaldschule on the Bergstrasse.

Concerned that such press coverage would damage the school and add to its reputation in reactionary circles as a "communist Jew school" and "hotbed of Marxism," Geheeb wrote to the paper, requesting a correction. The *Frankfurter Zeitung* never printed Geheeb's letter.[11]

On 11 March Goerendt appeared again in the Odenwaldschule, this time heading a contingent of approximately fifty armed SA and SS men, along with two policemen from Darmstadt. The findings of 7 March had apparently convinced Goerendt and his colleagues that their first raid had demonstrated the communist leanings of the Odenwaldschule and that a more thorough search was now appropriate. The Nazis ordered the students to go to their rooms and began a more systematic search.

According to alumni, the *Kameraden* responded to this second raid by jamming every toilet in the school with papers they wished to destroy and stuffing nooks and crannies with books they feared would be used to denounce themselves and the school. They supported each other throughout the ordeal. One dramatic instance of this mutual support concerned Carl von Ossietsky's daughter Rosalinde, who was a *Kameradin*. Ossietsky, the editor of the *Weltbühne*, had been arrested immediately after the Reichstag fire, and his daughter was grief-stricken by his incarceration. As the Nazis searched the Odenwaldschule, she purposely displayed her copies of the *Weltbühne* as a sign of loyalty to her father. Friends who recognized the seriousness of her protest tore the journals away from her, concealed them, and comforted her. Another instance of mutual student support concerned a communist *Kamerad*, Karl von Münchhausen, who was ill and in the small school clinic at the time of the raid. Geno Hartlaub, a *Kameradin* and daughter of Gustav Hartlaub, director of the Mannheim Museum, saved Münchhausen's political books by hiding them behind his house's roofing felt. Much of the material the Nazis took was apolitical, but since many of the more ignorant Nazis confiscated materials such as a Sanskrit dictionary (believing it to be Hebrew), the caution of the students appears warranted. The Nazis took books about travel to the Soviet Union, the collected works of Rosa Luxemburg, Marx's *Capital*, and all of the school's holdings on coeducation.[12]

In Paul Geheeb's study the Nazis ransacked his private papers and took his correspondence with Clara Zetkin, the communist and feminist Reichstag delegate from Berlin. One of the two policemen discovered a receipt from a contribution Geheeb had made to an anti-fascist organization. The policeman slipped the receipt to Geheeb confidentially, saying, "These gentlemen don't need to see this." He was probably one of the few remaining Social Democrats on the police force, all of whom would be dismissed by the Nazis in the coming weeks.[13]

This policeman's quiet decency contrasted sharply with his colleagues' treatment of two Jews in the school. Kurt Cassirer, Edith's brother, was struck in the face and kicked down a flight of stairs in Cassirer Haus by Goerendt and a storm trooper from nearby Bensheim. Esra Steinitz, the school's chemistry teacher, was kicked and shoved across the Goethe Court before the entire school; he was arrested and driven off to a jail in Darmstadt. Unlike Cassirer, Steinitz was politically active. He worked in the peace movement, and the Nazis had discovered a vast library on pacifism in his apartment.[14]

The *Kameraden* and *Mitarbeiter* of the Odenwaldschule were now much more thoroughly intimidated and helpless than after the first Nazi raid. The Nazis ended their intervention by promising that they would keep a close watch on the school and make sure that it aligned itself with national socialism. They then descended the Hambacher Valley towards Heppenheim, drinking until late that night in a local tavern. They were celebrating Goerendt's twenty-fifth birthday, which had been on the previous day.

Given the political turmoil of the period following the Nazi seizure of power, it was unclear to whom Geheeb could turn for effective assistance in warding off subsequent SA raids. Geheeb wrote no letters of appeal on either 11 or 12 March. On 13 March, however, the Hessian Parliament elected a National Socialist named Ferdinand Werner as Hessian State President. Geheeb immediately wrote Werner "to plead most urgently for protection and help" for his school. Arguing that the pedagogical atmosphere of his school was not only "disturbed, but even partially destroyed" through the SA searches, Geheeb again requested an official investigation of the school. Geheeb attempted to convince President Werner of his cooperative intentions, stating that "we would easily agree on all fundamental questions" in the course of a visit by the appropriate authorities. Appealing to the specifically German humanistic emphasis of the Odenwaldschule and Geheeb's personal connections to prominent German educators, Geheeb wrote that

I hope that the Odenwaldschule, which was founded in Imperial Germany and survived the difficult years of the war and the postwar period, thanks to the happy and enthusiastic work of both young and old, will continue to bloom and come ever closer to achieving its ideals under your government.

In a separate letter to Ferrière, Geheeb asserted that his letter to Werner was "thoroughly honest." Geheeb's preparedness to accommodate the new government cannot be taken at face value, however. Only two days after the letter to President Werner, he sent Ferrière a dramatically different message:

> Everything is much, much worse here than you can imagine. It is indeed the hardest time of my life. I can't tell you anything now because our correspondence is read by the police . . . If I were forced to give up my work here, could I then come to Switzerland with my best teachers and about one hundred children? . . . We'd like to come as early as April or May.

Ferrière's response to Geheeb's letter was enthusiastic. Ferrière wrote immediately to the Swiss national government in Bern and to eighteen separate cantonal authorities to inquire into the possibility of Geheeb's immigration with staff and students. President Werner, on the other hand, appears never to have replied to Geheeb's letter.[15]

These two letters to Werner and Ferrière inaugurate a complex double strategy, which Geheeb was to pursue for the rest of 1933. On the one hand, Geheeb extended himself to the Nazis in a manner which occasionally bordered on sycophancy, striving to find some way of continuing to work productively in the Odenwaldschule. On the other hand, Geheeb surreptitiously planned to emigrate, seeking a respite from the increasing controls the Nazis were imposing on his leadership. The two strategies sometimes contradicted one another and at other points actually undercut one another, but they gave Geheeb maximum flexibility in exploring both the readiness of the regime to endorse his work and the possibilities for a relatively frictionless transfer of his school to another country.

Although Paul Geheeb constantly kept his pedagogical principles in mind in pursuing this agenda, he was not entirely free of personal interests. He had to consider his own security and that of his wife and his step-father, and the Cassirers' Jewish background made him particularly vulnerable in negotiating with the Nazis. Beyond Geheeb's interests and those of his family, he was also entrusted with the well-being of almost 160 students, over twenty *Mitarbeiter,* and a small maintenance staff. The extensive property of the Odenwaldschule was also liable to expropriation without compensation, given the precarious legal situation.

Mixed with these definite interests were Geheeb's pedagogical values. For years he had been educating his students not only to cultivate their own individual personalities but also to learn and to practice social responsibility. It would have meant a betrayal of all that Geheeb had professed were he to abandon his school in the current situation, in spite of the fact that he was sixty-three years old and could easily have retired.

While Paul Geheeb groped for an effective response to the raids, Esra Steinitz remained in jail in Darmstadt, where he "had the feeling that every time the door opened, I could be taken out and shot." Edith Geheeb hired a prominent lawyer, Heinrich von Brentano, to release Steinitz. Conferring with him in his cell, Brentano urged Steinitz to sign an affidavit stating that he would no longer advocate communism. When Steinitz objected, insisting that he had never been a communist, Brentano told him, "That's irrelevant; the main thing is that we get you out of here." Brentano won Steinitz's release after two days, and the chemist returned to the Odenwaldschule. Upon coming home, Steinitz noticed that not a single person asked him about his treatment in jail. "Even then there was already an atmosphere of distrust in the country which made people afraid to talk about their heartfelt concerns," he observed. "Everyone was afraid to speak, even to open their mouths, and it was no wonder that they were silent about such things."[16]

The Odenwaldschule was still reeling from the raids of 7 and 11 March when Friedrich Ringshausen, the new Hessian Minister of Culture and Education, ordered celebrations of the National Socialist seizure of power in Hessian schools. The National Socialists officially took over state power in Hesse on 13 March with Werner's election and on the fourteenth Ringshausen ordered school classes suspended on the eighteenth to assure that Hessian youth would recognize the distinct characteristics of Nazism. Ringshausen's ordinance outlined the new spirit in German education as follows:

> In a struggle lasting for more than ten years we National Socialists have fought against the internationalist and antipatriotic beliefs which destroy virtue and character and have wrested state power from them ... It is our task to bring this victory of the German spirit to our people and to shape our youth into a self-confident, proud, powerful, and faithful species.

To begin this project, schools were to organize speeches celebrating the Nazis, to display the swastika, and to sing Nazi anthems such as the Horst Wessel song. They were also to report back to Ringshausen on the success of their festivals.[17]

The new ordinance provoked tremendous concern among the faculty of the Odenwaldschule. The *Mitarbeiter* agreed that history teacher Werner Meyer would give an address concerning the Nazis in which he would explain to the students that Germany had a new government. Paul Geheeb would display the swastika and explain that it should be accorded the respect attributed to all national flags since it was the new German flag. A *Kamerad* would read a chapter from Fichte's *Addresses to the German Nation* aloud, allowing the school to integrate one of its traditional "heroes" into the festival.[18]

These points of agreement ended when it came to singing nationalist songs. *Mitarbeiter* Alwine von Keller was the most resolute opponent of the songs. She sent a report to the Hessian Ministry of Culture, saying that

> Urging a public tribute (to Germany) from the school community does not fit in with the fundamental principles of the Odenwaldschule. Some of us believe we will overwhelm the children if we suddenly demand a tribute from them for which they are not sufficiently prepared.

Von Keller also claimed that the school was not prepared musically for singing together, attempting to displace a political disagreement with an aesthetic one.[19]

Although the staff ultimately did join in singing the national anthem, two young *Mitarbeiter*, Hans Neumeister and Otto Freidank, were critical of what they construed as the unpatriotic attitude of the staff. Neumeister and Freidank boycotted the festival and denounced the Odenwaldschule to the Ministry of Culture. According to *Mitarbeiter* Martin Wagenschein, Neumeister and Freidank were *"spiessig"* ("narrow-minded") and wanted "to distance themselves from this suspicious school." The denunciations of Freidank and Neumeister created yet another crisis situation to which Geheeb would have to respond.[20]

According to Wagenschein, Freidank and Neumeister told him that they were so repelled by the paucity of patriotism in the Odenwaldschule that they decided not only to denounce the school but also to leave it. Geheeb and Wagenschein subsequently discussed the situation in detail, and Geheeb told Wagenschein about his letters to President Werner requesting an official investigation of the school. The two agreed that Wagenschein would visit the Hessian Ministry of Culture to speak with Dr. Rudolf Blank, an official who joined the

Ministry on 15 March and was now responsible for overseeing the Odenwaldschule.[21]

Wagenschein made the trip to Darmstadt and spoke with Blank. Blank listened attentively and politely to Wagenschein's efforts to portray the school positively. He then ended the conversation with a smirk and the ambiguous comment that "Wagenschein is clever." The only immediate upshot of this awkward situation for the school was that Freidank and Neumeister decided to stay in the school and await its upcoming official investigation before undertaking any further action.[22]

Had the tumultuous changes in the Odenwaldschule prompted by the shift from the family system to the *Wartesystem* done much to prepare the school for the Nazi interventions? Apparently not. Most *Kameraden* were completely surprised by the raids. "We were absolutely not prepared for the change," Clewie Kroeker later recalled. "This political change was completely surprising and incomprehensible." Francis Marburg was also taken aback by the entry into the school of externally driven political forces. The raids were shocking because they "contrasted so sharply with what I had come to expect," he stated. "It was intervention from without by force—not persuasion—into our differently ordered world which had seemed self-contained." Several *Mitarbeiter* were equally surprised. One of them, Dr. Walter Bücheler, confessed he "had no idea" what was happening politically.[23]

The Odenwaldschule was just one small institution reflecting the broader suffocation of political life in Germany in March 1933. In nearby Heppenheim, communists had been arrested on 9 March and sent to the new Osthafen concentration camp near Worms. Before the end of the month the homes of prominent Jews in Heppenheim had been searched, including that of Martin Buber. On 23 March Hitler pushed a dictatorial "Enabling Act" through the Reichstag. The Nazis had arrested all of the Reichstag's communists and left-wing Social Democrats following the Reichstag fire. Only the remaining Social Democrats voted against the Enabling Act. The Nazis were successfully consolidating state power.[24]

As the public sphere in Germany was increasingly dominated by the Nazis, Geheeb drew upon his long association with the New Education Fellowship for assistance. After Geheeb reported about his difficulties to the NEF Central Office in London, Beatrice Ensor, president of the NEF, sent a telegram to Geheeb. Speaking in the name of educators from forty-eight countries, Ensor wrote that the NEF was "most grieved your school may be closed despite its work furthering understanding of German culture among children of other nations." Numerous other educators, informed by Ensor about the crisis in the school, sent similar messages. "I certainly believe these statements can help," Geheeb wrote to Ferrière. Referring to the Nazis, he held that "They are not indifferent to foreign opinion."[25]

As the end of March approached, Geheeb's requested official investigation of thc Odenwaldschule still had not occurred. Impatient with the delay, Geheeb turned to sycophancy. On 25 March he wrote a letter to Werner Goerendt requesting a discussion with the young SA leader. Geheeb wrote that he had discussed the political situation with a *Kamerad* named Goetz von Chelius who had convinced him that "you have overtaken a major responsibility for the local population in political matters and that you therefore have the right to be fully informed about our school life and the goals of my school." In light of this Geheeb offered Goerendt "confidential and complete information about the conditions in my school," particularly since "you and I follow fundamentally the same goals." Geheeb requested that Goerendt telephone him, and Geheeb would arrange to have Goerendt picked up and delivered by car.[26]

Goerendt took up Geheeb's offer, and Geheeb told Esra Steinitz that they had a long conversation. According to Paulus, the result of the meeting was that "We parted as friends." Steinitz was devastated. "A chill ran down my spine," he wrote, "and I knew that my days there were numbered."

Still, Geheeb's rapprochement with Goerendt was superficial. When Steinitz was later asked whether Geheeb's exchange with Goerendt was reflective of Geheeb's "inexhaustible faith in his own ability to educate," Steinitz responded that "this was indeed the case, and I would like to say, in a disastrous fashion! It wasn't in Paulus's nature to control this group of young hooligans," he continued. "Paulus was utterly undiplomatic, and naturally he couldn't handle such power-hungry people."[27]

On 31 March the SA again appeared in the Odenwaldschule and once more harassed Steinitz. On this occasion Edith intervened and was able to prevent a second arrest, but Steinitz decided he had had enough. Edith gave him some money and two *Kameraden* drove him to the train station at Mannheim, bypassing Heppenheim for fear that local Nazis would recognize him and invent a fresh pretext for incarcerating him. The next day Steinitz was in Switzerland, preparing for a new job at Ferrière's school, "Home Chez Nous," in Les Plèiades.

Steinitz was the first *Mitarbeiter* of the Odenwaldschule to leave as a consequence of the Nazi takeover. With this exception, the school population still held together. Yet no one knew if the school would be subjected to further spontaneous raids, if the regime would arbitrarily decide to close it permanently, or whether the worst fears were misplaced and the unrest in the school that March was only a temporary aberration in the history of the Odenwaldschule.

chapter 5

Accommodating the Regime: April–June, 1933

At the beginning of April 1933, Paul Geheeb clung to the hope that the official investigation of the Odenwaldschule would soon clear the name of the school and allow it to continue. In a letter to Rudolf Blank, the new Nazi official in charge of supervising the Odenwaldschule, Geheeb expressed "trust in continuing to work well under your government" and described the Odenwaldschule as "a reliable comrade in the fight against Marxism." Geheeb shared with Blank one of his major concerns, a drop in student enrollment in the period following the raids of 7 and 11 March. Yet rather than place the blame for this decline on the Nazis, Geheeb pointed to the negative press reports in the *Frankfurter Zeitung*, which strengthened popular perceptions about the Odenwaldschule as a school with communist sympathies. Unless the decline in student enrollment were arrested, Geheeb wrote, "financial collapse would force me to close my school." Geheeb also wrote that he needed to reverse foreign opinion about the situation in the Odenwaldschule. Foreign parents were pulling their children out of the school and the Ensor telegram provided clear evidence of concern among international professional educators. At no point did Geheeb suggest that Nazi policies had caused the crisis in the school.

Geheeb gave Blank three reasons for preserving the Odenwaldschule with its traditional structures intact. First, Geheeb wrote that he was concerned about both the young people in the school and those who could benefit from attending the school in the future. Closing the school would be a direct loss to these students. Second, Geheeb wished to protect the *Mitarbeiter* and staff who had lived in the school for many years and had made it their home. Third, Geheeb felt a debt to Hesse, the only German state bold enough to allow him to undertake his experiment with coeducation in 1910, and which derived economic benefits from the Odenwaldschule.

As for himself, Geheeb did not state any personal need to see the school continue:

> For myself personally, however, the destruction of my life's work would not touch me, because I believe I no longer need the atmosphere of the Odenwaldschule to fulfill my "Become who thou art." Incidentally, the sole purpose of my entire life has been to pass over this earth with a pure soul and clean hands.

Geheeb wrote that he could attain this goal just as easily in semi-retirement in the Rhön mountains of his childhood as he could in the Odenwaldschule.[1]

Several features in this letter were typical of Geheeb's correspondence with government authorities in the spring of 1933. First, Geheeb endeavored to depict the Odenwaldschule as an ally in the Nazis' struggle against communism. Given Geheeb's long interest in Social Democracy, this approach was clearly part of a strained effort to demonstrate some commonalities with the Nazis. Second, Geheeb criticized the consequences of Nazi actions in the Odenwaldschule (declining enrollment and negative press reports) while avoiding a direct attack on the Nazis. Third, Geheeb indirectly expressed resentment about the crisis the Nazis had created in the school. The use of the phrase "destruction of my life's work" implies deliberate action by the Nazis, and the reference to living "with a pure soul and clean hands" suggests that the regime was doing something different. In this and similar letters, Geheeb revealed his ambivalence regarding the proper manner to treat the Nazis.[2]

Geheeb's ambivalence had a tactical relevance. Consider the example of the decline in student enrollments which Geheeb took note of in his letter to Blank. From Geheeb's perspective, the decline in student enrollments could serve a dual purpose. First, the decline could be used to demonstrate that Nazi interventions in the school were destructive and that the authorities should be vigilant in protecting the security and autonomy of the school. Second, Geheeb's mention of the decline could serve to indicate that a future decision by him to close the school might stem from reasons which had nothing to do with his political opposition to the Nazis but rather from the fact that a private school cannot survive economically without students to pay tuition. The mention of declining enrollments became a means of cautiously beginning to close the school while escaping repercussions based on suspicions by the Nazis of political opposition. Geheeb was to convey such subtle and conflicting messages to the authorities on numerous occasions in 1933, and they became an important means of maintaining his independence in his relations with them.

One should not misinterpret Geheeb's letter to Blank as symptomatic of latent fascism. The rapid waves of arrests and public terror unleashed by the Nazis following the Reichstag burning and 5 March elections surprised even the most militant opponents of the Nazis. The mildest criticisms were defined as treason and individuals suspected of oppositional political convictions were targetted as the first victims. Geheeb's pacifism was to become an issue in the upcoming official investigation of the school. His desire to protect the seventy-six-year-old Max Cassirer as well as the children within his school placed a heavy obligation upon him to be cautious for their sakes, regardless of his own personal safety.

Easter vacation began for the Odenwaldschule on 7 April 1933. The majority of *Kameraden* and *Mitarbeiter* left Oberhambach to visit family and friends, while a small group remained to prepare for *Abitur* examinations or to enjoy the enchanting Odenwald forests and dales in springtime. Without prior notification, an entourage of armed Nazis headed by Ringshausen, Blank, and Goerendt drove up the winding Hambacher Valley at eleven o'clock on the morning of 7 April. Upon arrival they ordered all of the present members of the school community onto Paul Geheeb's balcony in Humboldt Haus, where they had to wait for interrogations by Ringshausen. The Minister of Culture sat on a chaise lounge in his apartment, underneath portraits of Goethe and Romain Rolland. The Geheebs and their students and teachers waited outside.

While Ringshausen occupied his apartment, Paul Geheeb meditated on the future of his school. What would the Nazis do with it? The Odenwaldschule was not a school like Minna Specht's "Walkemühle," where a combative left-wing socialism was taught and which the Nazis closed immediately after seizing power. Nor was it like the Hermann Lietz schools, which, under the leadership of Alfred Andreesen, quickly and enthusiastically aligned themselves with the Nazis. Rather, the Odenwaldschule existed in an unspecified and relatively apolitical cultural domain which necessarily opposed the Nazis on the basis of its ethical precepts, but which rarely took any explicitly political stance. It appeared to form a target which the Nazis might be able to penetrate and appropriate for their own ideological purposes, but which Geheeb might be able to protect with enough diplomacy and courage.

The Nazis could deploy a variety of tactics to change the Odenwaldschule. A massive and direct transformation was one option, but if it were done heavy-handedly it could reflect negatively on the new National Socialist Germany, which did not yet have the confidence to offend foreign opinion. Another option was to remove those institutional practices which were most noxious to National Socialist ideology—and Geheeb could only guess at what they were—and replace them with organizational arrangements more in line with Nazi *Weltanschauungen*. Finally, a mixture of psychological pressure and manipulative flattery might be combined to bring Geheeb to institute desired reforms.

These tactical considerations were complicated by the vagueness of Nazi educational ideology in 1933. Nazi pedagogical theories and practices did not originate within the domain of education proper, but were superimposed on it on the basis of political beliefs. Many examples of Nazi pedagogy could be glimpsed in organizations such as the Hitler Youth, where the segregation of young people on the basis of race and gender was a fundamental principle, and where the militaristic pedagogy of commanding and following stood in marked opposition to the Odenwaldschule's stress on individuation and egalitarian relationships. Yet it was not at all clear that the Hitler Youth would provide the blueprint for Nazi school reform. It was, in short, difficult to assess how militant the Nazis would be in attempting to reform schools, or how resilient schools might be in deflecting Nazi interventions.[3]

In addition to the unclarity of Nazi policy on education, the entourage of Goerendt, Blank, and Ringshausen which came to the Odenwaldschule on 7 April represented distinct and partially opposing tendencies within Nazism. Although the Nazis preferred to portray themselves as a tightly integrated political movement, "The party which appeared so resolute and disciplined outwardly was in reality anything but a unified force." Nowhere were conflicts within Nazism more evident than in the section of the Hesse-Darmstadt branch of the Party in the early 1930s, where observers of the movement were struck by its "disorder, malice, and utter confusion."[4]

Before his appointment as the Hessian Minister of Culture after the Nazi takeover, Friedrich Ringshausen had spent most of his professional life as a *Volksschule* teacher in the small city of Offenbach in Hesse. He joined the Nazi party in September 1923, when it was still quite small, and was appointed *Gauleiter,* or district chief of the party, in Hesse-Darmstadt in March 1927. In September 1930 he was elected as a Nazi delegate to the Reichstag, joining 106 other Nazis in their first major electoral victory.[5]

In spite of Ringshausen's political successes, he was a poor leader by many measures. He was a bad public speaker and members of the Nazi cadre complained that he was egotistical. On 6 January 1931, forty-three local Nazis who were disenchanted with Ringshausen's leadership sent a petition to Hitler in Munich requesting Ringshausen's removal from the *Gauleitung*. On 9 January the Führer intervened and dismissed Ringshausen.

It is not immediately evident why Ringshausen was appointed Hessian Minister of Culture by *Gauleiter* Jakob Sprenger after having been dismissed by Hitler from the Hesse-Darmstadt office. Although Ringshausen had demonstrated lack of talent, both Hitler at the national level and Sprenger at the local level were protective of loyal party members and rewarded them with official appointments after the takeover. Ringshausen's experience as a teacher recommended him for a position in education.

Rudolf Blank, the other Nazi from the Ministry of Culture who came to the Odenwaldschule on 7 April, was a Nazi "technocrat," the holder of a doctorate. Blank joined the Ministry on 13 March, after the formal transition of Hessian state power into the hands of the Nazis. He had previously visited the Odenwaldschule on 22 March to supervise *Abitur* examinations, and had accused Esra Steinitz of conducting the chemistry section too leniently.[6]

Werner Goerendt, the storm trooper who had led the two searches of the Odenwaldschule in early March, had his own personal agenda in his visit that day. Goerendt's anger at his father's alleged mistreatment by Max Cassirer made his actions more a personal vendetta than an overtly political intervention. For Goerendt, any reforms which compelled the Odenwaldschule to adapt his own Nazi convictions or which shut the school peremptorily would be likely to satisfy his cravings for revenge.

Prior to the visit to the Odenwaldschule on 7 April, the first major ordinance issued by Ringshausen as Hessian Minister of Culture appeared not to affect the Odenwaldschule. On 30 March Ringshausen dismissed "all Jewish teaching faculty and also all other international, pacifistic, and atheistically oriented teachers" from teaching the social sciences and German in Hessian public schools. Ringshausen's decree was the first step in the coordination, or *"Gleichschaltung,"* of Hessian schools with the Nazi movement. The decree outlined the key Nazi strategy in appropriating the state apparatus: a systematic purge of "politically unreliable" Germans and their replacement with others who were either active Nazis or sympathetic to Nazism. On 7 April Hitler promulgated a similar decree, the "Law for the Restoration of the Professional Civil Service," which applied to public school teachers in all of the German states. This law was the first nationwide school reform imposed by the Nazis and removed many of their opponents from teaching and administrative positions. Except for Prussia, where strict state laws compelled the dismissal of private school teachers with the stigmatized criteria, private schools such as the Odenwaldschule appeared spared. Ringshausen's visit to the school was to reveal how illusory such appearances could be.[7]

Friedrich Ringshausen led the interviews in Paul Geheeb's apartment. He began by calling in students to gather information about their perceptions of the Odenwaldschule. Many of his questions were innocuous, and simply concerned students' views on the strengths and weaknesses of their school.

Other inquiries were pathetically crude. One young *Kameradin* had just completed her *Abitur* and was on the verge of leaving the school when she was called in to speak with Ringshausen. "Sit down, Fräulein," he told her. "You've been here for years?"

"Yes, Herr Minister."

"And you liked it?"

"Yes, I truly love the school."

"You occasionally went on group hikes?"

"Yes, in the mountains."

"And probably sometimes just with another person. And when you were tired, you wanted to sit down. And just then a boy started moving closer and closer up to you?"

"What do you want, Herr Minister!"

In this artless manner, Ringshausen made it clear that coeducation was likely to be one of the day's casualties at the Odenwaldschule.

After several students and staff had been interviewed by Ringshausen, Geheeb himself was called into the apartment. Edith waited outside, convinced that her husband was going to be shot. It must have been an appalling sight for Paulus, who found a Nazi Minister of Culture occupying his favorite seat, with an armed storm trooper sitting by his side. Upon completing their introduction, Ringshausen told Geheeb that the Hessian Ministry of Culture had been informed of another denunciation against the school. At one point that spring a group of *Kameraden* had confronted Geheeb and demanded to know his opinions on Hitler and Germany's new government. Geheeb then told them that Hitler was a psychopath and the worst possible leader for Germany. Dr. Andreas Hohlfeld, a young *Mitarbeiter,* had eaves-dropped on the conversation and taken it upon himself to relate the incident to the authorities in Darmstadt.

When Ringshausen told Geheeb about the denunciation, Geheeb was so astonished that he reacted spontaneously. "I just couldn't con-trol myself," he later recalled, "and I burst out laughing right in his face." Ringshausen was appalled by Geheeb's response:

> He then became terribly uneasy . . . He had come to congratulate me on the famous school . . . and he hoped that it would conform with the spirit of the great Führer and then it would be even more famous. He was going to arrange that. And then he got this reaction, which really destroyed his plans. He was most reserved and only said, "Hold your tongue in the future."

Geheeb later recalled, "I can't say I was very careful. This story would have fully sufficed to have had me shot." Max Cassirer told Geheeb afterwards, "You really could have been shot six times already. That's how careless you are."[8]

Geheeb's laughter could have been viewed by the Nazis in many different ways—as an expression of open contempt, surprised embar-rassment, or simple incredulity. Once again, ambiguity played a key role in the relations between Geheeb and the authorities. Yet the pos-sible negative interpretations, buttressed as they were by denuncia-tions by three of the school's staff, must have made Geheeb vulnerable to the Nazis' charges of "political unreliability" and intensified their interest in securing the alignment of the school with Nazi educational policy.

Ringshausen made the power invested in his position as the Minis-ter of Culture and Education in Hesse clear to Geheeb before leaving Oberhambach on 7 April. Geheeb was accused of numerous ideolog-ical offenses in his leadership of the Odenwaldschule. These included promoting pacifism among his students, supporting social democracy, and subverting the principles and practices of the new Nazi state. As a consequence of these accusations, Ringshausen gave Geheeb two unnegotiable preconditions for the school's continued existence. The first precondition was the end of thorough coeducation by compelling boys and girls to live in separate houses. Nazi ideology was virulently anti-feminist, and coeducation was interpreted as a victory of the women's movement. Since Geheeb had often insisted that coeduca-tion was the foundation of all humanistic education, Ringshausen's reform was a major blow against the Odenwaldschule.[9]

The second precondition was equally serious. Geheeb was to dismiss almost his entire teaching staff and to replace them with young Hessian teachers known to be sympathetic to Nazism. The Nazi strategy of purging "the Weimar generation and replacing it with a specifically Nazi-recruited and indoctrinated group of pedagogues" would be implemented in the Odenwaldschule, as it was throughout the German educational system. Geheeb could appeal to Blank to maintain a few indispensable staff members, but most of the staff had to go. Geheeb had no time to consider his decision: "I was given the choice of either accepting the one alternative with its conditions or of closing the school." Unprepared to close the school with so little warning, Geheeb chose to accept the conditions. Yet the damage was done. "Today was the last day of the old Odenwaldschule," Martin Wagenschein lamented.[10]

The loss of most of the *Mitarbeiter* was a tremendous blow to the sense of internal cohesion in the Odenwaldschule. Many of the *Mitarbeiter* had worked in the school for years and had planned to spend the rest of their lives there. Geheeb observed,

> There was much crying and terrible unrest among the children. They were very attached to the *Mitarbeiter*. But at any rate I had to obey. That evening the older *Kameraden* stormed into my room and demanded to know how this was possible. I explained to them, "It's violence. We can't do anything against it."

Yet Geheeb did not mean this literally. On the contrary, he now undertook a wide series of actions to mitigate the effects of the last Nazi intervention in the Odenwaldschule and to attempt to preserve as much of the old school as possible. The absence of students and staff over the Easter vacation allowed him to devote the coming weeks to corresponding with the press, appealing to Blank in the Ministry of Culture, and coordinating strategy with *Mitarbeiter* and *Kameraden* for the coming summer term. This time between terms gave Geheeb a needed respite from the daily responsibilities of leading a school and allowed him to organize the most effective and sustained resistance he could in light of the new situation.[11]

Geheeb's first strategy was to contact the press to inform the *Frankfurter Zeitung* that the official investigation of the Odenwaldschule had been carried out and that "The result was a satisfactory understanding between the Hessian government and the leadership of my school, so the continuity of the school is guaranteed." Geheeb did not mention the reproaches he received at the end of the interview on 7 April, nor did he mention the reforms instituted by Ringshausen and Blank.[12]

Geheeb's second reaction was to write the school *Mitarbeiter* who were on vacation to urge them to come back to the Odenwaldschule to help him fight to retain their positions. In a letter to Werner Meyer, for example, Geheeb urged Meyer to interrupt his holidays in Holland:

> I rush to tell you that your position is greatly endangered because you are our history teacher, and they believe you are a Marxist. I urge you most strongly to shorten your stay in Holland as quickly as possible and to come back to discuss this with me to prepare for an interview with Dr. Blank.

Third, Geheeb wrote a series of long, detailed letters to Blank in which he defended himself and the Odenwaldschule and sought to conserve as much of the school's liberal atmosphere as possible.[13]

The first of these letters was sixteen pages long, and full of detailed repudiations of the charges made by the Nazis on their recent visit to the school. As part of their accusation concerning Geheeb's socialism, Ringshausen and Blank had shown Geheeb a student essay which had been confiscated in the Goerendt raids and was marked by militant support for social democracy. According to Ringshausen and Blank, the essay reflected the kinds of values Geheeb transmitted to his *Kameraden.* Geheeb was also accused of communist tendencies because the Odenwaldschule had conducted fundraising drives for the International Workers' Aid, an organization affiliated with communism. Geheeb's well-known pacifism was held to be yet another symptom of the international and unpatriotic spirit of the school.

Geheeb's reaction to the accusations was evasive. The socialist essay, he claimed, had not been written by a student at all but by her father, who was one of Germany's prominent religious socialists. Geheeb suggested that this showed that the Odenwaldschule did not spread socialist ideas but merely received them from beyond its institutional boundaries. Concerning the International Workers' Aid contributions, Geheeb claimed ignorance of its communist affiliations. Geheeb stated that he had been duped into believing the organization was apolitical, and that the Odenwaldschule's contributions did not reflect the school's political bias, but rather its ethical concerns (which had their ultimate foundation in Christ's sermon on the mount). He rejected accusations concerning communists in the Odenwaldschule as a "grotesque and fantastic presumption." That a small group of students had cooperated with communists in Heppenheim did not justify "massive exaggerations of the real facts," which were that communism was an insignificant persuasion among students. If students had any communist leanings at all, Geheeb claimed, they did not get them from the Odenwaldschule but from Germany's large cities, where many of them lived when not attending school.

Finally, Geheeb dodged the accusation of pacifism. He wrote Blank that he could not respond to this reproach until Blank defined what he meant by the term. Rather than deny his pacifism, Geheeb simply wrote that "I believe it would digress too much to discuss this issue here in any detail." He later wrote to Ferrière that the authorities had accurately confirmed his pacifism.[14]

After responding to the ideological objections, Geheeb then turned to the institutional reforms in the Odenwaldschule. Geheeb criticized the end of full coeducation in the Odenwaldschule as an intervention which would inflict substantial damage upon the quality of education in the school. According to Geheeb, it was a fundamental misunderstanding to believe that coeducation was a contingent principle which could be abrogated without penetrating to the heart of the Odenwaldschule's philosophy and practice. Coeducation was vital if students were to avoid sex role stereotypes and were to learn to respect students of the opposite sex as equal partners within the community of the school. Geheeb then protested the reforms of 7 April directly:

> In spite of this you have found it wise to implement a fundamental change in my school so that in the future boys and girls can no longer live in the same houses. I do not consider this to be an improvement but instead to be a force which will constrict the wonderful spontaneity which has hitherto characterized our youth of both sexes, but I submit to the superior force.

At the last NEF conference, Geheeb noted, Dutch educator J. J. van der Leeuw described the Odenwaldschule as the most perfectly developed coeducational school anywhere. The Nazi intervention would destroy the very feature of the school which had brought it fame.

After defending himself against the charges of ideological unreliability and fighting to defend coeducation, Geheeb then turned to the main theme of his letter, the dismissal of his staff. Geheeb urged Blank to grasp the unique character of the Odenwaldschule:

> [It is] not a school in the ordinary sense but instead a *Lebensgemeinschaft* dedicated to the purpose of education; it is therefore an organism. Thus your planned change implies a deep and violent operation which will provoke a crisis which must be of utmost concern.

According to Geheeb, ordinary teachers who wished to work for eight hours and then withdraw into their private lives were useless in a school like the Odenwaldschule. "Whoever considers being together with children outside of instruction to be an irritation—this person I cannot use." Geheeb referred to Georg Kerchensteiner's observation that only one teacher out of a thousand was really appropriate for the Odenwaldschule. For not only did the *Mitarbeiter* at the Odenwaldschule have to be specialists in their subjects and cultivated and dynamic personalities in their own right, but they also had to be so filled with pedagogical talent and commitment that they would bring these characteristics to bear in living together with children on a full-time basis. Blank was urged to recognize this in selecting new *Mitarbeiter* for the school.

Geheeb then turned to the actual composition of his staff. He first mentioned Heinrich Sachs, the Odenwaldschule's drawing teacher, "who is incidentally a thoroughly German person." Sachs' twelve-year residence in the Odenwaldschule and the participation of his wife and three children in the school made it particularly important that he be allowed to stay. Geheeb then referred to Werner Meyer, whom Geheeb presented as a "compassionate German man who has fought Marxist tendencies with deep conviction and great talent and success." Geheeb used this reference to digress and to attack communism, claiming that the Odenwaldschule was the "physical repudiation of Marxism" and that it drew its inspiration not from "Rathenau and other Marxist saints" but from the "heroes" of German classicism whose names were given to the houses of the school. Geheeb presented the case for each staff member, arguing for the retention of those whom he found to be in particular need of staying or who made a particularly outstanding contribution to the school.[15]

The result of Geheeb's letter to Blank was that Geheeb was able to retain Sachs, Meyer, and a few other staff members. Wagenschein and many more of the staff left the school and sought positions elsewhere—a challenging task, given the liberal reputation of the school and the ongoing pedagogical counterrevolution. Freidank and Neumeister, the two teachers who had denounced the school after the festival of 18 March, now decided to continue in the school. The rest of the staff was to be replaced by young teachers accredited by the Hessian Ministry of Culture and Education and appointed by Blank.[16]

It must have been most difficult for Geheeb to witness the departure of most of his staff, some of whom had been working in the school for years and had contributed substantially to the success of the Odenwaldschule. He once again wrote to Blank to express his concern over the reform:

A change in governmental politics cannot disturb my pedagogical work, regardless of how fundamental it may be. For my pedagogical ideals are completely apolitical and indeed transcendental. As a deeply religious person I am accustomed to viewing the laws of human development *sub specie aeterni.* If I had doubted whether I would be able to continue working under a National Socialist government I would have closed my school the day that Dr. Werner was elected president of Hesse.

In my forty years of educational activity I have worked under the most diverse authorities and have always been not only absolutely loyal but also straightforward and honest. I would never descend to the level of taking a certain position before a governmental representative and then carrying out the exact opposite of what I've said behind his back. I also will not change my character on this point. I am even positively convinced that I can continue to work well under the new government . . . and can contribute a modest part to the construction of the new Germany.

However unjustified and incomprehensible the measures appear which suddenly remove from the school the majority of my *Mitarbeiter*— who are neither politically nor pedagogically suspect in the slightest degree, and whose value has been confirmed by both external observers and the results of the last examinations—and which send me new and completely unfamiliar Hessian teachers, I do not see myself compelled to close my school. If, however, most honored doctor, you intend to force me, through this measure, to betray the educational experiences of forty years of my life's work and the pedagogical program which is incarnated in my personality . . . and to lead my school through the sudden directives of ministerial officials, then I would ask you to spare us all further trouble I could only plan in the face of this to close my school immediately. (With the intention, of course, that my father-in-law would be able to use the school's real estate and buildings for other purposes, but not that anyone else would establish an institute of education here.)

First Geheeb described the philosophical project behind his practical educational work, then he declared his readiness to cooperate with the new authorities if they allowed him to preserve and develop his educational autonomy, and finally he made it clear that he did not intend to cooperate with the authorities at all costs.

In addition to issuing press releases and communicating with his staff and with Blank, Geheeb responded to the investigation of 7 April by intensifying his correspondence with Ferrière. Although the authorities had given Geheeb permission to continue directing the Odenwaldschule, Geheeb wanted to secure a real alternative for himself and his school by laying the groundwork for continuing his educational work in a different form abroad. "I have no optimistic feelings regarding the future of my school here," he wrote to Ferrière. "Perhaps things will develop so that I close it this summer, so that I can then move it to Switzerland."

While Geheeb's letters to Blank imply that Geheeb was a politically neutral individual making an earnest effort to align his school with Germany's new nationalistic movement, his letters to Ferrière in April were filled with anger about the Nazis. He confided to Ferrière,

> In the last few weeks I would have given a great deal to see you and to be able to talk with you. It has probably been the most difficult period of my life: for weeks a constant tension—not anxiety, not fear!—in preparing myself to be arrested. Is it possible for you to have any real idea of what is happening in Germany? How many thousands sit in prisons? That they have already prepared four large concentration camps, each one for three to five thousand prisoners? And with what brutality they advance! The atmosphere is unbearable. Can you even imagine the truth? The German newspapers are not only prevented from printing the truth; they are forced to lie. For example, Jewish organizations are forced by the police to declare that the Jews are doing well, that they are not mistreated, etc. The conditions are so against all sense of culture and so terrible that one feels set back beyond the Middle Ages.

In this correspondence with Ferrière—which, it is important to note, usually escaped the censor by passing through friends who mailed the letters from abroad—Geheeb expressed his authentic perceptions clearly and adamantly, with none of the vacillation of his letters to Blank. He was unequivocally opposed to the Nazi transformation of Germany.[17]

Meanwhile, Ferrière sent Geheeb discouraging news about Swiss receptiveness to Geheeb's plans to emigrate. The Swiss were concerned about setting precedents and maintained strict controls on individual immigration; they were even more wary of allowing an entire school to move to their country. Furthermore, their own private schools had lost many students due to the financial depression and they were not eager to accommodate foreign competitors who might draw away their own students. Geheeb was not going to give up quickly, however. Since Ferrière was deaf and could not negotiate well for Geheeb, Geheeb urged Ferrière to ask his colleague Pierre Bovet to travel to Bern to plead on Geheeb's behalf.[18]

Nazi anti-Semitism influenced Geheeb's caution in dealing with the new Hessian school authorities. It was well known that Geheeb's wife was of Jewish descent and that the school legally belonged to Max Cassirer. Geheeb was in constant negotiations with his wife and father-in-law about different possibilities for saving the school. Cassirer's role in these discussions was to urge Geheeb to exercise diplomacy and prudence in his consultations with the Nazis. Frightened that the Nazis might confiscate the school property or punish Edith or him for ill-considered actions on Geheeb's part, Cassirer was convinced that a show of good will and cooperation by Geheeb would persuade the Nazis to leave the Odenwaldschule alone. As the year advanced, Geheeb and Cassirer were to experience numerous differences of opinion, with Cassirer convinced that Geheeb was going to bring about the school's doom through misplaced protests and Geheeb convinced that Cassirer was paralyzed by fear and incapable of perceiving the need to resist Nazi incursions. In April these differences were subdued, but Cassirer's cautious approach toward negotiating with the Nazis had already emerged in marked contrast to Geheeb's desire to assert his independence against the regime.

Geheeb experienced the pressures on him as so intense that he almost closed the Odenwaldschule before the beginning of its summer session. In a telephone conversation with Blank he notified the authorities that he intended to shut the school, but he backed down from this position in the course of an interview with Blank at the Ministry of Culture in Darmstadt. In this interview Geheeb became aware of divisions among the Nazi officials about the appropriate action to take with the Odenwaldschule. Hessian President Werner and Ringshausen both supported Goerendt and his two raids on the school in early March. Blank, on the other hand, was willing to use his limited power to secure a minimal amount of autonomy for the Odenwaldschule and would try to accommodate Geheeb's wishes to choose new *Mitarbeiter* on the basis of pedagogical and not only political considerations. Geheeb was encouraged and hoped Blank would be able to protect the school from Ringshausen, Werner, and Goerendt.[19]

When the *Kameraden* returned to the Odenwaldschule on 22 April, the future of the school was still indefinite. While most of the old staff had left the school, most of the new faculty had not arrived. In light of the transitional state in this and many other Hessian schools, the Ministry of Culture ordered the suspension of classes for the first week of the summer term, and the *Kameraden* and staff used their free time to work in the school's garden and to build an outdoor theater in the woods behind Herder House.

Meanwhile, the first government-sponsored boycotts of Jewish stores in Germany occurred in the first week in April. While the boycotts were largely unsuccessful, the Nazi repression of their opponents continued. One can well imagine the trepidation with which

Geheeb and his loyal staff and students entered upon the summer semester of the Odenwaldschule in 1933.

Geno Hartlaub led the *Warte* in the spring and summer of 1933, and wrote an article in *Der neue Waldkauz* describing students' reactions to the changes in the Odenwaldschule when they returned to the school on 22 April. "At first we were simply deeply pained, because we had to let all of the *Mitarbeiter,* whom we had known for a long time and who were intimately connected with the school, leave." According to Hartlaub, the loss of the old *Mitarbeiter* compelled the more mature students to realize that it was now their responsibility to uphold and preserve the Odenwaldschule as they had previously known it. The *Kameraden* and especially the *Warte* arranged numerous discussions with Geheeb to review the situation of the school. Unlike the silence which had earlier surrounded Steinitz, Geheeb and the *Warte* now discussed the political crisis in the school with one another. According to Hartlaub,

> We older *Kameraden* often came together with Paulus to reflect together on many things which were of utmost importance to us. We spoke completely openly with one another, everything superficial fell by the wayside, and that which was of vital importance emerged in full clarity.

Hartlaub neglected to define what was "superficial" or "of vital importance" for the readers of the school paper. Only in the postwar period did she make it clear that the *Warte* used their meetings to deliberate upon the best way to respond to the political situation in the school.[20]

The new situation was not just a contest between the Odenwaldschule and the Hessian Ministry of Culture; it was also a test of Geheeb's pedagogical achievements. If Geheeb's educational values had been realized and his students had developed a profound sense of autonomy and social responsibility, what would a change in the *Mitarbeiter* of the Odenwaldschule really effect? The *Mitarbeiter* lived separately from the students and the *Warte* oversaw the administration of the school. It was the *Warte* and not the *Mitarbeiter* who organized students' course schedules, finances, cleaning responsibilities, and health services. Since the *Wartekonferenzen* were closed meetings, with Geheeb the only adult in attendance, the *Wartekonferenz* actually exercised more power than the faculty meetings, which were dedicated almost solely to students' academic progress. By implementing the *Wartesystem* in 1931, Geheeb had given the Odenwaldschule an institutional mechanism for the continuation of student self-governance in spite of the threatening political climate.

According to Geheeb, the *Warte* were completely successful in their endeavor to protect the school against Nazi incursions. Rather than being intimidated by the arrival of the new Nazi staff, they took the offensive, saying, "We certainly will educate them." Geheeb was delighted and wrote Ferrière, "These young people are acting wonderfully, filled with enthusiasm and with the deepest sense of responsibility." Geheeb and the *Warte* decided not to antagonize or ostracize the new *Mitarbeiter,* but to so impress them with the dynamism and self-reliance of the Odenwaldschule community that they would put aside their political prejudices and give themselves over to the school's rich cultural life. Geheeb was so convinced of the superiority of the values of the Odenwaldschule to those of Nazism that he could not imagine the young *Mitarbeiter* would cling to their political ideologies once they experienced the emancipatory culture and structure of the Odenwaldschule. Inspired by the *Warte* and hopeful about Blank's desire to hire pedagogically talented staff, Geheeb felt at the end of the month that the Odenwaldschule had a good chance of recovering its vitality.[21]

By 2 May seven new Nazi teachers had arrived in the Odenwaldschule. Along with Freidank and Neumeister, there were now nine *Mitarbeiter* who had allegiances to the Nazi movement, among a faculty which fluctuated around twenty. This was a number large enough to cause significant damage to the school yet small enough to still allow the school to exert significant leverage upon them. For the moment, however, the only real power of the new *Mitarbeiter* lay in their privileged status vis-à-vis the Hessian Ministry of Culture and in their ability to denounce the school if they felt it was sabotaging Nazism. Barring such purely negative actions, the internal control of the school remained in the hands of Geheeb and the *Warte*.

The *Kameraden* had ambivalent reactions to the new *Mitarbeiter*. Some of them could not control their skepticism toward their new teachers, whom they treated as "second-class citizens." "We suddenly had these completely new teachers, to whom we responded with deep mistrust," Clewie Kroeker said. "We didn't make it easy for them." The Nazi teachers thought they could usurp student leadership roles and order *Kameraden* to carry out tasks according to their dictates, and that the *Kameraden* would obey. To their dismay, the *Kameraden* frequently refused. In one instance, the new *Mitarbeiter* decided that the traditional arrangement in which older *Kameraden* led the morning exercises was not rigorous enough, and they took the leadership in their hands themselves. The students objected, refused to follow the commands, and so effectively sabotaged the new leaders that they gladly returned to the traditional practice of student leadership of exercises. There appear to have been many small examples of passive resistance from *Kameraden,* who made a point of responding slowly and apathetically to *Mitarbeiter* requests.[22]

After the upheavals of March and April, the months of May and June were comparatively peaceful in the Odenwaldschule. There were no surprise raids on the school and no denunciations by the new staff. In spite of the surface peace, many *Kameraden* sensed that the atmosphere of the school had completely changed. Lore Fry felt that the separation of boys from girls in the houses brought about "a thorough transformation in the school in the briefest time." Kroeker observed that "The manner of interaction became much, much worse, with dirty jokes and the like. The tone of things changed absolutely." In their public statements, however, the *Kameraden* were more circumspect; Geno Hartlaub described the reorganization of boys and girls into separate houses as as "purely formal" in the student newspaper.[23]

In the first faculty meeting in the summer semester Geheeb gave a lengthy address which took up the time of the entire meeting. Geheeb spoke primarily to the new *Mitarbeiter,* most of whom were beginning teachers who were quite anxious about their new responsibilities. Rather than escalate tensions, Geheeb told them that there was no reason why the school could not cooperate with the new government and the new Nazi spirit in Germany:

> I would have to fail completely to understand the new national move-
> ment to presume that the Odenwaldschule cannot blossom and prosper
> in the Third Reich, especially as a dogmatic rigidity has never been a
> property of our *Lebensgemeinschaft.* We are always ready to discuss every-
> thing with new members of our community and to learn from them.

Geheeb urged the new staff to "Be completely honest, entirely yourselves!" He quoted Pindar's "Become who thou art!" and told the new *Mitarbeiter* that this dictum represented "not only our pedagogical leitmotif but our highest life maxim." Regardless of their affiliations with the Nazis, the new teachers were encouraged to pursue the same idealistic project that Geheeb had upheld ever since the inception of the Odenwaldschule.[24]

At the same time that Geheeb encouraged the new *Mitarbeiter* to bring themselves fully into the school community, he also confirmed that he was concerned about the school's future and stated that he would not retreat from defending his central pedagogical principles.

In Geheeb's presentation, the major threat to the Odenwaldschule at the current juncture lay not so much in the new *Mitarbeiter* as in the possibility of further surprise raids and interventions in the school by SA or SS troops and the Hessian government. Using naturalistic imagery, Geheeb stated that the dismissal of the old *Mitarbeiter* caused a "fever" in the school "organism." The intensity of this fever called for "a difficult operation, and it will probably require some time until the organism is healthy once again." Further surprise interventions in the Odenwaldschule would not result in superficial structural changes in the school but "would truly be a natural catastrophe, an earthquake, a real *force majeure* in the strictest sense." Practically speaking, such a catastrophe would begin if "the Hessian government were to intervene, make reforms, and so change the school that it would from my perspective at best be a caricature of that which I have always wanted." Should these reforms be forced through, Geheeb would respond by shutting the school immediately. "Either the Odenwaldschule survives with the conservation of its spiritual foundation or it closes."

Geheeb took special care in the first staff meeting to impress upon the new *Mitarbeiter* the central role which they played in either ensuring or destroying the continuity of the Odenwaldschule. If the *Mitarbeiter* showed a willingness to understand the unique atmosphere and purpose of the Odenwaldschule, one could anticipate their return in the fall and an upswing for the school after the instability of March and April. If, on the other hand, they held themselves back and criticized the school without attempting to adapt to it, they could destroy the school, if not through an overt denunciation then through parasitically taking from the community without giving of themselves to it. The Odenwaldschule would survive only through the mutual efforts of old and new members of the community.

The new *Mitarbeiter* were reserved in their reactions to Geheeb's address. One teacher claimed that a discussion of Geheeb's points was fruitless: "It isn't necessary to talk about this; our work will reveal whether we can cooperate." Others wanted more time to get to know the school and withheld further comment. Karl Gleiser, on the other hand, distinguished himself from the rest of the group by taking Geheeb's appeal to heart. Following the first two faculty meetings Gleiser wrote an article for the school journal in which he described his perception of the new situation in the school. According to Gleiser, the task of the new *Mitarbeiter* was to create "a synthesis between the theory of the new Germany and that of the founder and leader of the Odenwaldschule." Claiming that "Paul Geheeb is convinced of the possibility of such a synthesis," Gleiser defined the new overriding goal of the Odenwaldschule as

> the education of German youth to passionate and dutiful members of the *Volk* and state for our new National Socialist Germany under Adolf Hitler's leadership, the Germany of national greatness and of social justice.[25]

In spite of the complexity of the situation, it appears that the new *Mitarbeiter* adapted well to the principles and practices of the Odenwaldschule. Geheeb wrote to his friend Eduard Spranger that the work of the *Warte* in acclimating the *Mitarbeiter* to the school was "successful beyond all expectations." When the new *Mitarbeiter* criticized aspects of the Odenwaldschule, Geheeb asked them to withhold their complaints until they were more familiar with the school; "at that point their criticisms and proposed reforms ended." Geheeb was pleased by many of the new staff, whom he found to be friendly and hard-working. Most of the *Mitarbeiter* were accepted as distinct individuals who also had a certain role to play in the community. It appeared that the Odenwaldschule was en route to stability and prosperity in the Third Reich, just as Geheeb had claimed was possible.[26]

Geheeb nonetheless was deeply concerned about the future. On 22 June he wrote to former *Mitarbeiter* Martin Wagenschein,

> The process of cooperation between (*almost*) all of the new *Mitarbeiter* and me and the *Kameraden* is well underway, and I had hardly dared to hope that things could go so well. But, but—for many years I have had a (not always very pleasant!) intuition that has not yet deceived me! I see black clouds balling together on the horizon preparing for a terrible storm and it is slowly approaching. I have absolutely no factual reference, but I feel so strongly that some people outside are filled with hate and will not rest until they have moved against us.

Geheeb's intuition proved to be remarkably accurate. The "black clouds" broke open on 20 July, just one day before the students departed for summer vacation. On that morning Dr. Blank again made a sudden visit to the Odenwaldschule. Once again, the Odenwaldschule had been denounced, and the *force majeure* which Geheeb had feared was now unleashed.[27]

chapter 6

Emigration or Internal Migration?
July–August, 1933

At 7:00 in the morning on 20 July, Rudolf Blank visited the Oden-waldschule. Rather than discuss developments with Geheeb, however, he ignored the school's director and spent the entire morning with the new Hessian teachers. "His behavior toward me was the exact opposite of that in the series of friendly encounters we had had since last March," Geheeb lamented. When Geheeb finally was able to speak with Blank in the afternoon, he learned that the Odenwaldschule had been denounced not to the Ministry of Culture in Darmstadt but to the Reich Ministry of the Interior in Berlin. Blank told Geheeb that the Reich Ministry had reproached his office for its allegedly lacka-daisical supervision of the Odenwaldschule, saying that nothing had changed in the school since the National Socialist seizure of power. Blank charged that "Hardly anyone said 'Heil Hitler' at the beginning of class, no swastika flags were displayed, and everything continued just as it was before Hitler." He had now come to make certain that the Odenwaldschule would be brought into line with the principles and practices of National Socialist education.[1]

Blank's new intervention in the Odenwaldschule struck three blows against Geheeb's leadership. After meeting with the new Hessian *Mitarbeiter* for the entire morning Blank called together the *Wartekon-ferenz* in the afternoon. Blank then demanded the end of the *Warte-system* and of all student self-government in the Odenwaldschule. Blank's first attack on Geheeb's organization of the school was to inform the *Warte* of this change. Geheeb perceived the situation as follows:

> The central idea of our school life always was that of responsibility. All of our organizations and practices were designed with the purpose of filling our children at the earliest ages with a strong sense of responsi-

bility, which they learned to master with increasing maturity. Dr. Blank could not mock this enough and believed he was saying something pleasant to the young people (among whom there were numerous nineteen- and twenty-year-olds) when he proclaimed a new arrangement with these words: "Dear children, you really have it much easier when your teachers order and the students obey and leave all responsibility to the adults." I saw how the young people were infuriated. They nonetheless were able to control themselves and discussed tactfully and to the point.

Blank refused to entertain the objections of the *Kameraden* and student self-governance in the Odenwaldschule suffered a major defeat.[2]

After dismissing the *Wartekonferenz* Blank called the staff of the school together. Blank then explained the reasons for his intervention, which he traced back to a denunciation to the Reich Ministry in Berlin. He refused to identify the source of the denunciation and revealed the results of his meetings that morning with the new *Mitarbeiter*. Blank had gathered all their criticisms of the school and translated them into ministerial orders. These orders struck at the heart of Geheeb's school leadership and were Blank's second major attack on the school that day. Geheeb was no longer to lead the Odenwaldschule on his own. Dr. Freidank—one of the two teachers who had denounced the school after the 18 March celebration—was now to share the leadership with him. Foot-dragging on Geheeb's part was to be reported immediately to Blank by Freidank. Yet Freidank's rise in status did not mean that Geheeb could now resign as school headmaster. Blank told Geheeb that he had to continue as headmaster: the Nazis needed to use Geheeb's name for Nazi propaganda purposes, to help sway foreign opinion.

The third and harshest attack on the school on 20 July was Blank's refusal to allow Geheeb to close the Odenwaldschule. The regime would show no tolerance for such symbolic protest of National Socialist educational policy. Geheeb was infuriated when he learned of this prohibition, and said to Blank, "You don't understand anything about education! You've completely destroyed my school today!" Blank was unmoved, and responded, "You say that I've completely destroyed your school. If you should happen to think of closing the school, we've still got space for you in a concentration camp in this area. And that's where you'll go!" With this threat Geheeb was silenced. He was well informed about the new concentration camp at Osthafen near Worms. For all effective purposes he was now a prisoner in his own school.

The Odenwaldschule was now truly in crisis. Its headmaster was forced to share the school leadership with a zealous Nazi and was cut off from his power base in the students through the abolition of the

Wartekonferenz. Geheeb was being used as a figurehead for the purposes of a regime he detested.

After Blank's departure that evening the older *Kameraden* once more stormed into Geheeb's apartment. "Paulus, this is no longer the Odenwaldschule," they argued. "This is a farce, a Hitler school! You must close it immediately." "That is expressly forbidden to me," he replied. "All right, then *we* will close it," they shot back.[3]

The students and Geheeb then worked out a new plan to respond to the Nazi incursions in the Odenwaldschule. Rather than cooperate with the new ordinances or openly protest against them, Geheeb and the students would plan and implement the systematic depopulation of the school, destroying the school from within to prevent its usurpation by the Nazis. Geheeb would then be able to claim that he was forced to close the school for financial and not political reasons. The sooner all of the students left the school, the sooner Geheeb would be freed from his current entrapment.

There was one major complication to the plan. Approximately two dozen of the oldest *Kameraden* needed to take their *Abitur* in the fall or spring of the next school year. Closing the Odenwaldschule before they could graduate would interrupt their studies and jeopardize their graduation. Many of these students were among the most responsible *Warte* and Geheeb felt a particular duty to support them after their intense involvement in sustaining and protecting the Odenwaldschule during the summer session.

It was therefore difficult to close the school before the spring of 1934. In light of the situation for the older *Kameraden*, Geheeb and the students decided they would begin depopulating the school from below, starting with the kindergarten and escalating upward through the grades so that by the time the last students graduated their departure would complete the depopulation of the school. They hoped that the Geheebs could then close the school without suffering punishment by the Nazis.

There were tremendous risks involved in the new strategy. The Odenwaldschule had been denounced in Darmstadt and in Berlin and the Nazis openly read mail coming and going from the school. A new denunciation based on the disclosure of the strategy for depopulation could result in the confiscation of the school and the arrest, although probably not the execution, of the Geheebs. Concentration camps in 1933 were not the extermination camps of later years but more often bases of "re-education," a euphemism for the repression of dissidents to assure the end of their political involvement after their release.

A further danger in the plan lay in the many individuals who would have to participate in it to ensure its successful completion. New denunciations could come from students, their parents, the newly empowered Nazi *Mitarbeiter,* or the inhabitants of Oberhambach who might eavesdrop on a conversation among confidants and report it to the authorities. Yet the only other alternatives appeared to be either complete cooperation, which was abhorrent to Geheeb, or open protest, with the obvious consequence of internment in Osthafen. In light of these alternatives, Geheeb was more than ready to risk the new strategy.

As for the origin of the denunciation which led to the intervention of 20 July, Geheeb believed that it had come not from the new *Mitarbeiter* but from Andreas Hohlfeld, the same *Mitarbeiter* who had informed the Hessian Ministry of Culture of Geheeb's derisive comments about Hitler the previous spring. Hohlfeld had left the Odenwaldschule during Easter vacation and taken a position as an assistant to Ernst Krieck, one of the most prominent Nazi philosophers of education, who had been recently appointed rector at the University of Frankfurt. Hohlfeld had apparently written a denunciation of the Odenwaldschule which Krieck had endorsed. Geheeb wrote to a friend,

> I recently learned that it was Dr. H. who actually succeeded in urging his great boss to get involved; Professor E. K., who has never met me or been to my school, is warning the public about it as a "hotbed of Marxism" and apparently brought the Reich Ministry of Interior to move against us.[4]

The available historical documentation does not allow one to determine whether Geheeb's suspicion that Hohlfeld was behind the denunciation was accurate. Hohlfeld did become an assistant to Krieck in 1933 and wrote an essay for the first edition of Krieck's periodical, *Volk im Werden,* in which he attempted to redefine the tasks of *Landerziehungsheime* under Nazism. While not mentioning Geheeb or the Odenwaldschule by name, Hohlfeld's article attacked those *Landerziehungsheime* which did not link pedagogical reform with the political movement of Nazism. According to Hohlfeld, the initial social and idealistic goals which the *Landerziehungsheim* movement sought to address had become political and national goals in the early 1930s. Yet many *Landerziehungsheime* had failed to forge a connection to Nazism, a circumstance which "was not insignificantly related to the contemporary leaders." According to Hohlfeld, these leaders would have to learn that

Behind the new forces of the present stands a people which is erupting
and no longer has time for intellectual discussions. And that is the clear
foundation upon which this movement is based!

While it is impossible to prove whether Hohlfeld denounced Geheeb,
it seems clear that Hohlfeld would have considered such a denunciation to be completely consistent with his support for Nazism.[5]

To a certain extent it does not matter whether Hohlfeld was the
moving force behind the renewed denunciation or whether it came
from another source such as one of the new *Mitarbeiter,* for the key
structural reality to be grasped here concerns the sociological role of
denunciation under Nazism. Denunciation offered a triple opportunity to demonstrate loyalty to the regime, avenge oneself on scape-
goats, and enhance the upward mobility of the accuser through the
Nazi party and the state apparatus. Those who denounced others
with the motive of rising socially did so so often that they were nick-
named "job hunters" *(Postenjäger).* This social and psychological reality meant that individuals often went far out of their way to denounce
others, and it explains the factors which may have led Hohlfeld to
stigmatize Geheeb and the Odenwaldschule.[6]

For whatever reasons, Geheeb was certain that Hohlfeld was the
source of the new denunciation. He lamented, "It would be too infu-
riating if my life's work really were destroyed through the antagonistic
and denunciatory chatter of such a young man." Geheeb saw Hohlfeld as acting out of "a poisonous mixture of vanity and revenge" and
credited him with destroying years of labor which produced the elaborate cultural microcosm of the Odenwaldschule.

One particular incident in the Odenwaldschule after the end of the
summer session made clear to Geheeb that Blank's reforms were not
cosmetic changes. One of the new Hessian *Mitarbeiter,* Robert Niederhoff, had experienced insurmountable difficulties in adapting to
teaching and living in the Odenwaldschule. Geheeb planned to dismiss Niederhoff at the end of the summer term and was pleased when
Niederhoff came to him on his own initiative to state his intention
to leave the school. They both agreed that the Odenwaldschule did
not seem to be an appropriate work environment for Niederhoff,
whom Geheeb thought good-hearted but psychologically disturbed
and hopelessly incompetent. For both Geheeb and Niederhoff,
Niederhoff's work in the school ended with his departure from
Oberhambach.

Soon after, both Geheeb and Niederhoff were surprised when
Blank ordered Niederhoff to return to the Odenwaldschule for the

fall session. Blank's intervention was never justified to Geheeb and
Geheeb was outraged at being compelled to take Niederhoff back into
his faculty. Geheeb wrote to his old friend Philipp Harth,

> In this way the responsibility which I have to carry for everything is a
> complete illusion. I consider Herr N. to be not only incapable and useless
> but in light of his pathology to be harmful. I am responsible for all of
> the damage which he inflicts on the children, but my responsibility is
> completely illusory because I have no power to exercise it.[7]

In spite of the Nazi challenges to Geheeb's school leadership,
Geheeb was no more ready now to surrender without a fight than he
had been in March or April. He had long planned to attend a conference of the International Association of New Schools in Pont-Céard
(near Versoix in Switzerland) during his summer vacation. He now
decided to spend almost all of August in Switzerland. This would
enable him to investigate the possibilities of emigrating from
Germany to Switzerland and to coordinate strategy with Ferrière,
who had been working intensively on Geheeb's behalf since March. It
would also allow Geheeb to correspond confidentially with Max
Cassirer, who was planning to vacation in Karlsbad in Czechoslovakia.

Geheeb traveled from the Odenwaldschule to Switzerland at the
beginning of August. He felt a tremendous sense of relief and hope
upon crossing the border, and wrote to Edith,

> Every day I become more and more aware of how the misery which
> has penetrated Germany is a fortunate stroke of fate for myself insofar
> as it forces me to ascend from Dammersfeld to the Alps and from the
> German atmosphere to the international atmosphere of Switzerland,
> and finally to achieve the full realization of my personality. Only in this
> sense is the transference of our work from Odenwald to Switzerland
> justified and even necessary. Our community must reach a higher level
> of perfection than ever would have been possible in Germany.

For Geheeb, the prospect of a relocation in Switzerland was not necessarily tragic. While the Nazi takeover certainly was a disaster in
political terms, seen in light of his personal development it could serve
as a catalyst to realize his ideals more fully than ever would have been
possible in Oberhambach. Yet there was no doubting Geheeb's psychological break with his homeland. "Inwardly I am absolutely finished with Germany," he wrote. "It is no longer my fatherland. As
soon as I'm no longer needed at the school I never want to go to
Germany again."[8]

Geheeb's first stop was at the vacation home of Adolphe Ferrière in
Les Pléiades. Geheeb shared his frustration and uncertainty about the

situation, saying, "Everything is unclear because I myself am still very unclear about the future of the school." As August unfolded, however, Geheeb tried to develop a flexible yet cohesive strategy for steering the immediate crisis in the Odenwaldschule in a manner which would preserve his pedagogical principles.[9]

Although he was skeptical about achieving any positive results at this stage of the struggle, Geheeb felt obliged to explore every conceivable avenue. He thus endeavored to reverse Blank's ordinances of 20 July. It is difficult to assess Geheeb's motivations in attempting to recover the prior character of the Odenwaldschule at this point. His actions may have been guided by a stubborn spirit of courage in refusing to surrender the school without fighting to the last moment, a certain confusion about the appropriate way to respond to the last intervention, or a sense of obligation to his father-in-law, who was anxious about the fate of his real estate in Oberhambach and who feared its possible expropriation. All of these different motivations were probably at play as Geheeb attempted to save the Odenwaldschule.

Geheeb wrote to Harth again and asked him whether he would be willing to speak with Blank, Hessian president Werner, or Ernst Krieck, in an effort to revoke the new controls placed upon Geheeb's leadership of the Odenwaldschule. Geheeb hoped that a diplomatic third party might produce positive results that he himself could not. Geheeb also decided to ask two of Germany's most prominent philosophers of education to enter into discussions with the government on his behalf. Geheeb wrote Eduard Spranger at the University of Berlin and Peter Petersen at the University of Jena to ask each of them if they could help him gain a sympathetic audience with officials at the Reich Ministry of the Interior. Both Spranger and Petersen were political conservatives who might have more allies in the new government than Geheeb was likely to find. Petersen, at Jena, had been in contact with Dr. Wilhelm Frick, the new Minister of the Interior who had previously been the President of Thuringia; Geheeb hoped that Spranger's central location in Berlin had enabled him to establish positive professional relationships with officials in the Ministry of the Interior. Talking with Ferrière, Geheeb said that he had now "found the courage to travel to Berlin to grab the bull by the horns and to talk with the highest officials. Doing this I will naturally risk going to jail but I can't let this frighten me away." If Spranger and Petersen could use their connections to help Geheeb secure an audience with sympathetic officials it might be possible for Ministry of the Interior officials to rescind Blank's reforms in the Odenwaldschule.[10]

At the same time that Geheeb was trying to gain Harth's, Spranger's, and Petersen's assistance in saving the Odenwaldschule, he was exploring the real problems and challenges involved in emigrating to Switzerland. Ferrière had written Geheeb that it would be almost impossible for Geheeb to receive permission to open a school of his own in Switzerland. Geheeb was thus forced to modify his original plan. A solution was found through Geheeb's friendship with Wilhelm Gunning, the director of a small school called the Institut Monnier, which hosted the New Schools conference that August in Pont-Céard. Gunning had first visited the Odenwaldschule on Ferrière's recommendation in 1913 and Geheeb and Gunning had subsequently met at NEF conferences in the 1920s. Like the Odenwaldschule, the Institut Monnier practiced coeducation and attempted to realize various principles of progressive education. Geheeb had described the Institut in the school journal of the Odenwaldschule as one of the finest schools in Europe after visiting it in 1928. As a result of the depression, however, the Institut had fallen upon hard times and the student body had shrunk to twelve.[11]

Mutual need therefore led Geheeb and Gunning to join forces in planning to lead the Institut Monnier. Gunning needed new students with money to revive his school and hoped that Geheeb would bring these with him from the Odenwaldschule; Geheeb needed an established school in order to receive immigration papers from the Swiss authorities to carry on his work in a freer environment. Since Geheeb was indeed planning to bring many students with him to Switzerland from the Odenwaldschule, he believed it would be possible to convince the authorities that he would be an economic asset and not a disadvantage for Switzerland. Both Geheeb and Gunning were concerned about the difficulties of running a school with two headmasters, but they were willing to take on this challenge in light of their respective school crises.

Geheeb's pessimism about the future of the Odenwaldschule within a National Socialist Germany and his discussion with *Kameraden* after Blank's intervention in the school led him to play a major role in organizing the depopulation of the school that August. In addition to asking Spranger, Petersen, and Harth to intervene with the government to save the school and confirming plans with the Institut Monnier, Geheeb also used his month in Switzerland to write to parents to ask them not to send their children back to the Odenwaldschule for the fall semester. With parents whom Geheeb trusted and who lived outside of Germany or were vacationing abroad Geheeb shared his plans concerning emigration and asked that the parents continue to support his work by sending their children directly to the Institut Monnier for the fall semester. To provide Geheeb with protection against the suspicions of the German authorities, he asked that the parents send him letters stating their intent to withdraw their children from the school for nonpolitical reasons such as financial necessity or family problems. He also urged these parents to maintain absolute discretion about his plans:

> I hope that you can fully grasp how difficult, indeed how dangerous, my situation is still. I must urge you to speak with no one, but really no one, about the upcoming closure of the Odenwaldschule or about any of the facts concerning my school and the government. You can hardly imagine how brutal they are at the moment about such things. The government would only need the slightest intimation of that which I've told you to put me in prison and confiscate the entire school.

With parents who had younger or immature students, Geheeb asked the parents to keep the political motives for his emigration secret. Only absolute confidentiality would enable him to move to Switzerland, and he hoped that if everything went smoothly he would be able to start work at the Institut Monnier in October.[12]

What was Geheeb to do with the parents whom he did not really know and was hence not sure he could trust? Rather than write to these parents directly Geheeb decided to write to Hermann Kobbé, a former *Mitarbeiter,* to ask him to write these parents. Kobbé was an American who lived in France and had promised Geheeb in December 1932 that he would help Geheeb should the school be forced into a crisis in the event of a Nazi seizure of power. Geheeb sent Kobbé a mailing list of parents' addresses and asked Kobbé to inform them about the changes in the school without mentioning Geheeb's plans to emigrate. The letter should be composed to give the appearance that Geheeb had no part in it and should contain the following information, formulated in a rough draft by Geheeb:

> What the friends of the Odenwaldschule have been fearing for months has now become a painful reality. Inferior individuals have misused political struggles and weapons to satisfy their personal grudges and to denounce the Odenwaldschule to the Reich government, which subsequently ordered the Hessian Ministry of Culture to make an incisive intervention in the school. The pedagogical integrity of the school has been destroyed. Herr Geheeb is now powerless and has no real influence on the school leadership. He has even lost the right to dismiss completely incompetent *Mitarbeiter.* The school is governed by a narrow-minded bureaucrat and an equally blind young teacher.

My wife and I have just finished living in the Odenwaldschule for a year. We entrusted our children to the school. We took part in everything, including teaching. It was devastating to observe the destruction of the work which Paul Geheeb had built up over twenty-three years. Herr Geheeb has lost all freedom of decision making and of acting, including the freedom to shut the school according to the dictates of his pedagogical conscience.

As parents and friends of the earlier Odenwaldschule, we consider it to be our duty to inform you of these facts. If I can give you any advice, it would be to visit Herr Geheeb in the school, or if you do not wish to do this, to keep your children out of the school altogether.[13]

Complementing these letters to parents, Geheeb also prepared to send the Odenwaldschule's *Mitarbeiter* letters dismissing them from their positions. In spite of Blank's warnings that any one-sided or abrupt actions by Geheeb would be interpreted as sabotage of the Ministry's reforms, Geheeb evidently was willing to brave the regime's opposition. He hoped that the economic pretext he had invented with the students would provide a cover for the dismissals, and wrote to Edith,

I wanted to write you about the dismissals (on 15 August for 1 October). I am convinced that we must carry through with this. We will send Blank the letters in which the parents take their children out of the school. The closing of the school due to economic necessity will then be crystal clear, so that Blank will not be able to interpret it as a protest against 20 July.

These dismissals were intended to be provisional. In the event that Geheeb's planned visit to Berlin should yield positive results it would be possible to revoke them. Geheeb hoped that by mailing out the notifications of dismissal early it would be possible to close the Odenwaldschule quickly and efficiently.[14]

At the same time that Geheeb was corresponding with friends, colleagues, and parents from his Swiss retreat he was also in contact with his students. As with the parents, Geheeb had to exercise utmost caution in discriminating between students who could be trusted with confidential information and those who would share it with others, either out of immaturity or out of malice. Geheeb wrote one of the most moving and revealing letters from this time to a student who had reproached him with political naiveté. Since the letter reflects not only Geheeb's political analysis but also his pedagogical spirit it is worth quoting at length:

I can hardly express how deeply your wonderful letter of 31 July touched and pleased me. Dear friend, you ask most modestly whether you have ever understood my Odenwaldschule. I have always considered you to be one of the *Kameraden* who has been most filled with a deep and comprehensive understanding for the idea of our school, and this fact is not diminished because every now and then I had to scold you for lack of discipline . . .

In your letter you express your amazement that I was blind for such a long time to the growing cultural and political catastrophe and that a Dr. Blank first had to open my eyes for me. Believe me, I have seen everything clearly for a long time, but I considered it to be useless and (under the circumstances) damaging to speak with the *Kameraden* about it. I completely agree with you and other dear *Kameraden* in the interpretation that our school has been endangered for months but that now, on 20 July, it has been utterly ruined . . . I can no longer carry the responsibility involved in keeping the school open but also do not have the power to close it. As you know, Dr. Blank has taken away my right (which previously every headmaster had) to dismiss staff whom I consider inappropriate and to hire appropriate staff. He holds this to be his exclusive right. This means, for example, that I have heard through coincidence that Niederhoff will return to us after vacation and test you in geography. The Ministry does not even consider it necessary to inform me about this. These facts in themselves suffice to illustrate that I can no longer exercise the authority which I previously took for granted as part of our school life. It is therefore necessary to shut the school as quickly as possible.

Now comes the torturous situation I am in! The government has ordered that the school continue in accordance with Blank's "reforms." If I now explain that I refuse to cooperate, they would send me directly to the Osthafen concentration camp near Worms, perhaps for many years (and I would still have to pay taxes there, that's how cleverly the state arranges it!). They would just put a National Socialist teacher in my position. Beyond this, the government would confiscate the entire property of the Odenwaldschule, including houses and their contents, the library and our most important papers, letters, etc. My wife and I would be left with the clothes on our backs. It's also possible that they would send Edith, Sachs, and those who were loyal to me to concentration camps, or at least take away their passports so they couldn't travel abroad. Believe me, my dear boy, these are not apparitions I'm seeing! I have spoken with many knowledgeable people who know the political situation thoroughly and they see things in the exact same way.

What are my choices, then? I no longer have the freedom of action to close the school (out of conviction, out of a crisis of conscience), so we must wait and hope that our *Kameraden* will refuse to live under these unbearable circumstances and instead will leave the school so that we have to shut it down out of economic necessity. In this case, the government can make no reproach against us; we will have to regret, along with the Ministry, that the continuation of the Odenwaldschule is no longer possible financially. Then we will be freed from these tortures.

I hope that you understand my situation perfectly and do not consider my position to be cowardly. It is simply my duty to avoid provoking things so that I and possibly my relatives (including my seventy-six-year-old father-in-law) are condemned and the one and one-half million marks invested in the school are lost. We must therefore take up our work again at the end of the month, grit our teeth, and above all assure that your *Abitur* proceeds orderly and with the desired results.

Once more, my deepest personal thanks for your letter. I hope that we will always be close to one another, even when we should hardly see one another again.

Geheeb thus made it clear that he was counting on the *Kameraden* to depopulate the school to free him from "these tortures." At the same time, he expressed his delight that the concerned *Kamerad* had developed his sense of social responsibility to the point of confronting his school headmaster with what he felt to be inexplicable ethical compromises. Yet perhaps most striking in the letter is the sense of intimacy and equality with the student, and the conviction that both were allies, struggling to realize the same humanistic ideas in a time of increasing political repression.[15]

Taken together, Geheeb's August strategy included plans to make a last effort to save the Odenwaldschule by carrying negotiations to Berlin, notifications of a provisional dismissal of school staff, a wide range of correspondence with students and students' parents, and the coordination of plans to emigrate. But Max Cassirer quickly intervened to interrupt Geheeb's plans to send out notifications of dismissal. Cassirer had traveled from Berlin to the Odenwaldschule after Blank's last visit to the school and was alarmed by Geheeb's furious reaction to Blank's reforms. Cassirer was afraid that Geheeb would respond impulsively, with ill-considered counter-attacks that would not only jeopardize the Odenwaldschule as an institution but also the personal safety of those most intimately connected with the school. Cassirer therefore urged Geheeb to recognize that Blank could only interpret a notification of dismissal immediately following Blank's intervention as a retaliatory measure. Once more Cassirer pleaded with Geheeb to proceed prudently and to win the confidence of the new *Mitarbeiter*. While Geheeb was focusing on staff relations, Cassirer would work to sell the school—preferably to the Nazis, to assure them of Cassirer's benign intents.

Cassirer not only stated his opposition to Geheeb's plans to send out notifications of dismissal to the school's staff. He also attacked Geheeb's hopes of emigrating to Switzerland. Cassirer wrote,

If you carry out this plan you will totally endanger the school financially; I have no doubt that if you thus abandon the school the government will confiscate it. This would happen regardless of the legal situation, for the school does not belong to you but to me. But legal questions play a minor role today. The property with its enormous investments would have to be considered lost. One would also have to fear personal danger for those immediately concerned, for which we have abundant evidence from other cases. I can therefore only urge you once more to keep your temper under control and not to allow yourself to rush to measures from which we will not be able to recuperate.

As a response to Cassirer's concerns Geheeb decided against sending out the notifications of dismissal. He wrote to Ferrière to say that Cassirer's points were well taken and that Geheeb's visit to Switzerland that August would only increase the authorities' suspicions. As for his Swiss project, Geheeb recognized the legitimacy of Cassirer's concerns but did not consider them to be sufficient to surrender all hopes of emigrating.[16]

Eduard Spranger was quick to respond to Geheeb's appeal for assistance but confessed impotence in terms of helping Geheeb gain a sympathetic audience in the Reich Ministry of the Interior. Spranger had given up his position as rector of the University of Berlin after the Nazi takeover as a protest against anti-Semitism. He now gave tutorials to students at his home rather than at the university. Spranger urged Geheeb to recognize that the case of the Odenwaldschule was typical in terms of Nazi interventions in schools and that Geheeb's chances of appeal were limited. "Frankly, I don't know what one can do," Spranger wrote. "My only friendly advice can be to wait until the wind blows in another direction." Spranger did not see much value in protest: "Resistance is useless. One must go to the limits of one's pedagogical conscience."[17]

Compared to Cassirer and Spranger, Philipp Harth responded with enthusiasm to Geheeb's initiatives. Harth was able to arrange an interview with Blank and Freidank and reported positively back to Geheeb about his conversation. While Blank had not told Harth the source of the denunciation of the Odenwaldschule which had provoked Blank's latest reforms, Blank's comments to Harth supported the hypothesis that Hohlfeld was responsible. According to Harth, the complaint about the school had come from Frankfurt, where Hohlfeld was an assistant to Ernst Krieck at the university, and Krieck had written a supportive cover letter. The report had gone to the National Socialist League for German Culture in Berlin, which had sent it on to the Ministry of the Interior. The Ministry had then ordered a more decisive intervention in the school by the officials in Darmstadt.[18]

Harth attempted to make Geheeb aware of the positive aspects of the current situation in the Odenwaldschule. Harth stressed that the

Ministry of Culture in Darmstadt wanted to keep the school open, a real gain at a time when other private boarding schools had been summarily closed. Blank and Freidank both assured Harth that if Geheeb would overcome his inflexibility and simply adapt to the current arrangement he would realize that he was still very much the real headmaster of the Odenwaldschule. The Nazis held that Geheeb's years of experience in the Odenwaldschule and in educational circles in general made him far more powerful than Blank and Freidank, and that Geheeb was overlooking new opportunities that would be available to the Odenwaldschule if Geheeb would synchronize the school with the Nazi movement.

Harth also asked Geheeb to recognize that the new *Mitarbeiter* were still eager to work in the Odenwaldschule and that Gleiser's appeal for a synthesis of Nazi education with Geheeb's pedagogical practice had never been repudiated. Blank and Freidank had told Harth that many recent changes in the school were superficial and that a mere change of attitude on Geheeb's part would create a better Odenwaldschule than that which had existed under the Weimar Republic. In light of the positive atmosphere Harth had sensed when speaking with Blank and Freidank, Harth discouraged Geheeb from traveling to Berlin to undertake discussions in the Reich Ministry of the Interior, believing that a practical solution was at hand through intensified cooperation with Ministry of Culture officials in Darmstadt.

Geheeb was skeptical about Harth's encouraging words. From Geheeb's perspective, Blank and Freidank were essentially telling Geheeb that if he abandoned his educational principles and obeyed Blank's ordinances the Odenwaldschule would once again prosper. They did not recognize that the suppression of the *Wartesystem* and Blank's order that Niederhoff return to the Odenwaldschule struck at the very heart of Geheeb's sense of pedagogical autonomy and personal integrity. There was no mention in Harth's letter of any reconsideration or regret on Blank's part.

Finally, Peter Petersen wrote to Geheeb that he sent governmental officials

> a very, very long essay defending your work and offering practical suggestions. Unfortunately, this appears not to have worked. I also offered to discuss the matter. They neither responded nor did they take advantage of my offer. Only the arrival of my letter was confirmed.

Because of the overall climate of popular enthusiasm for the Nazi takeover and the increasing control of the Nazis over previously autonomous social institutions, Petersen held out little hope for the Odenwaldschule.[19]

As for Geheeb's correspondence with Odenwaldschule *Mitarbeiter*, his decision to postpone the notification of dismissals gave him more time to communicate with old faculty—such as Heinrich Sachs and Werner Meyer—who had escaped the purge of 7 April. Meyer in particular was concerned about the transformation of the school and the role he was playing in it. On 12 August he wrote Geheeb about his role in the Odenwaldschule since the Nazi seizure of power:

> I know that I have almost gone to the limit to win the approval of the new political leaders in Germany, where one begins to surrender his soul to the devil . . . Just believe one thing, dear Paulus: I may be able to help you . . . I hope you'll appreciate my help.

Many Germans decided after the Nazi seizure of power not to emigrate but to withdraw from political life in the hope of preserving a measure of autonomy from the regime. This strategy of "inner migration" was proposed by Meyer as the most appropriate way for the Odenwaldschule to deal with its current crisis:

> We must be silent about many things today, but that does not mean we should not live them. There is a part of our community into which the militaristic, the inhumane, and—as I more and more believe—the deepest lies of National Socialist politics cannot penetrate. We want to protect this part—and within Germany itself![20]

In contrast to Meyer, Paul Geheeb was ready to explore the possibilities of emigration but not to "surrender his soul to the devil." Geheeb was exhausted by all of the work he had accomplished during his stay in Switzerland, and on his way back to Germany wrote to Ferrière that "they were indeed difficult and demanding weeks." They had been worth it, however, for Geheeb had recovered his hope that the crisis in the Odenwaldschule could be resolved, even if the resolution involved his withdrawal from Oberhambach and the continuation of his work in the Institut Monnier. "I feel filled with *deep strength* and *great courage*," he wrote, "and return happily to my work."[21]

Paul and Edith Geheeb, 1909.

Max Cassirer, October 1928.

Werner Meyer.

Heinrich Sachs and Paul Geheeb, 1930.

Paul Geheeb and *Kameraden* during a meeting of the *Wartekonferenz*.

Air bath exercises at the Odenwaldschule.

Storm troopers in the Odenwaldschule in March 1933. This photograph was taken secretly by a student from the second floor of Goethe Haus.

Gender-segregated marches through the countryside, a practice initiated along with other Nazi reforms in the Gemeinschaft der Odenwaldschule.

The Gemeinschaft der Odenwaldschule prepares for sporting events in July 1935. This photo is taken from an informational brochure published in 1936.

Paul Geheeb with students at the Ecole d'Humanité in the postwar period.

chapter 7

The New Faculty's Reforms:
September–October, 1933

The Nazis in the Odenwaldschule were not idle while Geheeb was communicating surreptitiously with his trusted colleagues in Germany and with students and parents of the Odenwaldschule in August. Emboldened by Blank's intervention on 20 July, these *Mitarbeiter* were eager to experience their new powers and to demonstrate their nationalism by pushing through reforms which would explicitly align the Odenwaldschule with Nazism. Their initiatives, Geheeb's counter-thrusts, and the power-saturated interplay between *Kameraden* and *Mitarbeiter* in everyday life were to render the Odenwaldschule a psychological battlefield. The polarization in the school intensified in the autumn of 1933 and each side developed differentiated tactics and coalitions to either maintain or reform the Odenwaldschule in line with their pedagogical and political convictions.

The school was divided into three camps. Approximately half of the school's *Mitarbeiter* identified themselves with national socialism and sought to coordinate the school with the Nazi movement. These teachers found their major power base in their connection with the Hessian Ministry of Culture and its ability to transform the school through ministerial injunctions. At the opposite pole stood Geheeb, who was the most resolute of the old staff in opposing Nazism. Geheeb exercised a distinct power through his many successful years of leading the school, his charisma, and his alliances with the *Kameraden*. Although the *Warte* were now formally disempowered insofar as their closed meetings and far-reaching administrative tasks were concerned, they still maintained a certain cohesion through private discussions.

Between the ideologically motivated new Nazi teachers and Geheeb and his loyal followers lay the majority of the school population. Many

Mitarbeiter, Kameraden, and parents were concerned about the political situation in the school but felt that it was best under the circumstances that the school attend to its essential tasks of teaching and learning. These individuals wanted to strengthen the cohesion of the school community regardless of the political ramifications.

A dramatic decline in the school population before the reopening of school for the fall term attenuated the formation of these three groupings. In previous years the student population of the Odenwaldschule had fluctuated between 150 and 180. Eighteen students had left the school during the spring break in the previous April, and the school had not been able to replace them. At the beginning of the fall session, 51 students did not return, so that the student body dropped from 145 to 94. Some of these students may have left for reasons which had nothing to do with national socialism, but it is reasonable to assume that Geheeb's efforts played a major role in precipitating the sharp decline in the student body.[1]

While the Nazi movement had gained much power in German society by September 1933, it was not clear what direction the movement would take or whether it would be able to sustain the momentum it had built up over the spring and summer. There was much division in the Nazi movement as to how much "socialism" there actually was in national socialism, how literally Nazi anti-Semitism should be interpreted, and how strictly the Nazi synchronization of German society should be enforced. These ambiguities in the Nazi movement shifted frequently and unpredictably and caused "numerous separate, sometimes overlapping but seldom coordinated and frequently opposing processes." These created free zones and opportunities for flexibility for opponents of the movement, as long as one avoided an alignment with movements or parties which took an explicit stance against Nazism *in toto.*[2]

The Nazis on the staff of the Odenwaldschule initiated the fall term with four separate reforms to accelerate the alignment of the school with national socialism. Each of these reforms changed the atmosphere of the school, although Geheeb was able to deflect the one which he felt most directly threatened his educational philosophy. The reforms were not introduced as a unified agenda but as separate points supported by different *Mitarbeiter.*

Dr. Freidank used the first *Mitarbeiter* conference that September to introduce the reforms. A key component of Nazi education lay in military exercises and Freidank now stated that one afternoon a week in the school would be dedicated to military training for male students. The boys would practice spear-throwing, boxing, and grenade-throwing, and would eventually learn to shoot rifles. In addition, Frei-dank wanted *Kameraden* of both sexes to attend political education classes one afternoon each week. On this afternoon they would be informed about the leading figures and politics of Nazism and would participate in group activities such as the rehearsal of nationalistic songs. The *Kameraden* were then to sing these while marching in for-mation through the countryside.

Geheeb did not contest these first two reforms. His sole reaction was to inquire whether the Nazi staff all supported them. The new *Mitarbeiter* indicated that they did, and Freidank, probably anticipat-ing a negative reaction from Geheeb, said that "We don't intend to drill a company of soldiers. There is, doubtless, something like this in military sports, but we'll arrange things so that there is no compari-son." Rather than resisting, Geheeb encouraged Freidank:

> I'd like to ask you not to be too afraid with regard to these arrangements. One must regret that our sports have been very irregular and that what we have done has been particularly unsatisfying for a *Landerziehungsheim*. These kinds of beneficial exercises aren't possible without strict disci-pline and obedience. I'd like to ask you to be particularly active with the boys.

Freidank was evidently pleased with Geheeb's reaction and said, "We expect a positive influence on class discipline through these reforms." Freidank's initiatives were not open to discussion by the *Kameraden*, who were to be informed of the changes in a special *Schulgemeinde*. The democratic principles of the old Odenwaldschule were now replaced with the leadership principle, or *"Führerprinzip,"* emphasized by Nazi ideology.[3]

A third major change in the Odenwaldschule that September was the formation of a contingent of the Hitler Youth. Jakob Zahrt, a new Hessian *Mitarbeiter,* founded the Hitler Youth in the school on 3 September with seven students and the group expanded to thirty members over the fall term. The Hitler Youth held two meetings each week, appropriated a classroom which they decorated with Nazi par-aphernalia, and portrayed themselves in the student journal as the "connecting force between the ideas of the new Germany and those of our school." According to the editors of *Der neue Waldkauz,*

> We live in a time in which youth are particularly active and coordinated within the state. The contingent of the Hitler Youth, which was started under the leadership of Herr Zahrt after the summer vacation, forms a visible and disciplined group. One often sees them marching in forma-tion on our country roads and can hear their songs from far away.

Through meetings and common activities they are forming many connections with the Hitler Youth of our area, and they have recently begun
group evenings together with the Hitler Youth from Oberhambach.

All three of the new Nazi reforms separated students on the basis
of gender and ethnicity. Neither Jews nor girls could participate in
the military sports reserved for Aryan boys, and Jews were excluded
from membership in the Hitler Youth and its female subdivision, the
League of German Girls. This principle of exclusion and segregation
was a radical change in a school which had always emphasized intercultural exchange and gender equality. The inclusive spirit of coeducation suffered a critical defeat when boys trained in military sports
while girls were cleaning school rooms, learning cooking, and mend-
ing clothes.[4]

The fourth reform which the Nazi *Mitarbeiter* initiated in the fall
session concerned religious education. Rather than acquiescing, as he
did with the first three reforms, Geheeb adamantly opposed any
changes in the religious aspects of the Odenwaldschule. In the previous spring the Hessian government had ordered that every school
day open and end with prayers. When Geheeb learned of this he
wrote Blank to tell him that these practices would not be introduced
into the Odenwaldschule "because they would not fit in with our life-
style." Geheeb held that "problems of religious education" were "the
center of all of my pedagogical interests." In his account, the Odenwaldschule was to be "seen as a truly religious community," which
would not benefit by accepting commands from the state dictating the
school's character. Geheeb closed that letter by writing, "I hope that
you agree that the spirit of the ordinance in question is appropriate,
but that I should not have to follow the prescribed schema slavishly."
Blank never replied to Geheeb's letter.[5]

Now Geheeb was once again confronted with religious reforms, but
these were much more ambitious. They pertained to "school prayers,
school religious services, religious classes for separate denominations,
and obligatory church attendance." Geheeb did not go into a lengthy
discussion on these separate points but stated his general reaction:

> I must take the entire issue of these questions with the sharpest aware-
> ness of their seriousness and importance. What has been developed in
> this matter in the Odenwaldschule belongs in an organic and integrated
> way to the essence of the school, to the atmosphere and spiritual foun-
> dation which has developed here over decades. When we want to change
> that which is essential we must analyze it thoroughly and be fully con-
> scious of the responsibility we are exercising.

Geheeb was uncertain where the proposed changes in the religious practices of the Odenwaldschule originated: in the Ministry of Culture or with the *Mitarbeiter*. If they had come from Darmstadt and had been approved by Blank, Geheeb believed that the school would have to go along with the reforms: "We are the subordinates, the Ministry has the power." On the other hand, if the reforms had come from the *Mitarbeiter*, the staff would be urged to consider two factors. First, religious education was of great concern to many parents and it would not help the school if parents decided to pull their children out of the school because of heavy-handed reforms. Second, Geheeb referred to his childhood, in which he had experienced how compulsory religious education could stultify rather than awaken religious sensibilities. Geheeb did not want the same mistakes repeated in the Odenwaldschule.[6]

The Nazi *Mitarbeiter* heard Geheeb's objections to this last reform and the faculty meeting ended. A fortnight later, however, they began a new meeting with the same topic. They now insisted that the entire school join in prayer following each breakfast. Referring back to the ordinance of the previous spring, they held that it was the duty of the school to carry out directives issued by the state, and that Blank's lack of response to Geheeb's earlier letter on this point could not be equated with consent.

Geheeb reacted by returning to the position he had presented in the first *Mitarbeiter* conference that fall and developing it in greater detail. Noting that the Odenwaldschule often received circulatory letters from the Ministry of Culture which were not intended to be relevant to private schools, Geheeb contested the *Mitarbeiters'* assertion that Blank had not approved Geheeb's letter from the previous April. According to Geheeb, group prayer in the Odenwaldschule was more likely to promote a hollow facade of religiosity than a genuine ritual for experiencing and cultivating religious sensibilities. Geheeb noted that Lietz and he had experimented with religious education:

> We tried to use some beautiful school prayers, but we gave it up after a few weeks when we found that they no longer made the slightest impression on the students. Sheer routine plays an absolutely lethal role in most religious education and actually kills real religion. It's a terrible abuse of beautiful parables to use them for daily routines which lack true spirituality.

Geheeb claimed that he did not object to the motivations which lay behind the idea of school prayers. Rather, he was opposed to the practice, which he felt was an "empty formula." If the teachers really wanted their students to cultivate their religious awareness, he said, they should realize that the school's traditional *Andachten* on Sunday evenings and daily interactions with students provided infinite opportunities for religious education.

One of the new Nazi *Mitarbeiter*, Herr Hess, responded to Geheeb by criticizing Geheeb's neglect of Blank's ordinance from the previous spring. Hess defended the propriety of religious education based on denominational instruction. He wanted Geheeb to state the exact character of his religious convictions. Geheeb answered that although his own background was Protestant, he had little in common with Protestant rationalism and felt closest to the mystics in Protestantism and other religions. In relation to religious instruction, this meant that Geheeb's purpose as an educator was to enable the students in his classes to experience both that which was unique in each religion as well as the common threads of faith and revelation underlying all religions. Geheeb told Hess,

> I have always considered the central point to be the development of religiosity in children, so that they can experience Christianity thoroughly. I haven't concerned myself with whether the children were Jewish, Catholic, or Protestant. I have, for example, been very concerned that they recognize the wonderful strengths of Catholicism and haven't tried to convince them to become Catholic or to abuse Catholicism as though it were a blind superstition. I know that Jewish children were fascinated with Jesus' life. I've never been able to pin myself down to the boundaries of one denomination and to raise the children as mass-produced Jews, Protestants, or Catholics. I have tried to get them to experience something of all of these religions and have said to myself, "Wherever they end up I will leave to them and to God."

Another teacher, Herr Preusser, felt that Geheeb was missing the point. The key issue for the government, Preusser said, was not denominational instruction but the transmission of religious principles which would assist the German people to combat Marxism. For Preusser, it was not particularly important that the students learn about other religions, but he felt that they should understand something about their own inherited faiths: "They should not ponder this way or that, but fit in with their tradition." *Mitarbeiter* Frau Düffing felt the Odenwaldschule should encourage children to attend church. Geheeb resisted both of these points, arguing that "moral compulsion" exerted upon children inevitably destroyed true spirituality.

After much wrangling the conference turned to the *Andachten*, which had existed in the Odenwaldschule since its inception. Hess criticized Geheeb's leadership of the *Andachten*, holding that "in the place of their emphasis on Tolstoy and eastern traditions they should be more purely German." Frau Düffing agreed that "their contents had to be somewhat changed." In the only decision reached in the conference, the faculty then agreed to form an *Andacht* commission to discuss possible changes.[7]

How can one understand Geheeb's stubborn resistance to religious reforms in light of his acceptance of military exercises, nationalistic instruction, and the Hitler Youth? Much of the answer may be found in his biography. Geheeb's interest in theology had been stimulated by the death of his mother in his adolescence, and he had pursued religious studies at the University of Jena, which was the center of liberal Protestant theology in Germany in the 1890s. Upon completing his theology degree, Geheeb had not been afraid to provoke controversy by challenging literal interpretations of Christ's healing of the ill—in the only sermon he gave in his life—at the Schillerkirche in Jena. Much of Geheeb's correspondence with Berlin feminist Minna Cauer was dedicated to potential applications of Christianity to social problems, and his activities in the Society for Ethical Culture reflected his attempts to bring spiritual insights to bear on social concerns.

With Geheeb's turn to educational practice in the late 1890s his religious interests faded, but they did not disappear. By waging his intense conflict with Lietz over Jewish enrollments at Haubinda, by encouraging Margarete Moses to share parables from Hasidism in *Andachten,* and by defending the supradenominational religious character of the Odenwaldschule in his dispute in *Der neuen Waldkauz* with Ernst Zinn, Geheeb continued to assert the priority of religious concerns in his educational practice.

The denominational character of German schooling contained many of the seeds for Geheeb's reaction against religious instruction. Imperial Germany and the Weimar Republic institutionalized religious studies in schools, and in Geheeb's own childhood in the Second Empire, German elementary schools were strictly denominational. The imposition of religious creeds, endorsed and indeed imposed by the state as one component of a comprehensive campaign against social democracy, led many theologians and educational reformers of Geheeb's generation to react against religious instruction altogether. In their understanding, religiosity was a personal matter which could be enriched by separate doctrines and should never be imposed dogmatically.

Geheeb's theological beliefs were directly challenged by the Nazi proposals for the Odenwaldschule. Geheeb's conflict over religious reforms with the Nazis makes sense when viewed from the perspective of his prior insistence on the centrality of what he considered genuine religiosity to educational practice. From this perspective military sports, nationalistic dogma, and even the Hitler Youth were secondary phenomena. Damaging as they might be, there was still the chance that through adroit school leadership Geheeb could mitigate their more pernicious attributes. Religious indoctrination, on the other hand, would strike directly at the core of the child's spiritual and personal development.

In spite of Geheeb's opposition, the Nazis experienced partial success in transforming the spiritual atmosphere of the Odenwaldschule. Geheeb temporarily forestalled their plans for morning prayers and denominationally based religious instruction. The new teachers did take advantage, however, of his recommendation that they use the forum of the *Andachten* to express their deepest values. Geheeb had typically used the *Andachten* to convey his belief that all religions shared a common root in reverence for life, and had read to the *Kameraden* from authors as diverse as the Indian Rabindranath Tagore and the Swedish Selma Lagerlöf. The new *Mitarbeiter* now developed the *Andachten* for entirely new purposes by reading aloud passages from the diaries of German soldiers written during the First World War.[8]

The new *Mitarbeiter* made substantial advances in their control of the Odenwaldschule at the outset of the fall term. The Nazi presence in the school was much more overt than it had been in the summer. The Nazis supplanted traditional Odenwaldschule pacifism with military exercises and sports. They replaced the school's stress on international and multicultural awareness with the inculcation of Nazi dogma. The *Führerprinzip* of commanding and obeying took the place of the democratic principles which had informed the *Wartesystem* and *Schulgemeinden*. The Nazis imposed new social roles upon the students which separated the boys from the girls and the Aryans from the Jews and foreigners. The Hitler Youth was formed in the school and *Andachten* were used to underline nationalistic and militaristic principles. All of these reforms combined to destroy the liberal and tolerant *Weltanschauung* Geheeb had realized in the school's first twenty-three years.

The student response to the new reforms was complicated. On the one hand, some of the Jewish *Kameraden* were pleased that their ethnicity excused them from participating in Nazi activities. Sonja Neumann observed,

Sports were now very exact, with standing in formation and counting off. The Hitler Youth and the League of German Girls were formed, in which I was not allowed to participate. It was revealed to me that I had a Jewish grandmother and could not prove I was Aryan. All of the others envied me passionately; I was something special.

Geheeb felt that most *Kameraden* remained "absolutely loyal" to the old school, and expressed their loyalty by generally being cold and unresponsive to the new teachers. Yet there was a problem in that many young students or recent arrivals had not experienced the old school and were intrigued by the flags, uniforms, marches, and paraphernalia of the Nazi movement. If such trends continued, the school would eventually be filled with students who had never known the old Odenwaldschule and would easily be won over by the Nazis.[9]

In this context Geheeb began advising all Jews who expressed an interest in sending their children to the Odenwaldschule to place their children elsewhere. He wrote to a Jewish doctor in Berlin that while there were no formal prohibitions against Jewish children in the school, the Nazi reforms had so destroyed its community spirit that he could no longer recommend it to them:

> We now have organized military sports as well as the Hitler Youth, and we experience divisions which we never knew previously, such as German, Jewish, and foreign children. Previously we were a community; the children and young people called each other *Kameraden*. Race and nationality played no role whatsoever. The new emphasis on divisions has in the course of the last months contributed on a purely emotional level to the consciousness of differences and to discrimination. The younger Jewish children in particular feel more and more unhappy with every passing day.

From Geheeb's perspective, the Odenwaldschule had lost its distinctive spirit. Even though he was nominally still its director, he felt inwardly that the school's atmosphere was *de facto* determined by the Nazis.[10]

In spite of these fundamental transformations in the school, Geheeb still had grounds for anticipating a positive turn of events. He had loyal students and staff in the school and the option of a new start at the Institut Monnier in Switzerland. His plans to depopulate the school were relatively successful, and he had escaped renewed denunciations. Geheeb was waiting. Either the Nazis would have to revoke their reforms and restore his autonomy as a school headmaster, or he would continue to subvert the school by encouraging parents to withdraw their children and by discouraging new applicants.

In the interim, Geheeeb decided to engage the parents' assistance more fully than he had hitherto attempted. He started a Parents' Advisory Council, which he hoped would negotiate with the Hessian Ministry of Culture to protect the Odenwaldschule from further governmental incursions. Adolf Messer-Bicker, a National Socialist and industrialist from Frankfurt, was the leader of the parents on the Council. The Council composed circulatory letters sent to all of the students' parents, in which it repeated Geheeb's protests against Blank's intervention in the Odenwaldschule on 20 July. In a new twist, these protests were linked with explicit support for national socialism. In one letter, the Council wrote,

> The obvious precondition for the entire educational work of the Odenwaldschule is also for us parents the unconditional and enthusiastic integration of the school into the National Socialist seizure of power and into the construction of the German state under Adolf Hitler's leadership. This is consistent with the entire spirit of the Odenwaldschule.

From the viewpoint of the Council, however, the interventions by the Ministry of Culture in Darmstadt in the Odenwaldschule did little to further national socialism in the school and actually retarded the chances of its positive and organic development. According to the Council, the Ministry had hurt the school by forcing the old staff to leave, placing relatively inexperienced young *Mitarbeiter* in their place, and allowing Geheeb no influence over hiring or firing *Mitarbeiter*. The Parents' Advisory Council called upon parents to join their effort to support both Nazism and the Odenwaldschule by becoming active in the Council and entering into negotiations with the Ministry.[11]

While the parents were preparing to begin discussions with the Ministry in Darmstadt, Geheeb decided to surpass the Hessian Ministry of Culture and to find an ally in the central government in Berlin. On 2 September he wrote directly to Wilhelm Frick, the Minister of the Interior, to request an interview concerning the future of the Odenwaldschule. He hoped that if he could discover the origins of the denunciation which led to Blank's intervention on 20 July that he would have the chance of responding to the actual charges which had been brought against him and the school.

While Geheeb was preparing for further negotiations in Darmstadt and new discussions in Berlin, he refused to coordinate the Odenwaldschule into the Nazi movement. Throughout the spring and summer of 1933 many independent secondary institutions in Germany surrendered their autonomy and aligned themselves with new Nazi organizations as part of the *Gleichschaltung*. Autonomous educational organizations dissolved and joined Nazi groups such as the National

Socialist Teachers' League. Parallel changes transpired within religious, labor, and youth organizations, with widely fluctuating patterns of resistance and accommodation.

Geheeb had resisted ordinances from the National Socialist Teachers' League the previous May to join their organization. In correspondence with Alfred Andreesen, the headmaster of the Hermann Lietz Schools and the chairman of the Association of German *Landerziehungsheime,* Geheeb argued that the act of affiliating with Nazi organizations violated the autonomous heritage of their schools and should be resisted. The fact that the Nazis had closed one of the *Landerziehungsheime,* Bernhard Uffrecht's Free Work and School Community at Letzlingen, particularly angered Geheeb. Letzlingen was one of the more left-wing schools and had inspired Geheeb to introduce the *Wartesystem* in the Odenwaldschule. Geheeb urged Andreesen to use his position as chairperson of the German *Landerziehungsheime* to intervene on Uffrecht's behalf to enable him to reopen his school.

Andreesen was not responsive to Geheeb's request. "At the moment I don't believe any unified action by the Association regarding interventions in individual schools would have any success," he wrote. "Democratic methods are no longer applicable." Geheeb was infuriated. He wrote to Uffrecht,

> Your appeal to our "association" very much surprised me. When our school was in danger for several weeks in March, I immediately reported to the central office of the New Education Fellowship in London (which led to the successful result that our Ministry received many letters and telegrams . . .) But I never would have dreamed of asking our "association." You must be clear, my dear friend, as to the role you and I play in this illustrious circle. They've tolerated me because of my character as a veteran and my noble beard, and you because of your good jokes, which have enlivened our conferences. Fundamentally, however, they've long wished that we would both go to hell. And I believe that a self-satisfied smirk would be enjoyed by this circle if your school and mine were destroyed.

Geheeb had been disappointed with the character of the Association for many years, and he found in its reaction to the Nazi takeover a vindication of his hostile assessment. Instead of helping Uffrecht, Andreesen devoted himself to coordinating the Lietz Schools with the Nazi movement. He organized pro-Nazi rallies at his schools, which culminated in a massive festival for the Hitler Youth from all of the Lietz schools on 15 October. It must have particularly irritated Geheeb to learn that this festival was held at Haubinda—where

Geheeb had taught and led the school prior to his split with Lietz in 1906. In addition to these displays of loyalty to the regime, Andreesen began describing Lietz as a forerunner of national socialist education. Geheeb was infuriated by Andreesen and the spineless compliance of the directors of almost all of the *Landerziehungsheime* with the Nazis. "Oh, they're really shitting in their pants!" he fumed.[12]

In light of this antagonism it is hardly surprising that Geheeb boycotted a meeting of the German *Landerziehungsheime* at the Landschulheim am Solling on 23 and 24 September. The meeting was designed to coordinate the old association into a new "Reich Department of *Landerziehungsheime*." The absence of the Odenwaldschule—long one of Germany's best known boarding schools—could scarcely be overlooked at the conference. Geheeb's boycott of the meeting must have confirmed suspicions that he was inwardly opposed to Nazism.[13]

The Odenwaldschule was filled with tension and conflict in September and October. Rumors circulated that the Geheebs were planning to emigrate. The decline in the student population had palpable repercussions on the school and one could no longer deny the possibility that it might close. As more and more students left, two of the houses were shut in October to save on heating costs.

The impending collapse of the school evoked terrible arguments between Paul Geheeb and his father-in-law. Max Cassirer had long urged Geheeb to be prudent at all costs and to do nothing to suggest lack of loyalty and cooperation with the new Nazi authorities. He had opposed Geheeb's plans to send out notices of dismissal to the Odenwaldschule staff in August and was alarmed by Geheeb's plans to emigrate to Switzerland. Now, in the fall, as Geheeb's strategy of depopulating the school began to take effect and as he evolved new plans for negotiating with the Nazis and closing the school, their differences in theory became major differences in policy.

As soon as Geheeb returned to Oberhambach from Switzerland, his brother-in-law, Kurt Cassirer, tried to pressure him to continue leading the school. Geheeb told Ferrière in December that

> In the last months I have had tremendous difficulties with Edith and especially with her brother, her sister-in-law, and her father. You understand that all German Jews are now filled with fear psychoses. These fear psychoses were so great that they didn't want to do a single thing to work toward ending my school. They were afraid of the tiniest steps . . . I finally wrote a letter to the Reich Ministry of the Interior. I mentioned this to Edith on one occasion. Then the entire family fell upon me: my father-in-law in Berlin screamed at me on the telephone that I must have

lost my mind; my brother-in-law, who had read a copy of the letter, tried to prove to me that every sentence in the letter was wrong, stupid, and dangerous. I was supposed to have doomed the entire family. (Sometimes, when I was very tired and depressed, I thought of ending my life to escape the overpowering fear of my relatives.)

I sent the letter without telling anyone. My relatives would really prefer that I keep on fighting (in Germany). The main reason that my father-in-law decided to let the school close is because I am such an unpredictable, dangerous person, who will abruptly be imprisoned one day and will doom the entire family. Thus, it is better if I leave Germany. But my father-in-law still hoped in August and September that I would stay.

While Geheeb's comments capture the intensity of the antagonism between himself and the Cassirers, his defensiveness prevented him from seeing the legitimate aspects of the Cassirers' vantage point. Throughout his educational work, Geheeb had directed his attention more to single individuals than to social groups, and while this reaped many benefits in terms of pedagogical practice, the Cassirers may have justifiably doubted his ability to deal with a social movement as arbitrary and violent as Nazism. If Paul had not been able to prevail against educators such as Lietz at Haubinda and Wyneken at Wickersdorf, how could one imagine that he would triumph against Nazis in the Odenwaldschule? Cassirer may have thought that his son-in-law ought to show a bit more respect for his opinion, since it was only Cassirer's funding which had made the Odenwaldschule possible in the first place.[14]

Cassirer, in contrast to Geheeb, had extensive experience and success with political undertakings. His numerous social and philanthropic activities as a city councillor of Charlottenburg won him the title of "honorary citizen" of Berlin. He had tremendous financial success with his cellulose factory in Silesia. Cassirer certainly seemed more experienced, better placed, and more competent to handle negotiations with the Nazis.

Max Cassirer's caution was common among the many German Jews who had abandoned their religiosity to cultivate an inward identification with the German state. Cassirer had converted to Protestantism and Edith Geheeb was baptized in the Protestant church as a child. Separating from Judaism was tremendously difficult; many Jews undertook a step-by-step assimilation into mainstream German culture, only to be finally stigmatized, after years of identification with Germany, on the basis of a Jewish identity abandoned decades previously. Max Cassirer's pleas for prudence and diplomacy—which for

Geheeb were so incomprehensible and inappropriate—make a certain sense given his previous commitment to complete assimilation into mainstream German culture.

Paul's differences of opinion were not restricted to his relationships with Max and Kurt Cassirer. On one occasion when Max visited the Odenwaldschule, Paul and Edith were consulting with him on the best manner of coping with the Nazis. Max was interrupted by a telephone call and left the room to attend to it. As soon as he exited, Edith saw that her husband was upset. "Do you know how you look?" she asked him. "As if you'd like to divorce me." Paul retorted, "That's exactly what I'm going to do." He never followed through, however. The threat probably had little to do with his relationship with Edith, and was more likely an expression of Paul's frustration with the criticism he felt from her father and brother.[15]

That Paul Geheeb quarreled with the Cassirers in the fall of 1933 appears only natural in light of the tense situation. The Odenwaldschule had been pedagogically disemboweled, so to speak, ever since the first storm trooper intervention in March, and it was now limping toward an inglorious end. Following Werner Goerendt's raids the Nazis had imposed a sexual counterrevolution on the school, purged *Mitarbeiter,* introduced militaristic and fascist indoctrination, and strictly segregated *Kameraden* on the basis of their ethnicity. The permissive and, some would suggest, promiscuous spirit of the old school had been crushed. Genuine promiscuity still found places to continue in the broader society, however. On 29 September a son was born to Werner Goerendt—out of wedlock.[16]

chapter 8

Confrontation in the Conference: November–December, 1933

By the beginning of November Geheeb had prepared much of the groundwork for achieving his goal of either gaining greater autonomy for the Odenwaldschule or facilitating its closure. During November Geheeb traveled with Adolf Messer-Bicker of the Parents' Advisory Council to meet with Ministry of Culture officials in Darmstadt. He also went to the Reich Ministry of the Interior in Berlin for discussions.

On 27 November some of the Nazi *Mitarbeiter* confronted Geheeb in a faculty meeting with their suspicions about his plans for emigration and with questions about his real attitude toward the Nazi transformation of the Odenwaldschule. Wilhelm Stein, a new Nazi *Mitarbeiter,* was Geheeb's main antagonist on the school's staff. He replaced Steinitz, the chemistry teacher and pacifist who had been arrested by the Nazis the previous spring.

Just as Geheeb was starting the meeting, Stein interrupted him. "Before we go any further," he said, "I'd like to ask you an urgent question. Entirely apart from financial matters, does it seem likely that the school will continue after Easter, or do you want to close it? I've heard from *Kameraden* that the *Abitur* will still be completed but that the school will then close . . ."

"I am very thankful that you are addressing this question to me," Geheeb responded. "Such concerns should always be discussed immediately to prevent insecurity and unclarity. I believe that I can give you a clear answer, although it still isn't definite. Fundamentally, I still support the same position which I expressed so firmly in the conference many months ago. I believe I can still carry on the work of the Odenwaldschule in the new Germany and I am trying to do this with all of my strength. I have probably already told you that, ever since

April, some parents and good friends (who are competent people with trustworthy opinions) have been pessimistic and have attempted to persuade me to close the school. 'We're so different from the new Germany that we'll only experience senseless conflicts,' they've said. But I've already told you that I haven't changed my position."

Stein was not assured. "We believe that your trip to Berlin and your behavior after the summer vacation justify my previous comments," he said. "We believe that these things you're talking about lie in the past and came to an end with the summer vacation, and that you've changed your position since the vacation. We believe something is happening which we can't control. We don't know if the foreign *Kameraden* who have left or are going to leave intend to enter a similar school in Lausanne or Amsterdam. We don't believe that this massive flight began with things which we've done. Do you consider the situation to be the same as it was before summer vacation, or have things taken on a different shape for you? You yourself have said that you were in different ministries in Berlin and I believe that school issues led you there. We see that people who have nothing to do with the school are better informed than we are. It is aggravating to be made outsiders like this."

"I'd like to take up your last comment," Geheeb replied. "Be very skeptical of people who say things about the situation, the destiny and the future of the Odenwaldschule—outsiders who aren't part of the school as you are. Don't trust them! ... In times of crisis the air is filled with rumors. The individual can't be made responsible for this, least of all that individual—namely myself—who has to carry the responsibility.

"But I'm not finished with my response to your first question," Geheeb continued. "I said that I hold basically the same position which I have expressed repeatedly, and it's hard to shake my optimism. But since August a new issue has come about: an unusually large number of children have left. In the last twenty-three years it's often been the case that as many as twenty or even twenty-five children have left at Easter. It's never been so high in the summer. Some of them graduate, some of them leave for other reasons. But that such a number, sixty or seventy children, left in the fall, including the thirteen graduates—this is truly incredible. Now, I've never changed my mind about not shutting the Odenwaldschule for purely pedagogical reasons. Furthermore, I have been given the impression from the Hessian Ministry of Culture that I don't even have the right to close the school. This is absolutely clear and has been unequivocally expressed to me. So that when you ask whether I anticipate that the

Odenwaldschule will continue to exist a little while longer, that can only mean, do I believe that we will no longer be able to hold out financially? You know I've never had anything to do with finances and that I wouldn't trust my judgment about this. My wife is also not in the position to say anything definite. But without a specialized knowledge I can tell you that I think about it most pessimistically. I know that our school broke even with 180 or 190 children. We never sought profit and we never made a profit. There haven't been many students in the last few years. It was hard to make ends meet. You know the number has now dropped considerably. Therefore, I think very pessimistically and would like to assume that one will gain some clarity—this is a guess—in the next few weeks as to whether the school will continue to exist from a purely financial point of view. This is regardless of whether a significant number of students depart, not including the ten probable graduates next spring. I think that it will all be clarified in the coming weeks.

"You mentioned my recent trip to Berlin and have heard that I was asked to appear in the Ministry of the Interior," Geheeb said. "These negotiations in the Reich Ministry of the Interior served the sole purpose of trying once more to do everything to protect the school. I was asked to be discreet about these negotiations and I regret that I can't give out information about them. I was received very well and treated very kindly."

Stein was not placated. "You spoke about financial complications. I didn't include these in my question. You said that you've heard from the Hessian Ministry of Culture that you would not be granted the right to shut the school. I don't know if this is true—if this is the tendency—but you have the impression that it is. May I ask you if this would lead you to regard the school as a lost cause and whether you therefore might not favor closing the school? You say that you tried everything possible in the Reich Ministry of the Interior to keep the school going. I don't believe you tried to clarify financial difficulties in the Reich Ministry of the Interior."

"No," Geheeb responded.

"I believe they were discussions about *Weltanschauungen.*"

"About education."

"If the survival of the school depends on this, then it doesn't appear that financial reasons are that decisive."

"I would never go to a state official to talk about the financial situation of my school," Geheeb rejoined. "I would leave that to my wife or my father-in-law. You're right when you assume that it had to do with pedagogical questions. You can understand that I went there when you recall that Dr. Blank said on 20 July that he came to represent the Reich Ministry of the Interior. I can't remember his exact words. Up until then he had always reported positively about us. He then appeared to have received a reprimand from them, and was asked to undertake a new inquiry. The Ministry appears to have received different information from other sources that claimed to be better informed about us. His positive reports were held to be false. I asked him who had reported against us and what was held against us, but Dr. Blank wouldn't say.

"Now you'll understand that it was at the very least unpleasant for me that in the Reich Ministry of the Interior a complaint, or denunciation, or whatever you want to call it, was brought against us. Therefore, our discussions in the Reich Ministry of the Interior had to do only with education. You can see that this is one of the steps I've taken to ensure the school's continuation.

"Perhaps you've heard from your colleagues that due to the initiatives of Herr Messer-Bicker a Parents' Advisory Council has been started," Geheeb continued. "The Ministry wasn't antagonistic, but received Herr Messer-Bicker as the parents' representative, and I had to accompany him. This was on 4 November. But absolutely nothing changed. *Nothing* was accomplished. The Parents' Advisory Council was only formed for the purpose of securing the continuity of the Odenwaldschule on the educational level. This step has nothing to do with closing.

"Now you pose to me the question of whether I would be pleased or saddened if the Odenwaldschule were forced to close for economic reasons. I'm astonished by the question. In other words, is it fun for a sixty-three-year-old man to see his lifework collapse, or would he prefer to keep it going? I believe that you know my answer if you consider me to be psychologically normal."

"I might respond that you believe your work is already destroyed and that the collapse of your school is merely superficial," Stein interjected.

"You would have to know me more intimately to know and understand that I'm filled with a certain combative optimism. I'm not a fighter. People have often regretted that I am so little of one . . . I can emphasize the positive and I'm amazed that when everything seems thoroughly shattered new and rich strengths emerge within me which compel me to start anew. I can't imagine how I'll ever be finished off.

"I can imagine why you're thinking this way and why you're concerned," Geheeb continued. "I already told you that since spring I've heard so many well-informed people be very negative and pessimistic.

This has increased and reached a peak higher than ever before, especially after 20 July. So many older *Kameraden* became pessimistic all at once. To clarify the entire situation it would be important for you to understand how the conference which took place in this room with Dr. Blank on 20 July affected the *Kameraden*. I believe that for many of those *Kameraden* this was the unhappiest and most destructive day they had ever experienced here. None of you will be able to imagine to what extent these *Kameraden* held sacred some of our institutions, such as the *Schulgemeinden* and the *Wartekonferenzen*, as well as the precise form and style of these institutions. I myself don't want to take a major position in interpreting the situation. But a large number of the older *Kameraden* were very upset. They came to me that evening and yelled, 'The school is completely ruined! It isn't your school anymore! Close it today!' A large number of students who graduated this fall were among them. 'Forget graduation!' they said. 'The school must be closed immediately!' It took two hours before I could calm them down a little.

"Think of what it means for the school when a group of the oldest and most intelligent *Kameraden* feels this way, and when I have to muster up all of my strength to cool their tempers before they depart for the vacation. Surely you can understand that people will begin to think that the core of the Odenwaldschule has been destroyed, and that it has lost any right to exist and should be done away with. It would then make sense to wish that all of the children would leave, so that the school would be ruined financially and would be forced to close."

"Forgive me; I'm not satisfied with this," Stein protested. "If pedagogical issues were the basis for your visits to the Reich Ministry of the Interior and the Hessian Ministry of Culture then these must have had to do with changing the current conditions. If you weren't able to accomplish your goals, are you still prepared to help the school with the force of your entire personality? According to our opinion, this internal situation goes back to entirely different things. We aren't cooperating with each other. We're working against each other. I mean you, Herr Geheeb, and the teachers here. This schism must become apparent to each *Kamerad*, even the smallest, and it has become apparent. Thus, the school can no longer exist; it falls apart. If these visits [to the Ministries] were useless and things must remain the way they were after the visit from Dr. Blank, do you believe that you can still work and say you want to work for *this* Odenwaldschule?"

"I can only say that I have an unshakable faith in education. You will have to concede, it couldn't have escaped your attention, that after I accepted under protest the conditions of Dr. Blank I've done everything possible after the summer vacation to keep on working. I must protest when you say we've been working against each other."

Edith Geheeb intervened. "Herr Stein," she asked, "why do you say that the visits in Berlin and Darmstadt were unsuccessful?"

"I don't know, really."

"In both places they were friendly and understanding about the situation," she noted.

Paul Geheeb disagreed. "In Darmstadt they weren't understanding," he asserted. "They were friendly and even charming, but nothing changed. Incidentally, I didn't want to go to Darmstadt at all. I couldn't accept everything here on 20 July and then go to Darmstadt a few months later and argue about it. That would be simply illogical and childish. But I was convinced that Herr Messer-Bicker needed someone to accompany him who was informed. I was hesitant about asking Herr Sachs to go. I finally decided that I should go.

"I thought from the very beginning that I should play a subordinate role. I let Herr Messer-Bicker proceed and I answered only when I was spoken to . . . He said, for example, that 'It's impossible that Herr Geheeb should be forced to get his teachers only from Hesse . . . It should be obvious that he can appoint teachers from all of Germany!' At this point Herr Ringshausen answered angrily, 'But then we don't have the power to prevent politically undesirable people from joining the faculty.'

"I must say that we are not of one opinion regarding this visit. Three men were present: Herr Ringshausen, Dr. Leip, and Dr. Blank. Herr Messer-Bicker was so surprised by the charming character of these men that he left the room beaming after our one-and-one-half-hour-long conversation. Herr Ringshausen said that one can't say that Hesse is so impoverished that it doesn't have enough teachers for this small Odenwaldschule. Dr. Leip contradicted him and held that one could obtain the papers of a teacher from outside of Hesse to gather information about him. Then Herr Ringshausen said, 'Yes, if it happens that for one certain subject there isn't a single teacher in Hesse, then perhaps just one time we could get one teacher from Prussia.' In this manner the negotiations led nowhere . . ."

"You said that you worked with all your strength after the summer vacation, but that isn't our impression," Stein objected. "You were no longer with us after summer vacation. Who isn't *with* us is *against* us. You've never again made *one* single decision. You've complained that you're no longer the master in your own house. You've never *tried* to be the master in your house. You've never attempted to make decisions. You said to one of us, 'Just look at how you all come back again!' With this division the school will soon collapse! We believe that financial issues are only a consequence of this division. Should this split which is destroying our school continue or shall we put an end to it?"

Geheeb disagreed. "You aren't accurately describing the situation when you say that in reality we've worked against each other and not with each other. When I receive directives from the Ministry concerning national holidays or some special National Socialist question and pass these on to Dr. Freidank or some other especially competent person, I have no objection. I'm thankful for the division of labor. It's more important to you, and you understand much better how to organize these things. I've cooperated with you. The conferences have been conducted just like they were before summer vacation. You can't think that I've participated in them with any less interest . . .

"On the other hand we are all clear that our school is more than a school. We love to call ourselves a *'Lebensgemeinschaft.'* Here people really live with each other, are interested in each other, and cultivate personal relationships with each other. If you recall, you'll have to admit that I did my utmost to reach out to each of you before summer vacation—I'm talking to the young Hessian colleagues now. And now consider what happened on 20 July. I told you, 'My ladies and gentlemen, realize what you are destroying today!' I'm convinced that you young colleagues destroyed, completely destroyed the relationship of personal trust which we had established. You did it with your supervisor's support. I'm not alone in thinking this way. I said so then, and could find no other way to express it. You put a wall between yourselves and me, under the leadership of your superiors. And what have I done after my return from the vacation? I've respected this fact. I haven't attempted with a *salto mortale* to overcome this schism but have sought diplomatically to accept it.

"Although it was a very emotional afternoon for me I was able to preserve enough inner composure to foresee how the inner condition of the school would be after this destruction and after the vacation," Geheeb continued. "It was absolutely clear to me that our school would have to proceed in an impossible, almost unbearable fashion. So please don't be unjust! What happened on 20 July, this destruction, has happened. The consequences are most painful and embarrassing for you, as they are for me and for the entire school. We feel this every day and every hour. Don't be unfair and try to get around these consequences or try to make them pretty or imagine that I am the cause of these circumstances, which are unbearable for all of us. You have to eat this bitter soup just as I do."

Stein objected. "You said before that you tried to work on day-to-day matters with us," he said. "You also said that we are more than a school. Ninety percent of school affairs aren't arranged in the conferences. It's impossible to work when the headmaster of a school continually treats us as nonentities or with hostility."

"That isn't true, Herr Stein. You've said you can't bridge this gap. On that day you had the inner composure to imagine what the Odenwaldschule would be like after the vacation. I believe this about you. In the excitement of that day you developed an image of us and now you are treating us according to that image. Don't you want to check to see if the image is accurate? You can never say that I've been impolite to you or showed you disrespect. I'd like to assure you in particular that even after 20 July I don't have the slightest trace of resentment. I can only say that you all made me extremely sorry for your helplessness on 20 July."

"Herr Geheeb," Stein protested, "there is a politeness which kills."

Another new *Mitarbeiter*, Karl Gleiser, now addressed Geheeb. "I said to you right after summer vacation and again yesterday that we don't see this division. If you're always going to be referring to this division, this creates a situation which doesn't facilitate our work. This work happens not only in conferences but also outside of them. I think I can say that we can ignore the differences and continue to work just as before. But you must see that the work becomes far more difficult if you hold this position against us and keep up the division. The work for the teachers doesn't consist in just teaching two courses. Even the youngest students notice it, and the fourteen-year-olds ask, 'Isn't it strange how Paulus and the teachers walk past one another? How long will the Odenwaldschule continue to exist?' One can't work in such an atmosphere. When the *Kameraden* write home about this one can't be surprised when the parents take their children out of the school. We can't do anything more than respond to what is around us."

"I've already said that I find the atmosphere to be unhealthy and difficult," Geheeb asserted. "But give me advice. I've come to the conclusion that one needs much time and patience to overcome the situation."

"In this time the school will collapse," protested Stein. He later added, "We believe that you aren't working in the current situation with the strength required to keep the school going. This makes us sorry because those of us who are sitting here have really done our best to achieve a worthwhile goal here."

"Believe me, I see the entire situation," Geheeb said. "I see how you work and suffer and would be thankful to each person who tells me how I can be more helpful."

"Don't you believe that a great deal of subjective resentment is playing a role?" Stein asked.

"You don't know me well enough; otherwise the thought wouldn't even cross your mind. But I'd like to answer every question. You said before that foreign children from here are going to a school in Lausanne or Holland. This is completely unknown to me."

"I don't know anything about it," Stein admitted. "But we've had the feeling that you'd try to get another school going somewhere else. You know that Herr Kobbé intends to start a school in Holland. We know that another school has gone to England. You mustn't hold it against us that we think that one day the tent over our heads is going to disappear."

"If the thing collapses, you don't need to be interested in what I'll do," Geheeb later continued, "whether I tend cattle in Dammersfeld or continue my pedagogical work elsewhere."

"One has to cooperate better," Werner Meyer urged, "so that the children won't be frightened by things they could misinterpret."

Edith spoke to Paul, "I think that the teachers should leave neither you nor me in peace but instead should come to us with every single question they have. They shouldn't wait for you to take care of things but should do it themselves immediately."

"You won't expect from me that I participate in the military exercises. In and of itself I enjoy such things. But I haven't had the time to feed my animals for months. But I repeat the request of my wife: if you have concerns or complaints, please come to me directly, so that we can clarify things."[1]

When one knows the concealed story of Geheeb's coordination of the student depopulation of the Odenwaldschule, Geheeb's rage over Blank's intervention of 20 July, and his hatred of Nazism in general, his leadership of this conference demonstrates a masterful fusion of emotional self-control, intellectual adroitness, and theatrical chutzpah. That Geheeb was able to insist on his innocence about the sources of the decline in student population and to affirm that he had no plans to emigrate without provoking an enraged protest by the Nazi *Mitarbeiter* testifies to his remarkable achievement in deceiving the new faculty about his real intentions.

Geheeb's plans to depopulate the school and emigrate remained completely secret to the Nazis. Not one faculty member suggested that Geheeb himself had taken a leadership role in urging students to leave the school. Apparently no parents, *Mitarbeiter,* or *Kameraden* who knew about Geheeb's plans denounced Geheeb. Nor did the Nazi *Mitarbeiter* gain access to this information by eavesdropping or reading misplaced letters. Stein's commentary that foreign students were leaving the Odenwaldschule to enroll in similar schools in Lausanne or Amsterdam suggests that some information may have been leaked, but it evidently was not enough to incriminate Geheeb.

Geheeb stumbled at just one point. He initially claimed that the meetings in Darmstadt and Berlin were solely concerned with securing the financial continuity of the Odenwaldschule. Stein easily compelled Geheeb to admit that those meetings also dealt with educational and political issues. Geheeb attempted to deflect this concession by truthfully asserting that the trip to Berlin was motivated by his desire to learn more about the denunciation which had led to Blank's intervention on 20 July. He also suggested that Stein perversely thought that Geheeb was enjoying the ongoing crisis in the Odenwaldschule.

Stein's response was to challenge Geheeb by asserting that Geheeb was no longer fighting to save *this* Odenwaldschule. From Stein's perspective, Geheeb's obvious lack of cooperation with the new staff reflected an intolerable political opposition, and he vented his anger at this by stating, "Who isn't with us is against us." Yet by constantly focusing on strictly pedagogical issues in the Odenwaldschule, Geheeb succeeded in deflecting the discussion away from any political opposition to national socialism and eventually brought it into the comparatively tepid domain of interpersonal relationships among the faculty.

Although Geheeb did not dwell on the point, one important part of the discussion with the faculty concerned internal schisms between the officials at the Hessian Ministry of Culture. Ringshausen appears to have taken the hardest line against the school in his most recent meeting with Geheeb, and Blank was relatively silent on that occasion. A new official, Dr. Hans Leip, had dared to oppose Ringshausen when the Minister of Culture wanted to restrict Geheeb to hiring his teachers from Hesse. While Leip's formal subordination to Ringhausen prevented him from supporting Geheeb more overtly, Geheeb and the *Mitarbeiter* learned that there was at least one official in the Ministry who appeared willing to speak up on behalf of the school.

Geheeb withheld from the Nazi *Mitarbeiter* one important development in his discussions with officials at the Reich Ministry of the Interior in Berlin. Geheeb had the fortune to be received at the Ministry by Dr. Ludwig Niessen, who unexpectedly showed great interest in and support for the Odenwaldschule. Although Niessen greeted Geheeb with the Nazi salutation, "Heil Hitler!" he listened sympathetically to Geheeb's account of his difficulties with the Hessian Ministry of Culture. In Niessen's view, Blank had overreacted to the denunciation which had made its way to his Ministry and only worsened the situation through the 20 July intervention. Geheeb later wrote Ferrière, "The Reich government (in Berlin) forced me to tell them about every stupidity which the Hessian government had imposed on me. The Reich government was furious."[2]

Niessen apparently believed Geheeb's claim that the Odenwaldschule would have to close because of financial difficulties. He gave Geheeb a tentative agreement to issue letters of dismissal to the school staff. It appears that Niessen wanted to clear this procedure with higher officials; for the time being he asked Geheeb to keep the negotiations discreet. Max Cassirer subsequently met with Niessen on several occasions to facilitate the closing of the Odenwaldschule.

Niessen's willingness to bring about the end of Geheeb's leadership of the Odenwaldschule was much appreciated by Cassirer. Cassirer had been alarmed by what he viewed as his son-in-law's volatile relationships with the Nazis, and was delighted to find that Niessen was far more accessible than school officials in Hesse. After several meetings with Niessen, Cassirer wrote to Geheeb,

> In my long experience I have never met an official with as much understanding and good will as governmental council N. Simply this circumstance imposes the duty upon you and upon all of us to be most cautious and to avoid the slightest action which could bring us and therefore also him into difficulties.

Niessen's helpfulness stood in marked contrast to the attitude of Hessian officials. Cassirer had written to the Hessian Ministry of Culture as well as to the Ministry of State on 26 October to request an interview. In these letters Cassirer stated that the Odenwaldschule was experiencing financial difficulties and that it was urgent that he be granted the chance to discuss these with Hessian officials. On 27 November the Hessian Ministry of State responded to Cassirer that they had consulted with the Ministry of Culture and that there was no need for an interview because "your fears are ungrounded."[3]

Niessen's unexpected support for Paul Geheeb and Max Cassirer reflected the contradictions between different levels of government and administration in Germany in the fall of 1933. Civil servants at the Ministry of the Interior possessed a high social status and a strong professional ethos, and were an indispensable part of the state administration; they could not be purged and replaced by political appointees without a serious destabilization of many vital institutions and procedures. Although as early as 7 April the regime had passed a "Law for the Restoration of a Professional Civil Service," which purged non-Aryans and political dissidents from the bureaucracy, at most two percent of civil servants were directly affected. The vast majority of civil servants continued their work with the same dedication to legally established rules and guidelines they had employed during the Weimar Republic.

Under the federal system of the Weimar Republic, it would have mattered little what Niessen thought about developments in the Odenwaldschule, for educational matters lay entirely in the hands of the individual states, with the Ministry of the Interior playing a purely advisory role. One clear goal of the Nazi takeover, however, was to supplant the old federal framework of the Bismarckian and Weimar constitutions with the centralization of state power in Berlin. Reich Minister of the Interior Wilhelm Frick quickly made it one of his major policy goals to establish the absolute hegemony of his Ministry over and against the decision-making organs of local governments. While this transformation had not been legally codified in the fall of 1933, the antifederal biases of Nazi ideology were indisputable. Differences of opinion between the Reich Ministry of the Interior and the Hessian Ministry of Culture would be resolved by recalling that the "leadership principle" of national socialism compelled a complete subordination of local administration to all branches of the Reich government in Berlin.

The different responses of the Ministry of the Interior in Berlin and the Ministry of Culture in Hesse to developments in the Odenwaldschule offer striking evidence of the manner in which the unevenness of the Nazi *Gleichschaltung* created openings for opponents of the regime to wrest a measure of freedom from the government. Ironically, the Nazis' desire to centralize power with the goal of establishing a more absolute control over the population was compromised by their dependency on the Reich civil service. In the case of the Odenwaldschule, the tilt toward centralization shifted the balance of power out of the hands of the Nazi militants in the Hessian Ministry of Culture and into the domain of the relatively unpurged Reich Ministry of the Interior.[4]

Thanks to Niessen's mediation, Geheeb and Cassirer obtained permission to issue notifications of dismissal to the Odenwaldschule staff at the end of December. Yet Cassirer apparently wanted to reassure the government that his intentions were benign. He thus refrained from stating that the school would shut permanently, and suggested that some new development might take over after a transitional period. Cassirer wrote to Edith,

> We have the ardent wish to keep the school as such going, first because we believe that under the government's leadership positive things can happen, and second because we place great value upon employing our loyal *Mitarbeiter* and not removing them in the current situation. My entire direction is to preserve and to develop, not to tear down.

A crucial ambiguity was built into the dissolution of the old Odenwaldschule. Niessen enabled Geheeb to close the Odenwaldschule as it had previously existed, but because of Cassirer's mediation, it appeared that some kind of pedagogical institution would probably be constructed in its place. Although Geheeb had previously stressed that he did not want a new school established in the Odenwaldschule if it were closed, Cassirer disagreed and pursued an alternative strategy. In December and January, Cassirer attempted to sell the school to either the Hessian or the Reich government to establish a school of their own on the property.[5]

On 20 December Geheeb sent letters of dismissal to his faculty. He avoided any hint of controversy. "It will no longer surprise you to learn that we are forced through the economic situation of our school to release you provisionally on 31 March 1934," he wrote. "We hope very much that you will succeed in finding another satisfying place to work, and thank you very much for your loyal services."[6]

Two days later Geheeb traveled to Switzerland to spend the Christmas holidays with Adolphe Ferrière and his family. In spite of his success at avoiding internment in the Osthafen concentration camp, Geheeb recognized that one did not need to be imprisoned to suffer under national socialism. Geheeb told Ferrière of his experiences and of a discussion he had with Eduard Spranger in Berlin:

> I can hardly express how happy I am to see you again. In autumn I sometimes thought I would *never* see you again. More and more of my friends and colleagues went into concentration camps, and many didn't come out alive. When I was in Berlin I was most shaken by my encounter with Spranger. I once mentioned "concentration camps." He then said very seriously, "Dear friend, in Germany one can now be destroyed *without* concentration camps." I noticed that he was talking about himself.[7]

chapter 9

The Splintering of the School: January–March 1934

By January 1934 it was clear that Paul Geheeb was going to close the Odenwaldschule. For Max Cassirer, the parents of the *Kameraden*, and many of the school staff, however, Geheeb's maneuvers did not foreclose the possibility of establishing a different kind of school on the same property in Oberhambach. Cassirer wrote to Paulus's brother,

> One can have different opinions about whether the school will be able to continue. Only one thing is definite, and that is that Paul (to whom I don't want to address the slightest reproach) is not in the position to do this . . . He has led the education of children for decades with principles which he cannot and does not want to give up, because he is not in the position to make any concessions . . . The only issue now is what will happen with the school. One idea which I'd like to see is that the Reich or Hesse would take it over and continue it with the principles which they consider correct. I am ready to sacrifice a great deal for this plan and would sell the entire institution to the state for a very modest mortgage . . . I write you this in all openness, but would ask you to keep the entire affair *strictly confidential*. It would probably be the best thing if you would destroy this letter as soon as you have read it.[1]

On the same day Werner Meyer sent Cassirer a letter with an essay on "Some Suggestions for the Odenwaldschule as a *Landerziehungsheim* in the National Socialist State." According to Meyer, discussions with Dr. Hans Leip at the Hessian Ministry of Culture revealed a strong interest by both Leip and the Reich Propaganda Ministry in the continuation of the school. Although Geheeb made it clear that he would no longer be leading the Odenwaldschule, Meyer wished to inform Cassirer that there were government officials who were interested in keeping the school going, and that Geheeb's departure from

Oberhambach might allow for the transformation of the Odenwald-schule in a new direction with the support of Nazi officials.

Max Cassirer thanked Meyer for this initiative, which he viewed as "valuable material for the solution of the entire question," but abstained from endorsing Meyer's plan. "I really do not know how one should progress in the entire issue," Cassirer wrote to his daughter. If a new school were started after the Geheebs' departure, parents sympathetic to the Geheebs would probably not send their children to it, for they were likely to believe that the new school "had departed from its previous principles." It was too late to persuade the Geheebs to keep on with the school. Cassirer wrote to Edith that Germans "would have reservations entrusting their children to you because Paul doesn't go far enough, and because they do not consider him to be a one hundred percent National Socialist." He was skeptical about Meyer's proposal: "Nothing is to be achieved by continuing the school through a transformation."[2]

Cassirer was hardly alone in his confusion, for the entire Oden-waldschule was filled with rumors in January 1934. "We had no idea what was going on," alumna Marina Jakimow later recalled. Instead of staying in Oberhambach to steer the school through this difficult period, Paul traveled throughout Switzerland and Germany, negotiating with government officials, deliberating with friends, and attempting to ease the closure of the Odenwaldschule to prepare for emigration. Edith was left with the burden of trying to dispel rumors and create a modicum of stability in this difficult phase. She wrote to Paul, "As you can imagine, everyone is wondering if the school can continue. What should we say to the children? Can we say that something new will be created?"[3]

Geheeb's negotiations with Niessen at the Reich Ministry of the Interior and with officials at the Foreign Office finally resolved the situation to his satisfaction. Paulus was eager to arrange a cordial departure from Germany with the officials, because a confrontational exit would endanger the likelihood that German students would attend the Institut Monnier, regardless of how sympathetic their parents may have been to his work. Geheeb told Niessen that he was deeply disappointed in the collapse in the Odenwaldschule, but that the Institut Monnier now provided an ideal opportunity for him to work on behalf of German culture abroad. To Paul's delight, Niessen said that the Ministry would raise no objections should he choose to transfer his educational work to Switzerland. Exhilarated with this victory, Paul wrote to Edith on 18 January that he had received official permission to move to Pont-Céard, and "everyone can now know about it."[4]

Did Niessen actually suspect Geheeb's opposition to national socialism? Since Niessen knew about the politically motivated denunciations of Geheeb, it may be that Niessen saw Geheeb's desire to move to Switzerland as an ideal opportunity to rid Germany of a nuisance who would only generate hostile publicity about the regime. On the other hand, Niessen may have represented a relatively moderate element within the civil service, which accepted national socialism in general while deploring the violence perpetuated by storm troopers like Goerendt and the heavy-handedness of "old fighters" like Ringshausen. In this case, Niessen may have genuinely regretted the Nazi reforms in the Odenwaldschule and wished to compensate for them by assisting Geheeb. Whatever his motives, Niessen's positive reception of Geheeb gave the veteran educator what he had desired ever since Blank's reforms on 20 July: official approval of his desire to emigrate and to begin his work anew in Switzerland.[5]

Meanwhile, the future of the school in Oberhambach was as unclear as ever. At this point, a creature of Geheeb's own making—the Parents' Advisory Council—became energized and began exploring the possibility of keeping some kind of school in place in Oberhambach. Adolf Messer-Bicker, the leader of the Council, was a Nazi party member, and he felt that Geheeb was overreacting to the Nazi reforms. Messer-Bicker had established positive contacts with many parents during the fall, and he now began forging a new coalition between teachers and parents to create a new school in the houses of the old Odenwaldschule after the departure of the Geheebs for Switzerland.

Looking for support among the faculty, Messer-Bicker first turned to Heinrich Sachs and Werner Meyer, two of the school's oldest and most committed *Mitarbeiter*, to see if they had any interest in leading a new Odenwaldschule. Following Messer-Bicker's inquiries, Sachs and Meyer traveled to Mannheim and Heidelberg in January to visit parents and to "confirm personally how much interest there is in continuing the school." They found that many parents valued the Odenwaldschule greatly and would gladly send their children to an offshoot of the Geheebs' work in Oberhambach. For many of these parents the political conflicts between Paul Geheeb and the Nazis were an unfortunate side effect of the Nazi takeover which had no direct bearing on educational issues. They believed that the Geheebs' departure should not preclude their children from receiving a quality private school education in a new institution led by two of the most popular teachers from the old school.

Taking note of this mood among the parents, Messer-Bicker wrote to Max Cassirer that the "parents believe that continuing the Odenwaldschule is necessary, regardless of the difficulties entailed in a transformation." If Cassirer would be willing to rent his property to a new school, Messer-Bicker reasoned, there was no reason that a new institution led by Sachs and Meyer should not be able to flourish. "The decision about the continuation of the Odenwaldschule is now in your hands," he wrote to Cassirer.[6]

Max Cassirer knew that his son-in-law was opposed to the Nazis for matters of principle, and that the creation of a new school led by two of his closest colleagues would sabotage all of Geheeb's efforts to close the school permanently. He further knew that Paul felt that by closing the Odenwaldschule he would be sending a strong message, however veiled by diplomacy, that he disapproved of the regime. On the other hand, what would Cassirer do with the school if he turned down Messer-Bicker's proposal? At the very best, the real estate would stand vacant, a clear enough symbol of his son's disenchantment with the Nazis; at the worst it might be expropriated by the regime as an arbitrary and punitive expression of their disapproval of Geheeb's emigration. Messer-Bicker offered a solution which would take effect immediately after Edith and Paulus's departure, generate at least some income, arise more or less organically out of the participants of the old Odenwaldschule, and probably win the approval of the Hessian Ministry of Culture. Given the lack of a viable alternative, Cassirer notified Messer-Bicker that he would approve a lease for a new school to begin in April. "I fundamentally agree to offer rooms on a provisional basis," he wrote to Edith, "and I will stay with this commitment and show as much interest as possible."[7]

As Cassirer had anticipated, Edith and Paul were hostile to this new development. The Geheebs had hoped that Sachs and Meyer would emigrate with them and assist them in setting forth their work at the Institut Monnier. To find out that they preferred to stay in Oberhambach to start a new kind of Odenwaldschule was a "bitter disappointment" to the Geheebs, which complicated their plans in several ways.[8]

The first and most obvious way that the initiation of the new school upset the Geheebs was the simple matter of principle. Geheeb had made it clear to Blank that in the event of his closing the Odenwaldschule he did not want another school established in the school's houses. He had fought with the Hessian Ministry of Culture to keep Sachs and Meyer in the school after the dismissal of most of the Odenwaldschule's staff the previous April. He had conferred with *Kameraden* to carry out the depopulation of the school at tremendous personal risk. After finally winning approval from the authorities to close the school in December, Geheeb now learned that two men—who were not only among his most loyal *Mitarbeiter* but were also personal friends—were going to exploit this opportunity to start a school of their own with themselves as its directors.

Not only did this destroy Geheeb's efforts to close the Odenwaldschule as a matter of principle, but it also undercut his plans to emigrate with as many students as possible to Switzerland. Sachs, Meyer, Messer-Bicker, and even Edith's father were making it easy for many students to stay in Oberhambach and enroll in the new school. They were undermining the Geheebs' financial base in starting a tremendously risk-laden project abroad.

Finally, the Geheebs believed that Sachs and Meyer were naive to believe that they could start a new Odenwaldschule with pedagogical integrity in Germany. Sachs and Meyer were going to make concessions to the Nazi government which Geheeb had refused to make. While one could not be certain how much the regime would demand of them in conforming to Nazi reforms, one could be sure that many of the new practices in the Odenwaldschule—such as the meetings of the Hitler Youth, segregated residences for boys and girls, and the overall subordination of the school to the dictates of the state—were most likely to intensify the more the Nazis consolidated their control of civil society. However much Sachs and Meyer might desire and attempt to carry on the spirit of the Geheebs' Odenwaldschule, their new work would have to be hindered from the very start by major compromises concerning student self-government, coeducation, and internationalism.

Paul Geheeb made it clear that he was opposed to the new school by speaking directly to Sachs and Meyer about it. According to Elizabeth Sachs, the wife of Heinrich, there was an element of personal resentment in transferring the leadership of the Odenwaldschule to Sachs and Meyer. "Paulus did not want *his* unique and famous school continued," she asserted. "Yes, he was straightforward about this."[9]

It would be a mistake, nonetheless, to view the Geheebs' reaction to the new school as only negative. Paul wrote that "I feel most skeptical about this new project, which is born of sentimentality, but would of course be pleased if something beautiful were created here." In conversation with Ferrière, Geheeb stated that although he regretted the loss of children who would have gone to Switzerland with him, "that doesn't destroy the friendship between Sachs and me! He has the best intentions." Max Cassirer's support for the new school probably influenced the Geheebs in suppressing their criticisms of the project.[10]

Sachs, Meyer, and Messer-Bicker had no difficulties receiving the approval of the Hessian Ministry of Culture to start the new school. On 9 February they had their first negotiations with the Ministry to propose their school and on 17 February they had a second meeting to confirm an agenda for establishing the school. Together they agreed that on 17 March an opening assembly would be held in the Odenwaldschule to lay the groundwork for the school.

It was now clear that the Odenwaldschule would split in three directions with the onset of Easter vacation in March. One group of *Kameraden* would depart with the Geheebs to continue their studies at the Institut Monnier in Pont-Céard. A second group would join Sachs and Meyer in beginning a new school in Oberhambach in April. Finally, a third group would join neither of these two endeavors, but would either graduate or continue their studies in another setting. The school was filled with rumors as the students and their parents deliberated on which option was most appropriate for their needs and values. Alumna Marina von Jakimow later recalled,

> Everything was in transition and everyone knew that everything was in transition. The thought was: "What are you doing? Are you going to Switzerland? Are you staying here? What are you going to do?"

By March the outlines of the dissolution of the old school were relatively clear. Twenty-five *Kameraden* would leave with the Geheebs for the Institut Monnier. Thirty *Kameraden* would remain with Sachs and Meyer to start a new school in Oberhambach. Ten *Kameraden* would graduate, and the rest would scatter to other institutions to begin new lives elsewhere.[11]

Adolf Messer-Bicker gave the introductory address at the opening assembly of the new school on 17 March, three days before the old Odenwaldschule was officially to end. The originators of the new school sought to perpetuate the best aspects of the Geheeb's Odenwaldschule in the new historical context. The tension between Geheeb's values and legacy and those of the new school were conflated and disguised in the very name of the new school—the "Gemeinschaft der Odenwaldschule," or "Community of the Odenwaldschule." Those who were familiar with the old Odenwaldschule knew that Paul Geheeb had always recognized the responsibility of the individual for the community, but they also knew that Geheeb repeatedly emphasized that "fundamentally the individual does not exist for the community, but the community for the individual." This individualistic approach to community was now either masked or done away with by the new Nazi stress on community as the suppression of individual differences for the sake of German national unity. Since this kind of linguistic clarification had potentially dangerous political components, one can wager that few participants in the new school dared to discuss the ramifications of the new title publicly. As a consequence, the title of the new school embodied an enigmatic and contradictory project, a confused and impossible reconciliation of Paul Geheeb's philosophy of education with the jargon of Nazism.

In his address, Messer-Bicker set the new tone by declaring strong support for national socialism:

> In the first year of its existence the National Socialist government has pulled our Germany out of the deepest misery and saved it from collapse ... We must stand with a free spirit and full enthusiasm on the foundation of our National Socialist government ... We want to lead the Gemeinschaft der Odenwaldschule entirely in the spirit of the National Socialist government.

Messer-Bicker praised Paul Geheeb for his work in the first twenty-four years of the Odenwaldschule and the parents gathered at the assembly voted unanimously to elect Geheeb the first honorary member of the new school. The parents thereby perpetuated the fiction—that Geheeb himself had promoted—that his approach to education could coexist with Nazi school reforms. The key difference appears to have been that Geheeb knew that he was distorting his perspective for political reasons, whereas a Nazi party member such as Messer-Bicker apparently fully believed in the compatability of Geheeb's principles with those of the Nazis.[12]

On 19 March, the last full day of the Geheebs' Odenwaldschule arrived. *Abitur* examinations were given that day, attended by Dr. Hans Leip from the Hessian Ministry of Culture. Although he was working with the National Socialist government, Leip had been impressed by Geheeb in their first encounter in Darmstadt on 4 November, and had spoken up on that occasion against Ringshausen's reforms. Leip now sought to convince him to stay in Germany and take over the leadership of the new school. To his chagrin, Geheeb discovered from Leip that the Gemeinschaft der Odenwaldschule would have many positive features which the Odenwaldschule had lost in its last year. Sachs and Meyer would be given the freedom to hire teachers from anywhere in Germany. The new small school would also be able to give its own *Abitur* examinations, a privilege for which Geheeb had fought for twenty-one years before receiving it in 1931. It appeared that Messer-Bicker, Sachs, and Meyer were being rewarded for their open support of the National Socialist government. Geheeb was embarrassed by Leip's attempt to recruit him to the new school. "I was in an awkward position," he later told Ferrière, "because I couldn't tell him that I can no longer live in Germany."

Ironically, Geheeb's visits with Niessen at the Reich Ministry of the Interior worked to the advantage of the Gemeinschaft der Odenwaldschule. Niessen had placed pressure on the Hessian Ministry of Culture to restore more autonomy to the Odenwaldschule after Geheeb had told Niessen of his grievances. "The Hessian government only said 'yes' to everything" about the Gemeinschaft der Odenwaldschule, Geheeb said, "because they were afraid of Berlin." Since Geheeb was now leaving Germany, it would not be his school, but rather the new Gemeinschaft der Odenwaldschule which stood to gain from his protests.[13]

The final *Schulgemeinde* of the Geheebs' Odenwaldschule was held on the evening of 19 March. Geheeb described that last meeting years later:

> 19 March 1934 was, I believe, the last *Abitur* examination, and that evening there was a great farewell assembly announced in the meeting hall. Many people, parents and friends from outside, traveled to us. The assembly hall was overflowing ... I then presented very clearly and exactly what I had always wanted and what I would always want. Frau von Keller and many other *Mitarbeiter* spoke, many tears flowed, and the *Kameraden* also spoke briefly. It was therefore a very emotional ending, and a Beethoven quartet was played. On the next day everything disappeared. The houses were empty, completely emptied. All the *Mitarbeiter* were gone and all the children were gone.

The Geheebs were then left with closing down their operations, packing the furniture, papers and other possessions which they wished to bring with them, and making their departure. Geheeb wrote to Ferrière on 25 March that "Edith and I are about to collapse" from the strain of the transition. Paul left for Switzerland on 31 March; Edith followed with two *Mitarbeiter* and twenty-five *Kameraden* one week later.[14]

part III

Consequences

chapter 10

The Ecole d'Humanité, 1934–1945

Twenty-four children followed the Geheebs from the Odenwald-schule to the Institut Monnier at Pont-Céard near Versoix. The move was full of complications. One Russian child was not allowed to enter Switzerland at the border, apparently a victim of Swiss anxiety that he might come from a family with communist convictions. The Geheebs had to claim that property they owned belonged to Geheeb's secretary Lisbeth Hartig, who was a nationalized Swiss, in order to bring furniture and office supplies out of Germany. The Institut Monnier was situated in a completely different milieu from that of the Odenwald-schule; it stood close to a major highway from Lausanne to Geneva and lacked the expansive forests of the Odenwald. When the Geheebs arrived they found that the student population in the Institut had dropped to ten and that the school was deeply in debt. The Institut was in a French-speaking part of Switzerland, so the children who followed the Geheebs from Germany had to learn a new language as part of their adaptation to their new home.[1]

In spite of the difficulties, Paul Geheeb was determined to make the best of the new situation. On 17 April he opened the first *Schul-gemeinde* at the Institut Monnier with the same Goethe quotation he had used to open the Odenwaldschule twenty-four years earlier. In the address which followed, Geheeb reiterated many of the major themes of his philosophy of education, stressing the importance of idealistic self-cultivation, responsibility for one's community, and reverence toward life in general. He also brought international concerns to the fore in a hitherto unprecedented manner. Geheeb resented the loss of the "eternal Germany," which he identified with the idealist tradition, to the "political noise" coming from his homeland. "You all know," he said, "that you have come here for political and economic and many other reasons." Yet rather than mourn the unfortunate situation in Germany, Geheeb sought to win the students' enthusiasm for a fundamentally new project. "The highest mission of our community we have apparently not been able to fulfill within the Odenwaldschule, within the boundaries of our home," he said. The relocation in Switzerland provided an opportunity not only for an outward change but also for an inward renewal:

> We don't want simply to continue, nor do the same things we've done for decades in the Odenwald, but rather do something higher, something better and more beautiful in every sense, to move closer to the perfection of the human community . . . If we succeed in realizing that which I imagine, we will be neither a French, nor a German, nor an English, nor a Swiss school in the next few years, but the School of Humanity.

As a pedagogical response to national socialism, Geheeb hoped that such a "School of Humanity" might emerge from within and perhaps ultimately supplant the Institut Monnier. If Geheeb could be successful in founding and leading such a school, then his emigration from Germany would go beyond a purely formal *reaction* to take the shape of a vigorous and humanistic *action* on behalf of the principles he had always held dear.[2]

The transplantation of Paul Geheeb's work to Switzerland was received with great interest by many Swiss educators who had heard of the Odenwaldschule or been active in the Swiss section of the New Education Fellowship. In September 1934 Paul attended his first meeting of the Swiss NEF and further developed the ideas he had first presented in the *Schulgemeinde* meeting the previous April. For Geheeb, the "ubiquitous bacteria of nationalism and fascism" prompted him to leave Germany and compelled all humanistic educators to intensify their efforts on behalf of cross-cultural understanding and international reconciliation. "One ideal stands unshakably before us," he said, "that of the economic and cultural cooperation of mankind bound together in one brotherhood. Such a macrocosm should be mirrored in its essential features in the microcosm of the school community."[3]

How would such a school look in practice? A future "School of Mankind," Geheeb thought, should take the form of a *Landerziehungsheim,* in which five or six separate cultural communities "would find their happy synthesis in the consciousness of representing ideally the culture of mankind." Each culture would occupy its own house so that the children could acquire a sense of connectedness to their own culture while also being in regular contact with children from other cultures in their class and work situations. Although English, French, and German would be the privileged languages, the school would aspire to transcend Western cultures and would seek to integrate other cultural groups into its community. Geheeb's stress on responsibility would continue to be paramount: "The kind of school we are thinking about presupposes that the principle of education for self-government shall be bravely carried through to its ultimate consequences." Fully aware that his proposal "may perhaps appear utopian to many," Geheeb shared it at the Swiss NEF conference because he was convinced that "there was no forum more interested or more competent to discuss it in a friendly spirit."[4]

Perhaps because of his ambitious project, Geheeb rapidly came into conflict with Willem Gunning, the founder of the Institut Monnier and Geheeb's *de facto* host in Switzerland. Throughout his educational career, Paulus had scorned what he perceived as the artificial pleasures of material acquisitiveness and sensual indulgence. While many of the children in the Odenwaldschule had come from wealthy backgrounds, he had always taken it to be his educational responsibility to teach them that life's greatest rewards were to be found in intellectual self-cultivation and physical abstinence. To his chagrin, Paulus quickly discovered that Gunning, his current pedagogical partner, was just the kind of aesthete whom he had frequently berated before his students. Gunning loved expensive cigarettes, fine wines, and expensive cars, and had little aversion to introducing older students to these delights. He often slept late into the day, long after the students had attended their first classes, and could be seen meandering between buildings in his bathrobe, nursing a cup of coffee and indulging in idle conversation with passersby. Since Geheeb's approach to education emphasized teaching by example, he found himself bridling at the kind of role model Gunning offered to the students. It must have been hard for him to believe that he had fended off the Nazis and emigrated to Switzerland only to end up as the junior partner to a man who was pleasant enough in his outward disposition but relatively hollow when it came to the educational principles Geheeb so earnestly sought to propagate.[5]

In spite of his difficulties with Gunning, Paul Geheeb held back his criticisms of his colleague for his first months in Pont-Céard. It was imperative that the new team of directors establish a spirit of unity and cooperation in this transitional period, for the Geheebs suffered continued difficulties with the German government. On 17 April Max

Cassirer wrote Paul Geheeb to let him know that yet another "notifi-cation has reached the Reich Ministry of the Interior, where attention is brought to the fact that Geheeb was intending to go to Switzerland to agitate against Germany, and that one must prevent this." Cassirer once more urged Geheeb to be cautious in his public statements and to give the Nazis no reasons to move against him or the new Gemein-schaft der Odenwaldschule.[6]

The Gcheebs were fortunate to find support from the German Consulate in Geneva. A sympathetic official visited the Institut and subsequently sent a report to the Foreign Office in Berlin, saying that the Geheebs' work could "only be greeted as in German cultural and political interests." This positive report enabled Edith Geheeb to make regular trips to Berlin and Oberhambach, so that she could keep apace with developments in her family and the Gemeinschaft der Odenwaldschule.[7]

Unfortunately, Edith's visits to her childhood home in Berlin were filled with conflict. Although he had helped to ease the Geheebs' emi-gration to Switzerland, Max Cassirer was convinced that his daughter and son-in-law had made a terrible mistake and that they should return to Oberhambach. Paul Geheeb told Ferrière in January 1935,

> My father-in-law insists that I travel to Germany in February to visit the government in order to reopen the school in Odenwald. That is out of the question! Then he said, "What Sachs can do, you also must be able to do!" In addition, the ministerial official who observed the *Abitur* in the Odenwaldschule in September had a discussion with Sachs afterwards. He praised my personality, my character, and my importance for edu-cation in the highest terms. He deeply regretted that I had emigrated and said that he expected that I would once more take over the leader-ship of the school in the spring.
>
> That made a great impression on my father-in-law. They *can* be decent. But this ministerial official could be in a concentration camp tomorrow. You know I'm not *afraid,* but I see clearly that I would risk being shot, placed in a concentration camp, or at least deprived of my passport. The German government isn't unified and is completely unpredictable.
>
> Edith is in a difficult position. If she were to tell her father politely that she shares my opinion he would throw her out of the house. So she just says that I'm crazy and that she can't do anything about it.

The ministerial official who wanted Geheeb to return was Hans Leip, who had spoken up on Geheeb's behalf during the conference at the Hessian Ministry of Culture in November 1933 and who had attempted to persuade Geheeb to stay in Oberhambach as late as

March 1934. In spite of Leip's interest and Cassirer's pleadings, Geheeb could not imagine returning to Germany. As a consequence, his relationship with his father-in-law remained strained.[8]

Paul intensified his work in the Institut Monnier that spring and summer. He was thrilled with its development, and wrote,

> I believe I have never been so active and influential in my entire life as I am here. My new school has developed wonderfully. It has become a real community with a harmonious atmosphere and a strong spiritual lifestyle.

Yet life in the Institut Monnier was anything but idyllic. On the contrary, the overall climate in the school was one of almost spartan rigor and self-discipline. Theda Henle was an American *Kameradin*, whose mother had admired the Odenwaldschule from afar for many years and was determined that her children should experience the kind of education practiced there. When the Geheebs moved to Switzerland, it was natural that the three Henle children should come to the Institut Monnier. What they found was an intense community of young people who took almost complete responsibility for their own educations:

> The students were aggressive, dedicated, and too old for their years. And *they* ran the school. Most of them were refugees from Germany who could pay only an exceedingly small sum each month, some nothing at all. Paulus never turned a pupil away. They were brilliant, defensive, and, many of them, tragically maladjusted. Children who have seen their parents shamed, mistreated and, in some cases, jailed or killed are not children . . . They wanted to work and work and work. They wanted to build themselves into people who could fight back. Under their rigid discipline we worked and studied and worked from the cold early morning exercises until bedtime. Even our recreational moments had to have a purpose.
>
> They knew how hard it was for the school to keep going, and through their student government, and it was a complete student government, they saw that all the chores of keeping the school clean and fed were carried out. The emotional strain was unbearable for some . . . The German mail plane—with the swastika on its wings—flew over the vegetable garden every afternoon around 4:00 and those of us working in the garden screamed and yelled curses in uncontrollable hate . . .
>
> This was progressive education—harsh and exaggerated to be sure. This was Paul Geheeb's educational experiment—living still in poverty and exile . . . This was an experience none of us will ever forget.[9]

In spite of the relative successes of the Institut Monnier, Geheeb became convinced in the course of 1935 that it would be necessary to terminate the relationship with Gunning and to leave Pont-Céard. Geheeb had come to hate Gunning and he found the location of the school close to a major thoroughfare dissatisfying. The student body of the school had risen to more than fifty students and Geheeb believed the school would be more feasible financially on its own than as a vehicle to pay off Gunning's debts. Since the Swiss immigration authorities were almost certain to refuse Geheeb the permission to direct a school of his own, Geheeb asked Elisabeth Huguenin to take over the nominative leadership of a new school. Huguenin had visited the Odenwaldschule during the First World War, was a resident of Neuchâtel, and had written the first popular description of the Oden- waldschule, which had been published in French and German.[10]

Throughout the rest of 1935 and all of 1936, the Geheebs searched for an appropriate location for a new "Ecole d'Humanité," which would realize the principles put forth in Geheeb's 1934 address to the Swiss section of the NEF. The key impediments were cantonal per- mission to open the school and inexpensive and appropriate housing. Due to the strict Nazi laws against exporting capital by Jews, Max Cassirer was no longer in a position to help the Geheebs. Cassirer's correspondence to Paul Geheeb throughout the middle and late 1930s was filled with doubts about the wisdom of continuing educa- tional work in Switzerland. Cassirer was convinced that his son-in-law lacked any political diplomacy or financial sense and that this would lead to catastrophic consequences for the children of the school, his daughter, and Paul himself. A letter from Cassirer to Paul in 1936 about the Geheebs' intention to start a new school reflected this mood:

> The times in which one could realize such plans have passed. Certainly you've had some successes and the foundation of a *Landerziehungsheim* does not require millions. But the times in which one found benefactors who helped eagerly are over. I also have lost every opportunity to help you, regardless of how much I might desire to, because the economic context has completely changed and the export of money is totally blocked. With your attitude you won't place much value on my objec- tions, and I don't hold that against you. I just hope that you won't expe- rience disappointments in your endeavors which could have disastrous consequences for Edith and you.[11]

True to character, Paul Geheeb disregarded Cassirer's warnings. The Geheebs explored possibilities in four different cantons. They then went through the labor-intensive procedure of applying for permis- sion to open a new school in an abandoned hotel in Corbeyrier near Aigles in Vaud in August 1936. To their great disappointment their application was denied. They then applied for permission to open a school in Neuenburg. This request was also rejected.

It is easy to understand why the Swiss refused the Geheebs' applications. Enjoying the benefits of spectacular natural settings, an international milieu, and well-trained teachers, the Swiss had numerous private boarding schools of their own to protect in the 1930s. These schools had lost many students during the depression and did not want competition from the Geheebs, however worthy their projects might be. As if to validate Max Cassirer's worst intuitions about his son-in-law's tactlessness, Paulus attacked Swiss boarding schools as a "pedagogical industry." From Geheeb's point of view, traditional private schools had no right to exist, since they only served to maintain the interests of what he perceived as an affluent and uncreative status quo. The organization of private school directors, called the "Association des Directeurs," did not take well to Geheeb's criticisms, and used its leverage to dissuade governmental officials from granting the Geheebs residency status. The Association implied that Paul was a communist of whom the Nazis were justly suspicious, and held up the "air baths" of the Odenwaldschule as evidence of his allegedly perverse interest in nudism. Observing these smear tactics, Edith complained that the Swiss were "even worse than the Nazis."[12]

Both the Geheebs and Ferrière were infuriated by the negative decisions from Vaud and Neuenburg. Max Cassirer urged the Geheebs to give up: "a horrible end is always better than endless horror." Fortunately, the Geheebs received permission to stay in Canton Geneva. In spite of Paul's animosity to Willem Gunning, the founder of the Institut Monnier was willing to let the Geheebs continue to work in Pont-Céard. Gunning now volunteered to close his school to enable the Geheebs to start an institution of their own. Under the new arrangement, the Geheebs would pay rent to Gunning, but all of the pedagogical decisions would be left up to them. The Geheebs agreed to take advantage of this opportunity. The Institut Monnier dissolved in the summer of 1937 and the groundwork was laid for the Ecole d'Humanité to take its place when the academic year resumed in September.[13]

Other forces now intervened to plague the Geheebs. Paul had to undergo a series of operations for ear and jaw disabilities and was hospitalized in Geneva when the new school opened. In his absence, Ferrière gave the opening address on 2 September 1937. While Geheeb was still in the hospital Swiss fascists slandered his new school in their paper, *Action Nationale*. Two weeks after Geheeb returned to Pont-Céard, Leonardo Segovia—the son of the classical guitarist

Andrés Segovia and a student in the school—had a fatal accident on nearby train tracks. His best friend, who reported the incident, was the son of Loucien Trouchet, a well-known anarchist who lived in Geneva. Ferrière wrote to Geheeb, "The fact that the police would meet precisely *him* now isn't going to help the Ecole!" The Geheebs persevered through this crisis as they had so many others.[14]

The Ecole d'Humanité operated in Pont-Céard for a little over one year. Unfortunately, the number of students in the new school dropped from around sixty at its inception to roughly thirty by December 1938. According to Geheeb, most of the students who left were German Jews whose parents decided to emigrate to other countries after experiencing the rising anti-Semitism in Germany that peaked on Crystal Night. The decline in enrollments created yet another crisis for the Geheebs. Paulus told Adolphe Ferrière, "Gunning knew my international reputation and expected that hundreds of children would rush to me and that he could make a great profit through me. He is therefore deeply disappointed that the number of children declined over the year." After a trial period of sixteen months, Gunning believed he had erred in allowing the Geheebs to start the Ecole d'Humanité and decided that he would reopen the Institut Monnier on his own. He terminated their contract and forbade them to return to the schools' houses after Christmas vacation.[15]

The Geheebs would have been completely stranded were it not for the hospitality of the ever-protective Ferrière, who invited them to spend the holidays with their students at his vacation home in Les Pléiades. Cantonal authorities agreed to let the Geheebs stay in Vaud while they looked for a new school, but gave them only a brief period of grace—until 15 February 1939. Whether from wisdom or from ignorance, Paul Geheeb refused to give up, and found solace in his students. He wrote to Romain Rolland,

> For this harmonious community which has developed in these years, consisting of a few dozen children from the most different countries, idealistic young teachers, and myself, our present destiny is fundamentally a positive experience. We are all filled with an unshakable belief in the primacy of the spiritual world over the material . . . Our youth, our boys and girls from eight to nineteen years old, learn in this crisis . . . to live for a great idea and to stand in the rows of those fighting for a better human condition.

The Geheebs needed their idealism. Shortly before the calamity with Gunning, Max Cassirer had arrived in Pont-Céard. His confidence in his ability to deal rationally with the Nazis had finally been shattered when he was compelled to sell his factory in Silesia. Broken-hearted, he decided to emigrate to Britain, and planned his journey so that he could see the Ecole d'Humanité. By emigrating he lost almost all of his savings to the German government. Cassirer and the Geheebs were now all homeless. Within a five-year period their possessions had been decimated, and their fame did not carry enough clout to win permission from cantonal authorities to start a new life in Switzerland. Meanwhile, the Ecole d'Humanité was mocked as an *"école des juifs,"* or "school of Jews," by anti-Semitic opponents.[16]

Once again, however, the Geheebs' resilience paid off. Immigration officials in Vaud extended permission for the Geheebs to stay in Les Pléiades until April and in March an Odenwaldschule alumnus referred the Geheebs to Schloss Greng, an estate near Lake Murten. The building was vacant and the owners appeared eager to take in the new school. Max Cassirer and Edith Geheeb visited the estate and found the conditions promising. To the Geheebs' delight, cantonal authorities in Fribourg posed no hindrance. With a tremendous sense of relief, they moved to Schloss Greng in March.

Yet Schloss Greng also proved to be a disaster. The owner, Leo Schermann, was economically motivated and wanted to derive a handsome profit from the new school. Ambiguities in the contract, the Geheebs' belated discovery that vast portions of the old building had minimal or no heating facilities, and the decision by the Swiss military to make use of the Schloss as soldiers' quarters after the beginning of the Second World War in September provoked yet another crisis. Paul wrote in October,

> I freely admit that our immediate existence is hideous. We have two hundred soldiers and another twenty officers and their subordinates. They have taken the classrooms and the few heated rooms . . . On top of this I have so much work and don't have the time continually to do gymnastics to warm up . . . The attitude of the children is beautiful, truly heroic. From the oldest to the youngest they work for our project and give their best. Nonetheless, at least a half dozen are now ill with colds.

Meanwhile, the Geheebs were more and more cut off from their old friends in their homeland. "In Germany one can't address a letter to an 'Ecole d'Humanité' without hesitation," Eduard Spranger wrote to them while visiting Switzerland. "I have heard of your difficulties and hope with you . . . that you have found a final place of refuge for 'Humanité.'"[17]

Paul Geheeb was now sixty-nine years old and had no financial security. After so many years of success in the Odenwaldschule he was almost back in the same vulnerable position he had been in after leaving Haubinda and Wickersdorf. Yet, with the same tenacity which had served him so well before, he refused to abandon the Ecole d'Humanité. His stamina more and more validated his utterance to Stein in the *Mitarbeiter* conference in November 1933, "I can't imagine how I'll ever be finished off." Paulus now carried less of the work, and it was Edith who again found the next location for the Ecole, at the empty Hôtel du Lac at Schwarzsee south of Bern. The school moved to its new location on 26 October.

The first brochures for the new school emphasized the quality of the school as a "germ cell for a future Ecole d'Humanité," which hoped to earn its name by attracting students from many different nations. The brochures showed the rugged quality of life students would face at Schwarzsee, with students gathering potatoes, cleaning shoes and attending to other daily tasks; gone were the majestic houses of the Odenwaldschule and its meticulously cultivated educational atmosphere. The Geheebs found the natural setting of the lake magnificent, and Paul rose early each morning for a refreshing swim in its waters.

Although Schwarzsee represented all that the Geheebs had been longing for ever since their first plans to emigrate in 1933, the war threatened to decimate the school. Many parents called their children home. By November only twenty students remained.

To complicate matters even more the Geheebs now confronted litigation with Leo Schermann, the owner of Schloss Greng. In their desperation to find a site for the school after losing the building at Pont-Céard and struggling through the winter at Les Pléiades, Paul unwittingly signed a contract with Schermann in which he assumed partial responsibility for previous debts incurred in running the estate at Greng. In light of the Geheebs' financial difficulties, Schermann was infuriated by their practice of taking in students at half-price or without any tuition at all based on the students' ability to pay. The Geheebs lost the court case and were forced to pay Schermann 8200 francs. Paul wrote Ferrière after the hearing that Schermann had *"completely ruined* the existence of the school and Edith's and my personal security."[18]

It now looked as though all of the efforts of the Geheebs to begin a school of their own since their emigration from Germany were doomed. Paulus pleaded for help in an open letter to his old friends,

The existence of the Ecole d'Humanité is endangered. As a consequence of the unusual developments in international politics the number of children who come from abroad to Switzerland has grown smaller and smaller . . . In our epoch of illegality, racial hatred, and the most brutal violence, no other institution has a more important claim to legitimacy or is more urgently needed than an Ecole d'Humanité. In the last years I have received hundreds of letters from almost every country on earth which assure me that the mere fact that somewhere in the world there is an Ecole d'Humanité represents an incomparable comfort and a constant source of encouragement.

The Geheebs spent that summer hoping that their letter would generate action, especially in the United States. "If we don't get almost three thousand dollars we'll have to stop on 31 August," Paul lamented, "and then Edith's and my personal security is also destroyed."[19]

On 11 August the Geheebs received a response from friends who had tried to raise funds in the United States. Paul wrote,

> Yesterday our so deeply desired telegram from the U.S. finally arrived. The result of my open letter is almost entirely negative. A few poor (German) immigrants, earlier students of the Odenwaldschule, and a few poor teachers sent contributions of between five and twenty dollars. All of the rich Americans didn't give a cent. They apparently think that Switzerland is also a lost cause and that there's no way that I can keep my school . . . We will now dissolve the school in the next weeks.

Ferrière urged Geheeb to recognize that he was in a *"situation de guerre"* and should declare bankruptcy. "That you can get through the war years and live with Edith is the most that one can ask of such a time," he advised.[20]

In spite of the grim situation, the Geheebs reversed their decision to shut the school. They moved out of the Hôtel du Lac and resettled across the lake in a small house named the Chalet Aurore. They now had only eleven students. The school limped through the rest of 1940, and in 1941 the student body dropped to nine.

The Geheebs now received yet another blow, this time from the German government. They learned in 1941 that the Nazi regime had revoked their citizenship. The papers supporting the expatriation were organized by the Gestapo and approved by the Reich Ministry of the Interior in Berlin. In the eyes of the Gestapo,

> Geheeb was the leader of the Odenwaldschule in Oberhambach, which was known as a stronghold of the German Communist party until the seizure of power. The private school students from Germany and abroad took part in Communist party demonstrations with the consent of the school leadership and distributed Communist party literature to the

population. Geheeb subscribed to Marxist publications. He commented when he emigrated in 1934 that he would never step on German soil again. According to the political department of the local National Socialist office in Heppenheim, he is completely unreliable politically.

The loss of citizenship made the Geheebs' legal status in Switzerland even more tenuous, but they realized that in many ways it had been a foregone conclusion. They suffered a more serious loss on 15 January 1943, when Max Cassirer died in London. In spite of their many differences of opinion over the years, Paul deeply mourned his father-in-law's passing. He wrote to Ferrière that "this man, who stemmed from a completely different social world from my own, had a tremendous significance for my life as did few others, and it certainly wasn't just superficial."[21]

After several years of unrelenting poverty and hardship, the tiny Ecole d'Humanité finally began expanding in the summer of 1943. A philanthropic association in Bern called the "Swiss Assistance Agency for Emigrant Children" established contact with the Geheebs and began sending refugees with small stipends to the school. Of twenty-five children in the Ecole d'Humanité in the fall of 1943, twenty were refugees. Most of these children came into Switzerland from France and Belgium and were interned in camps before being sent on to Schwarzsee.

The revival of the Ecole d'Humanité filled Paul and Edith with trepidation. Alwine von Keller visited the school at Schwarzsee and found that many of the refugee children were "shattered and perhaps destroyed forever" by the traumas they had experienced. Simply keeping the new children clothed, well sheltered, and fed was a challenge for the Geheebs, since their quarters were small and their resources scarce. With time, however, they were excited to discover that the children were extraordinarily receptive and "eager to make up for the years in which they had not been able to learn." "In spite of all the changes and real problems, we nonetheless are a real community, now that we have more than twenty children here," Edith wrote to her brother. "Previously we were always more or less private tutors for rich children. You can imagine how much more I enjoy the present work."[22]

For many of the children, the Ecole d'Humanité was a dream and a haven from months or years of anguish. Heinz Goldstein was a German Jew who had caught a ship to Cuba with other émigrés but was not able to land; the vessel finally made its way to France, whence he was passed from one refugee camp to another until he arrived at the

Ecole. Eva Schöneberg and her mother were deported to Theresien-
stadt, where her mother died; Eva was one of a small and fortunate
group of children delivered into asylum in Switzerland who also made
her way to the Ecole. Hanna Reich, a Jewish refugee from Berlin, also
found shelter in the Ecole. All of these children had been traumatized
by the attempted Nazi genocide of the Jews and the Second World
War. One refugee from Belgium described her path to the Ecole
d'Humanité and the conditions she found in the school in a letter to
a pen-pal in England:

> I had to try twice to enter France, and after a short time already we could
> no longer stay in France. We decided then to leave for Switzerland; it
> was not very easy: the first time we tried, we were betrayed by our
> "leader" who was to bring us over the frontier, and the second time we
> succeeded by passing over the mountains in December. Edith, with the
> help of the Red Cross . . . succeeded in liberating me, and that is how I
> manage to enter our school, last March.
>
> I have met so many wicked men in Belgium and in France (and those
> who were not wicked, were indifferent) that I disbelieved at this moment
> in the word "Humanity." After a few days of our school life I found hope
> and faith again.
>
> We lead a simple and happy life. There are nearly 25 pupils from nine
> to sixteen years here. Most of us are refugees, and are as I am liberated
> from the camps by Edith and Paulus. We are all very happy to have the
> possibility of living together in this school. We have come from many
> different countries and we speak French or German. We all have passed
> bad moments recently; some of us even have their parents deported; but
> just these are the most courageous of us. They live full of hope and
> expectation for the day when they will see their relatives healthy and
> safe again, hoping that their parents will find their little boy or girl some-
> body worthy of the word "Man" . . .
>
> We also have a "School-Community." Once more, we are gathered
> around the table of our biggest room; the School-Community is
> announced by Paulus at dinner-time and mostly begins at half past four
> in the afternoon. This School-Community, where we discuss all our
> problems, where we bring forth our newest ideas, in one word where we
> speak about all kind of subjects related to our school-life, is one of the
> most important things of our school; it is the foundation of our princi-
> ples and our practices.
>
> This is a little, a very little of our life. Can you see from my writing
> that we are happy to live in this way, so many refugees together, to be
> able to enjoy such a wonderful nature and learn so much?[23]

More and more refugees filled the Ecole in 1944, bringing the student body to sixty *Kameraden* who lived in the huts and cabins sur-

rounding Schwarzsee. The conditions were so crowded that some of the *Kameraden* entered and left their rooms through their windows rather than the door so that every inch of floor space could be used for bedding. The students who prepared meals had to be especially quiet so as not to disturb the students who were attending class a few yards away in the dining room.

The rise of student enrollments allowed the Geheebs for the first time in many years to recreate many of the old practices of the Odenwaldschule. Academic classes were held in the morning, and at the end of each term the students shared their results with each other in a *Kursschlussschulgemeinde*. Alwine von Keller was present on one occasion, and was impressed with the way

> in which the children who had just come out of the camps reported in such an independent and enthusiastic manner on their achievements in their courses and displayed their accomplishments. Even in the Odenwaldschule I rarely saw such fine presentations. And what was especially delightful was that such an intense cultural atmosphere penetrated and uplifted everything, even in the very primitive circumstances.

Paul began each lunch with one of his traditional quotes from the classics, and he introduced the new *Kameraden* to the works of Tolstoy, Tagore, and Lagerlöf during *Andachten*.[24]

Like Alwine von Keller, Odenwaldschule alumnus Klaus Mann also made his way to Schwarzsee and was excited with the school community created by the Geheebs. He considered the Ecole to be "the scene of what is perhaps the most important educational experiment in war-torn Europe today," where students from the most diverse national backgrounds coexisted peacefully with one another:

> The scions of old Swiss patrician houses mingle with Czech refugees and young German Jews who have witnessed the horrors of Belsen, Oranienburg, and other Gestapo infernos . . . There are little Poles and little Hungarians; children who were driven from their homes in Holland when the Germans moved in and children who were evacuated from one of the destroyed German cities, where their parents may still lie buried under debris and rubble. Two melancholy-looking girls with oversized heads and bloated limbs spent most of their childhoods in Theresienstadt, the fortress near Prague used by the Nazis as a ghetto town for Jews from Czechoslovakia and other countries.

Mann was deeply moved by the Geheebs' persistence in pursuing their educational vision throughout the entire Nazi period and by their hopes for the school in the postwar era. He continued,

I could not help thinking of some of the young people now under Paulus's care—the sad-eyed boy whose parents were gassed at Auschwitz; the two pathetic girls with their oversized heads—and the old man's unabated faith struck me as more admirable than ever.

"Of course," I told him—and curiously, I felt much older, more skeptical and more tired than my white-haired companion seemed to be— "of course, you'll have your school."

"Naturally, I will," the old man smiled, his eyes radiant with hope and confidence. "What you've seen here today is just a beginning, a nucleus. It will develop, grow. One has to be very patient."

It would be easier to be patient and less difficult to keep up one's faith if more were like you, Paul Geheeb.

Paulus worked closely and supportively with the traumatized children in his care. A young girl in the school had been so terrified by the war that she stopped speaking. One day she and Paulus were seeing who could spit cherry pits the farthest out of a window on the second floor of the Chalet Aurore when Edith passed by underneath. Edith could not see who was doing the spitting and called out that they should stop. Paul playfully hid from Edith with the girl below the window, and after this experience the girl began speaking again.[25]

chapter 11

The Gemeinschaft der Odenwaldschule, 1933–1945

The Gemeinschaft der Odenwaldschule began in April 1934 with thirty-two boarding students and seven day students. The first convocation of the new school was held in Plato Haus. Heinrich Sachs welcomed the students and stated that Werner Meyer and he would now be leading the school. The assembly tried to sing the German national anthem and the Horst Wessel song, but the effort failed. Apparently, enough *Mitarbeiter* and *Kameraden* from the old school felt that such a beginning "really didn't fit; it just wasn't appropriate."[1]

In spite of this opening attempt to conform to the rituals of the Nazis, Sachs, Meyer, and many *Kameraden* made a strong effort to preserve the climate and values of the Geheebs' Odenwaldschule. The directors mustered up scholarships for students familiar with the old school to enable them to help found the new one. One *Kamerad,* Michael Hartlaub, ritualistically shook the old "Odenwaldschule spirit into a bottle, so that it could continue to influence us." Dankwart Rüstow, who had entered the old Odenwaldschule in April 1933, recalled,

> Even the youngest *Kameraden,* to whom I then belonged, felt largely subconsciously that they had a tradition to continue, and that they should acclimate the "new ones" to this lifestyle through their example and their stories about how community life was in the old school. Very quickly it was such that a "new one" no longer meant someone who had recently come to the school but rather someone who had never known the "proper" school. And the more "new ones" that came, the more conscious we few "old ones" were of our task to continue to sustain the old tradition.

There were enough leaders among the *Kameraden* in the new school that a core group, intimately familiar with the spirit and practices of the old Odenwaldschule, could carry forth its traditions. These included Geno Hartlaub, who had led the *Warte* in 1933, and Thomas Cassirer, nephew of Paul and Edith, who returned to the school to be with his friends over the objections of his émigré parents. Because of their presence and the leadership of Sachs and Meyer, who had come to the old Odenwaldschule in 1921 and 1927 respectively, there was at least a fighting chance for many of the old traditions to survive.[2]

Countless concessions were nonetheless imperative. Many changes had to do simply with appropriating Nazi jargon. The very title of the school, with the incorporation of the Nazi obsession with *Gemeinschaft*, was just part of a pattern. The intimacy and nurturance implied by the pedagogical "families" of the Geheeb era now became suspect; henceforth, the families became *"Kameradschaften."* Rather than call the *Mitarbeiter* who led these groups "family heads," a title with greater affinities to national socialism was created—the *"Kameradschaftsführer."* "Cassirer Haus" and "Humboldt Haus" offered too open praise to a Jew and a liberal; the two buildings were renamed "Bach Haus" and "Dürer Haus" respectively. Finally, one could even give patriotic names to rooms; in Schiller Haus in 1936 several of them were named after the portions of Germany which had been lost in the Treaty of Versailles, such as Upper Silesia, Danzig, and the Saar.[3]

Other changes in the school touched more deeply on the fabric of everyday life. The Hitler Youth continued and expanded, with regular meetings, marches through the countryside, and omnipresent uniforms. The segregation of boys and girls into separate houses persisted and became part of a new routine. The old, democratic *Schulgemeinden* of the Geheeb era were abandoned.

In spite of these disruptions many aspects of life persisted from the old Odenwaldschule. The flexible course system continued completely undisturbed. The history courses taught by Meyer made no references to the Nazis or to their views on the German past. Sachs, like Geheeb, approached the young people in his care as individuals and with such a mild leadership style that the *Kameraden* gave him the nickname of "gentle Heinrich." Nazi rituals, such as greeting others with "Heil Hitler!" were completely ignored. Several of the *Kameraden* who continued in the school did not even move out of the houses or rooms they had previously inhabited, and many of them did not change their primary instructors after the founding of the new school.[4]

The contradictory nature of the Gemeinschaft der Odenwaldschule was particularly evident in an informational brochure developed by

Sachs and Meyer for prospective students in August 1936. On the one hand, many themes and photographs from the Geheebs' school were incorporated directly and without commentary into the brochure. Martin Wagenschein—who had been forced by Ringshausen to leave the old Odenwaldschule in April 1933—was shown teaching a physics class. Familiar quotes from Goethe were juxtaposed with photographs of students engaged in hands-on learning. Plato and Pestalozzi were described as "the eternal mentors of true community education." "The highest and most demanding form of self-education and self-discipline" had nothing to do with national socialism, but lay in "aesthetic activity, in language, music, and art. Here the entire person is challenged and can reach his full potential." Theater was particularly important: "The great works of Shakespeare and German authors, and skits which we compose ourselves, lift our community out of its everyday routine and fill it with magical beauty."

The lovely effect generated by lyrical passages in the brochure was rendered problematical by the selective incorporation of the symbols and jargon of national socialism. In the midst of photographs of small groups of students reading, sculpting, and sewing lay a picture of the entire school standing at attention under a swastika banner. Readers were informed that students heard stories of "bravery, solidarity, and heroism from the World War and the present" on Sunday evenings. Matter-of-fact statements that Tuesday and Wednesday evenings were reserved for meetings of the Hitler Youth were inserted between enthusiastic descriptions of musical events on Monday and Thursday nights.[5]

In spite of these concessions to national socialism, Max Cassirer continued to visit Oberhambach to confer regularly with Sachs and Meyer. His visits, and Thomas Cassirer's attendance in the school until his graduation in 1936, demonstrated that a partial continuity with the old Odenwaldschule was indeed intact. "For the children, there *was* a real continuity," Thomas Cassirer later observed. "I have very good memories of it."[6]

Although unresolved tensions persisted between Sachs and the Geheebs, Sachs appears to have done his best to protect the Geheebs while leading the new school. By electing Paul Geheeb the first honorary member of the new school Sachs created a certain symbolic continuity between the two schools. In an interview with government officials in May 1934 "Sachs adamantly denied that the transference of Geheeb's work from Hambach to Pont-Céard in Canton Geneva was influenced by any other than purely financial reasons." Sachs thus protected the Geheebs by assuring the government that the Geheebs' given reasons for emigrating were accurate.[7]

Although Sachs disappointed the Geheebs by founding the Gemeinschaft der Odenwaldschule, he scarcely had strong affinities for national socialism. He had given himself the nickname of "Erasmus" because of his love of the Dutch humanist and pacifist—hardly an auspicious beginning for a fledgling Nazi sympathizer. In 1933 Geheeb thought that any Nazi retaliations against him would necessarily include only two other people, Edith and Sachs. Geheeb had considered Sachs to be his closest friend among his colleagues, and the similarities between the two men were striking. "Both were so quiet and reserved, shy, without temperamental outbursts," Marina Jakimow observed. "Both never fully revealed their innermost thoughts."[8]

Although the close friendship between Geheeb and Sachs was tested by Sachs's decision to found the Gemeinschaft der Odenwaldschule, it seems that Geheeb was able to put these differences behind him. The two corresponded after the Geheebs' emigration, and Sachs referred prospective Jewish students to the Institut Monnier and then the Ecole d'Humanité, where several went to continue their educations and avoid the stigmatization they would have encountered in German schools. The Geheebs likewise referred students to the Gemeinschaft der Odenwaldschule when they needed a German *Abitur*. Sachs idolized Paul Geheeb and was delighted that their friendship was intact. "My springboard for the present and for the beyond will always be you, dear Paulus," he wrote. "The only thing which I still hope for from this life is to see you again, to speak with you, and to be happy in your presence." In guarded language, Sachs tried to convince Paul of his desire to protect the school from the Nazis. "We want to place all of our strength in our work and not turn outside," he wrote.[9]

Although Geheeb had expressed negative sentiments to Sachs about the new school before his departure, he also extended his support to the Gemeinschaft der Odenwaldschule in its first years. In 1936 he wrote to Meyer, "You will believe me when I tell you that I follow the development of your school with great empathy and that your personal destiny will always have my warmest interest." Meyer responded to Geheeb by assuring him that in the Gemeinschaft der Odenwaldschule "the good and strong memory of its origins remains."[10]

Sachs and Meyer refrained from making public statements about their enthusiasm for the old Odenwaldschule. As the school expanded they had to hire new teachers, and occasionally teachers were simply sent to them from the Hessian Ministry of Culture. Some of these teachers were sympathetic to national socialism and found the spirit and structure of the Gemeinschaft der Odenwaldschule decidedly out of step with the times. One of these, Dr. Walter Mann, a French language teacher, wrote a letter to his superiors describing the school:

> A few weeks after beginning my work in January 1936 I had to let Herr Sachs know in response to his inquiries that I am convinced that there is still a great deal of individualism and Geheebian educational ideology present in the new Gemeinschaft der Odenwaldschule . . . The work in the Gemeinschaft der Odenwaldschule appeared to me to be too limp, soft and not masculine enough, and that also means not enough national socialism. That one said that they didn't want to talk about national socialism but to live it appeared to me unsatisfying . . .
>
> In close connection with this question stands the problem of punishment . . . While at first even the word "punishment" was anxiously avoided, Herr Sachs represented his standpoint with the slogan of "no formalism," meaning that every punishment must correspond to an individual action. In practice this means the rejection of a clear position and plodding on in the same old trot. The tendency of most of the colleagues to punish violations of existing rules was rejected by Herr Sachs as not creative enough. If a student in a quiet period slammed doors shut in spite of the rules, he would have thought it sensible to let the student practice shutting the door for a half-hour under supervision! Pure individualism! . . . In addition, I am convinced that the headmaster does not always state his views openly and clearly—an opinion I share with other *Mitarbeiter.*

Fortunately for Sachs, Mann's letter—which bordered on a denunciation—appeared to attract no official action, and Sachs was able to continue his work relatively untroubled.[11]

Daily work with Nazis such as Mann in the school led Sachs to pursue a cautious strategy in which he endeavored to protect its autonomy as much as possible without provoking the anger of the regime. When sufficiently provoked, however, Sachs deliberately refused to implement Nazi ordinances. In 1936 Bernhard Rust, the head of the Ministry of Education in Berlin, ordered the abolition of private elementary schools because they "contradict the spirit of the National Socialist *Volksgemeinschaft.*" In response, Sachs claimed that the elementary school in the Odenwaldschule should be exempted from Rust's decree because it provided a home for German children who came from troubled settings or who had parents who were working abroad. Sachs was able to persuade the central authorities of this, much to the astonishment of Dr. Hans Leip, the local supervisor of the school in the Hessian Ministry of Culture. Sachs also kept the Hitler Youth contingent in the Gemeinschaft der Odenwaldschule separate from that of the surrounding area so that the *Kameraden* were not pulled into the broader National Socialist movement. Dr. Leip, who had encouraged Geheeb to stay in Germany and who had impressed Max Cassirer, now quietly assisted Sachs in his efforts to sustain the principles of the old Odenwaldschule.[12]

As a result of the isolated setting of the Gemeinschaft der Odenwaldschule and Sachs' desire to protect it from larger social developments, the school was able to maintain a distance from the many political events transpiring in Germany in the first years of the Third Reich. "We really felt happy," enthused Viktor Dahm. "We were on a beautiful, wonderfully beautiful and secluded island." For Hedi Schlimmer, the *Mitarbeiterin* who led the League of German Girls, her years in the school were "the happiest time in my life."[13]

Not everyone was so enthusiastic. Dankwart Rüstow was appalled by the local manifestations of Nazi brutality:

> By far the worst of these were the days of "Crystal Night." Heppenheim also had an old synagogue, like most of the medium-sized cities in Hesse and southern Germany, and it was well known due to the activity of Martin Buber. What happened in that night— that uniformed SA men smashed the chandelier, destroyed the sacrament and set part of the house on fire with gasoline—all of that was discussed the next day, but (at least among my friends) only in whispers.
>
> And a surprising and strange result: one could see in the next days precisely where everyone stood politically by reading their facial reactions. Some of the worst Nazi rowdies among the *Kameraden* slapped each other on the fat of the thigh or on the *Lederhosen* as if to say "That's the way, keep on going." Less fanatical Nazis or half-Nazis laughed a bit self-consciously and shrugged their shoulders: "That's the way it is in the new Germany." Others simply pursued their daily work without looking to the right or left. And only a very few, such as my sister and I . . . and maybe a half dozen others, went about deeply disturbed, completely silent, with quiet and disgusted countenances.
>
> It was absolutely shocking to see how few shared our spontaneous human reactions. But on the other hand it brought for me as an almost fourteen-year-old an inestimable profit: from now on one knew exactly where everyone stood on the political spectrum, from whom one must protect oneself in these still terrible times and who the few were on whom one could completely rely.

Like Rüstow, *Mitarbeiter* Ingeborg Halm found it absolutely essential to know who to trust:

> We knew that we lived in a "pedagogical province" in an ideal and a political sense. We wanted—insofar as it was possible—to work in Geheeb's spirit. With this "we," however, not all *Mitarbeiter* were included. But between those of us who had this goal there was always a silent understanding.

Secrecy remained an unwritten law in the Gemeinschaft der Odenwaldschule, and it is difficult even today to reconstruct precisely which individuals belonged to the regime's opponents, and which were loyal enough to the Nazis that they would denounce a colleague.[14]

The Gemeinschaft der Odenwaldschule developed rapidly in terms of student enrollment. In part this was due to the recovery of the German middle class as the depression waned; in part it was due to the Nazi decision to close Martin Luserke's *Landerziehungsheim,* the "Schule am Meer," in the spring of 1934, which sent a host of students to Oberhambach. By 1939 ninety-three *Kameraden* were attending the Gemeinschaft der Odenwaldschule. To accommodate them, Sachs and Meyer rented from Max Cassirer not only Plato Haus and Pestalozzi Haus but also five other houses.[15]

While general student enrollments climbed in the 1930s, the participation of Jews appears to have been drastically reduced. During Geheeb's tenure Jews made up close to twenty percent of the student body, whereas from 1934 to 1943 only two percent of the *Kameraden* were Jewish, and most of these enrolled prior to 1937. According to Sachs's official count, from 1937 to 1942—the year of the final tabulation including race—only one Jew remained in the school.[16]

The decline in Jewish enrollment is thrown into relief by contrasting it with the partial continuity of coeducation. The boldest experiment in coeducation undertaken by the Geheebs concerned the innovation of boys and girls living in the same houses. This facet of the school was destroyed by Ringshausen's intervention in April 1933, when he demanded the end of coeducation in terms of cohabitation as one of the conditions for the continuation of the Odenwaldschule. In spite of this prohibition, coeducation in terms of common classroom instruction continued in the Gemeinschaft der Odenwaldschule throughout the Nazi era, regardless of repeated proclamations by the government that it intended eventually to make the school an institution for boys only.

In other domains coeducation suffered further restrictions. In the

Geheeb's Odenwaldschule, pedagogical families were always made up of both boys and girls; in the Gemeinschaft der Odenwaldschule many *Kameradschaften* were made up exclusively of one sex. The traditional hikes of the old Odenwaldschule had always included both sexes; in the new school, hikes were divided on the basis of sex. Eventually even the comprehensive pedagogical agenda aimed at both sexes was divided, and the Gemeinschaft der Odenwaldschule became a school for boys with only a home economic program for girls. By 1943 Sachs was so convinced that the coeducational aspect of the Odenwaldschule was about to be destroyed that he wrote to the directors of girls' boarding schools asking them if they had vacant spaces for his female students. His anxieties appeared to be misplaced, however, for the coeducational aspect of the school was never completely dismantled.[17]

Given the animosity of Nazi ideology to coeducation, its persistence in the Gemeinschaft der Odenwaldschule appears surprising. However, historians have noted that Nazi policy was remarkably lenient on coeducation, given the misogynistic shrillness of much Nazi rhetoric. Part of the explanation may lie in the practical difficulties of segregating schools, particularly when they were located in areas of low population density. Another part of the explanation might consider the importance of the Second World War in interrupting the belated Nazi attempt to institutionalize single-sex schools. Whatever the causes, coeducation appears to be one area in which the intensity of Nazi rhetoric was offset by a relative laxness in effort. In the example of the Odenwaldschule, although female enrollment dropped slightly in the Third Reich, the magnitude of the decline is so small as to be statistically insignificant.[18]

The opening of hostilities in the Second World War played a major role in hastening the regimentation and politicization of life in the Gemeinschaft der Odenwaldschule. According to a chronology kept by *Mitarbeiter* Joachim Boeckh, Werner Meyer began reading aloud to *Kameraden* from *Mein Kampf,* and leading "Sieg Heil!" chants before the student body. Dankwart Rüstow, who had greatly admired Meyer, was disillusioned:

> In the late 1930s Meyer's quotes worsened. He began to quote here and there from the "intellectual" Nazis or their precursors, like Alfred Rosenberg or Ernst Jünger. And once on a Nazi holiday he quoted a high Nazi before lunch for the first time (I believe it was Goebbels himself). Then I thought in great sorrow, "Now the good old Odenwaldschule has really been finished off."

The old course system in the school, one of the few practices left from the Geheebs' period, was the next casualty. Following new state ordinances in 1939, regular grade levels on the model of the traditional German public school now replaced the old flexible course schedule, and classes were broken up into smaller time periods. Grades were now assigned instead of the old written reports, rules were codified to regulate the relationships between boys and girls, lists of transgressions and punishments were drawn up and carried out. Only Rüstow and a handful of *Kameraden* from the days of the Geheebs' Odenwaldschule still remained in Oberhambach to witness the final destruction of the old schedule. "We eight or ten old ones who were still in the school then," he recalled, "spoke a lot about our 'freedom' that was stolen from us and often became very bitter." To add a more militaristic flavor to the school, plans were now drawn up to establish a shooting range where the nude "air baths" of the earlier Odenwaldschule had taken place.[19]

A new introductory brochure, written by Sachs in the fall of 1939, reflected the changes. Whereas the 1936 brochure had maintained a critical distance from the regime, the new brochure was saturated with the jargon and values of national socialism. Sachs dutifully praised all things German, from art to history to landscape, and made it a major principle of the school to transmit those "essential components which have shaped our *Volk* and will continue to shape it in the future." "We want to work in harmony with parents and national youth organizations [the Hitler Youth] to prepare the young people in our trust so that they will dedicate themselves with their entire bodies and souls to serve their *Volk*," Sachs wrote. "Leading and following is the premise of our community." Foreign students were welcome to the school, not to facilitate a real cross-cultural exchange, but so that they could learn about "German ways." Sachs accepted the Nazi distrust of intellectual learning: "It is self-evident that we must place a major emphasis on physical education." Finally, Sachs passed no comment on the destruction of the old course system. Instead, he simply noted that "Our elementary and secondary schools teach the same curriculum that has been approved for the public schools."

Even at this late date, Sachs still attempted to qualify certain aspects of Nazi ideology. He wrote, "the social integration of every individual into the community is the law that governs our lives," but instantly added, "our constant goal, however, is cooperation that is voluntary and that springs from the heart." The stress on physical education was offset by an altogether separate comment that "instruction and learning form the core of our work." Fully absent, however, was any hint of the old individualism or tolerance for others of different backgrounds. At least from the vantage point of its printed matter, the Gemeinschaft der Odenwaldschule was in complete accord with Nazi ideology.[20]

On 1 January 1940 Sachs officially joined the Nazi party. Meyer had already joined in 1938; shortly after the outbreak of the Second World War he was drafted and sent to the eastern front. It appeared that each man had been proved wrong in believing it would be possible to maintain a measure of independence from the regime in Nazi Germany.[21]

In the early 1940s, the Nazis began to obliterate the last shreds of autonomy in German private schools. On 11 August 1941 Max Cassirer was deprived of his German citizenship and all of his property in Oberhambach was confiscated by the regime. On 31 August 1941, the Gemeinschaft der Odenwaldschule and all previously private boarding schools in Germany were placed under the supervision of August Heissmeyer, an SS officer designated Inspector of German Boarding Schools. Heissmeyer visited all of the schools and began replacing their staffs with hand-picked, doctrinaire Nazis who were determined to synchronize the schools completely with Nazi educational ideology and practices. In this manner the *Landerziehungsheime* at Kirchberg, Birklehof, Schondorf, Neubeuern, Urspring, and Wickersdorf were nationalized and lost all independence from the state.[22]

Heissmeyer ordered Sachs to prepare the Gemeinschaft der Odenwaldschule for nationalization on 26 June 1943. As part of this preparation, Sachs was ordered to renovate Goethe House, which had been vacant since the Geheebs departed in 1934. Sachs delayed the renovation, fearing that its completion would seal the fate of the school, and claimed that technical difficulties made it difficult for him to carry out the work. He was subsequently informed that the deadline for nationalization was 1 September 1944. Once again, Sachs procrastinated, and then learned that the final date would fall on 1 April 1945. In the meantime, the campus was visited by commissions from the army, the Nazi party, and the Hessian government, all of whom hoped that they could find a way to gain control of the property. Deeply alarmed, Sachs appealed to Dr. Leip for assistance, claiming that the frequent visits were arousing the anxiety of the school's children, who were afraid that they were about to lose their *de facto* home.

In the meantime, Sachs had a host of other preoccupations. As the war wound on, and particularly as it entered its final phases after the Soviet victory at Stalingrad, the procurement of supplies was an exhausting challenge. Food was strictly rationed, and the *Kameraden* found themselves dedicating more and more of their time to working in the school's garden in an effort to grow as much of their own produce as possible. Coal also was rationed, and became increasingly scarce in the last winters. As the war drew to a close many of the male teachers and alumni of the Gemeinschaft der Odenwaldschule were killed in combat. These *Mitarbeiter* included Jockel Zahrt, who had been one of the Hessian teachers Ringshausen ordered to replace the old staff in 1933, and Walter Mann, who had taught in the school since 1936 and had condemned Sachs's individualism in his report to his superiors in 1938. Newsletters with the title *"Der Lindenstein"*—the name of the inn which was transformed into Goethe Haus after the Odenwaldschule was built—were sent to alumni and to soldiers at the front, informing them of casualties and providing information on the impending nationalization. By December 1944 all of the male teachers except Sachs had been drafted into the *Volkssturm*—the last-ditch militias composed of elderly males and young adolescents—and the older boys had left Oberhambach to assist with air weaponry units or the Reich Labor Service.[23]

From 1943 to 1945 the Allied bombing of Germany became increasingly intense. The night sky above the Hambacher Valley was often brightly illuminated as Darmstadt burned under Royal Air Force bombardment. Sachs was burdened with an "insane sense of responsibility" at this time. He organized the *Mitarbeiter* so that they made rounds in the small hours of the morning to make sure no lights were left burning when there were bombing raids and devised elaborate escape plans for students and teachers in the event of a German defeat.[24]

By early 1945 twelve female teachers and Sachs were the only adults in the Gemeinschaft der Odenwaldschule to care for eighty *Kameraden* under fifteen years old. For Marina Jakimow, "To preserve the spiritual and physical health of these children in the last months of the war had increasingly become the single task of the school." Most of these children had lost contact with their parents, who had preferred that the children remain in the relative security of the countryside rather than suffer the Allied air attacks on cities. Victorious American troops entered Oberhambach on 27 March 1945—four days before the projected nationalization of the Gemeinschaft der Odenwald-schule by the SS.[25]

chapter 12

Postwar Developments and Geheeb's Legacy

The Nazi government surrendered on 7 May 1945. In the following months it was unclear what would happen in the Odenwaldschule. In addition to the daily struggle to acquire sufficient food and materials to care for the children in the school, Sachs worried about how he would be judged by Paul Geheeb, his old friend and mentor. Although he believed that he had preserved the best spirit of the old Odenwaldschule under the most oppressive of conditions, he knew that he would be viewed with some suspicion because of the manner in which he had started the school in 1934 and his membership in the Nazi party. Sachs had been warned by the Gestapo to stop corresponding with the Geheebs after their expatriation in 1941, so they had heard nothing at all from him in the worst of the war years.

To rectify the situation, Sachs sent a long letter to Paulus in late July, which was lost in the mail. The first correspondence the Geheebs received from him came in the form of a postcard ten days later, signed by Sachs and his wife, Elisabeth. The Sachses wished the Geheebs well and requested an affidavit from them in which Erasmus would be empowered to serve as their executor in the school until further notice. He appeared ready to return the school to the Geheebs, and wrote, "I will be happy when the day comes that I can give everything back to you again, undamaged."[1]

For their part, the Geheebs were not at all sure as to how they should respond to the new situation. On the one hand, Sachs was a link to their own past in the school and his recent correspondence appeared to be a sincere expression of goodwill. On the other hand, they still harbored doubts about Sachs's motives in starting the Gemeinschaft der Odenwaldschule and leading it throughout the Third Reich, and they questioned whether he would be the appropriate person to reestablish its original democratic and humanistic spirit in the postwar period. Edith wrote a perplexed letter to her brother and sister-in-law in late August in which she agreed that "for the time being, Sachs is the person who should take care of things." Yet she also feared that Sachs, "in his sneaky way, will try to gain influence," and that "Sachs would shake us off if he could."[2]

Because Max Cassirer had bequeathed the school to Edith and her brother Kurt, the odds were against Sachs, but the situation in Germany was still so unstable that any number of things could happen. Hoping to secure the return of the school to the Geheebs and Cassirers, friends from across the Atlantic became involved. On 29 August 1945 émigré author Thomas Mann, Columbia University Dean Harry Carman, and Odenwaldschule alumna Truda Weil wrote a letter to the United States State Department requesting that leadership of the school be returned to the Geheebs.[3]

To his chagrin, Sachs did not receive any response from the Geheebs. In mid-September he wrote them an emotional letter pleading for support:

> Once again I try to reach you. It has been months now; I call into emptiness. Don't you hear me? Can't you come and do something? In these difficult years I have given many children a home, preserved a paradise, kept all of the barbarism which would destroy the soul and spirit of the innocents far away. Parents visit me from all sides and thank me that I dedicated our hearts to humanism, and that in spite of all of the compromises I *never*, not for one second, lost sight of the higher goal. I carried a massive load by myself, without a friend; even Elisabeth came to know nothing more about me and my inner secret and my oath: to protect this beloved piece of land, cost my life if it must. I turned to stone, inhuman behind my mask, suffering; this time was a scorching purgatory for me. The more I suffered, the more I had to say no, the more passionately, but also silently, did I dare to do what my conscience commanded. And I know what I say: I have repeatedly risked my life for good things—a shot in the back of the head or torture would have been certain for me.

In spite of Sachs's pleas, the Geheebs were not moved to intervene. They had been bitterly alienated from Germany during the Third Reich, and they were not certain that they wanted to contribute to its reconstruction. "I could not yet have any trust in the new Germany," Paulus reflected, "but rather found my former home to be a chaos in which cultural work in my sense would be impossible for many years."[4]

Kurt Cassirer then intervened with a proposal. Cassirer had worked at a Quaker school in Britain after emigrating from Germany and had met Minna Specht there. Specht was a feminist and socialist who had led the most left-wing boarding school in Germany, the Walkemühle, before emigrating with students to Denmark in 1933 and then to Britain in 1938. She had participated in the British-based committee on German Educational Reconstruction headed by Karl Mannheim and had written an essay, *Gesinnungswandel,* which outlined an approach for the democratic reeducation of German youth in the postwar period. Cassirer mailed the manuscript to the Geheebs and it won their wholehearted approval. The Geheebs then communicated to the occupying American authorities that they wanted Specht to take over the Odenwaldschule as soon as possible.[5]

Meanwhile, the Odenwaldschule remained relatively stable under Sachs's leadership. The major issue for the rest of 1945 was survival, and *Kameraden* and *Mitarbeiter* alike worked day after day planting, harvesting, or cleaning, depending on the immediate task at hand. In an abrupt intervention, Sachs had his school leadership taken away by the United States Office of Military Government for Hesse on 25 September, but received it again on 3 October. The school then experienced an autumn of stability and reconstruction, followed by the celebration of the first peaceful Christmas in six years.

From the perspective of Heinrich Sachs, the Odenwaldschule was now in better shape than it had been for ages. Although there were many material hardships, the school appeared to be slowly recovering its old identity, shorn of the threats to its autonomy which typified the Nazi years. Yet oddly enough, Sachs did little to actually restore the pre-Nazi structure of the school. No *Schulgemeinde* sessions were held to reconstitute community self-governance; the old course plan was not recreated; and the symbolic names, such as those given to the houses to deemphasize the school's affiliation with liberalism and Jews, did not change. Many students and teachers were too preoccupied with survival to care, but others found the lack of response a troubling indication that Sachs did not really understand the political ramifications of these pedagogical phenomena. Klaus Fuchs-Kittowski came to the Odenwaldschule in August 1945 from a family which had been active in the German resistance, and he was alarmed to find "that the situation was unchanged in regard to Nazism." While no major Nazi rituals transpired, nothing was being done to educate the students on the immorality of the Third Reich or to prepare them for the tasks of democratic citizenship.

Perhaps because of this situation, the United States Military Government intervened on 3 January 1946. The Sachs family was arrested along with most of the teachers from the old Gemeinschaft der Odenwaldschule. These *Mitarbeiter* were placed under house arrest in Unterhambach and forbidden to visit the school again. The United States Military Government was implementing a policy of "denazification" in the postwar era, in which individuals affiliated with the Nazi government were removed from their positions. Sachs had escaped this policy throughout 1945, but it appears that a denunciation finally made its way to the United States authorities and a thorough purging of the school ensued. A *Mitarbeiter* named Robert Killian—to whom Sachs had given a teaching position after the Nazis closed the Waldorf School in Stuttgart—took over the school leadership until Minna Specht's arrival in March.[6]

Following his removal Sachs began compiling a manuscript justifying his school leadership and defending himself against suspicions that he was sympathetic to national socialism. Calling upon the parents of students as well as upon former *Mitarbeiter* and friends, Sachs pulled together the testimony of Jews, communists, pacifists and other opponents and victims of the regime to support his case. From these documents emerged a hidden history of the Gemeinschaft der Odenwaldschule, which revealed a new dimension to the development of the school and Heinrich Sachs's personal integrity.

Several testimonies on Sachs's behalf came from people who had been persecuted by the Nazis for political reasons. Rudi Vogel, a member of the Communist party who was arrested in the first mass imprisonment of communists in March 1933, sent his children to the Gemeinschaft der Odenwaldschule because he wanted them to receive an education "with as little Nazi influence as possible." "I must say I never regretted this decision," he stated. His daughter Liselotte later remarked, "we had the impression that we were handled particularly gently, whereas I can't say that of the school where I was previously." Emil Fuchs, a prominent religious socialist, had sent two of his children, Gerhard and Christel, to the Odenwaldschule in the 1920s, and it was Gerhard who had challenged the Odenwaldschule to address the political crisis of the Weimar Republic at the school's twentieth anniversary festival. Both Fuchs and his son had taken part in the anti-Nazi resistance in the 1930s by surreptitiously transporting opponents of Nazism out of the country to safety—an act for which they were arrested and imprisoned. Fuchs affirmed that Sachs had been a splendid teacher for his children, and had taught them "true humanism and respect for all people." Sachs also received praise from Paul Geheeb's old friend Philipp Harth, who had been arrested once by the Gestapo for creating "decadent art" and attempted to avoid a second arrest for three months in the summer of 1944 by concealing himself in the Gemeinschaft der Odenwaldschule. Harth wrote that he

> was astonished to experience how Herr Sachs succeeded in spite of the terror to lead the school in a similar spirit as earlier. As long as I was in the school I never heard the Nazi greeting, from either a student or a teacher. I was often concerned and frightened for Herr Sachs because I myself had terrible experiences due to denunciations. I anticipated that he would be arrested on some occasion due to an oversight and an anti-Nazi remark.

Harth left the Gemeinschaft der Odenwaldschule when he heard that the authorities had discovered his presence in the school and that he was in danger of being arrested once again.

In the final years of the war, any sign of the slightest political opposition to the regime could be taken as grounds for incarceration or even execution. Yet in this perilous context, Sachs dared to accept Uta Maass—the daughter of a cleric and union activist who had been hanged for complicity in the 20 July 1944 assassination attempt against Hitler—into the Gemeinschaft der Odenwaldschule. As late as October 1944 he hired a *Mitarbeiter* who had been labeled "politically unreliable" by the regime. According to that teacher, "Sachs knew that I had conversations with numerous teachers and employees which brought up the struggle against Hitler." Yet Sachs never reprimanded him, and this failure to do so implicated him in the resistance: "Sachs consciously tolerated my antifascist agitation and let me act. If something were betrayed, we would have been lost."[7]

Sachs received favorable affidavits not only from political opponents of the Nazis. Unbeknown to many *Mitarbeiter* and *Kameraden*, Sachs had protected several students and *Mitarbeiter* with Jewish backgrounds. One such *Mitarbeiter*, Eduard Zuckmayer, was hired by Sachs after Martin Luserke's Schule am Meer was dissolved. Zuckmayer thanked Sachs for protecting him for close to two years "in spite of massive resistance and attacks from the side of the Nazis." Many parents also were grateful. One mother wrote,

> I, Lilli Feit . . . am of non-Aryan heritage, and my children are therefore of mixed background according to Nazi laws. This fact made it gradually more and more impossible for us to send our children to school in Aschersleben, where our background was known, if we wished to avoid dealing with being banned from classes, the denial of any further education, moral defamation and persecution, and worse.
> In this terrible crisis I turned at Easter 1939 to Herr Director Sachs,

who was recommended to me by a friend. I gave him a complete description of the circumstances and asked him to help me and to give my children asylum in the Odenwaldschule, and in this way to enable my children to continue to attend school. What I had hardly dared to hope for in light of the unpitying terror of the National Socialists happened. Herr Director Sachs took it upon himself to resist the prohibitions and terror of the Nazis. He took our three children into his school.

In the following period he made it possible, through his tireless personal commitment, for my children to enjoy an untroubled youth and an undisturbed unfolding of their personalities at ages which are so important, as well as an education which made it possible for all three to take their *Abitur* at the school . . .

Obviously it was only possible for Herr Sachs and the school to follow an exemplary path when his true convictions were shielded through the fulfillment of external demands which the Nazis imposed on all educators and schools. Thus, for example, I found it to be self-evident and unavoidable that Herr Director Sachs had to be a party member by title and that the Hitler Youth and the League of German Girls were allowed to keep up a facade . . . My children are thankful to Herr Director Sachs and the Odenwaldschule for their lives and their health; my husband and I for the maintenance of our family.

Another mother also testified on Sachs's behalf:

I am Jewish . . . My husband was an anti-fascist. In the course of the liquidation of Jewry all of my relatives, over fifty persons, were killed in concentration camps. In 1944 we were warned in time by friends that my husband would be brought to Buchenwald and we fled with my two daughters from Berlin. We found a place to stay in Oberhambach and hid there for five months until the liberation by American troops. Among the most "reliable" people our host told about our presence were Herr Sachs and his step-sister Maria Neumann. Everyone who experienced the Hitler regime knows what it means to shelter four people illegally. I know our host asked Herr Sachs for advice; I know that when certain "commissions" were coming to visit and in other times of danger he telephoned to warn us. In February 1945 our youngest daughter, who had been completely healthy until then, became gravely ill. It was impossible to call a doctor. Caring for our child, who was often screaming or unconcious, almost made us lose our wits . . . And also here, it was Herr Sachs, next to Maria Neumann, who made connections and gave advice, entirely in the background, helpfully assisting . . . Does one require any further proof for the inner conviction of these two people, for their courage and self-sacrifice in a situation of the gravest danger?

Michael Balaszeskul was a Jewish student who was in the school from 1939 to 1944. Sachs never reported Michael's racial background on the student enrollment forms that he was required to send to the regime. "Sachs protected us with the greatest personal risk," Balaszeskul later said. "I am convinced that some of my friends and I owe our lives to Herr Sachs." Michael's father concurred, and wrote to Sachs that "I will never forget this, and will always remember your way of acting as a rare and courageous human triumph." When all was accounted for, Sachs could claim that he had saved the lives of six Jews and sixteen children of mixed racial backgrounds.[8]

After Sachs and many of the staff were forbidden to return to the Odenwaldschule, Killian and the remaining *Mitarbeiter* struggled to keep the school functioning. In this crisis the staff sent out emergency telegrams which called upon alumni and old *Mitarbeiter* to return to the school to help rebuild it. This call was successful and several alumni returned.

Many of the most idealistic alumni who returned to Oberhambach were determined to root out the vestiges of Nazism in the Odenwaldschule. They assumed that Sachs had compromised the integrity of the old Odenwaldschule and sought to resurrect the progressive school community of the Geheebs' era. One of these alumni, Ewa Liesegang, wrote that "The inhabitants of the school struck us as unsuspecting angels. That the Nazi era ended three-quarters of a year previously didn't appear to have penetrated through to here." In January and February the school was polarized between the *Mitarbeiter,* who defended the accomplishments of the Gemeinschaft der Odenwaldschule, and the returning alumni, who wished to make a sharp break with the Nazi past. The alumni were eager to reestablish the democratic and humanistic principles which had originally motivated the Geheebs to found the Odenwaldschule.

The first major institutional transition in the postwar Odenwaldschule was a *Schulgemeinde* convened on 2 February 1946. To mark the transition out of Nazism, the returned alumni proposed that the school restore the original names to houses which had been retitled during the Nazi years. Liesegang described the atmosphere in the *Schulgemeinde* as the motion was introduced:

Dürer Haus again Humboldt Haus; Bach House again Cassirer House. It was said quietly and gently but the atmosphere was so tense, indeed so terribly strained that the silence itself could have ignited an explosion. The name of Humboldt was the catalyst. We struggled and screamed at one another. First it was just Humboldt, who was irrelevent for some and meant a great deal to others. We fought about Humboldt, about Humboldt's ideas, about freedom and about all of that which the Odenwaldschule meant to us. The others fought about Dürer and the work they had built up here.

We won a sad victory. They granted us Humboldt; we granted them Bach. We had forgotten that we didn't have equal opponents before us. They were already beaten, in Easter 1945, and in January 1946 through the expulsion of their colleagues and through the command of the Americans to take us in. We were left with a taste of bitterness.

Reflecting on the tensions from a later vantage point, Liesegang wrote, "I believe we were merciless, without consideration in our fanatic desire to wash away here all of the disgrace which hung on Germany." Marina Jakimow, from the other side, complained, "Oh, they couldn't see what we were—a small group of exhausted and apolitical people just trying to survive."[9]

At the same time that the Odenwaldschule underwent major transformations, the Sachs family endeavored to clarify its position with the Geheebs. Through friends who had visited the Geheebs in Switzerland, Heinrich and Elisabeth learned that the Geheebs were critical of their leadership of the Odenwaldschule during the Nazi years. Elisabeth Sachs wrote to Paul Geheeb,

> If we stayed in Germany and didn't go with you, and also not to the Quaker School in Holland or the German School in Italy, this wasn't, dear, dear Paulus, to betray you. You are said to have said this about us, and it has been made clear to us once more. We stayed here because this appeared to be our duty, not the easiest, but a hard duty. We believed that with our strengths we could accomplish the most here, in Germany, which we loved. We believed that it was up to each individual who stayed here to fight for the good in an endangered country. How terrible everything would develop was something we indeed did not guess.

Yet the Geheebs had abundant difficulties of their own to cope with at this time. They were compelled to leave the Chalet d'Aurore in the spring of 1946 so that the clientele which used the building in peacetime could once again have access to it. They finally found a new location for the Ecole d'Humanité in Goldern on the Hasliberg in the Bernese Oberland. While the community council of the Hasliberg rejected their application to settle in Goldern, cantonal authorities in Bern intervened so that the school could move to its new site on 25 May 1946. Once again, the Geheebs started their school in a new location, and organizing the transference of their work took up much of their time and energy that year.[10]

In this same time period, however, the Ecole d'Humanité received the international attention it had so badly needed during the war. On

6 May *Life* magazine printed an article on the school which began with a full-page photograph of Paul Geheeb holding Christian Keller, the son of a former German soldier, in his arms. Other photographs showed *Kameraden* convening in a *Schulgemeinde*, gathering wood, and serving dinner in the library of the Chalet d'Aurore. A short article described the Ecole d'Humanité as "an oasis in the desert of European education" and Geheeb as a "seventy-five year old German educator who salvages war-torn lives of children." The article ended with a plea for support: "More philosopher than businessman, Geheeb is now in danger of losing his school for lack of funds because the majority of the students are refugees from all over Europe who are unable to pay tuition." As a result of the article, Odenwaldschule alumni in the United States gathered $3000 to mail Geheeb to assist the Ecole d'Humanité.[11]

Paul Geheeb finally responded to the Sachses' urgent inquiries on 20 August 1946. To their dismay, Geheeb made it clear that he approved of the steps taken to remove Sachs from the school leadership. Whatever his personal achievements, Geheeb held Sachs at least partially responsible for the terror which had besieged Europe during the Third Reich, and no individual who was thus compromised could reconstruct the democratic foundation of the old Odenwaldschule. "My dear Erasmus," he wrote,

> At the end of June I received a warm letter from Hermann Maass, a priest in Heidelberg, who expressed the greatest concern for you. I was overworked and believed I could let the letter go unanswered because my wife had just written a friendly letter to your wife.
>
> I certainly wish that we could once more see each other and talk with each other again; we could then probably understand each other better than is possible through letters. I hope, dear Erasmus, that you know me well enough to never be disappointed in my position. I hope you will therefore understand that I am completely disgusted by the rumor that you are again in Unterhambach and are trying to force your way into the Odenwaldschule. Your action seems very egotistical to me and proves that you don't care to gain an overview on the entire situation. According to my convictions you can never again come in question for working in the Odenwaldschule. If you have ever loved my project properly, then you must also be capable of completely renouncing your part in it—in spite of your personal crisis and in spite of your efforts to maintain the educational institution that you led under the name of the "Odenwald-schule." Before you complain about injustices you should think about the uncounted millions who have been annihilated in the last twelve years through the brutalities of politics. I lay the greatest value upon the

development of the Odenwaldschule under Dr. Minna Specht's leadership for its unshakable and undisturbed progress.

With best wishes for you and your dear family I am,

Your old,
Paul Geheeb

Geheeb's critical letter expressed an anger felt by many émigrés toward their friends and colleagues who had remained in Germany in the Nazi years. From Geheeb's vantage point, the Allied victory over Germany had established the preconditions for a reconstructed, democratic Germany. By charging that Sachs did not "care to gain an overview on the entire situation," Geheeb made clear that he wanted a clean break with all of the compromises Sachs had made during the Nazi period. In light of the apocalyptic scope of the Nazi destruction, Geheeb felt, Sachs should have understood that the Odenwaldschule would have to begin anew as one part of the effort to reestablish a democratic Germany.[12]

Marina Jakimow visited Sachs in Stuttgart shortly after he received Geheeb's letter, and she found him haggard and depressed. Sachs had suffered from a heart condition and lung infections throughout the last years of the war, and it was only because of his physical frailty that he escaped military service. Since his departure from the Odenwaldschule he was broken in spirit. "Look at the letter Paulus sent me," he told Marina. He wept silently as she read it.

Sachs saw himself as very much a victim of the Third Reich and a person who risked his life repeatedly to protect those whose lives were threatened by the Nazis. Sachs and Geheeb never resolved their differences. Only two months after receiving Geheeb's letter, Sachs died, and his death exacerbated the rift between those who saw him as a martyred idealist and those who criticized him as an opportunist who exploited political change to take control of the Odenwaldschule.[13]

Sachs was not the only figure to attempt to seek a reconciliation with Geheeb. In 1947 Werner Meyer wrote Geheeb a letter for the first time in twelve years and sought to explain his role in founding the Gemeinschaft der Odenwaldschule:

> My decision in 1934 not to go to Switzerland or Holland but rather to attempt to continue the work in Oberhambach had the inevitable consequence that one had to make compromises with the inhuman development of world events. Until 1938 one could do this in a bearable fashion. We could, on the contrary, do many good things in our small Gemeinschaft der Odenwaldschule, especially with Jewish children and others who came to us to escape the public schools and for reasons of their spiritual development. But in the school year 1938–1939 the polit-

ically powerful got us more and more in their grip. In much of what we did we deceived ourselves. Sometimes it was truly nauseating for us. Only in the quiet, hidden areas was a genuine educational influence from one person to another possible . . .

Not all educators could emigrate or sacrifice themselves in the resistance. Perhaps it was a necessary service to keep our children alive and to take care that the sparks of the humane in their hearts were not fully extinguished.

Different interpretations of Sachs and Meyer persist to this day. Many Odenwaldschule alumni believe that Sachs and Meyer performed a valuable service for which they have not received sufficient acknowledgement. Dankwort Rüstow stated at the seventy-fifth anniversary of the Odenwaldschule in 1985 that Sachs had enabled him to receive an unpolitical education, and that in the Third Reich this was a courageous political act. There is no doubt that Sachs's work in protecting Jews easily could have led him to internment in a concentration camp and a death sentence. This aspect of his emotional letter to Geheeb was not exaggerated.[14]

Minna Specht arrived and became the new director of the Odenwaldschule in March 1946. Specht brought an entirely new spirit to the school. She had been a disciple and comrade of the Göttingen philosopher Leonard Nelson, who combined a strict interpretation of Kantian ethics with a Spartan commitment to militant socialism. By translating her political values into educational work, Specht had labored for years to inculcate young people with analytical precision and political insight. She hoped that the Odenwaldschule could serve as an experimental school in which the humanistic principles of the Geheebs' Odenwaldschule would be united with political education for Germany's working class. "For myself, as an old socialist and unionist," she wrote, "it is completely unthinkable that I would lead a school which is only open to children of the well-to-do."[15]

Specht also gave a new direction and meaning to the feminist legacy in the Odenwaldschule. Not only was Specht a powerful and charismatic woman herself, but she also hired many politically aware women as *Mitarbeiter* to reconstruct the Odenwaldschule. The result was that "the women governed and that the men played a peripheral role" for the first time in the history of the school. According to postwar *Mitarbeiter* Wolfgang Edelstein, Specht led a true revolution in the Odenwaldschule as she recruited many "people like Ernst Jouhy and people like myself: Jews and émigrés and resisters who had been fighting Germany, who had been fleeing Germany." According to

Edelstein and Jouhy, the remarkable feature of the postwar Odenwaldschule was the rapidity and the earnestness with which its members attempted to address Germany's recent past—a project rarely
undertaken in schools in the immediate postwar era. The students
also found that "a really new pedagogical and social and political spirit
emerged in the school." An exciting new phase had begun in the history of the Odenwaldschule.[16]

As the new Odenwaldschule stabilized under Specht's leadership, the
attempt to reassess the heritage left by the Geheebs and to appropriate its most vital and humanistic elements was catalyzed by the fortieth
anniversary of the school in 1950. A committee of *Mitarbeiter* formed
to plan a celebration of the anniversary and linked it with Paul
Geheeb's eightieth birthday in the same year. Geheeb was invited to
attend the festival and he agreed to return to Oberhambach for the
first time since his departure in 1934.

   Although there was much excitement about the upcoming festival
in the Odenwaldschule, Trude Emmerich, one of the most involved
Mitarbeiter planning the event, knew that many *Mitarbeiter* and *Kameraden* were afraid of polarization among groups at the anniversary. For
Emmerich, a "standard reunion" in which old friends swapped stories
without any serious consideration of the ramifications of the Nazi
epoch on their lives and the history of the Odenwaldschule was out
of the question. On the other hand, the planners also wanted to avoid
acrimonious reproaches between émigrés and those who stayed in
Germany during the Third Reich. Finally, there was concern about
how Geheeb would judge the reconstituted Odenwaldschule and the
different life paths taken by his students and colleagues.

   A series of opening addresses were given at the first convocation of
the festival on 26 July. Because Minna Specht was ill, *Mitarbeiter* Kurt
Zier, a returned émigré, welcomed the guests. Theodor Scharmann,
a former *Schulgemeinde* leader, articulated the latent political issues
confronting the assembly by pointing out that the Odenwaldschule
had passed through many different periods in its forty-year history.
In Scharmann's account, it was central to ask, "which Odenwaldschule
celebrates its fortieth anniversary today?" While preferring to leave
"final judgments" about "individual actions to a time which has more
distance," Scharmann called for an explicit "allegiance to that other
Germany, to the spirit of living humanity, to the ideals of a genuine
democracy and an open-minded and cosmopolitan citizenry." Former
Mitarbeiter Eva Cassirer followed Scharmann's address by asking for a
moment of silence for those who died in the Nazi era. Finally, Paul

Geheeb rose and asked for a special moment of commemoration for Max Cassirer in particular.

The following morning a *Schulgemeinde* of the current student body, alumni, and old teachers convened, "which had the greatest symbolic meaning for the whole meeting." The *Schulgemeinde* opened with numerous questions from *Kameraden* to alumni. Most of the questions concerned institutional arrangements and practices such as curricula and homework. Yet "no one asked about the principles, no one asked about the ideas which were the foundation of the old school."

After a pause, Paul Geheeb rose to bring in the points he felt required discussion. Emmerich described his concerns:

> For him, he said, there is only one essential question: does our school have to do with humanistic education (*Menschenbildung*) in Goethe's sense or with the development of a method to make a lot of money as quickly as possible? If we want the first, then there are certain logical consequences, as the great educator Georg Kerschensteiner taught us. But the most important thing is: do we want humanistic education? Do we want to educate our children in line with Pindar's saying: "Become who thou art!"?
>
> The discussion now penetrated to the essential and was led only by adults until the end of the *Schulgemeinde*. For many of us (for example, *Kameraden* of the old school) the saying "Become who thou art!" appeared too vague, and the question surfaced as to "How do I know who I am?" Don't people not only have a good side, but also a bad side which can develop in them? In the contemporary situation can we simply repeat phrases like that from Pindar or those from Goethe, Humboldt, etc., without interpreting them anew for our generation? Can we even understand today the questions which moved Goethe and Humboldt?
>
> The disgusted reaction from Paulus, "Is Goethe then dead in Germany today?" could not keep several from commenting that it was precisely in Goethe's homeland that the barbarism of national socialism originated and developed. Need one wonder that we and especially our youth are skeptical of the words and values of German idealism?
>
> A *Mitarbeiter* of the present school attempted to explain to Paulus and the alumni the concrete situation of today. "We have in common with you that we also don't think we will be 'completed people.' We are questioners and we want to educate our children to question and to search. The real difference with previous times is that you had common values, whereas we are in search of ours."[17]

For Geheeb's critics, his intervention in the *Schulgemeinde* revealed that he had indeed learned little, either from Gerhard Fuchs's criticisms of the old Odenwaldschule more than two decades earlier, or from the educational lessons to be derived from the Nazi years.

From their perspectives, the unreflected idealization of a Goethe, Humboldt, or Kerschensteiner in postwar Germany could not be ritualistically repeated in the wake of national socialism without trivializing the cataclysm of the Third Reich. They believed that German idealism provided little of value for the kinds of practical political issues that confronted their country in 1950. For these critics, it was time for a belated recovery of analytical sharpness and critical discourse. Neither Goethe nor Gcheeb should be idealized in this endeavor.

Just as Fuchs had done in 1930, the conference participants identified the Achilles' heel of Geheeb's approach to education. Geheeb constantly privileged aphorisms and episodic pedagogies which were more suggestive than systematic, and he rarely emphasized the importance of a rigorously intellectual approach to virtually any subject matter. The conference participants had tired of Geheeb's recitations of quotes from Pindar, Goethe or Kerschensteiner, and sought a more sustained kind of knowledge that would enable them to confront the tremendous political and economic problems facing postwar Germany. That Geheeb could urge them to return to his "heroes" with the same conviction that he did in the pre-Nazi era must have struck them as the height of pedagogical naiveté.

From Geheeb's perspective it must have seemed that his alumni failed to discriminate between the idealistic legacy he attempted to transmit in the Odenwaldschule and the perversion of idealism under national socialism. If he were a more argumentative personality, Geheeb might have responded by noting that Goethe's writings were filled with questions; he might have insisted that effective political education can only occur when children develop a firm sense of their own identities and convictions, and that such crucial psychological development can only occur in a setting in which children slowly learn to cultivate their own interests and talents. As it was, Geheeb maintained his silence, perhaps sensing that his own beliefs in the validity of idealism had been displaced by new historical imperatives.

Paul Geheeb enjoyed many tributes in the next few years. American officials in the Federal Republic of Germany invited him to give a series of public lectures throughout their zone of occupation, and Geheeb spoke to enthusiastic audiences in Frankfurt, Kassel, Darmstadt, and Wiesbaden in the summer of 1951. He was one of thirty-one candidates nominated in 1952 for the Nobel Peace Prize, which he failed to receive, and he was awarded a medal of honor the following year from the Federal Republic. On that occasion he was too frail to give a public address, but he characteristically and humbly quoted a dictum from Goethe, which he repeated twice: "What you are, you owe to others."

In 1955 Geheeb suffered a nearly fatal kidney infection and was subsequently compelled to pass almost all of the leadership of the Ecole on to Edith and two younger *Mitarbeiter*, Armin and Natalie Lüthi-Peterson, of Swiss and American backgrounds respectively. In 1959 A. S. Neill, the founder of Summerhill in Britain, brought his daughter Zoe to the Ecole. Zoe was unhappy at Summerhill and Neill hoped that the Ecole would be the kind of school she needed. Unfortunately, Zoe detested the Ecole even more than Summerhill, and she quickly returned to Britain after a series of altercations with the Ecole's students and teachers. She did, however, afford an opportunity for Geheeb and Neill to meet after corresponding with one another since the 1930s. On encountering Geheeb, Neill was thrilled: "I felt at once the amount of love he had to give out; I felt his warm humanity, his modesty, his selflessness. His influence on modern education must have been tremendous."[18]

Paul Geheeb had little energy to spare in his declining years, and devoted himself as best he could to maintaining his correspondence with his many friends and colleagues. He was delighted to receive a deluge of mail from admirers scattered around the world congratulating him on his ninetieth birthday in 1960. He grew progressively weaker in the following months and rarely ventured beyond the second floor of an old, ramshackle wooden house which he shared with *Kameraden* and *Mitarbeiter*. He died in the early morning on 1 May 1961.

Conclusion

The story of Paul Geheeb's leadership of the Odenwaldschule, the splintering of the school community into the Ecole d'Humanité and the Gemeinschaft der Odenwaldschule, and the postwar conflict between Geheeb and Sachs raises a plethora of questions about how we should interpret the clash between Nazi policies and the educational principles of the Odenwaldschule. It also raises a number of questions (and provides a few answers) that are currently debated by historians and educationalists. Recognizing that one case study necessarily involves limitations, one can nonetheless derive a number of insights from this particular history that enrich our understanding of both past conflicts and certain perennial pedagogical topics which possess a relevance for our approach to education and politics today.

The major issue left unresolved in the history of the Odenwaldschule in the Third Reich is the schism between Geheeb and Sachs. When I first began examining this breakdown in communication, the evidence appeared to indicate that Geheeb was a truly heroic émigré and Sachs more or less a collaborator who misused a regime change to advance his career. The more I delved into the past, however, the more I came to feel that such a picture was a simplification, and that while the two men were very different, they also had much more in common than was immediately evident.

To suggest that Geheeb was only heroic would certainly be a misrepresentation. In the first months after the Nazi seizure of power, Geheeb repeatedly made overtures to the Nazis suggesting that there were no outstanding reasons why the Odenwaldschule should not be able to thrive under the new regime. Geheeb flattered Goerendt, who had led two searches of the Odenwaldschule, brutalized Kurt Cassirer, and arrested Esra Steinitz; he identified himself with the crude anti-communism of the Nazis in his letters to Blank; he was ready to compromise with the Nazis on many minutiae of school reform even after they purged much of his faculty. Only after Blank's intervention on 20 July 1933 did Geheeb seriously undertake the depopulation of the Odenwaldschule, and this effort was combined with last-ditch attempts to reverse Blank's reforms, in which Geheeb allied himself with Adolf Messer-Bicker, a Nazi industrialist who took on a leadership role in the Parents' Advisory Council. Even after his emigration to Switzerland, Geheeb sought affadavits from the German government supporting his work at the Institut Monnier, and when the final break with Germany came, it was initiated by the Third Reich itself, not by Geheeb.

Heinrich Sachs accommodated Nazi school policies much more extensively than Geheeb. Sachs publicly endorsed Hitler and national socialism—a step Geheeb refused to take—and he tolerated far deeper restrictions in the school than Geheeb would have allowed. The racially determined membership in the Hitler Youth, the segregation of boys and girls not only for living but also for innocuous events such as hikes, and the destruction of the old flexible course plan in the school were all incidents which would have bridled Geheeb's conscience and compelled his protest. Perhaps because he was a more compliant individual, Sachs appears to have put up with these incursions with scarcely a murmur. Simultaneously, however, he undercut the regime by sheltering the children of Jews and dissidents, and he deliberately falsified records to conceal these children's presence in the Gemeinschaft der Odenwaldschule. These activities were so dangerous during the war years that Sachs indeed could have been executed by the regime. To this extent his opposition to Nazism was just as tenacious as that ever manifested by Geheeb, even though it found much more surreptitious expression.

If Geheeb and Sachs shared many points in common, however, it is also important to recognize their differences. Geheeb understood that there was a link between external political repression and the reforms that were being imposed on the Odenwaldschule. On the one hand, this achievement is little short of miraculous, given his mandarin-like fixation on the classics of German idealism and his baffling propensity for transforming all practical and political issues into rarefied philosophical ones. It was just this philosophical grounding, however, which enabled Geheeb to see what many more "realistic" individuals could not—that the Nazi regime was endeavoring to eradicate all individuality, autonomy, and difference under the suffocating grip of a specious *Volksgemeinschaft*. Max Cassirer, Heinrich Sachs, and Werner Meyer misinterpreted the far-reaching ambitions and the potency of

Nazi ideology, and found themselves slowly losing more and more autonomy until they were driven into exile, robbed of virtually all pedagogical independence, and drafted to serve in the German army on the eastern front respectively.

Geheeb's early recognition of the tyrannical nature of the Nazi regime enabled him to emigrate at an early date and to establish a school which became a haven for refugee children victimized by the Third Reich. Yet by emigrating early, Geheeb did more than transplant his work into a freer society. He also expressed his conviction, however obliquely, that he could no longer continue to work in Germany because of his problems with the new regime. Even the title of the new school, the "Ecole d'Humanité," made it clear that Geheeb was opposed to the idea that a school should be constituted with race or gender as an organizing principle. By contrast, Sachs's role in founding the new Gemeinschaft der Odenwaldschule indicated that a reconciliation between the old school and the new regime was indeed possible. However much Paul and Edith may have disavowed any hostility between the founders of the new school and themselves in the 1930s, it must have been impossible on a purely human level not to view the new initiative as a betrayal of their principles and their past.

Paulus's anger with Sachs only surfaced in 1946, a full dozen years after his emigration from Germany, at a time when Sachs was desperately in need of some support from his former mentor. Certainly, Geheeb's resentment was founded in an accurate reading of the situation. Given all of Sachs's compromises during the Third Reich, and given his puzzling sluggishness to reconstitute the democratic principles of the old Odenwaldschule after the Nazi defeat, he could hardly be the best director of the school in the postwar period. Minna Specht, on the other hand, embodied the best and most progressive principles of the *Landerziehungsheim* tradition, combined with a longstanding commitment to feminism and an uncompromised resistance to national socialism. The problematic aspect of the transition in school leadership did not reside in the fact that Sachs was summarily dismissed from his directorship. It was the manner in which Geheeb broke with his old admirer (a manner that presumed that Sachs had been a more active supporter of the Nazis than was in fact the case) and Sachs's subsequent untimely death, which prevented a later reconciliation between the two men, that combined to make Sachs a deeply tragic figure.

If one steps back from the interpersonal conflict between Geheeb and Sachs and turns to some of the recurrent themes in the history of the

Odenwaldschule in the Nazi years, a number of patterns of development which can cast some light on our understanding of this period in general become evident. One of the major areas of contention among historians of Nazi Germany for years has been the degree to which the Nazi state was totalitarian—which implies an exhaustive control, from the top down, of all sectors of civil society—or "polycratic"—that is, divided into rival loci of power and control which compete with one another and produce a social totality much more driven by internal conflict than by centralized state directives. In the history of the Odenwaldschule in the Nazi period, we have seen abundant evidence of the manner in which Nazi reforms were, if not totalitarian, at least "totalizing" in their mutually reinforcing propensity to saturate the school with the principles and structures typical of National Socialist organizations. Werner Goerendt's personal vendetta against Max Cassirer, Friedrich Ringshausen's curtailment of coeducation and faculty purge, and Rudolf Blank's destruction of the *Wartesystem* with the attendant threats of concentration camp internment directed against Geheeb catalyzed far-reaching transformations in the Odenwaldschule in the first year after the Nazi takeover. These included the segregation of girls from boys in housing; the introduction of the Hitler Youth and political indoctrination; the segregation of Jews and foreigners from sports activities designated for Aryans; and the introduction of militaristic themes in *Andachten*.[1]

After Geheeb's departure the statements of formal allegiance to national socialism made by Sachs and Meyer and the increasing accommodation of the Gemeinschaft der Odenwaldschule to Nazi ordinances reflect the further penetration of Nazi ideology and practices in the school. Houses with names like "Humboldt" and "Cassirer" were given new names with less problematic connotations ("Bach" and "Dürer"); the flexible course plan of Geheeb's Odenwaldschule was abolished and replaced with a schedule indistinguishable from that of a public school, and quotes from Nazis rather than humanists were read to the student body. In spite of the multiple challenges to Nazi reforms made by Geheeb and then by Sachs, the Nazis set in motion an externally driven dynamic which annihilated the cohesive subculture of the "pedagogical province," scattered its members, and manipulated the remaining enclave with ever-increasing ideological control backed by state terror.

Although the Nazi interventions were rapid and incisive in the period following the takeover, there were niches in the system which changed in light of ongoing historical developments. Internal conflicts between Nazis provided several openings for Paul Geheeb to gain greater flexibility in his relations with the government. At different periods, Geheeb found support from both Rudolf Blank and Hans Leip in attempting to circumvent Friedrich Ringshausen's reforms. Cleavages between the Hessian Ministry of Culture and the Reich Ministry of the Interior provided the vital passageway for Geheeb to emigrate and continue his pedagogical project in the Ecole d'Humanité. After Geheeb's exit, Sachs was able to deflect state mandates to abolish the elementary grades in the Odenwaldschule, and a near-denunciation by one of his faculty indicated that he continued to preserve much of the spirit of the old school, however much its structural character may have been compromised. When the school was threatened with dissolution and takeover by branches of the army, the Nazi party, or the local government, Hans Leip intervened on Sachs's behalf to prevent visits from these organizations to the school grounds. These maneuvers, combined with Sachs's tactics of stalling the renovation of Goethe Haus as part of an effort to delay the impending nationalization of the Odenwaldschule, succeeded in frustrating the designs of the SS to transform the school and to appropriate it for its own purposes.

Taken together, these kinds of factors validate "polycratic" interpretations of Nazism, and suggest openings in the regime that individuals could use to wrest a measure of autonomy from the system. These openings must not be romanticized; nor should they be conflated with the kinds of taken-for-granted liberties enjoyed by citizens in liberal and democratic societies. They do demonstrate, however, that undue emphasis on the "totalitarian" aspects of Nazism can prohibit us from understanding many developments in German society which derived more from internal conflicts than from systematic and centrally dictated reforms. Without an appreciation of these internal conflicts, it would be impossible to understand how it was that Geheeb was able to emigrate, how it was that he received approval from the regime for his work in Switzerland, and how Heinrich Sachs was able to prevent the nationalization of the Gemeinschaft der Odenwaldschule. In other words, we would be able to understand very little of the development of the Odenwaldschule in the Third Reich. The validity of contemporary "polycratic" interpretations of Nazism which emphasize internal schisms and disruptions within the regime is confirmed by the history of the Odenwaldschule.

Can one generalize from the history of the Odenwaldschule to other German schools during the Third Reich? Given the deliberately individualistic and innovative character of the Odenwaldschule during the Second Empire and Weimar Republic, any attempts to generalize from this particular history must be followed with caution. It would be a radical misinterpretation of my intent and findings to presume that the kinds of opposition which Geheeb and Sachs expressed to the Nazi regime could be projected to German educators at large. On the contrary, teachers appear to have been one of the Nazis' most enthusiastic constituencies. By May 1933, only about five percent of the German adult population had joined the Nazi party, but the membership of teachers was almost five times greater. Even at that early date, almost a quarter of all teachers belonged to Nazi paramilitary groups such as the storm troopers and the SS. Former teachers were fully fourteen percent of party functionaries, as compared to only six percent for other civil servants. "And, more ideologically motivated than perhaps any other single section of the population, they could be relied upon to provide solid and dependable backing for Nazi policies if and when necessary." Whatever exceptions there may have been, Ian Kershaw has commented, "the pro-Nazi sentiments of substantial sections of the teaching profession cannot be denied."[2]

Although the nonconformist spirit of Geheeb and Sachs was unusual, the character of their opposition fits into a common pattern of Nazi reforms and societal dissent. The combination of local storm trooper violence supplemented by the power and authority of the state affected not simply liberal schools like the Odenwaldschule, but the whole spectrum of the German Left:

> In early 1933 the Nazis' opponents faced apparently spontaneous attacks by marauding bands of storm troopers as well as the authority of the police, and the effectiveness of each was enhanced by the other: the storm troopers presented all the more a threat because behind them—somewhere—stood the State, and police repression was all the more effective because it was enhanced by the extra-legal threat of the SA.

In spite of Goerendt's personal vendetta against the Cassirer family, the Odenwaldschule fits into a double-barreled strategy of Nazi reforms, in which the spasmodic and deliberate use of violence, coupled with state ordinances, proved highly effective in intimidating and controlling the regime's opponents.[3]

A second example of the overall pattern of Nazi educational reforms implemented in the Odenwaldschule involved the systematic purging of Geheeb's faculty. In all strata of both public and private education, the Nazis intervened by either compelling school directors to fire or transfer opponents of the regime or by removing directors themselves from their posts. In the regime at large, the purge followed in the wake of Hitler's "Law for the Restoration of the Profes-

sional Civil Service." This edict was implemented on the same day—
7 April 1933—that Ringshausen visited the Odenwaldschule and
demanded that Geheeb remove his faculty as one condition for the
continuation of the Odenwaldschule. In all, some 3,000 teachers are
estimated to have lost their positions for political reasons during the
Gleichschaltung. Schools with social democratic, communist, or other
oppositional perspectives were particularly hard hit, and the boldest
of these—such as Minna Specht's Walkemühle, Fritz Karsen's Karl-
Marx-Schule, and Bernhard Uffrecht's Freie Schul- und Werkge-
meinschaft—were simply terminated.

The Odenwaldschule, however, did not belong to this radical wing
of the school reform movement, however much sympathy and admiration Geheeb may have had for its advocates. Recognizing the difference between the Odenwaldschule and the radical schools, the
Nazis sought to maintain Geheeb as its director while curtailing his
autonomy and purging his faculty. While this paradoxical policy of
preserving a prestigious reform educator as director of a school while
undercutting his overall project was not common, it also was not
unique to the Odenwaldschule. Hermann Nohl—whom Geheeb
hoped would head the German section of the NEF during the Weimar Republic—found himself in a similar situation at the University
of Göttingen. The strategy proved an effective way of preserving the
credibility of the regime vis-à-vis foreign opinion—an important Nazi
goal in 1933—while curtailing and controlling the activities of potential critics.[4]

In many other ways the Odenwaldschule experienced the increasing "Nazification" of everyday life typical of German schools in the
Third Reich. The introduction of the Hitler Youth, militaristic exercises, political indoctrination, the segregation of girls from boys and
Jews from Aryans—all of these reforms were part and parcel of a
broader national educational agenda of transforming German society from a differentiated and internally divided liberal democracy
into a monolithic and militaristic *Volksgemeinschaft.* The Nazi-imposed
reforms in the Odenwaldschule were probably more incisive and trau-
matic than elsewhere because the school had so many unusual features, such as coeducation, student self-government, and a flexible
course schedule. Yet the general dynamic of reforms dictated by the
state and accommodated by the schools describes the overall development of the Odenwaldschule in the Third Reich.

A final area in which the Odenwaldschule was representative of the
general process of Nazi school reform and educational response was
in its overwhelmingly *defensive* reaction. Both Paul Geheeb and Hein-

rich Sachs withstood spontaneous raids by storm troopers and racist and sexist state interventions which shattered much of the pedagogical integrity of the school. They both counteracted Nazi policies conscientiously and at great personal risk. Yet at no point did they venture into contact with the *political* resistance. In this attitude of defensiveness, which placed educational autonomy above all else, Geheeb and Sachs—however exemplary their conduct in the most difficult moments—found kinship with other German educators who resented Nazism subjectively but never translated their disillusionment into political practice. In settings as diverse as rural Catholic schools, urban reform pedagogical schools, as well as other *Landerziehungsheime*, the predominant character of pedagogical disenchantment with national socialism stemmed not so much from political objections to Nazi reforms but from professional grievances due to the loss of independence. The strength of this opposition (its unmediated, personal, and visceral character) was also its limitation—its failure to develop a strategy and organizational support for a specifically *political* resistance to the Nazi state.[5]

A recurrent topic of investigation for historians of modern German education concerns the possible affinities between German reform pedagogy and Nazi educational policies. The example of the Odenwaldschule suggests that the linkages between its reform pedagogical features and the Nazi incursions it suffered were so weak and improbable as to render the historical project of mapping out their affinities suspect. The principles of coeducation in Geheeb's Odenwaldschule were supplanted by sexual counterrevolution, the undifferentiated equality of *Kameraden* was replaced by ethnic divisions, the "air baths" of the old school were threatened with replacement by a shooting range in the Gemeinschaft der Odenwaldschule, the student self-government of the *Schulgemeinde* was terminated and replaced by faculty dictation of school policy. The few points of vague similarity—such as the reform pedagogical emphases on learning by doing and the Nazi criticism of intellectualism, or the reform pedagogical interest in student self-government and skewed Nazi interpretations of adolescent autonomy through the Hitler Youth—appear specious when one apprehends the humanistic context and intentions of reform educators such as Geheeb and contrasts them with the militaristic and fundamentally anti-democratic stance of Nazi doctrine. Examining the debate in light of the Odenwaldschule, it appears that historians have more fruitful projects and more problematic relationships to pursue than to search for points of identity between such mutually exclusive educational philosophies as pedagogy "from the child's point of view" and the Nazi educational *Weltanschauung*.

The Odenwaldschule, however, cannot be construed as a typical reform pedagogical school. Few German schools pursued such vigorous contact with foreign innovators in the progressive education movement. The very fact that the Odenwaldschule was a private boarding school makes it somewhat unusual in terms of the broader movement, which—outside of other *Landerziehungsheime*—occurred in day schools. More importantly, there were numerous conflicts between Geheeb and other reform educators within the *Landerziehungsheim* movement. Even before the Nazi seizure of power Geheeb experienced fierce altercations with Hermann Lietz and Gustav Wyneken. These differences did not involve marginal issues of school organization or curricular preferences but intense political and pedagogical differences. The problems were so extreme that Geheeb was compelled to surrender his leadership of both the *Landerziehungsheim* at Haubinda and the Free *Schulgemeinde* at Wickersdorf.

Geheeb's differences with other reform educators did not end with Lietz's death in 1919 and Wyneken's final banishment from Wickersdorf after a homosexual incident with two students in 1920. Geheeb could scarcely tolerate his relationship with the educators in the Association of *Landerziehungsheime* and Free *Schulgemeinde*. In the Weimar Republic, Geheeb was revolted by what he saw as their philistinism and preoccupation with economic prosperity. After the Nazi takeover, Geheeb warned Bernhard Uffrecht that not only would the Association provide no solidarity for him but that other members would positively gloat over his school's demise. Geheeb further made it clear that he expected that the Odenwaldschule, which he placed on "the extreme left-wing" of the Association, would receive the same lack of support.

The diametrically opposed reaction of the New Education Fellowship to Geheeb's appeals for help illuminates the break between German school reformers and their foreign colleagues. The NEF responded swiftly and effectively to Geheeb's appeals in the spring of 1933. From Geheeb's correspondence with Uffrecht, it is clear that the difference between the reactions of the two organizations cannot be explained away by observing the foreign status, and hence unendangered circumstances, of the NEF. If Geheeb was right in his suspicion that the directors of the other *Landerziehungsheime* would be gratified by the demise of the Odenwaldschule, then the NEF indeed represented a more liberal and progressive political and pedagogical outlook than the Association. From this vantage point, it would appear that German reform pedagogy had more authoritarian strains than its foreign analogues.

Is there then a German *Sonderweg*, or "special path," which made its school reformers peculiarly illiberal during the era when progressive education movements were blossoming in other countries? It is possible that the power and autonomous culture of the German youth movements were a singular phenomenon, although the rise of groups such as the Boy Scouts in Britain and the United States suggests similar developments in other western countries. In most respects the motifs of German reform educators belong squarely within the parameters of the romantic, anti-mechanistic, and child-centered pedagogies which arose and spread as part of a broad cultural reaction against industrialization and modernization in the eighteenth century. Modern progressive educators throughout Europe were indebted to Rousseau and Pestalozzi, two Swiss visionaries who had profound impacts not only on the spread of romanticism in France and England but also on the entire heritage of German idealism. Herder, Kant, Schiller, and Goethe were all enthralled with Rousseau's *Emile,* and we have seen the impact that Pestalozzi's work had on Fichte's *Addresses to the German Nation,* which so inspired Geheeb. Even if one follows Hermann Nohl in tracing the character of reform pedagogy back to the "German movement" of *Sturm und Drang* and romanticism, then, one should surely be aware that the "German movement" had deep roots within the continent at large.[6]

A second argument against a German *Sonderweg* in school reform has to do with the origins of the modern *Landerziehungsheim* movement. One errs in attributing too much attention to Hermann Lietz as the founder of the "new schools" in Germany. It was Cecil Reddie, a Briton, who was recognized by German directors of *Landerziehungsheime* as the "grandfather" of their schools when he toured them in the 1920s. And Reddie was hardly more enlightened or liberal than his German colleagues. On the contrary, Reddie's misogyny, his authoritarianism, and his adoration of Kaiser Wilhelm even during the height of the First World War all suggest that irrationalist currents were alive and well among school reformers outside of Germany.[7]

Many educators within the reform pedagogical movement evinced a striking opposition to national socialism. No other incident offers such striking evidence of those antifascist orientations as the diaspora of its liberal and radical wings after the Nazi seizure of power. Not only did Paul Geheeb carry his work into Switzerland and Minna Specht hers to Denmark and Wales, but many other reform educators transplanted their educational projects abroad. Anna Essinger abandoned her boarding school at Herrlingen and started a new one at Bunce Court in Britain; Kurt Hahn, prohibited from continuing his leadership of Schloss Salem, emigrated to Britain, where he started a new school at Gordonstoun and the now world-renowned Outward Bound program; Hans Weil, a former student of Paul Geheeb, moved to Recco, Italy, and began the "Schule am Mittelmeer"; Max Bondy, compelled to leave the school he had started at Marienau, subsequently began the Windsor Mountain School in Windsor, Vermont. In their new host countries these educators linked up with native advocates of progressive school reform, exchanged ideas, and assisted in the broader diffusion of innovative pedagogical practices.[8]

Within Germany, each of the remaining reform pedagogical boarding schools evolved its own response to the regime's incursions. Lietz's schools fully incorporated Nazi principles and practices into their pedagogy and curricula, offering a singular example of complete "self-coordination," or *Selbstgleichschaltung*, with the Nazi movement among the *Landerziehungsheime*. Wickersdorf suffered massive Nazi interventions as Thuringia became the first German state to elect a Nazi majority before the national takeover, and Gustav Wyneken responded with an opportunistic brochure in which he compiled selections from his writings to identify his pedagogical program with that of Nazism. Most of the schools adopted defensive postures and developed individual responses to Nazi reforms. From the point of view of ensuring institutional continuity, this strategy proved tenable up until 1939; with the outbreak of the Second World War, however, the increasing militarization and regimentation of German society wrought radical changes in all of the remaining schools. Heinrich Sachs's fears of massive Nazi interventions in the Gemeinschaft der Odenwaldschule were not phantoms; several independent boarding schools were nationalized, others experienced a complete turnover of faculty, and the independent spirit of all of the schools was severely curtailed.[9]

Given the current state of research, it would be premature to offer a definitive interpretation of the extent to which German reform educators may have been more "illiberal" than foreign colleagues in the progressive education movement. We lack comparative studies of the "new education" which analyze not only the theoretical proclamations of reformers in different countries but also the substance of their innovations and the form of their political engagement. When such research is undertaken, I anticipate that the results will be more complex and less susceptible to sweeping generalizations than one might expect. While there will be no denying that German reform educators were by and large more conservative than their American colleagues, for example, this conservatism will have to be approached more as a phenomenon to be explained than a fact to be condemned. We will have to find ways to understand how Leonard Nelson, a Jew and a socialist, deeply admired and borrowed heavily from the work of Hermann Lietz, an anti-Semite and a monarchist. We will have to challenge our stereotypes of "progressives" and "conservatives" to understand how it was that Peter Petersen, who led the Laboratory School at the University of Jena for all twelve years of the Third Reich, nonetheless incorporated into his work so many elements from the work of pacifists (Paul Geheeb), democratic socialists (John Dewey and William Heard Kilpatrick), and communists (Célestin Freinet). Only such differentiated analyses, which link and contrast German reformers among themselves and with foreign innovators, will move us beyond simplistic condemnations or celebrations of the "new education" in Germany.[10]

When Geheeb began the Odenwaldschule in 1910, the classics of German idealism still played a powerful role among the educated middle classes, and the ritualized idealization of figures like Goethe struck a highly responsive chord among *Kameraden* and *Mitarbeiter*. By 1950, when Geheeb returned to the Odenwaldschule for the first time in sixteen years, his desire to resurrect the idealistic legacy in the school appeared anachronistic to the alumni who had endured the trauma of national socialism. Much has been written in the postwar era to suggest similarities between the idealist heritage and Nazism in the domain of education. Geheeb's response to the Nazi reforms indicates, however, that the idealist legacy could provide a source of opposition to the regime.

On the one hand, many aspects of the Odenwaldschule from the pre-Nazi era suggest a negative model of citizenship education from the vantage point of today. Geheeb's "mandarin" posturing, his obsession with inner pedagogical reforms at the cost of outer-directed political vigilance, and his romantic celebration of individual differences to the detriment of serious intellectual analysis and critique remain the most negative components of his legacy. All of these deficiencies derive from his reading of the idealist tradition; not one of them shares any meaningful affinities with National Socialist education. On the other hand, Geheeb's role in humanizing student-teacher relationships, encouraging student autonomy and responsibility, and emphasizing multicultural awareness and even reverence remain among the most enduring and meritorious challenges for educators today. The complexity enters in when one considers that all of these discrete phenomena can be interpreted as legacies of German idealism, which remains a remarkably fecund and multifaceted intellectual tradition for all of its shortcomings. In the example of Geheeb, his stress on the principle of individuation impelled him to leave a Germany where massive conformity to Nazism militated against his strongest values, and his insistence on the autonomy of his "pedagogical province" made his accommodation to the Nazi interventions impossible. Geheeb's example demonstrates that whatever accusations one might wish to make against the idealist tradition should be levied judiciously, and that historical evenhandedness demands a balanced representation of both the upholders and the perverters of German idealism in the Nazi period.[11]

I stated above that it would be a mistake to view Paul Geheeb in a simplistic, hagiographic manner. We have seen that Geheeb was "human, all too human" on many occasions. Although talented in some areas, he was fundamentally incompetent in the early years of his career; he only thinly veiled his intention to benefit from his wife and father-in-law by accepting their financial support for the Odenwaldschule; he flattered the Nazis, even after they had physically abused two Jews in the school; he peremptorily dismissed Sachs's need for friendship and solace when his old friend was banished from the school to which he had dedicated a quarter-century of love and labor. Yet, even with all of these shortcomings, Geheeb offers an example of "humanized" heroism, the kind of heroism which persists in the face of overwhelming obstacles to uphold life-affirming and threatened principles, regardless of the cost. When Geheeb emigrated from Germany he left a home behind him which promised him complete security if only he would accept the Nazi reforms. For the next eleven years he lurched, once again, "from catastrophe to catastrophe," almost as if he were recapitulating the painful decade before the founding of the Odenwaldschule. The key difference, however, was that he was willing to accept this fate rather than accommodate the Nazis, and in the process he brought a new school, an "Ecole d'Humanité," into being, which created a haven for children who were escaping from the turmoil of the Second World War. By so doing, he gave a newer and far more profound meaning to the ideas and practice of progressive education he had expressed in peacetime, and left a permanent legacy of pedagogical integrity and civic courage.

Selected Bibliography

Archival Material

ARCHIVES OF THE GERMAN YOUTH MOVEMENT
Correspondence of Gustav Wyneken with
Walter Benjamin
Paul Geheeb

LEO BAECK INSTITUTE
Julie Braun-Vogelstein Collection
Correspondence between Lily and Otto Braun

BERLIN DOCUMENT CENTER
National Socialist Central Registry
National Socialist Culture Chamber
National Socialist Party Correspondence
National Socialist Teachers' Association
Non-biographic Collection
Supreme Party Court Records

ECOLE D'HUMANITE
Correspondence of Paul Geheeb with
Bernhard Adelung
Alfred Andreesen
Paul Baumann
Rudolf Blank
Albrecht Johann Calmberg
Christiane Calmberg
Kurt Cassirer
Max Cassirer
Minna Cauer

Adolphe Ferrière
Wilhelm Frick
Edith Geheeb
Karl Gleiser
Werner Goerendt
André Golay
Willem Gunning
Philipp Hardt
Elisabeth Huguenin
Marina Jakimow
Hermann Kobbé
Friedrich Kraft
Fritz Künkel
Hans Leip
Hermann Lietz
Werner Meyer
Ludwig Niessen
Peter Petersen
Romain Rolland
Heinrich Sachs
Alice Salomon
Heinrich Simon
Eduard Spranger
Bernhard Uffrecht
Martin Wagenschein
Correspondence of Edith Geheeb with
Eva Cassirer
Kurt Cassirer
Max Cassirer
Adolphe Ferrière
Marina Jakimow
Alwine von Keller
Elisabeth Sachs
Correspondence of Max Cassirer with
Reinhold Geheeb
Adolf Messer-Bicker
Werner Meyer
Ludwig Niessen
Transcripts of faculty meetings in the Odenwaldschule, June-December
1933

FOREIGN OFFICE ARCHIVES AT BONN
Political Archives

HESSIAN STATE ARCHIVES AT DARMSTADT
Department of State

INSTITUTE JEAN-JACQUES ROUSSEAU
Adolphe Ferrière Files

ODENWALDECHULE ARCHIVES
Correspondence of Paul Geheeb with
  Klaus Mann
  Thomas Mann
  Werner Meyer
  Martin Wagenschein
Correspondence of Edith Geheeb with
  Eva Cassirer
  Kurt Cassirer
Manuscript of Paul Geheeb interviewed by Walter Schäfer, December 1959
Protocol of *Schulgemeinde* meetings, 1910–1934
School records of correspondence with Hessian Ministry of Culture, 1934–1945

Primary and Secondary Sources Relating to Paul Geheeb and the History of the Odenwaldschule

Alexander, Thomas, and Beryl Parker. *The New Education in the German Republic.* New York: John Day, 1929.

Andreesen, Alfred. *Hermann Lietz: Der Schöpfer der Landerziehungsheime.* Munich: J. F. Lehmanns, 1934.

Becker, Gerold, Wolfgang Edelstein, and Walter Schäfer. *Probleme der Schule im gesellschaftlichen Wandel: Das Beispiel Odenwaldschule.* Frankfurt: Suhrkamp, 1971.

Cassirer, Eva, Ewa Liesegang, and Max Weber-Schäfer, eds. *Die Idee einer Schule im Spiegel der Zeit.* Heidelberg: Lambert Schneider, 1950.

Cassirer, Eva, Wolfgang Edelstein, and Walter Schäfer, eds. *Erziehung zur Humanität.* Heidelberg: Lambert Schneider, 1960.

Cassirer, Heiner. "Worte zur Einweihung des Paul-Geheeb-Hauses." *OSO-Hefte,* vol. 11, no. 2, May 1965, p. 86.

———*Seeds in the Winds of Change: Through Education and Communication.* Norfolk: Peter Francis, 1989.

Cleve, Christoph. "Die Geschichte der deutschen Landerziehungsheime während der Zeit des Nationalsozialismus—dargestellt am Beispiel der Hermann-Lietz-Schulen und der Odenwaldschule." Unpub. ms., 1984, OSO.

Diller, Edward. "With Paul Geheeb from the 'Odenwaldschule' to the 'Ecole d'Humanité.'" *The Journal of Educational Thought,* vol. 17, no. 1, April 1983, pp. 23–28.

Feidel-Merz, Hildegard, ed. *Schulen im Exil: Die verdrängte Pädagogik nach 1933.* Reinbek bei Hamburg: Rowohlt, 1983.

Ferrière, Adolphe. *Das Landerziehungsheim und die wissenschaftliche Zentralstelle für Landerziehungsheime.* Berlin-Fichtenau: Verlag Gesellschaft und Erziehung, 1920.

————*The Activity School.* New York: John Day, 1928.

————"A l'Ecole d'Humanité." *L'Essor,* 29 October 1937, p. 3.

————"Le Bureau International des Ecoles Nouvelles." In Kreis der Förderer der Odenwaldschule, eds. *Erziehung und Wirklichkeit. Festschrift zum 50 jährigen Bestehung der Odenwaldschule.* Braunschweig: Georg Westermann, 1960, pp. 65–70.

Fishman, Sterling. *The Struggle for German Youth: The Search for Educational Reform in Imperial Germany.* New York: Revisionist Press, 1976.

Fuchs, Emil. *Mein Leben.* 2 vols. Leipzig: Koehler & Amelang, 1959.

Geheeb, Paul. *Zur Abwehr! Akten und Erläuterungen zur Wickersdorfer Katastrophe.* Munich: Wühlthaler's Buch und Kunstdruckerei, 1909.

————"Entwurf des Planes einer privaten Lehr- und Erziehungsanstalt, deren Gründung im Odenwald bei Darmstadt beabsichtigt wird." Unpub. ms., 1909. Archives of the Odenwaldschule.

————"Die Zukunft des Landerziehungheimes." *Blätter für Volkskultur,* vol. 19, 1 October 1911, pp. 371–377.

————"Die Odenwaldschule." In *Heim-, Heil-, und Erholungsanstalten für Kinder in Deutschland.* Halle: Marhold, 1915, pp. 1–5.

————"Die Einrichtung der Andachten in der Odenwaldschule." *Der neue Waldkauz,* vol. 1, no. 4, May 1927, pp. 40–45.

————"IV. Weltkongress für Erneuerung der Erziehung." *Der neue Waldkauz,* vol. 1, no. 8, September 1927, pp. 89–104.

————"The Odenwaldschule—After Twenty Years." *The New Era,* vol. 11, no. 48, December 1930, pp. 187–190.

————"An Ovide Decroly." In Le comité organisateur de la Manifestation Decroly, eds., *Hommage au Dr. Decroly.* Saint Nicolas, Belgium: Scheerders-Van Kerchove, 1932, pp. 81–83.

————"Ansprache von Paul Geheeb an seine Mitarbeiter und Zöglinge anlässlich der Aufnahme seiner erzieherischen Arbeit in Versoix am 17. April 1934." *Schweizerische Erziehungsrundschau,* vol. 7, June 1934, pp. 69–70.

————"A School of Mankind." *The New Era,* vol. 17, no. 3, March 1936, pp. 76–78.

————"Ein Dank." *Neue Zürcher Zeitung,* 7 July 1946.

————*Briefe: Mensch und Idee in Selbstzeugnissen.* Ed. Walter Schäfer. Stuttgart: Klett, 1970.

Grunder, Friedrich. *Land-Erziehungsheime und Freie Schulgemeinden: Aus vieljährige Praxis in Deutschland, England, Frankreich und der Schweiz.* Leipzig: Klinkhardt, 1916.

Hamaker-Willink, Agaath. "Die gänzliche Verantwortung tragen." *Neue Sammlung,* vol. 25, no. 4, October-December 1985, pp. 521–562.

Helmer, Siegfried. "Martin Buber und die Odenwaldschule." *OSO-Hefte,* vol. 6, 1981, pp. 5–16.

Hierdies, Helmut. "Die Schulgemeinde in der Odenwaldschule unter Paul Geheeb." In Lenz Kriss-Rettenbeck and Max Lietke, eds., *Regionale Schulentwicklung im 19. und 20. Jahrhundert: Vergleichende Studien zur Schulge-*

schichte, *Jugendbewegung und Reformpädagogik im süddeutschen Sprachraum.* Bad Heilbrunn: Julius Klinkhardt, 1984, pp. 273–281.

Hohlfeld, Andreas. "Der politische Ort des Landerziehungsheimes und die völkische Bewegung." *Volk im Werden,* vol. 1, no. 1, 1933, pp. 40–44.

Huguenin, Elisabeth. *Die Odenwaldschule.* Weimar: Hermann Böhlau, 1926.

Kupffer, Heinrich. *Gustav Wyneken.* Stuttgart: Klett, 1970.

Kurzweil, Zwi Erich. "Die Odenwaldschule: 1910–1934." *Paedagogica Historica,* vol. 13, no. 1, 1973, pp. 23–56.

Kutzer, Elisabeth, ed. *Hermann Lietz: Zeugnisse seiner Zeitgenossen.* Stuttgart: Klett, 1968.

Lange, Thomas. "Der 'Steglitzer Schülermordprozess' 1928." In Thomas Koebner, Rolf-Peter Janz, and Frank Trommler, eds., *"Mit uns zieht die neue Zeit": Der Mythos Jugend.* Frankfurt: Suhrkamp, 1985, pp. 412–437.

Lennert, Rudolf. "Ursprung und Frühzeit der deutschen Landerziehungsheime." *Neue Sammlung,* vol. 8, no. 3, May–June 1968, pp. 247–259.

———"Neue Literatur zur Geschichte der Landerziehungsheime." *Neue Sammlung,* vol. 12, no. 2, March–April 1972, pp. 90–103.

Mann, Klaus. *Anja und Esther.* Berlin: Oesterheld, 1925.

———*Vor dem Leben.* Hamburg: Gebrüder Enoch, 1925.

———*Kind dieser Zeit.* Reinbek bei Hamburg: Rowohlt, 1982.

———"Portrait of a Pedagogue." *Tomorrow,* vol. 7, no. 1, September 1947, pp. 36–40.

———*Der Wendepunkt.* Munich: Nymphenburger, 1969. 2nd edition.

Meyer, Adolph E. *Modern European Educators and their Work.* New York: Prentice-Hall, 1934.

Müller-Holz, Henner. "Warten auf das Wartesystem?" *OSO-Hefte,* vol. 1, 1973–74, pp. 48–62.

Näf, Martin. "Paul Geheeb: Wesen und Entwicklung." Unpub. ms., n.d., EDH.

Nohl, Hermann. *Die pädagogische Bewegung in Deutschland und ihre Theorie.* Frankfurt: Vittorio Klostermann, 1988. 10th edition.

Nohl, Hermann, and Ludwig Pallat. *Handbuch der Pädagogik.* 5 vols. Langensalza: Beltz, 1930.

Noth, Ernst Erich. *Erinnerungen eines Deutschen.* Hamburg and Düsseldorf: Classen, 1971.

Ossietsky, Rosalinde von. "Einführung." In Bäbel Boldt et al., eds. ". . . aber von dir wird gesprochen." Oldenburg: Littman, 1981.

Petersen, Peter. *Die neueuropäische Erziehungsbewegung.* Weimar: Hermann Böhlaus, 1926.

———"Vorwort." In Adolphe Ferrière, *Die Schule der Selbsttätigkeit oder Tatschule.* Weimar: Hermann Böhlaus, 1928, p. 1.

Prellwitz, Gertrud. *Drude.* Oberhof im Thüringen Wald: Main-Verlag, 1920.

Reddie, Cecil. *Abbotsholme.* London: George Allen, 1900.

Röhrs, Hermann. *Die progressive Erziehungsbewegung.* Hannover: Schroedel, 1977.

————*Die Reformpädagogik: Ursprung und Verlauf in Europa.* Hannover: Schroedel, 1980.

————"Die Schulen der Reformpädagogik—Glieder einer kontinuierlichen internationalen Bewegung." In Röhrs, ed., *Die Schulen der Reformpädagogik heute.* Düsseldorf: Schwann, 1986, pp. 13–63.

Schäfer, Walter. *Die Odenwaldschule: Der Weg einer freien Schule, 1910–1960.* Oberhambach: Werkstatt der Odenwaldschule, 1960.

————"Edith Geheeb zum 5. August 1975." Ober Hambach: Werkstatt der Odcnwaldschule, 1975.

————*Paul Geheeb.* Stuttgart: Klett, n.d.

Scheibe, Wolfgang. *Die Reformpädagogische Bewegung, 1900–1932.* Weinheim and Basel: Beltz, 1973.

Schwarz, Karl, ed. *Bibliographie der deutschen Landerziehungsheime.* Stuttgart: Klett, 1970.

Seidelmann, Karl. "Wyneken und Geheeb: Historische Prominenz aus der Frühzeit der Landerziehungsheime." *Jahrbuch des Archivs der deutschen Jugendbewegung,* vol. 3, 1971, pp. 75–83.

Wagenschein, Martin. *Erinnerung für Morgen.* Weinheim and Basel: Beltz, 1985.

Secondary Sources on Education

Albisetti, James C. *Secondary School Reform in Imperial Germany.* Princeton: Princeton University Press, 1983.

————*Schooling German Girls and Women: Secondary and Higher Education in the Nineteenth Century.* Princeton: Princeton University Press, 1988.

Allen, Ann Taylor. "Spiritual Motherhood: German Feminists and the Kindergarten Movement, 1848–1911." *History of Education Quarterly,* vol. 22, no. 3, Fall 1982, pp. 319–339.

————"'Let Us Live with Our Children': Kindergarten Movements in Germany and the United States, 1840–1914." *History of Education Quarterly,* vol. 28, no. 1, Spring 1988, pp. 23–48.

Axhausen, Silke. *Erziehungswissenschaft und Bildungspolitik: Zur Kritik des pädagogischen Idealismus.* Meisenheim: Forum Academicum, 1980.

Bernfeld, Siegfried. "Die Schulgemeinde und ihre Funktion im Klassenkampf." In *Antiautoritäre Erziehung und Psychoanalyse,* vol. 3. Frankfurt: März, 1971, pp. 923–949.

Blackburn, Gilmer W. *Education in the Third Reich: A Study of Race and History in Nazi Textbooks.* Albany: State University of New York Press, 1985.

Bohrer, Reiner, and Birgit Renner. "Historisch-kritische Untersuchung der pädagogischen Konzeption und organisatorischen Struktur der Hermann Lietz-Schulen." Unpub. ms., 1982, OSO.

Dick, Lutz von. *Oppositionelles Lehrerverhalten, 1933–1945: Biographische Berichte über den aufrechten Gang von Lehrerinnen und Lehrern.* Weinheim and Munich: Juventa, 1988.

Eilers, Rolf. *Die nationalsozialistische Schulpolitik: Eine Studie zur Funktion der Erziehung im totalitären Staat.* Cologne and Opladen: Westdeutscher Verlag, 1963.

Feiten, Willi. *Der Nationalsozialistische Lehrerbund: Entwicklung und Organisation.* Weinheim and Basel: Beltz, 1981.

Flessau, Kurt-Ingo. *Schule der Diktatur: Lehrpläne und Schulbücher des Nationalsozialismus.* Munich: Ehrenwirth, 1977.

Flitner, Wilhelm. *Goethes Pädagogische Ideen.* Godesberg: Küpper, 1948.

——*Theorie des pädagogischen Weges und der Methode.* Weinheim: Beltz, 1950.

Flitner, Wilhelm and Gerhard Kudritzki, eds. *Die deutsche Reformpädagogik.* 2 vols. Düsseldorf and Munich: Küpper, 1961 and 1962.

Fuhr, Christoph, ed. *Zur Schulpolitik der Weimarer Republik.* Weinheim and Basel: Beltz, 1970.

Gallin, Alice. *Midwives to Nazism: University Professors in Weimar Germany.* Macon, Georgia: Mercer University Press, 1986.

Gamm, Hans-Joachim. *Führung und Verführung: Pädagogik und Nationalsozialismus.* Frankfurt and New York: Kampus, 1984.

Habermas, Jürgen. "The Intellectual and Social Background of the German University Crisis." *Minerva,* vol. 9, no. 3, July 1971, pp. 422–428.

Heinemann, Manfred, ed. *Erziehung und Schulung im Dritten Reich.* 2 vols. Stuttgart: Klett-Cotta, 1980.

Hermann, Ulrich, ed. *"Die Formung des Volksgenossen." Der "Erziehungsstaat" des Dritten Reiches.* Weinheim and Basel: Beltz, 1985.

Hermann, Ulrich, and Jürgen Oelkers, eds. *Pädagogik und Nationalsozialismus.* Weinheim and Basel: Beltz, 1989.

Hochmuth, Ursel and Hans-Peter de Lorent, eds. *Hamburg: Schule unterm Hakenkreuz.* Hamburg: Hamburger Lehrerzeitung, 1985.

Kanz, Heinrich, ed. *Der Nationalsozialismus als pädagogisches Problem: Deutsche Erziehungsgeschichte 1933–1945.* Frankfurt: Peter Lang, 1984.

Kassner, Peter, and Hans Scheuerl. "Peter Petersen, sein pädagogisches Denken und Handeln." *Zeitschrift für Pädagogik,* vol. 30, no. 5, October 1984, pp. 647–661.

Keim, Wolfgang. "Verfolgte Pädagogen und verdrängte Reformpädagogik." *Zeitschrift für Pädagogik,* vol. 32, no. 3, June 1986, pp. 345–360.

Keim, Wolfgang, ed. *Pädagogen und Pädagogik im Nationalsozialismus—Ein unerledigtes Problem der Erziehungswissenschaft.* Frankfurt, Bern, and New York: Peter Lang, 1988.

Klewitz, Marion. *Lehrersein im Dritten Reich: Analysen lebensgeschichtler Erzählungen zum beruflichen Selbstverständnis.* Weinheim and Munich: Juventa, 1987.

Kneller, George Frederick. *The Educational Philosophy of National Socialism.* New Haven: Yale University Press, 1941.

Köhler, Manfred. *Die Volksschule Harsum im Dritten Reich: Widerstand und Anpassung einer katholischen Dorfschule.* Hildesheim: August Lax, 1985.

Kunert, Hubertus. *Reformpädagogik und Faschismus.* Hannover: Schroedel, 1973.

Lassahn, Rudolf. "Das unerschlossene Erbe der Reformpädagogik." *Pädagogische Rundschau*, vol. 38, no. 3, May–June 1984, pp. 273–294.

Leschinsky, Achim. "Waldorfschulen im Nationalsozialismus." *Neue Sammlung*, vol. 23, no. 3, May–June 1983, pp. 255–283.

Lingelbach, Karl Christoph. *Erziehung und Erziehungstheorien im nationalsozialistischen Deutschland*. Weinheim: Beltz, 1969.

——"Unkritische Bildungshistorie als sozialwissenschaftlicher Fortschritt?" *Zeitschrift für Pädagogik*, vol. 34, no. 4, July 1988, pp. 519–534.

Mosse, George L. *The Crisis of German Ideology: Intellectual Origins of the Third Reich*. New York: Schocken, 1981. 2nd edition.

Müller, Gerhard. *Ernst Krieck und die nationalsozialistische Wissenschaftsreform: Motive und Tendenzen einer Wissenschaftslehre und Hochschulreform im Dritten Reich*. Weinheim and Basel: Beltz, 1978.

Nabel, Gunter. *Verwirklichung der Menschenrechte: Erziehungsziel und Lebensreform: Hans Maeder und die Stockbridge School in den USA*. Frankfurt: dipa, 1985.

Nielsen, Birgit S. *Erziehung zum Selbstvertrauen: Ein sozialistischer Schulversuch im dänischen Exil, 1933–1938*. Wuppertal: Peter Hammer, 1985.

Nixdorf, Delia and Gerd. "Politisierung und Neutralisierung der Schule in der NS-Zeit." In Hans Mommsen and Susanne Willems, eds., *Herrschaftsalltag im Dritten Reich: Studien und Texte*. Düsseldorf: Schwann, 1988, pp. 225–260.

Oelkers, Jürgen. *Reformpädagogik: Eine kritische Dogmengeschichte*. Weinheim and Munich: Juventa, 1989.

Olson, James M. "Radical Social Democracy and School Reform in Wilhelmian Germany." *History of Education Quarterly*, vol. 17, no. 1, Spring 1977, pp. 3–16.

Otto, Hans-Uwe, and Heinz Sünker. *Soziale Arbeit und Faschismus: Volkspflege und Pädagogik im Nationalsozialismus*. Bielefeld: Kritische Texte, 1986.

Paulsen, Friedrich. *Geschichte des Gelehrten Unterrichts*. 2 vols. Leipzig: Verlag von Veit & Co., 1897.

Ringer, Fritz. *The Decline of the German Mandarins: The German Academic Community, 1890–1933*. Cambridge: Harvard University Press, 1969.

Rödler, Klaus. *Vergessene Alternativschulen: Geschichte und Praxis der Hamburger Gemeinschaftsschulen, 1919–1933*. Weinheim and Munich: Juventa, 1987.

Salzmann, Christian, ed. *Die Sprache der Reformpädagogik als Problem ihrer Reaktualisierung: Dargestellt am Beispiel von Peter Petersen und Adolf Reichwein*. Heinsberg: Agentur Drieck, 1987.

Scholtz, Harald. *Erziehung und Unterricht unterm Hakenkreuz*. Göttingen: Vandenhoeck & Ruprecht, 1985.

——"Zum Stand der erziehungsgeschichtlichen Erforschung der Schule unter der NS-Herrschaft." *Zeitschrift für Pädagogik*, vol. 24, no. 6, December 1986, pp. 965–973.

Schonig, Bruno. *Irrationalismus als pädagogische Tradition*. Weinheim and Basel: Beltz, 1973.

Seidelmann, Karl. "Reformpädagogik—ins Zwielicht geraten." *Zeitschrift für Pädagogik*, vol. 20, no. 5, October 1974, pp. 783–788.

Specht, Minna. *Gesinnungswandel: Die Erziehung der deutschen Jugend nach dem Weltkrieg*. Welwyn Garden City, Herts, Eng.: Renaissance, 1943.

Tenorth, Heinz-Elmar. *Zur deutschen Bildungsgeschichte 1918–1945: Probleme, Analyse und politisch-pädagogische Perspektiven*. Cologne and Vienna: Böhlau, 1985.

———"Deutsche Erziehungswissenschaft 1930 bis 1945." *Zeitschrift für Pädagogik*, vol. 32, no. 3, June 1986, pp. 299–321.

———*Geschichte der Erziehung: Einführung in der Grundzüge ihrer neuzeitliche Entwicklung*. Weinheim and Munich: Juventa, 1988.

———"Erziehung und Erziehungswissenschaft von 1933–1945." *Zeitschrift für Pädagogik*, vol. 35, no. 2, 1989, pp. 261–280.

Ueberhorst, Horst. *Elite für die Diktatur: Die nationalsozialistische Erziehungsanstalten, 1933–1945*. Düsseldorf: Droste, 1969.

General Secondary Sources

Abraham, David. *The Collapse of the Weimar Republic: Political Economy and Crisis*. New York: Holmes and Meier, 1986. 2nd edition.

Allen, William Sheridan. *The Nazi Seizure of Power: The Experience of a Single German Town, 1922–1945*. New York: Franklin Watts, 1984. 2nd edition.

———"Farewell to Class Analysis in the Rise of Nazism: Comment." *Central European History*, vol. 17, no. 1, March 1984, pp. 54–62.

Arendt, Hannah. *Origins of Totalitarianism*. New York: Harcourt, Brace, Jovanovich, 1973. 2nd edition.

Arns, David E. "Grassroots Politics in the Weimar Republic: Longterm Structural Change and Electoral Behavior in Hessen-Darmstadt to 1930." Ph.D. diss., State University of New York at Buffalo, 1979.

Blackbourn, David, and Geoff Eley. *The Peculiarities of German History: Bourgeois Society and Politics in Nineteenth-Century Germany*. New York: Oxford University Press, 1984.

Bracher, Karl Dietrich. *The German Dictatorship*. New York: Praeger, 1970.

Bracher, Karl Dietrich, Wolfgang Sauer, and Gerhard Schulz. *Die nationalsozialistische Machtergreifung*. Cologne and Opladen: Westdeutscher, 1962.

Broszat, Martin. *The Hitler State: The Foundation and Development of the Internal Structure of the Third Reich*. London and New York: Longman, 1981.

Broszat, Martin, Elke Fröhlich, and Falk Wiesenmann, eds. *Bayern in der NS-Zeit*. 6 vols. Munich and Vienna: R. Oldenburg, 1977.

Bruford, W. H. *Culture and Society in Classical Weimar, 1775–1806*. London: Cambridge University Press, 1962.

———*The German Tradition of Self-Cultivation*. London: Cambridge University Press, 1975.

Caplan, Jane. *Government without Administration: State and Civil Service in Weimar and Nazi Germany*. New York: Oxford University Press, 1988.

Childers, Thomas. *The Nazi Voter: The Social Foundations of Fascism in Germany, 1919–1933.* Chapel Hill: University of North Carolina Press, 1984.

————"Who, Indeed, Did Vote for Hitler?" *Central European History,* vol. 17, no. 1, March 1984, pp. 45–53.

Craig, Gordon A. *Germany, 1866–1945.* New York: Oxford University Press, 1978.

Dahrendorf, Ralf. *Society and Democracy in Germany.* New York: Norton, 1967.

Diehl-Thiele, Peter. *Partei und Staat im Dritten Reich.* Munich: C. H. Beck, 1969.

Eley, Geoff. *Reshaping the German Right: Radical Nationalism and Political Change after Bismarck.* New Haven and London: Yale University Press, 1982.

————"Educating the Bourgeoisie: Students and the Culture of 'Illiberalism' in Imperial Germany." *History of Education Quarterly,* vol. 26, no. 2, Summer 1986, pp. 287–300.

————*From Unification to Nazism: Reinterpreting the German Past.* Boston: Allen and Unwin, 1986.

Evans, Richard J. *The Feminist Movement in Germany, 1894–1933.* London and Beverly Hills: Sage, 1976.

Evans, Richard J., ed. *Society and Politics in Wilhelmine Germany.* New York: Harper and Row, 1978.

————*Rethinking German History: Nineteenth-Century Germany and the Origins of the Third Reich.* London: Allen and Unwin, 1987.

Fichte, Johann Gottlieb. *Reden an die deutsche Nation.* Hamburg: Felix Meiner, 1978.

Franz, Eckhart G. "Vom Biedermeier in die Katastrophe des Feuersturms." In Friedrich Battenberg et al., eds., *Darmstadts Geschichte.* Darmstadt: Eduard Roether, 1980.

Frecot, Janos, Johann Friedrich Geist, and Diethart Krebs. *Fidus: Zur ästhetischen Praxis bürgerlichen Fluchtbewegungen.* Munich: Rogner and Bernhard, 1972.

Gillessen, Günther. *Auf verlorenem Posten: Die Frankfurter Zeitung im Dritten Reich.* Berlin: Siedler, 1986.

Goethe, Johann Wolfgang. *Wilhelm Meisters Wanderjahre.* Stuttgart: Reclam, 1982.

Gordon, Sarah. *Hitler, Germans and the "Jewish Question."* Princeton: Princeton University Press, 1984.

Hackett, Amy. "The Politics of Feminism in Wilhelmine Germany, 1890–1918." Ph.D. diss., Columbia University, 1976.

Hamilton, Richard F. *Who Voted for Hitler?* Princeton: Princeton University Press, 1982.

————"Braunschweig 1932: Further Evidence on the Support for National Socialism." *Central European History,* vol. 17, no. 1, March 1984, pp. 3–36.

Hennig, Eike, ed. *Hessen unterm Hakenkreuz: Studien zur Durchsetzung der NSDAP in Hessen.* Frankfurt: Insel, 1983.

Hirschfeld, Gerhard, and Lothar Kettenacker, eds. *Der "Führerstaat": Mythos und Realität*. Stuttgart: Klett-Cotta, 1981.

Hüttenberger, Peter. "Vorüberlegungen zum Widerstandsbegriff." In Jürgen Kocka, ed., *Theorien in der Praxis des Historikers*. Göttingen: Vandenhoeck & Ruprecht, 1977, pp. 117–137.

Iggers, Georg G. *The German Conception of History: The National Tradition of Historical Thought from Herder to the Present*. Middletown, Conn.: Wesleyan University Press, 1983. 2nd edition.

Jarausch, Konrad H. *Students, Society, and Politics in Imperial Germany: The Rise of Academic Illiberalism*. Princeton: Princeton University Press, 1982.

———"Illiberalism and Beyond: German History in Search of a Paradigm." *Journal of Modern History*, vol. 55, no. 2, June 1983, pp. 268–284.

———*The Unfree Professions: German Lawyers, Teachers, and Engineers, 1900–1950*. New York: Oxford University Press, 1990.

Jens, Walter. "The Classical Tradition in Germany: Grandeur and Decay." In E. J. Feuchtwanger, ed., *Upheaval and Continuity: A Century of German History*. London: Oswald Wolff, 1973.

Koshar, Rudy. *Social Life, Local Politics, and Nazism: Marburg, 1880–1935*. Chapel Hill: University of North Carolina, 1986.

———"From *Stammtisch* to Party: Nazi Joiners and the Contradictions of Grass Roots Fascism in Weimar Germany." *Journal of Modern History*, vol. 59, no. 1, March 1987, pp. 1–24.

Krieger, Leonard. *The German Idea of Freedom: History of a Political Tradition*. Boston: Beacon Press, 1957.

Laqueur, Walter. *Weimar: A Cultural History, 1918–1933*. New York: Putnam, 1974.

———*Young Germany: A History of the German Youth Movement*. New Brunswick, N J : Transaction, 1984.

Linz, Juan J. "Some Notes Toward a Comparative Study of Fascism in Sociological Historical Perspective." In Walter Laqueur, ed., *Fascism: A Reader's Guide*. Berkeley and Los Angeles: University of California Press, 1976, pp. 3–124.

Loewenberg, Peter. "The Psychohistorical Origins of the Nazi Youth Cohort." *American Historical Review*, vol. 76, no. 5, December 1971, pp. 1457–1502.

Maier, Charles S., Stanley Hoffmann, and Andrew Gould, eds. *The Rise of the Nazi Regime: Historical Reassessments*. Boulder and London: Westview, 1986.

Metzendorf, Wilhelm. *Geschichte und Geschicke der Heppenheimer Juden*. Lorsch: Laurissa, 1982.

Muthesius, Hans. *Alice Salomon: Die Begründerin des sozialen Frauenberufs in Deutschland*. Berlin and Cologne: Heymann, 1958.

Offen, Karen. "Liberty, Equality, and Justice for Women: The Theory and Practice of Feminism in Nineteenth-Century Europe." In Renate Bridenthal, Claudia Koonz, and Susan Stuard, eds., *Becoming Visible: Women in European History*. Boston: Houghton Mifflin, 1987, pp. 335–375.

Peukert, Detlev. *Inside Nazi Germany.* New Haven: Yale University Press, 1987.
Peukert, Detlev, and Jürgen Reulecke, eds. *Die Reihen fast geschlossen: Beiträge zur Geschichte des Alltags unterm Nationalsozialismus.* Wuppertal: Peter Hammer, 1981.
Pingel, Henner. *Das Jahr 1933: NSDAP Machtergreifung in Darmstadt und im Volkstaat Hessen.* Darmstadt: n.p., 1978.
Rebentisch, Dieter. "Der Gau Hessen-Nassau und die nationalsozialistische Reichsreform." *Nassauische Annalen,* vol. 87, 1978, pp. 129–162.
————"Nationalsozialistische Revolution, Parteiherrschaft und totaler Krieg in Hessen (1933–1945)." In Uwe Schultz, ed., *Die Geschichte Hessens.* Stuttgart: Konrad Theiss, 1983, pp. 232–248.
————"Persönlichkeitsprofil und Karriereverlauf der nationalsozialistischen Führungskader in Hessen, 1928–1945." *Hessisches Jahrbuch für Landesgeschichte,* vol. 33, 1983, pp. 293–332.
Sarah, Elizabeth, ed. *Reassessments of "First Wave" Feminism.* Oxford: Pergamon, 1982.
Schmädeke, Jürgen, and Peter Steinbach, eds. *Der Widerstand gegen den Nationalsozialismus: Die deutsche Gesellschaft und der Widerstand gegen Hitler.* Munich and Zurich: Piper, 1985.
Schneider, Ulrich, ed. *Hessen vor 50 Jahren: 1933.* Frankfurt: Röderberg, n.d.
Schoenbaum, David. *Hitler's Social Revolution: Class and Status in Nazi Germany, 1933–1939.* New York: W. W. Norton, 1980. 2nd edition.
Schön, Eberhart. *Die Entstehung des Nationalsozialismus in Hessen.* Meisenheim am Glan: Anton Hain, 1972.
Stephenson, Jill. *Women in Nazi Society.* New York: Harper and Row, 1975.
Stern, Fritz. *The Failure of Illiberalism.* London: George Allen and Unwin, 1972.
————*The Politics of Cultural Despair: A Study in the Rise of the Germanic Ideology.* Berkeley: University of California Press, 1974, 2nd edition.
Strzelwicz, Willy, Hans-Dietrich Raapke, and Wolfgang Schulenberg. *Bildung und gesellschaftliches Bewusstsein.* Stuttgart: Ferdinand Enke, 1966.
Veblen, Thorstein. *Imperial Germany and the Industrial Revolution.* Westport, Conn.: Greenwood Press, 1984.
Vondung, Klaus, ed. *Das Wilhelminische Bildungsbürgertum.* Göttingen: Vandenhoeck & Ruprecht, 1976.
Wehler, Hans-Ulrich. *Das Deutsche Kaiserreich, 1871–1918.* Göttingen: Vandenhoeck & Ruprecht, 1973.
Weinstein, Fred. *The Dynamics of Nazism: Leadership, Ideology and the Holocaust.* New York: Academic, 1980.
Weitzel, Kurt. "Nationalsozialistische Propaganda in Hessen am Ende der Weimarer Republik." *Archiv für hessische Geschichte und Altertumskunde,* vol. 43, 1985, pp. 351–376.

Notes

Introduction

1. The major published reference works on Paul Geheeb and the Oden-waldschule in German are Elisabeth Huguenin, *Die Odenwaldschule* (Wei-mar: Hermann Böhlaus, 1926); Eva Cassirer, Ewa Liesegang, and Max Weber-Schäfer, eds., *Die Idee einer Schule im Spiegel der Zeit* (Heidelberg: Lambert Schneider, 1950); Walter Schäfer, *Paul Geheeb: Mensch und Erzieher* (Stuttgart: Klett, n.d.); Walter Schäfer, *Die Odenwaldschule: Der Weg einer freien Schule, 1910–1960* (Oberhambach: Werkstatt der Oden-waldschule, 1960); Eva Cassirer, Wolfgang Edelstein, and Walter Schäfer, eds., *Erziehung zur Humanität* (Heidelberg: Lambert Schneider, 1960); Paul Geheeb, *Briefe: Mensch und Idee in Selbstzeugnissen,* ed. Walter Schäfer (Stuttgart: Klett, 1970). For English-language accounts, see Thomas Alexander and Beryl Parker, *The New Education in the German Republic* (New York: John Day, 1929), pp. 201–205; Adolph E. Meyer, *Modern European Educators and their Work* (New York: Prentice-Hall, 1934), pp. 139–159; Sterling Fishman, *The Struggle for German Youth* (New York: Revisionist Press, 1976), pp. 72–79; Edward Diller, "With Paul Geheeb from the 'Odenwaldschule' to the 'Ecole d'Humanité,'" *The Journal of Educational Thought,* vol. 17, no. 1, April 1983, pp. 23–28. For a listing of further references on Paul Geheeb and the Odenwaldschule, see the out-dated but still invaluable work by Karl Schwarz, *Bibliographie der deutschen Landerziehungsheime* (Stuttgart: Klett, 1970), pp. 19–33 and pp. 207–224. Detailed citations for the historical events described above are provided in Chapters 4 and 5.
2. The designation of two paradigmatic approaches here is deliberately schematic and intended primarily to offset the focus on popular responses to Nazi school reform. For examples of the first paradigm, see Rolf Eilers, *Die nationalsozialistische Schulpolitik* (Cologne and Opladen: Westdeutscher Verlag, 1963); Horst Ueberhorst, *Elite für die Diktatur* (Düsseldorf: Droste, 1969); Elke Nyssen, *Schule im Nationalsozialismus*

(Heidelberg: Quelle & Meyer, 1979); Kurt-Ingo Flessau, *Schule der Diktatur* (Munich: Ehrenwirth, 1977); Hubertus Steinhaus, *Hitlers Pädagogische Maximen* (Frankfurt: Peter Lang, 1981); Hans-Joachim Gamm, *Führung und Verführung* (Frankfurt and New York: Kampus, 1984); Heinrich Kanz, ed., *Der Nationalsozialismus als pädagogisches Problem* (Frankfurt: Peter Lang, 1984); Gilmer W. Blackburn, *Education in the Third Reich* (Albany: State University of New York Press, 1985); Harald Scholtz, *Erziehung und Unterricht unterm Hakenkreuz* (Göttingen: Vandenhoeck & Ruprecht, 1985); Kurt Flessau, Elke Nyssen, and Günther Pätzold, eds., *". . . und sie werden nicht mehr frei ihr ganzes Leben!"* (Cologne: Böhlau, 1987). This list and the lists in the four following notes could all be much longer.

3. See George Frederick Kneller, *The Educational Philosophy of National Socialism* (New Haven: Yale University Press, 1941); Fritz Stern, *The Politics of Cultural Despair* (Berkeley: University of California Press, 1974); Karl-Christoph Lingelbach, *Erziehung und Erziehungstheorien im nationalsozialistischen Deutschland* (Weinheim: Beltz, 1969); Fritz Ringer, *The Decline of the German Mandarins* (Cambridge: Harvard University Press, 1969); Hubertus Kunert, *Reformpädagogik und Faschismus* (Hannover: Schroedel, 1973); Bruno Schonig, *Irrationalismus als pädagogische Tradition* (Weinheim and Basel: Beltz, 1973); George Mosse, *The Crisis of German Ideology* (New York: Schocken, 1981), 2nd ed.; Heinrich Kupffer, *Der Faschismus und das Menschenbild der deutschen Pädagogik* (Frankfurt: Fischer, 1984); Alice Gallin, *Midwives to Nazism* (Macon, Georgia: Mercer University Press, 1986).

4. See Martin Broszat, Elke Fröhlich, and Falk Wiesenmann, eds., *Bayern in der NS-Zeit* (Munich and Vienna: R. Oldenburg Verlag, 1977), 6 vols.; Ian Kershaw, *Popular Opinion and Political Dissent in the Third Reich* (New York: Oxford University Press, 1983); Kershaw, *The Nazi Dictatorship* (Baltimore: Edward Arnold, 1985); Kershaw, *The Hitler Myth* (New York: Oxford University Press, 1987); Detlev Peukert and Jürgen Reulecke, eds., *Die Reihen fast geschlossen* (Wuppertal: Peter Hammer, 1981); Detlev Peukert, *Inside Nazi Germany* (New Haven: Yale University Press, 1982). Also valuable are Richard Bessel, ed., *Life in the Third Reich* (New York: Oxford University Press, 1987) and Jürgen Schmädeke and Peter Steinbach, eds., *Der Widerstand gegen den Nationalsozialismus* (Munich and Zurich: Piper, 1985).

5. There has been some debate about whether Nazism should be approached as an example of fascism—as I believe is appropriate—or as a unique historical phenomenon. See Kershaw, *Nazi Dictatorship*, pp. 18–41. For recent examples of educators' responses to Nazism, see Dieter Galinski, Ulrich Herbert, and Ulla Lachauer, eds., *Nazis und Nachbarn* (Reinbek bei Hamburg: Rowohlt, 1982); Klaus Van Eickels, *Das Collegium Augustianum Gaesdonck in der NS-Zeit, 1933–1942* (Cleve: Boss, 1982); Hermann Schnorbach, ed., *Lehrer und Schule unterm Hakenkreuz* (Königstein: Athenäum, 1983); Hildegard Feidel-Merz, ed., *Schulen im Exil*

(Reinbek bei Hamburg: Rowohlt, 1983); Arbeitsgruppe Pädagogisches Museum, ed., *Heil Hitler, Herr Lehrer* (Reinbek bei Hamburg: Rowohlt, 1983); Ulrich Herrmann, ed., *"Die Formung des Volksgenossen"* (Weinheim and Basel: Beltz, 1985); Ursel Hochmuth and Hans-Peter de Lorent, eds., *Hamburg: Schule unterm Hakenkreuz* (Hamburg: Hamburger Lehrer-zeitung, 1985); Manfred Köhler, *Die Volksschule Harsum im Dritten Reich* (Hildesheim: August Lax, 1985); Birgit S. Nielsen, *Erziehung zum Selbstvertrauen* (Wuppertal: Peter Hammer, 1985); Reece C. Kelly, "German Professoriate under Nazism: A Failure of Totalitarian Aspirations," *History of Education Quarterly*, vol. 25, no. 1, Fall 1985; Reiner Lehberger and Hans-Peter de Lorent, eds., *"Die Fahne Hoch,"* (Hamburg: Ergebnisse, 1986); Lucie Schachne, *Erziehung zum geistigen Widerstand* (Frankfurt: dipa, 1986); Wilhelm Damberg, *Der Kampf um die Schulen in Westfalen, 1933–1945* (Mainz: Matthias-Grünewald, 1986); Marion Klewitz, *Lehrersein im Dritten Reich* (Weinheim and Munich: Juventa, 1987); Lutz von Dick, *Oppositionelles Lehrerverhalten, 1933–1945* (Weinheim and Munich: Juventa, 1988); Wolfgang Keim, ed., *Pädagogen und Pädagogik im Nationalsozialismus* (Frankfurt: Peter Lang, 1988); Delia and Gerd Nixdorf, "Politisierung und Neutralisierung der Schule in der NS-Zeit," in Hans Mommsen and Susanne Willems, eds., *Herrschaftsalltag im Dritten Reich: Studien und Texte* (Dusseldorf: Schwann, 1988), pp. 225–260; Ulrich Herrmann and Jürgen Oelkers, eds., *Pädagogik und Nationalsozialismus* (Weinheim and Basel: Beltz, 1989); Marianne Doerfel, "Der Griff des NS-Regimes nach Elite-Schulen: Stätten Klassischer Bildungstradition zwischen Anpassung und Widerstand," *Vierteljahresheft für Zeitgeschichte*, vol. 37, no. 3, July 1989, pp. 401–456; Wolfgang Keim, ed., *Erziehungswissenschaft und Nationalsozialismus* (Marburg: Forum Wissenschaft, 1990); Konrad H. Jarausch, *The Unfree Professions: German Lawyers, Teachers, and Engineers, 1900–1950* (New York: Oxford University Press, 1990).

6. There is an extensive literature on German reform pedagogy. Critical accounts include Mosse, *Crisis of German Ideology;* Karl-Heinz Günther et al., *Geschichte der Erziehung* (Berlin: Volk und Wissen, 1966), pp. 563–577; Kunert, *Reformpädagogik und Faschismus;* Schonig, *Irrationalismus als pädagogische Tradition;* Silke Axhausen, *Erziehungswissenschaft und Bildungspolitik* (Meisenheim: Forum Academicum, 1980); Achim Leschinsky, "Waldorfschulen im Nationalsozialismus," *Neue Sammlung*, vol. 23, no. 3, May-June 1983, pp. 255–283; Heinz-Elmar Tenorth, *Zur deutschen Bildungsgeschichte, 1918–1945* (Cologne and Vienna: Böhlau, 1985) and *Geschichte der Erziehung* (Weinheim and Munich: Juventa, 1988), pp. 203–219; Jürgen Oelkers, *Reformpädagogik: Eine kritische Dogmengeschichte* (Weinheim and Munich: Juventa, 1989). Sympathetic interpretations are given by Alexander and Parker, *The New Education in the German Republic;* Meyer, *Modern European Educators*, pp. 81–159; Hermann Nohl, *Die pädagogische Bewegung in Deutschland und ihre Theorie* (Frankfurt: Vittorio Klostermann, 1988), 10th ed.; Wilhelm Flitner and Gerhard Kudritzki, eds., *Die deutsche Reformpädagogik* (Düsseldorf and Munich: Helmut Küp-

per, 1961 and 1962), 2 vols.; Wolfgang Scheibe, *Die Reformpädagogische Bewegung, 1900–1932* (Weinheim and Basel: Beltz, 1973); Karl Seidelmann, "Reformpädagogik—ins Zwielicht geraten," *Zeitschrift für Pädagogik,* vol. 20, no. 5, October 1974, pp. 783–788; Fishman, *The Struggle for German Youth;* Hermann Röhrs, *Die Reformpädagogik: Ursprung und Verlauf in Europa* (Hannover: Schroedel, 1980), pp. 298–333, and "Die Schulen der Reformpädagogik—Glieder einer kontinuierlichen internationalen Bewegung," in his anthology, *Die Schulen der Reformpädagogik heute* (Düsseldorf: Schwann, 1986), pp. 13–63; Feidel-Merz, *Schulen im Exil;* Christian Salzmann, ed., *Die Sprache der Reformpädagogik als Problem ihrer Reaktualisierung* (Heinsberg: Agentur Dieck, 1987); Klaus Rödler, *Vergessene Alternativschulen: Geschichte und Praxis der Hamburger Gemeinschaftsschulen* (Weinheim and Munich: Juventa, 1987); Hans-Peter de Lorent and Volker Ulrich, eds., *Der Traum von der freien Schule* (Hamburg: Ergebnisse, 1988); Hildegard Feidel-Merz and Jürgen P. Krause, *Der andere Hermann Lietz: Theo Zollmann und das Landwaisenheim Veckenstedt* (Frankfurt: dipa, 1990). Lawrence Cremin, the primary historian of American progressive education, made only a passing reference to the international character of the "new education" movement in *The Transformation of the School* (New York: Vintage, 1964) and *American Education: The Metropolitan Experience* (New York: Harper & Row, 1988). Patricia Albjerg Graham provided brief comments on the relationship between American and European "new educators" in her *Progressive Education: From Arcady to Academe,* but also noted that the relationship between them "has never been fully explored," an observation which remains true more than a quarter century later (New York: Teachers College Press, 1967), p. 183.

1. Paul Geheeb's Youth and Educational Apprenticeships, 1870–1909

1. Paul Geheeb to Albrecht Johann Calmberg, Geisa, 26 December 1878, Archives of the Ecole d'Humanité (henceforth EDH); Paul Geheeb to Christiane Calmberg, 3 August 1886, Fulda, EDH; Geheeb, *Briefe,* p. 33; see also an unpublished, untitled, undated, and invaluable scrapbook compiled by Anna Geheeb, EDH. Documents in the EDH are not numbered and are organized alphabetically by correspondent. All translations from the German throughout this book are my own.
2. Geheeb, *Briefe,* p. 117.
3. Geheeb, *Briefe,* p. 33; Paul Geheeb to Christiane Calmberg, 3 August 1886; Paul Geheeb to Adolphe Ferrière, Les Sapins, 16 August 1926, EDH.
4. Hermann Calmberg to Paul Geheeb, Fulda, 9 October 1887 and 8 March 1889, EDH; Paul Geheeb to Christiane Calmberg, Fulda, 3 August 1886, EDH; Anna Geheeb's scrapbook, p. 3.
5. Geheeb, *Briefe,* p. 34; Paul Geheeb to Friedrich Kraft, Geisa, 13 November 1890, EDH.
6. Paul Geheeb to the members of the Allgemeiner Deutscher Burschen-

bund, Berlin, 23 October 1890, EDH. For additional information on student organizations in this period, see Konrad H. Jarausch, *Students, Society, and Politics in Imperial Germany* (Princeton: Princeton University Press, 1982).

7. Paul Geheeb to Minna Cauer, Berlin, 9 November 1891, 15 November 1891, and 21 November 1891, EDH. Cauer's feminism is described in Else Lüders, *Minna Cauer: Leben und Werk* (Gotha: Leopold Kloss, 1925); Richard J. Evans, *The Feminist Movement in Germany, 1894–1933* (London and Beverly Hills: Sage, 1976); Amy Hackett, "The Politics of Feminism in Wilhelmine Germany, 1890–1918" (Columbia University: Ph.D. dissertation, 1976); Barbara Greven-Aschoff, *Die bürgerliche Frauenbewegung in Deutschland, 1894–1933* (Göttingen: Vandenhoeck & Ruprecht, 1981); Gabriele Braun-Schwarzstein, "Minna Cauer: Dilemma einer bürgerlichen Radikalen," *Feministische Studien*, vol. 3, no. 1, 1984, pp. 99–116. On Cauer and Geheeb, see Lüders, *Minna Cauer*, p. 77 and p. 106; Geheeb, *Briefe*, pp. 16–17.

8. On Geheeb's years in Berlin, see Eva Cassirer, "Paul Geheeb," in Cassirer et al., eds., *Die Idee einer Schule im Spiegel der Zeit* (Heidelberg: Lambert Schneider, 1950), pp. 1–7. The Ecole archives contain a copy of a letter from August Bebel to Geheeb, dated 12 December 1891, in which the Social Democratic leader explained to Geheeb why Christianity was irreconcilable with the Marxist interpretation of class struggle. (I was unable to locate the original, however.) Geheeb had earlier written Bebel a sixteen-page letter suggesting a synthesis of "applied Christianity" with socialism, apparently following the wishes of Moritz von Egidy. He refers to that letter in correspondence to Minna Cauer, Berlin, 11 December 1891, EDH. On Egidy, see Heinrich Driesman, ed., *M. von Egidy: Sein Leben und Wirken* (Dresden and Leipzig: G. Pierson's, 1900), 2 vols.

9. Paul Geheeb to Minna Cauer, Berlin, 27 February 1892, EDH.

10. Emmy Bélart, who was deaf, apparently suffered from paranoia. She was so afraid that others would talk about her that she forbade Anna to talk with her father at the dinner table. She also forbade Anna to visit the grave of her dead mother. See Anna Geheeb's scrapbook, pp. 26–27.

11. Transcribed interview of Paul Geheeb by Walter Schäfer, unpub. ms., Goldern, Switzerland, Winter 1959, Odenwaldschule Archives, p. 59. Henceforth, this manuscript shall be referred to as the Geheeb-Schäfer interview, and the archives as OSO. As with the EDH, documents at the OSO are generally organized alphabetically and are not numbered.

12. Johann Gottlieb Fichte, *Reden an die deutsche Nation* (Hamburg: Felix Meiner, 1978).

13. The use of only the male possessive is appropriate here, since Goethe's pedagogical province was populated only by males. See Johann Wolfgang Goethe, *Wilhelm Meisters Wanderjahre* (Stuttgart: Reclam, 1982), pp. 165–184. It should be noted in passing that the section on the pedagogical province is open to many different readings; I omit these here in the interests of brevity. Commentaries are provided by Wilhelm Flitner in

> *Goethes Pädagogische Ideen* (Godesberg: Küpper, 1948), pp. 185–234; Thomas Mann, "Geist und Wesen der deutschen Republik," in *Reden und Aufsätze* (Oldenburg: Fischer, 1965), pp. 53–60; Karl Otto Conrady, *Goethe: Leben und Werk* (Königstein: Athenäum, 1985), pp. 513–531.

14. Geheeb, *Briefe,* p. 34, and his "Die Odenwaldschule im Lichte der Erziehungsaufgaben der Gegenwart," in Cassirer et al., eds., *Erziehung zur Humanität* (Heidelberg: Lambert Schneider, 1960), pp. 132–138. The above presentation of *Bildung* is deliberately schematic. Valuable discussions of *Bildung* which explore its philosophical complexity and historical development can be found in two works by W. H. Bruford: *Culture and Society in Classical Weimar* (London: Cambridge University Press, 1962) and *The German Tradition of Self-Cultivation* (London: Cambridge University Press, 1975); essential German sources are Friedrich Paulsen, *Geschichte des Gelehrten Unterrichts* (Leipzig: Veit & Co., 1897), vol. 2, and Hans Weil, *Die Entstehung des deutschen Bildungsprinzips* (Bonn: Cohen, 1930). The routinization of *Bildung* in the nineteenth century was described by Friedrich Paulsen in "Bildung," in Wilhelm Rein, ed., *Encyklopädisches Handbuch der Pädagogik* (Langensalza: Hermann Beyer & Söhne, 1903), 2nd ed., vol. 1, pp. 658–670; by Ringer in *Mandarins;* by Walter Jens in "The Classical Tradition in Germany: Grandeur and Decay," in E. J. Feuchtwanger, ed., *Upheaval and Continuity: A Century of German History* (London: Oswald Wolff, 1973), pp. 67–82; and by Klaus Vondung in "Einleitung," in Vondung, ed., *Das Wilhelminische Bildungsbürgertum* (Göttingen: Vandenhoeck & Ruprecht, 1976).

15. See James C. Albisetti, *Secondary School Reform in Imperial Germany* (Princeton: Princeton University Press, 1983), pp. 16–56; Jürgen Herbst, *And Sadly Teach* (Madison: University of Wisconsin, 1989), pp. 32–56; David Landes, *The Unbound Prometheus* (New York: Cambridge University Press, 1969), pp. 342–348. As Herbst points out, the admiration of foreign observers for German schools may be taken with skepticism, for many of them were quite selective in their perception and were mostly interested in gathering fodder for their own efforts at school reforms in their home countries.

16. Ringer, *Mandarins;* James C. Albisetti, *Schooling German Girls and Women* (Princeton: Princeton University Press, 1988); Stern, *Cultural Despair,* which regrettably omits Nietzsche, the most important of the cultural critics; James M. Olson, "Radical Social Democracy and School Reform in Wilhelmian Germany," *History of Education Quarterly,* vol. 17, no. 1, Spring 1977, pp. 3–16.

17. Geheeb-Schäfer interview, p. 60.

18. The original German "Uebungsschule des pädagogischen Universitätsseminar" I translate as the "laboratory school," which captures its spirit more directly than a literal rendering would provide. No confusion with John Dewey's laboratory school at the University of Chicago is intended. See Hermann Lietz, "Was bedeuten Pädagogisches Universitäts-Seminar und Uebeungsschule in Jena für die Deutschen Land-Erziehungs-

Heime?" in Balthasar Hofmann, ed., *Das Lebenswerk Professor Doktor Wilhelm Reins* (Langensalza: Beyer & Mann, 1917), pp. 120–126.

19. See B. M. Ward, *Reddie of Abbotsholme* (London: George Allen & Unwin, 1934), pp. 323–324; Robert Skidelsky, *English Progressive Schools* (Middlesex, Eng.: Penguin, 1969), pp. 69–120; Jonathan Gathorne-Hardy, *The Public School Phenomenon* (London: Hodder & Stoughton, 1977), pp. 279–283; Friedrich Grunder, *Land-Erziehungsheime und Freie Schulgemeinden: Aus vieljährige Praxis in Deutschland, England, Frankreich und der Schweiz* (Leipzig: Klinkhardt, 1916), pp. 8–55.

20. Geheeb-Schäfer interview, p. 60.

21. Lietz's correspondence to Geheeb while Lietz was composing *Emlohstobba: Roman oder Wirklichkeit?* (Berlin: Ferdinand Dümmlers, 1897) is in the EDH. Unfortunately, Geheeb's correspondence to Lietz has been lost. It was probably destroyed in a fire in Schloss Bieberstein in 1908. Lietz's problematic autobiography, *Lebenserinnerungen* (Veckenstedt am Harz: Verlag des Land-Waisenheimes, 1922), regrettably suppresses any mention of Geheeb. On the numbers of students at the Lietz schools, see Theodor Lessing, "Eine deutsche Schulreform," in Elisabeth Kutzer, ed., *Hermann Lietz: Zeugnisse seiner Zeitgenossen* (Stuttgart: Klett, 1968), p. 102.

22. Cassirer, "Paul Geheeb," pp. 3–4; Geheeb-Schäfer interview, p. 41.

23. Paul Geheeb to Paul Baumann, Goldern, 29 September 1959, EDH; Geheeb, *Briefe*, pp. 35–39.

24. One alumnus of Abbotsholme during the First World War recalled Reddie's instruction at this time: "Teaching, what there was of it, was thrown completely to the winds, and instead we suffered tirades against the English, against women and against public schools. Only Germany was extolled, although at that very time German bullets were tearing old Abbotsholmians to death." Cited in Gathorne-Hardy, *The Public School Phenomenon*, p. 282.

25. Lietz and Geheeb publicized their differences. From Lietz's perspective, see the "Bericht über die Versammlung von Eltern von Schülern des D.L.E.H.'s Haubinda zu Berlin," a brochure recording an evening meeting of parents and school representatives in Berlin on 7 July 1906, Archiv der Deutschen Jugendbewegung (henceforth ADJ); from Geheeb's side, see his "Ein Brief an die Eltern einiger Kinder, die mir seither im D.L.E.H. Haubinda anvertraut waren," a forty-four–page account composed at the end of July in Munich, EDH. For Wyneken's recollections, see "Erinnerungen," pp. 103–104. Lessing described his confrontation with Lietz in "Gerichtstag über mich selbst," *Junge Mensch*, vol. 6, no. 10, October 1925, pp. 238–244. Secondary source accounts are in Alfred Andreesen's apologetic *Hermann Lietz: Der Schöpfer der Landerziehungsheime* (Munich: J. F. Lehmanns, 1934), p. 131, and in Mosse, *Crisis of German Ideology*, pp. 160–170. Mosse does not refer to either of the key primary sources produced by Lietz and Geheeb, and incorrectly states the exit of Wyneken and Geheeb as occurring in 1903 rather than in 1906. It

is worth noting that the issue of anti-Semitism, which is presented by Mosse as the dominating issue dividing Lietz and the liberal teachers, is not even mentioned by Geheeb in his published reproach to Lietz. This is not to deny Lietz's anti-Semitism; it is to suggest that his anti-Semitism was only one of many factors which provoked the secession of Geheeb and Wyneken from Haubinda. For a defense of Lietz, see Kutzer's "Anmerkungen," in *Hermann Lietz*, pp. 136–138.

26. Geheeb, "Ein Brief an die Eltern einiger Kinder," pp. 30–32.

27. Ibid. Although Wyneken later claimed that he founded Wickersdorf, it was Geheeb who carried out all of the official transactions which started the new school. See Geheeb's reproduction of correspondence with the Thuringian Ministry of Culture in Meiningen in Geheeb, *Zur Abwehr! Akten und Erläuterungen zur Wickersdorfer Katastrophe (zugleich ein Beitrag zur Geschichte des Idealismus)* (Munich: Wühlthaler's, 1909), pp. 4–5.

28. The concept of the *Schulgemeinde* at Wickersdorf was taken from the Swiss *Landesgemeinden,* or local assemblies, in which citizens deliberated on issues of common concern. See Helmut Hierdies, "Die 'Schulgemeinde' in der Odenwaldschule unter Paul Geheeb," in Lenz Kriss-Rettenbeck and Max Lietke, eds., *Regionale Schulentwicklung im 19. und 20. Jahrhundert: Vergleichende Studien zur Schulgeschichte, Jugendbewegung und Reformpädagogik im süddeutschen Sprachraum* (Bad Heilbrunn: Julius Klinkhardt, 1984), pp. 273–281. For the general principles of the new school, see Paul Geheeb and Gustav Wyneken, "Programm der Freien Schul-Gemeinde Wickersdorf," June 1907, OSO.

29. Coeducation was not on the feminist agenda in the 1890s when Geheeb was working with Minna Cauer, but it had won several advocates by the early 1900s, including Helene Lange, Helene Stöcker, Hedwig Dohm, Klara Zetkin, Marianne Weber, and Lily Braun. It is possible that Geheeb's interest in coeducation may have been stimulated by Wilhelm Rein, who preceded many feminists in advocating coeducation. See Albisetti, *Schooling German Girls and Women*, pp. 172–173, and his unpub. ms., "The Debate over Secondary Coeducation in Imperial Germany," paper presented at the History of Education Society annual meeting, 1985, pp. 3–4. On Lily and Otto Braun see Julie Braun-Vogelstein, ed., "Einleitung," *Fragment der Zukunft* (Stuttgart: Deutsche Verlags-Anstalt, 1969), p. 13; Lily Braun, *Memoiren einer Sozialistin* (Berlin-Grunewald: Hermann Klemm, n.d.), pp. 500–503; correspondence between Otto and Lily Braun, Julie Braun-Vogelstein Collection, Box 3, Folder 1, Leo Baeck Institute, New York. On feminist interest in Wickersdorf see Clara Zetkin, *Revolutionäre Bildungspolitik und Marxistische Pädagogik* (Berlin: Volk und Wissen, 1983), p. 238; Lily Braun, "Children's Liberation," in Alfred G. Meyer, ed., *Selected Writings on Feminism and Socialism: Lily Braun* (Bloomington: Indiana University Press, 1987), pp. 218–232, especially pp. 229–230; Hedwig Dohm, "Das männliche Geschlecht muss die Gleichwertigkeit der Frau erfahren," in Elke Frederiksen, ed., *Die Frauenfrage in Deutschland, 1865–1915* (Stuttgart: Reclam, 1981), pp. 170–

173, and "Einheitsschule und Koedukation," in Frederiksen, *Frauenfrage,*
pp. 232–239. Zetkin and Braun did not mention Wickersdorf by name;
however, it is clear from the context that they are both referring to the
new school.

30. Gustav Wyneken, *Zweiter Jahresbericht der Freien Schulgemeinde Wickersdorf*
(Jena: Eugen Diederichs, 1910), p. 4.

31. The Wyneken-Nachlass at ADJ contains numerous primary documents
regarding the conflict between Wyneken and Geheeb. See Geheeb's *Zur
Abwehr!* and Wyneken's response, *Die "Katastrophe" des Herrn Geheeb* (Jena:
Anton Kämpfe, 1909). For secondary source interpretations of the conflict, see Heinrich Kupffer, *Gustav Wyneken* (Stuttgart: Klett, 1970),
pp. 55–59, and Karl Seidelmann, "Wyneken und Geheeb: Historische
Prominenz aus der Frühzeit der Landerziehungsheime," in the *Jahrbuch
des Archivs der deutschen Jugendbewegung,* vol. 3, 1971, pp. 75–83. On the
German youth movement, see Walter Laqueur, *Young Germany,* 2nd ed.
(1962; rpt. New Brunswick, N.J.: Transaction, 1984).

32. Paul Geheeb quoted by Edith Geheeb, "Aus meinem Leben," in Armin
Lüthi and Margot Schiller, eds., *Edith Geheeb-Cassirer: Zum 90. Geburtstag*
(Meiringen: Brügger, 1975), p. 16.

33. On the Pestalozzi-Froebel Haus, see three essays by Ann Taylor Allen:
"Spiritual Motherhood: German Feminists and the Kindergarten Move-
ment, 1848–1911," *History of Education Quarterly,* vol. 22, no. 3, Fall 1982,
pp. 319–339; "'Let Us Live with Our Children': Kindergarten Movements in Germany and the United States, 1840–1914," *History of Educa-
tion Quarterly,* vol. 28, no. 1, Spring 1988, pp. 23–48; and "The City as
Household: Henriette Schrader-Breymann and the Pestalozzi-Froebel
Haus," *Central European History,* vol. 10, no. 10, 1988. On Anna von
Gierke, see Marie Baum, *Anna von Gierke: Ein Lebensbild* (Weinheim and
Berlin: Beltz, 1954); on Alice Salomon, see Hans Muthesius, *Alice Salo-
mon: Die Begründerin des sozialen Frauenberufs in Deutschland* (Berlin and
Cologne: Heymann, 1958).

34. Edith Geheeb, "Aus meinem Leben," pp. 10–11.

35. Alice Salomon to Paul Geheeb, Berlin, 29 February 1908, EDH.

36. Edith Geheeb, "Aus meinem Leben," pp. 12–15. Quotations from the
conversation between Paul Geheeb and Alice Salomon are given as cited
by Edith Geheeb.

37. Ibid., pp. 10–12.

38. On coeducation in "new schools," see Ward, *Reddie of Abbotsholme,* pp. 71–
74, and the Geheeb-Schäfer interview, p. 25.

39. Geheeb-Schäfer interview, pp. 5–7.

40. Geheeb-Schäfer interview, pp. 4–7; Philipp Harth, "Besuch von Paul
Geheeb 1958," in Cassirer et al., *Erziehung zur Humanität,* pp. 38–42;
Peter Petersen, "Vorwort," in Elisabeth Huguenin, *Die Odenwaldschule*
(Weimar: Hermann Böhlau, 1926), pp. xxxvi–xlii; Albisetti, *Schooling
German Girls and Women,* pp. 282–283.

41. Geheeb, *Briefe,* pp. 76–87, for a portion of the proposal; for the entire

document see Paul Geheeb, "Entwurf des Planes einer privaten Lehr- und Erziehungsanstalt, deren Gründung im Odenwald bei Darmstadt beabsichtigt wird," unpub. ms., August 1909, OSO.

42. Geheeb's emphasis on differentiation had its limitations. He betrayed a homophobic attitude when he claimed that boys who lived in single-sex boarding schools suffered from an "unhealthy, unbearably homosexual atmosphere," whereas boys in coeducational schools were "much more delicate in their manners and more polite." Geheeb, *Briefe,* pp. 84–85. On the differences between "relational" and "individualist," or "equal rights," feminism, see Karen Offen, "Liberty, Equality, and Justice for Women: The Theory and Practice of Feminism in Nineteenth-Century Europe," in Renate Bridenthal, Claudia Koonz, and Susan Stuard, eds., *Becoming Visible: Women in European History* (Boston: Houghton Mifflin, 1987), pp. 335–375; Allen, "Kindergarten Movements," p. 48; Elizabeth Sarah, ed., *Reassessments of "First Wave" Feminism* (Oxford: Pergamon, 1982).

43. Edith Cassirer to Paul Geheeb, Wilmersdorf, 6 May 1909, EDH; Edith Geheeb, "Aus meinem Leben," pp. 17–18; Edith Geheeb interviewed by Walter Schäfer, Winter 1959, Goldern, unpub. ms., pp. 64–65, OSO; Geheeb-Schäfer interview, p. 40.

44. Geheeb-Schäfer interview, pp. 39–41; Paul Geheeb, "Ansprachen am 5. Oktober," *Der neue Waldkauz,* vol. 4, nos. 10–11, November 1930, p. 112. *Der neue Waldkauz* was the student newspaper of the Odenwaldschule from 1927 to 1934 and will henceforth be designated *DNW.* Geheeb's relationship with Cassirer was typical of the alliances reform educators needed to build with wealthy philanthropists in order to fund their pedagogical projects. "The foundation of the homes was only possible practically in the form of private schools. Therefore an alliance with prosperous citizens was necessary, who at the same time had interests which extended beyond their own social circles and were willing to become involved in innovative pedagogical works." Hermann Rieche, *Der soziale Gedanke in den Landerziehungsheimen und Schulgemeinden Deutschlands* (Dresden: M. Dittert, 1935), p. 52. Hermann Harless contrasted Lietz's fiscal struggles with Geheeb's security in the Odenwaldschule in "Von Hermann Lietz zu Paul Geheeb," in Cassirer et al., *Erziehung zur Humanität,* p. 53.

2. The Odenwaldschule, 1910–1930

1. Geheeb, *Briefe,* p. 42; Otto Erdmann, "Die Oso in den Kinderschuhen," in Cassirer et al., eds., *Die Idee einer Schule,* p. 15.

2. Erdmann, "Die Oso in den Kinderschuhen," p. 14; Hans Grunsky, "Erinnerungen an die Anfänge der Odenwaldschule," in Cassirer et al., eds., *Erziehung zur Humanität,* p. 43; Edith Geheeb, "Aus meinem Leben," pp. 19–20; Schäfer, *Odenwaldschule,* p. 25.

3. Paul Geheeb, "Rede zur Eröffnung der Odenwaldschule," in Cassirer et al., eds., *Die Idee einer Schule*, p. 10; Geheeb-Schäfer interview, p. 43.
4. Esther Bueckers, "Die ersten Schulgemeinden," *DNW*, vol. 1, no. 10, November 1927, pp. 129–130; Gerhard Fuchs, "Die Schulgemeinde," ibid., pp. 130–132; Gertraudt Schaefer, "Ueber das Stimmrecht," ibid., pp. 134–135; Geheeb, *Briefe*, pp. 35–39; Ward, *Reddie of Abbotsholme*, pp. 129–131.
5. On Lietz's quotations before meals, see Erich Meissner, "Hermann Lietz," in Kutzer, *Lietz*, pp. 21–22. Ernst Erich Noth held that the *Mitarbeiter* in conferences "discussed more important things than in the *Schulgemeinde*." See his *Erinnerungen eines Deutschen* (Hamburg and Düsseldorf: Classen, 1971), p. 159.
6. Paul Geheeb, "Koedukation als Lebensanschauung," in Cassirer et al., eds., *Erziehung zur Humanität*, pp. 116–127; Marilisbeth Niederhöffer-Trusen, "Erinnerungen," in Cassirer et al., eds., *Die Idee einer Schule*, p. 43; Henry Cassirer, "Die Podiumsdiskussion," *OSO-Hefte*, 1986, vol. 11, p. 19. "Die Podiumsdiskussion" is a transcript of a large group discussion by alumni of the Odenwaldschule at the seventy-fifth anniversary of the school in Oberhambach in June 1985. In this and following citations I have identified the speaker for the sake of precision.
7. The clearest elaboration of the course plan in the Odenwaldschule is given by Otto Erdmann in "Die Arbeitsorganisation," in Cassirer et al., eds., *Die Idee einer Schule*, pp. 19–24.
8. Edith Geheeb, "Aus meinem Leben," p. 22.
9. Peter Petersen, *Die neueuropäische Erziehungsbewegung* (Weimar: Hermann Böhlaus, 1926), p. 60; Meyer, *Modern European Educators*, pp. 146–153.
10. Hans Grunsky, "Erinnerungen an die Anfänge der Odenwaldschule," in Cassirer et al., eds., *Erziehung zur Humanität*, p. 48; Erdmann quoted in Schäfer, *Odenwaldschule*, p. 29.
11. Paul Geheeb, "Die Odenwaldschule im Lichte der Erziehungsaufgaben der Gegenwart," in Cassirer et al., eds., *Erziehung zur Humanität*, pp. 131–133.
12. The phrase "child-centered education" did not achieve the same currency in German as in American progressive education; a rough analogue to Geheeb's viewpoint was expressed by Harold Rugg and Ann Shumaker, *The Child-Centered School* (Yonkers-on-Hudson, New York: World Book, 1928). Friedrich Nietzsche used Pindar's dictum repeatedly in his writings and Geheeb may have initially encountered it either in *Ecce Homo*, where it is the subtitle, or in *Also Sprach Zarathustra*, where it is one of the aphorisms. See Alexander Nehamas, *Nietzsche: Life as Literature* (Cambridge: Harvard University Press, 1985), pp. 170–199. The quote is from Paul Geheeb, "Die Odenwaldschule. Geistige Grundlagen," in Cassirer et al., eds., *Erziehung zur Humanität*, p. 157.
13. Geheeb, "Grundlagen," pp. 163–164; Geheeb, "Erziehungsaufgaben," p. 134.

14. Geheeb, "Grundlagen," pp. 158–159.
15. Paul and Edith Geheeb, "Die Odenwaldschule," n.p., n.d., OSO; Geheeb, *Briefe*, p. 52. The concept of responsibility did not emerge as strongly in Geheeb's theoretical writings as in his pedagogical practice. While Geheeb often stated that "fundamentally the individual does not exist for the community, but the community for the individual," he also wrote on one occasion that "the individual must learn to love the community in which he is placed, and to love it completely and to serve it to the point of self-sacrificc." The latter quote, which is almost unique within Geheeb's writings, is one of the few instances in which he suggested a certain priority of the community before the individual. In general his writings argue that all social structures "are only means of assisting the individual to the fulfillment of his personality." Geheeb, "Grundlagen," pp. 157–158. Silke Axhausen distorts this aspect of Geheeb's philosophy in *Erziehungswissenschaft und Bildungspolitik*, pp. 78–87. Axhausen quotes this single passage from Geheeb's writing and subsequently identifies Geheeb with Lietz's anti-individualism, without addressing either Geheeb's constant eulogies to individual self-realization or his actual pedagogical practice.
16. Geheeb, "Grundlagen," p. 159; Geheeb, "Erziehungsaufgaben," p. 133.
17. Geheeb, "Erziehungsaufgaben," p. 135. See Georg Kerschensteiner, *Das Grundaxiom des Bildungsprozesses und seine Folgerungen für die Schulorganisation* (Berlin: Union Deutsche Verlagsgesellschaft, 1931).
18. The incident is recounted in the Geheeb-Schäfer interview, pp. 20–21.
19. See Flitner and Kudritzki, *Die deutsche Reformpädagogik;* Scheibe, *Bewegung;* Röhrs, *Reformpädagogik;* Stern, *Cultural Despair*. My presentation differs from that of Wilhelm Flitner, who suggested that the German reform pedagogical movement evolved through three phases in his *Theorie des pädagogischen Weges und der Methode* (Weinheim: Beltz, 1950). Flitner's periodization was accepted and expanded upon by Röhrs, "Die Schulen der Reformpädagogik," pp. 14–19. In Flitner's account, the first phase lasted from the late 1890s to 1912, when reformers began isolated projects; the second phase began in 1912 and continued to 1924, and was a period of rapid transformation in schooling; a third period of stabilization followed. By ignoring the decisive break in German history marked by the November Revolution and the responsiveness of the Weimar Republic to new trends in education, however, Flitner demonstrated the unfortunate consequences of treating the history of education as autonomous from political developments. For this reason, more coherent and persuasive accounts were provided by Alexander and Parker, *New Education*, and Tenorth, *Bildungsgeschichte*, pp. 17–48.
20. It is impossible to map out all of the ways in which the "new education" movement had an impact on German public schools. Alexander and Parker held in 1929 that "A visit to a German rural school gives proof that the reform of education has penetrated to the remotest corners of the land, making the *activity method* and *education through experience* common-

place realities to the village schoolmaster and realities in his daily practice." However, they also noticed that the pace of development was extremely uneven, and that traditional schools could often be found within a few city blocks from the most daring examples of progressive practice. See Alexander and Parker, *New Education*, pp. 243–296, quote from p. 260; for the most fully developed examples of progressive practices in public schools, see Rödler, *Vergessene Alternativschulen*.

21. For the first figure, see Schäfer, *Odenwaldschule*, p. 100; the second is cited in Paul Geheeb's letter to Hessian President Bernhard Adelung, Oberhambach, 29 November 1932, EDH. The following figures on student enrollment are taken from Schäfer, *Odenwaldschule*, p. 100, and describe *only* the years from 1910 to 1925, excluding 1915–16. The documents on the Odenwaldschule which were housed at the Hessian Ministry of Culture in Darmstadt were destroyed in 1944, "predominantly by the officials themselves." See Albrecht Eckhardt, ed., *Hessisches Staatsarchiv und Stadtarchiv Darmstadt* (Darmstadt: Verlag des Historischen Vereins für Hessen, 1975), p. 76. Additional damage was caused by the bombing of Darmstadt by the Royal Air Force. It appears that the Geheebs either destroyed many of their files from the first twenty years of the school in 1934 or took them with them in emigration, in the course of which they were lost.

22. On the Jews, see Sarah Gordon, *Hitler, Germans and the "Jewish Question"* (Princeton: Princeton University Press, 1984), pp. 7–24. Figures cited from the Kaiserliche Statistische Amte, *Statistik des deutschen Reichs*, vol. 240, *Die Volkszählung im Deutschen Reiche am 1. Dezember 1910* (Berlin: Puttkammer & Mühlbrecht, 1915), pp. 134–135; Statistische Reichsamt, *Statistik des Deutschen Reichs*, vol. 401, *Volkszählung: Die Bevölkerung des Deutschen Reichs nach den Ergenbissen des Volkszählung 1925*, part 2 (Berlin: Reimar Hobbin, 1930), p. 596. As a point of comparison from the public schools, Catholics made up roughly twenty-eight percent of the *Volksschule* population in the 1920s, with Jews providing only three-tenths of a percent. See Christoph Fuhr, *Zur Schulpolitik der Weimarer Republik* (Weinheim and Basel: Beltz, 1970), p. 345.

23. On the Catholics, see David Blackbourn, "The Problem of Democratisation: German Catholics and the Role of the Center Party," in Richard J. Evans, ed., *Society and Politics in Wilhelmine Germany* (New York: Harper and Row, 1978), pp. 160–185; quote from Henry Cassirer in "Die Podiumsdiskussion," p. 19.

24. Henner Müller-Holz, director of the Odenwaldschule Archives, estimated that the cost of a month's tuition in the Odenwaldschule probably equalled the monthly earnings of a worker. Interview, Oberhambach, 1 March 1986. For some different interpretations comparing the financially exclusive aspects of education in *Landerziehungsheime* with their innovative pedagogical reforms, see Ernst Reisinger, *Hermann Lietz und die Weiterentwicklung der deutschen Landerziehungsheime* (Munich: Josef Kösel & Friedrich Pustet, 1904), p. 7; Wilhelm Hausenstein, "Geistige

Bewegung," *Sozialistische Monatsheft,* July 1910, pp. 980–981; P. Hoche, "Landerziehungsheime," *Deutscher Courier,* 29 January 1912, p. 132.

25. See Sonja Latk, "Erinnerungen," in Cassirer et al., eds., *Die Idee einer Schule,* pp. 74–75; Emil Fuchs, *Mein Leben,* vol. 2 (Leipzig: Koehler & Amelang, 1959), pp. 127–130; Erich Ernst Noth, *Erinnerungen;* and Thomas Lange, "Der 'Steglitzer Schülermordprozess' 1928," in Thomas Koebner, Rolf-Peter Janz and Frank Trommler, eds., *"Mit uns zieht die neue Zeit": Der Mythos Jugend* (Frankfurt: Suhrkamp, 1985), pp. 412–437. Klaus Mann's short story "Der Alte" satirized Geheeb and provoked an angry reaction from him. See Klaus Mann, *Vor dem Leben* (Hamburg: Gebrüder Enoch, 1925), pp. 137–141, and Geheeb, *Briefe,* pp. 43–45 and pp. 194–195. Klaus Mann used Geheeb as the basis for a more positive character in his first play, *Anja und Esther* (Berlin: Oesterheld, 1925).

26. "Paulus spricht zu Eva Cassirer," unpub. ms., 25 August 1955, p. 4, OSO. Eisner is mentioned by name in Edith Geheeb, "Aus meinem Leben," p. 26. Geheeb said that students in the Odenwaldschule came "in the first place from artistic circles. They showed the greatest, most enthusiastic, most instinctive and direct understanding for that which I want and understand as humanistic education. In the second line were doctors . . . In the third line were people of scientific professions: industrialists, engineers. Finally, the colleagues." Geheeb-Schäfer interview, p. 5.

27. Wagenschein's works include *Natur physikalisch gesehen* (Braunschweig: Westermann, 1975), *Die Pädagogische Dimension der Physik* (Braunschweig: Westermann, 1976), and *Naturphänomene sehen und verstehen* (Stuttgart: Klett, 1980). His autobiography recounts the importance of the Odenwaldschule for the development of his pedagogy; see his *Erinnerung für Morgen* (Weinheim and Basel: Beltz, 1985), pp. 31–38 and pp. 53–58. Janos Frecot, Johann Friedrich Geist, and Diethart Krebs describe the founding of the St. George's Union by Fidus, Prellwitz, and von Keller in their study, *Fidus: Zur ästhetischen Praxis bürgerlichen Fluchtbewegungen* (Munich: Rogner and Bernhard, 1972), p. 253. Prellwitz's novel is *Drude* (Oberhof im Thüringer Wald: Main-Verlag, 1920).

28. Bollnow's writings include *Die Geschichte der Pädagogik* (Stuttgart: Kohlhammer, 1952), *Existenzphilosophie und Pädagogik* (Stuttgart: Kohlhammer, 1959), *Die pädagogische Atmosphäre* (Heidelberg: Quelle & Meyer, 1964), *Krise und neuer Anfang* (Heidelberg: Quelle & Meyer, 1966), and *Sprache und Erziehung* (Stuttgart: Kohlhammer, 1966); Jacoby's essays are collected by Sophie Ludwig in *Jenseits von "Begabt" und "Unbegabt"* (Hamburg: Hans Christians Verlag, 1981) and *Jenseits von "Musikalisch" und "Unmusikalisch"* (Hamburg: Hans Christians Verlag, 1984). Suhrkamp's publishing house, Suhrkamp Verlag, publishes the works of Bertolt Brecht, Hermann Hesse, Theodor Adorno, and many other prominent twentieth-century German authors. On Suhrkamp in the Odenwaldschule, see Siegfried Unseld and Helene Ritzerfeld, *Peter Suhrkamp: Zur Biographie eines Verlegers in Daten, Dokumenten, und Bildern* (Frankfurt:

Suhrkamp, 1975), pp. 60–63. On Buber, see Siegfried Helmer, "Martin Buber und die Odenwaldschule," *OSO-Hefte*, vol. 6, 1981, pp. 5–16; Geheeb, *Briefe*, p. 70.

29. Agaath Hamaker-Willink, "Die gänzliche Verantwortung tragen," *Neue Sammlung*, vol. 25, no. 4, October–December 1985, p. 558.

30. Interview with Jane and Reinhard Bendix, Berkeley, California, 30 March 1989. The Bendixes had discussed this incident with Edith Geheeb.

31. Paul Geheeb, "Zu Stadtrat Max Cassirer's 70. Geburtstag," *DNW*, vol. 1, no. 9, October 1927, pp. 113–114; Eva Cassirer, "Der Stadtrat," in Cassirer et al., eds., *Erziehung zur Humanität*, pp. 63–65.

32. Dankwart Rüstow, "Die Verwandlung der alten Schule," in Cassirer et al., eds., *Die Idee einer Schule*, p. 101; Reingart Ahrem, "Von der Staatschule zur OSO und wieder zurück," in ibid., pp. 48–52.

33. Marilisbeth Niederhöffer-Trusen, "Erinnerungen," pp. 41–43; Dodo Kroner quoted in "Die Podiumsdiskussion," pp. 38–39; Gideon Strauss, "Ueber die Schulgemeinde," *DNW*, vol. 1, no. 10, November 1927, p. 132.

34. Niederhöffer-Trusen, "Erinnerungen," p. 43; Geheeb, "Koedukation als Lebensanschauung," p. 121.

35. Hans Grunksy, "Erinnerungen," p. 49; Walter Matuschke, "Menschenbildung bei Paul Geheeb," in Cassirer et al., eds., *Erziehung zur Humanität*, p. 95; Friedel Hellmund, "Aus Tagebüchern," in Cassirer et al., eds., *Die Idee einer Schule*, p. 29; Klaus Mann, *Der Wendepunkt* (Munich: Nymphenburger, 1969), p. 101.

36. Uschl Schön-Friend, "Erinnerungen," in Cassirer et al., eds., *Die Idee einer Schule*, pp. 45–48; Ahrem, "Von der Stattschule zur OSO und wieder zurück," in ibid., p. 51; Walter Matuschke, "Menschenbildung bei Paul Geheeb," in Cassirer et al., eds., *Erziehung zur Humanität*, p. 94; Ruth Blunden-Bachert, "Erinnerungen," in Cassirer et al., eds., *Die Idee einer Schule*, p. 53.

37. Ruth Blandon, "Education for Tolerance," in Cassirer et al., eds., *Erziehung zur Humanität*, p. 101; Fuchs quoted in Hans Grunsky, "Erinnerungen," p. 47.

38. Geheeb, *Briefe*, pp. 70, 91–93, 99, 104–105, 108–109.

39. Elisabeth Johnson, "Die Podiumsdiskussion," p. 36; interview by Dennis Shirley of Friedburg Lorenz, Heppenheim, 6 June 1985.

40. Ernst Zinn, "Die Einrichtung der 'Andachten' in der Odenwaldschule," *DNW*, vol. 1, no. 1, February 1927, p. 3; Paul Geheeb, "Die Einrichtung der 'Andachten' in der Odenwaldschule," *DNW*, vol. 1, no. 4, May 1927, pp. 40–45.

41. Richard Erdoes, *Lame Deer: Seeker of Visions* (New York: Simon and Schuster, 1972), p. 272; Paul Geheeb to Heinrich Simon, Oberhambach, 10 March 1933, EDH.

42. On Ferrière's significance as the "Lord Chancellor" of reform pedagogy, see Peter Petersen's forward to Ferrière's *Schule der Selbsttätigkeit oder Tat-*

schule (Weimar: Hermann Böhlaus, 1928), p. 1. On the Institut Jean-Jacques Rousseau, see Pierre Bovet, *Vingt Ans de Vie* (Neuchâtel: Delachaux & Niestlé, 1932).

43. Paul Geheeb, "IV. Weltkongress für Erneuerung der Erziehung," *DNW*, vol. 1, no. 8, September 1927, pp. 89–104; Paul Geheeb, "Höhepunkte des Lebens," *DNW*, vol. 2, nos. 7–8, August–September 1928, pp. 73–83; Paul Geheeb, "New Education," *Progressive Education*, vol. 7, no. 6, October 1930, p. 271; Paul Geheeb, "The Odenwaldschule—After Twenty Years," *The New Era in Home and School*, vol. 11, no. 48, December 1930, pp. 187–190; Geheeb, *Briefe*, p. 131. On the Fairhope School, see John and Evelyn Dewey's enthusiastic description in *Schools of Tomorrow* (New York: E. P. Dutton, 1915), pp. 17–40.

44. Paul Geheeb to Eduard Spranger, Goldern, 2 May 1960, EDH; Geheeb, *Briefe*, pp. 125–127. Geheeb's letter to an unidentified *Staatsrat*—presumably in the Hessian Ministry of Culture—further elaborates this perspective (Oberhambach, 6 December 1930, EDH).

45. Hermann Nohl and Ludwig Pallat, *Handbuch der Pädagogik* (Langensalza: Belz, 1930), vol. 4, p. 336; Alexander and Parker, *New Education* (New York: John Day, 1929), p. 201; Adolphe Ferrière, *Das Landerziehungsheim und die wissenschaftliche Zentralstelle für Landerziehungsheime* (Berlin-Fichtenau: Verlag Gesellschaft und Erziehung, 1920).

46. For a socialist interpretation of the *Schulgemeinde* and its ramifications for the education of working-class youth see Siegfried Bernfeld, "Die Schulgemeinde und ihre Funktion im Klassenkampf," in *Antiautoritäre Erziehung und Psychoanalyse*, vol. 3 (Frankfurt: März, 1971), pp. 932–949; quote from Klaus Mann in his *Kind dieser Zeit* (Reinbek bei Hamburg: Rowohlt, 1982), p. 152.

47. On academic achievement in the Odenwaldschule, see the "Aussprache auf der Tagung der früheren Mitarbeiter und Kameraden," *DNW*, vol. 5, nos. 1–2, January-February 1931, pp. 24–25; on autonomy, see Hamaker-Willink, "Verantwortung," pp. 557 and 539.

48. Quote on idealism from Anne Cross to Dennis Shirley, San Leandro, California, 22 October 1989; Felix von Mendelssohn, "Nach-Gedanken," *OSO-Hefte*, vol. 11, 1986, p. 30; Felix von Mendelssohn to Dennis Shirley, Munich, 24 February 1986.

49. Theodor Scharmann to Walter Schäfer, Linz, 1 May 1972, copy in my possession sent by the late Dr. Scharmann.

3. Outer Dangers and Inner Reforms, 1930–1932

1. Paul Geheeb, "Neue Erziehung," *DNW*, vol. 3, no. 11, December 1929, pp. 121–136.
2. Paul Geheeb, "Abgangszeugnis," 8 June 1928, Gerhard Fuchs file, OSO.
3. Gerhard Fuchs, "Problem der alten Kameraden," *DNW*, vol. 4, no. 4, May 1930, p. 41–47.
4. Walter Solmitz, "Beitrag zu Gerhard Fuchs Aufsatz, 'Problem der alten

Kameraden'," *DNW*, vol. 4, nos. 6–7, July–August 1930, pp. 79–83; Werner Meyer, "Beschäftigung mit Zeitfragen," *DNW*, vol. 4, no. 5, June 1930, pp. 53–55.

5. Paul Geheeb, "Ansprachen am 5. Oktober," pp. 111–112.
6. Alwine von Keller, introducing the "Aussprache auf der Tagung der früheren Mitarbeiter und Kameraden," *DNW*, vol. 5, nos. 1–2, January–February 1931, p. 1.
7. Gerard Fuchs, in "Aussprache," p. 5. It is interesting to note that Fuchs was essentially calling for the intensification of reform pedagogical principles in the Odenwaldschule by bringing together cognitive and experiential learning for purposes of citizenship education. It is questionable whether Buber used the term "shock troops" (*Stosstrupps*). This was nonetheless the term Fuchs used in "Aussprache," p. 7.
8. Noth, *Erinnerungen eines Deutschen*, pp. 158–159; Scharmann to Schäfer, 1 May 1972.
9. Paul Geheeb, in "Aussprache," p. 21.
10. Werner Meyer quoting Paul Geheeb in "Zielsetzung für die politische Arbeitsgemeinschaft," *DNW*, vol. 6, nos. 1–2, January–February 1932, p. 14.
11. The Geheebs reported on their visit to Letzlingen in *Schulgemeinden* in the Odenwaldschule in the fall of 1930. See Liesel Motteck and Otto Leitolf, "Die Arbeitsgemeinschaften und Schulgemeinden über die Stellung der Kameraden zur Wirtschaft der Odenwaldschule," *DNW*, vol. 4, nos. 10–11, November 1930, pp. 148–149. On Geheeb's comparison of Letzlingen's founder Bernhard Uffrecht with A. S. Neill, see the *Briefe*, p. 53.
12. Paul Geheeb, "Die Neugestaltung der Schule," *DNW*, vol. 5, no. 4, April 1931, p. 62. On Geheeb's proposal as a result of the October 1930 conference see Henner Müller-Holz, "Warten auf das Wartesystem?" *OSO Hefte*, vol. 1, 1973–74, p. 50.
13. In the original German, the *Ordnungswart* was responsible for cleanliness, the *Hygienewart* oversaw the health of *Kameraden*, the *Studienwart* counseled *Kameraden* on their curricula, the *Urlaubswart* regulated the departure and arrival of *Kameraden* from the school, and the *Finanzwart* oversaw the individual financial needs and expenditures of *Kameraden*. Other *Warte* were also designated in the school, so that younger *Kameraden* would be *Kreidewarte*, responsible for providing chalk and other classroom materials.
14. Paul Geheeb, "Neugestaltung," p. 63.
15. According to Schäfer's history of the Odenwaldschule, the *Schulgemeinde* had become unwieldy due to the growth in the student body as early as November 1927. At that point the *Schulgemeinde* was bracketed into three "work groups" based on age gradations. The development of decentralized "project groups" oriented around problems in community living also threatened to subvert the central role of the *Schulgemeinde* in communal decision making, for it appears that the project groups were inconsistent in reporting their decisions and initiatives back to the *Schulgemeinde* for

confirmation. Heiner Cassirer wrote a lead article for *Der neue Waldkauz* in February 1930 in which he addressed the gradual atrophy of the assembly in the school and Geheeb's role in furthering decentralization. See Schäfer, *Odenwaldschule,* p. 33 and Heiner Cassirer, "Krise der Schulgemeinde," *DNW,* vol. 4, no. 1, February 1930, pp. 6–8.

16. Lily Schesinger, "Erfahrungen einer Kameradin im ersten Odenwaldschuljahr," *DNW,* vol. 6, nos. 3–4, March–April 1932, pp. 41–42; Otto Leitolf, "Meine Erfahrungen bei der Bildung einer Hausgemeinschaft," *DNW,* vol. 5, no. 12, December 1931, pp. 170–171.

17. Heinz Schlee, "Ueber die Schülerselbstverwaltung in der Odenwaldschule," unpub. ms., OSO.

18. Schlee, "Schülerselbstverwaltung," p. 24.

19. Alumni quotes from personal interviews with Rosemarie Varga, Goldern, 25 June 1985, and with Marina Jakimow, Wallersdorf, 28 January 1986, and from a letter from Felix von Mendelssohn to Dennis Shirley, Munich, 24 February 1986. The quote from Edith Geheeb is taken from a taped interview with Dr. Otto Kopp, Goldern, 1970, EDH.

20. Paul Geheeb to the *Schulgemeinde,* Canton Waadt, Switzerland, 31 August 1931, OSO.

21. Paul Geheeb to Frau Barth, Oberhambach, 17 December 1931, EDH; Zwi Erich Kurzweil, "Die Odenwaldschule, 1910–1934," *Paedagogica Historica,* vol. 13, no. 1, 1973, pp. 23–56, especially p. 53.

22. McGregor Gray, "What the OSO Meant to Me," *OSO-Hefte,* vol. 11, 1986, pp. 177–180, quote from pp. 178–179.

4. A Storm Trooper's Revenge: January–March, 1933

1. Edith Geheeb, "Aus meinem Leben," p. 29.

2. Ibid.

3. Gordon A. Craig, *Germany, 1866–1945* (New York: Oxford University Press, 1978), pp. 474, 571–572.

4. On the Nazi seizure of power in Hesse, see Eberhart Schön, *Die Entstehung des Nationalsozialismus in Hessen* (Meisenheim am Glan: Anton Hain, 1972); Eike Hennig, ed., *Hesse unterm Hakenkreuz* (Frankfurt: Insel, 1983); Henner Pingel, *Das Jahr 1933: NSDAP Machtergreifung in Darmstadt und im Volkstaat Hessen* (Darmstadt: n.p., 1978); Ulrich Schneider, ed., *Hessen vor 50 Jahren: 1933* (Frankfurt: Röderberg, n.d.); Eckhart G. Franz, "Vom Biedermeier in die Katastrophe des Feuersturms," in Friedrich Battenberg et al, eds., *Darmstadts Geschichte* (Darmstadt: Eduard Roether, 1980), pp. 289–482, especially pp. 453–482; Kurt Weitzel, "Nationalsozialistische Propaganda in Hessen am Ende der Weimarer Republik," *Archiv für hessische Geschichte und Altertumskunde,* vol. 43, 1985, pp. 351–376. See also three essays by Dieter Rebentisch, "Persönlichkeitsprofil und Karriereverlauf der nationalsozialistischen Führungskader in Hessen, 1928–1945," in *Hessisches Jahrbuch für Landesgeschichte,* vol. 33,

1983, pp. 293–332; "Der Gau Hessen-Nassau und die nationalsozialistische Reichsreform," *Nassauische Annalen*, vol. 87, 1978, pp. 128–162; "Nationalsozialistische Revolution, Parteiherrschaft und totaler Krieg in Hessen (1933–1945)," in Uwe Schultz, ed., *Die Geschichte Hessens* (Stuttgart: Konrad Theiss, 1983), pp. 232–248. Two contemporary perspectives are given by Bernhard Adelung, *Sein und Werden* (Offenbach: Bollwerk, 1952), pp. 359–378 and Eugen Schmahl and Wilhelm Seipel, *Entwicklung der völkischen Bewegung* (Giessen: Emil Roth, 1933).

5. The information on Clemens and Werner Goerendt is drawn from files on Werner Goerendt at the Berlin Document Center (henceforth "BDC") in the collections of the NSDAP central registry, the Party correspondence, the supreme Party court records, and the non-biographical collection. (These files are arranged alphabetically by category and are not numbered.) Additional information is provided in Max Cassirer's letter to Paul Geheeb, Berlin, 21 October 1933, EDH.

6. Quote from Werner Goerendt in a letter to the "Hilfskasse der NSDAP," Gelnhausen, 27 November 1939, BDC.

7. Peter Loewenberg has argued persuasively that the generation of German youth born between 1900 and 1915 was traumatized by the First World War and fixated on this trauma in the postwar years. According to Loewenberg, the disruption of traditional German society during the war and during the Weimar Republic led German youth to seek an uncompromising ego-ideal untainted by defeat, the treaty of Versailles, or postwar compromises with the Allied powers. This need was manipulated and satisfied by Hitler and the Nazi party. Werner Goerendt was born in 1908—in the exact center of this generational cluster. See Peter Loewenberg, "The Psychohistorical Origins of the Nazi Youth Cohort," *American Historical Review*, vol. 76, no. 5, December 1971, pp. 1457–1502.

8. The literature on institutional reform in the first months following the Nazi takeover reflects a differentiated and highly uneven pattern of development. Generally speaking, openly nationalistic schools, such as the Hermann Lietz *Landerziehungsheime*, were not raided, whereas more left-wing schools, such as Letzlingen, were summarily closed. Most schools, which stood somewhere between these two extremes, experienced haphazard interventions by the Nazis, which were determined more by local idiosyncracies than by state policies. On the patterns of Nazi social reforms in general, see William Sheridan Allen, *The Nazi Seizure of Power*, pp. 295–296, and Jürgen Schmädeke and Peter Steinbach, eds., "Einleitung," in *Der Widerstand gegen den Nationalsozialismus*, pp. xxii–xxiii.

9. The information on this first raid is drawn from the correspondence from Paul Geheeb to U. Urstadt, Oberhambach, 8 March 1933, EDH; Paul Geheeb to Dr. Heinrich Simon (head of the editorial board of the *Frankfurter Zeitung*), Oberhambach, 10 March 1933, EDH; and Geheeb, *Briefe*, p. 145. Geheeb had a friendly relationship with Simon, who sup-

ported the school by providing fellowships for students. Hans von Bredow of the Frankfurter Societäts-Druckerei to Dennis Shirley, Frankfurt, 20 May 1988.

10. For the timing of Nazi interventions in Hesse, see Peter Diehl-Thiele, *Partei und Staat im Dritten Reich* (Munich: C. H. Beck, 1969), p. 39.

11. "Haussuchungen in Hessen," *Frankfurter Zeitung und Handelsblatt,* 10 March 1933, second morning edition, p. 2. It is difficult to gauge why Geheeb's letter was not printed. On the one hand, Heinrich Simon may have wished to avoid challenging the Nazis by printing Geheeb's letter, which was sarcastic and critical of Goerendt and the SA. On the other hand, Simon may have had more political sense than Geheeb and may have wished to protect him from what was certain to have been a dangerous Nazi response to his letter. On Simon and the *Frankfurter Zeitung* in this time period, see Günter Gillessen, *Auf verlorenem Posten* (Berlin: Siedler, 1986), pp. 91–151.

12. Personal interviews with Marina Jakimow, Wallersdorf, 24 January 1986; with Geno Hartlaub, Hamburg, 20 August 1985; with Maria Funk-Rüstow, Oberhambach, 1 March 1986. Rosalinde von Ossietsky described the search from her vantage point as a student in Bäbel Boldt et al., eds., ". . . *aber von dir wird gesprochen*" (Oldenburg: Littman, 1981), pp. 7–9. Kurt Cassirer to the Military Government of Hesse, Wetherby, England, 13 March 1948, EDH.

13. Geheeb-Schäfer interview, pp. 31–32.

14. Kurt Cassirer to the Military Government of Hesse, 13 March 1948; Esra Steinitz to Dennis Shirley, Jerusalem, 30 October 1985, 12 December 1985, and 1 January 1986.

15. Geheeb, *Briefe*, pp. 144–148. Paul Geheeb to Adolphe Ferrière, Oberhambach, 15 March 1933; Adolphe Ferrière to Paul Geheeb, 17 March 1933, EDH.

16. Esra Steinitz to Dennis Shirley, Jerusalem, 30 October 1985; 7 December 1985; 1 January 1986.

17. Friedrich Ringshausen to the "Direktion und Leiter der höheren Schulen und die Kreis- und Schulämter," Darmstadt, 14 March 1933, EDH.

18. Paul Geheeb to the Hessian Ministry of Culture and Education, Oberhambach, 20 March 1933, EDH.

19. Alwine von Keller, "Bericht," n.d., EDH.

20. Telephone interview by Dennis Shirley with Martin Wagenschein, 28 February 1986.

21. E. G. Franz of Hessisches Staatsarchiv in Darmstadt (henceforth "HSAD") to Dennis Shirley, Darmstadt, 19 October 1987.

22. Telephone interview with Martin Wagenschein, 28 February 1986.

23. Interviews with Geno Hartlaub, Hamburg, 20 August 1985, Marina Jakimow, Wallersdorf, 24 January 1986, and Walter Bücheler, Frankfurt, 3 March 1986; Clewie Kroeker in "Uebergänge," in *OSO-Hefte*, vol. 11, 1986, p. 47; Francis Marburg, "A Personal Assessment of the 'OSO Experience,'" ibid., p. 203. "Uebergänge" is a transcript of a small group

discussion by alumni of the Odenwaldschule at the seventy-fifth anniversary of the school in Oberhambach in June 1985. In this and following citations I have identified the speaker for the sake of precision.

24. Wilhelm Metzendorf, *Geschichte und Geschicke der Heppenheimer Juden* (Lorsch: Laurissa, 1982), p. 185.
25. Geheeb, *Briefe*, p. 198; Paul Geheeb to Adolphe Ferrière, Oberhambach, 29 March 1933, EDH.
26. Paul Geheeb to Werner Goerendt, Oberhambach, 25 March 1933, EDH.
27. Esra Steinitz to Dennis Shirley, 7 December 1985 and 1 January 1986.

5. *Accommodating the Regime: April–June, 1933*

1. Paul Geheeb to Rudolf Blank, Oberhambach, 2 April 1933, EDH.
2. Geheeb voted for Hindenburg for president in 1932 and not for the communist candidate Ernst Thälmann because he was convinced that Thälmann's politics threatened the Odenwaldschule as much as Hitler's. Letter from Theo Scharmann to Walter Schäfer, Linz, 1 May 1972, pp. 10–11.
3. Dr. Rudolf Benze, the director of the German Central Institute for Education, observed that "National Socialist education has not grown primarily out of pedagogical theory, as former systems of education may have . . . but out of the political activity of the movement." Quoted in George Frederick Kneller, *The Educational Philosophy of National Socialism* (New Haven: Yale University Press, 1941), p. 4.
4. Rebentisch, "Persönlichkeitsprofil," p. 307.
5. Background information on Ringshausen is available at the BDC in the NSDAP central registry and the collections on Party correspondence, the supreme Party court, the culture chamber, the NS Lehrerbund and the non-biographical files.
6. Esra Steinitz to Dennis Shirley, 30 October 1985.
7. Ringshausen's decree is reprinted in Heinrich Kanz, ed., *Der Nationalsozialismus als pädagogisches Problem* (Frankfurt: Peter Lang, 1984), p. 73; Eilers, *Schulpolitik*, p. 69.
8. Geheeb-Schäfer interview, pp. 28–30; all of the dialogue cited was quoted by Geheeb from memory.
9. See Jill Stephenson, *Women in Nazi Society* (New York: Harper and Row, 1975), pp. 116–129; Eilers, *Schulpolitik*, pp. 18–21.
10. Tenorth, "Deutsche Erziehungswissenschaft," p. 305; Geheeb, *Briefe*, p. 152; Martin Wagenschein to Werner Meyer, n.d., n.p., OSO.
11. Geheeb-Schäfer interview, p. 33.
12. Paul Geheeb to Heinrich Simon, Oberhambach, 8 April 1933, EDH.
13. Paul Geheeb to Werner Meyer, Oberhambach, 8 April 1933, OSO.
14. Geheeb, *Briefe*, p. 155.
15. Paul Geheeb to Rudolf Blank, Oberhambach, 10 April 1933, EDH.
16. Even the released custodians suffered from their association with the Odenwaldschule, which now more than ever was perceived as a "com-

munist school." Interview with Richard Geiss, Oberhambach, 15 June 1985.

17. Geheeb, *Briefe*, pp. 148–154. Odenwaldschule alumnus John Kobbé carried several secret letters for Geheeb from Germany to Switzerland, concealing them in such innocuous places as tent posts. Telephone interview with John Kobbé, 23 October 1989.

18. Adolphe Ferrière to Bernhard Nater, Siders, 20 April 1933. Nater was a Swiss *Mitarbeiter* at the Odenwaldschule. Geheeb and Ferrière occasionally communicated through him, apparently believing that the police would be less likely to read his mail than Geheeb's.

19. Geheeb's description of the interview is in the *Briefe*, pp. 155–156. "I have been able to convince myself that Dr. Blank is very much trying to understand my school and to select the new *Mitarbeiter* according to pedagogical and not political critieria."

20. Geno Hartlaub, "Ein Kamerad zur neuen Situation," in *DNW*, vol. 7, nos. 7–8, July–August 1933, p. 71; interview with Geno Hartlaub, Hamburg, 20 August 1985.

21. Geheeb-Schäfer interview, p. 34; Geheeb, *Briefe*, p. 156.

22. Dankwart Rustow and Clewie Kroeker, in "Uebergänge," p. 13 and p. 50; Sonja Neumann, "Erinnerungen an die OSO," *OSO-Hefte*, vol. 11, 1986, p. 215. The description of the new teachers as "Nazi teachers" should be read advisedly, since it is not clear how much the new teachers were truly loyal to the regime and how much they were merely willing to gain personal advantage from the new jobs which the regime created for them by purging alleged opponents of Nazism. Whatever their initial orientations, however, once the new teachers were in the Odenwaldschule they played a major role in escalating the regime's control and transformation of the school. On the level of conduct, then, one need have no hesitations about referring to them in general as "Nazi teachers."

23. Lore Fry and Clewie Kroeker in "Uebergänge," p. 50; Hartlaub, pp. 70–71.

24. "Protokoll der 6 Juni 1933 Konferenz," unpub. transcript of faculty meeting, EDH. The faculty meetings in the summer and fall of 1933 were stenographed, typed, signed by three faculty members, and mailed to the Ministry of Culture.

25. Karl Gleiser, "Die Stellung der neuen Mitarbeiter zur Odenwaldschule," *DNW*, vol. 7, nos. 7–8, July–August 1933, p. 70.

26. Paul Geheeb to Eduard Spranger, Les Pléiades, 9 August 1933, pp. 4–6, EDH.

27. Paul Geheeb to Martin Wagenschein, Oberhambach, 22 June 1933, EDH.

6. Emigration or Internal Migration? July–August, 1933

1. Geheeb to Spranger, 9 August 1933, p. 5; Geheeb quoted Blank from memory, Geheeb-Schäfer interview, p. 34.

2. Geheeb to Spranger, p. 5.
3. Geheeb quoted Blank and the *Kameraden* from memory, Geheeb-Schäfer interview, pp. 35–36.
4. Paul Geheeb to Peter Petersen, Les Pléiades, 18 August 1933, EDH.
5. Andreas Hohlfeld, "Der politische Ort des Landerziehungsheimes und die völkische Bewegung," *Volk im Werden*, vol. 1, no. 1, 1933, pp. 40–44.
6. On the role of ordinary citizens' denunciations in persecuting opponents of the regime and consolidating National Socialism, see Martin Broszat, "Politische Denunziationen in der NS-Zeit," *Archivalische Zeitschrift*, vol. 73, 1977, pp. 221–238, and Robert Gellately, "The Gestapo and German Society: Political Denunciation in the Gestapo Case Files," *Journal of Modern History*, vol. 60, no. 4, December 1988, pp. 654–694.
7. Paul Geheeb to Philipp Harth, Les Pléiades, n.d. (circa August 1933); Paul Geheeb to Philipp Harth, Les Pléiades, 19 August 1933, EDH.
8. Paul Geheeb to Edith Geheeb, Les Pléiades, 4 August 1933 and 15 August 1933, EDH. Edith Geheeb was vacationing in Saas-Fee in Canton Vallis in Switzerland in August, which meant that this correspondence from her husband escaped the fear of police control which would have inhibited their communication had she been in Germany.
9. Geheeb visited Ferrière in Les Pléiades at the beginning of August. Ferrière was deaf, and to communicate with him Geheeb wrote down his half of their conversations. These notes have survived in the Archives of the Ecole d'Humanité and will be referred to here as "Geheeb-Ferrière conversation." The date for this quote is 2 August 1933.
10. Geheeb-Ferrière conversation, 2 August 1933.
11. Paul Geheeb, "Höhepünkte des Lebens," *DNW*, vol. 2, nos. 7–8, August–September 1928, p. 80.
12. Geheeb, *Briefe,* p. 169.
13. Paul Geheeb to Herman Kobbé, Les Pléiades, 20 August 1933, EDH.
14. Paul Geheeb to Edith Geheeb, Les Pléiades, 7 August 1933, p. 3, EDH.
15. Geheeb, *Briefe,* pp. 161–163.
16. Max Cassirer to Paul Geheeb, Karlsbad (Czechoslovakia), 8 August 1933, p. 1, EDH; Paul Geheeb to Adolphe Ferrière, Les Pléiades, 11 August 1933, EDH.
17. Eduard Spranger to Paul Geheeb, Berlin, 12 August 1933, EDH. On Spranger's response to the Nazi takeover, see his "März 1933," *Die Erziehung*, vol. 8, no. 7, April 1933, and "Mein Konflikt mit der nationalsozialistischen Regierung 1933," *Universitas: Zeitschrift für Wissenschaft, Kunst und Literatur*, vol. 10, no. 5, 1955, pp. 457–473. For commentaries, see Gallin, *Midwives to Nazism*, pp. 97–98; Ringer, *Mandarins*, p. 439; and Adalbert Rang, "Reaktionen auf den Nationalsozialismus in der Zeitschrift 'Die Erziehung' im Frühjahr 1933," in Hans-Uwe Otto and Heinz Sünker, eds., *Soziale Arbeit und Faschismus* (Bielefeld: Kritische Texte, 1986), pp. 35–54; Uwe Henning and Achim Leschinsky, "'Widerstand im Detail': Eduard Sprangers Rücktrittsaktion vom Frühsommer 1933 im Spiegel bürgerlicher Presseberichte," *Zeitschrift für Pädagogik*, vol. 36, no.

4, July 1990, pp. 551–572; Heinz-Elmar Tenorth, "Eduard Sprangers hochschulpolitischer Konflikt 1933—Politisches Handeln eines Preussischen Gelehrten," ibid., pp. 573–596.

18. Philipp Harth to Paul Geheeb, Cologne, n.d., EDH. Regretfully, an exhaustive archival search did not produce a copy of the alleged denunciation by Hohlfeld or Krieck.

19. Peter Petersen to Paul Geheeb, Jena, 4 January 1934, EDH.

20. Werner Meyer to Paul Geheeb, Amsterdam, 12 August 1933, EDH.

21. Paul Geheeb to Adolphe Ferrière, en route from Stuttgart to Bensheim, 29 August 1933, and en route from Romanshorn to Lindau, 27 August 1933, EDH.

7. The New Faculty's Reforms: September–October, 1933

1. Paul Geheeb to Wilhelm Frick, Reich Minister of the Interior, Oberhambach, 2 September 1933, EDH.

2. Martin Broszat, *The Hitler State: The Foundation and Development of the Internal Structure of the Third Reich* (London and New York: Longman, 1981), p. 347.

3. "Protokoll der 1 September 1933 Konferenz," unpub. transcript of faculty meeting, EDH.

4. Hermann Lamby, "Hitler-Jugend in der Odenwaldschule," *DNW*, vol. 7, nos. 11–12, November–December 1933, p. 116. The editors of *DNW*, "Chronik," ibid., p. 113.

5. Paul Geheeb to Rudolf Blank, Oberhambach, 26 April 1933, EDH.

6. "Protokoll der 1 September 1933 Konferenz, unpub. transcript of faculty meeting, EDH."

7. "Protokoll der 15 September 1933 Konferenz," unpub. transcript of faculty meeting, EDH.

8. The editors of *DNW*, "Chronik," p. 114.

9. Neumann, "Erinnerungen an die OSO," p. 215; Geheeb-Ferrière conversation, 23 December 1933.

10. Paul Geheeb to Dr. Fritz Künkel, Oberhambach, 16 October 1933, pp. 1–2, EDH.

11. Der Elternbeirat der Odenwaldschule, "Stellungsnahme des Elternbeirats der Odenwaldschule zu deren gegenwärtiger Situation," n.d., unpub. ms., EDH.

12. Alfred Andreesen to Paul Geheeb, Schloss Bieberstein (Fulda), 10 May 1933, EDH; Geheeb, *Briefe*, p. 141; Paul Geheeb to Edith Geheeb, n.p., 24 May 1933, EDH. See the special issue of the Lietz school journal *Leben und Arbeit* on the Hitler Youth meeting at Haubinda, vol. 26, no. 3, 1933–34.

13. The meeting is reported on in the "Sonderdruck der Innengemeinde zur Gründungsfeier der Reichsfachschaft," a publication of the Landschulheim am Solling, September 1933.

14. Geheeb-Ferrière conversation, 23 December 1933.

15. Notes by Armin Lüthi from a conversation with Edith Geheeb, Goldern, 25 August 1966, EDH.
16. See the application from Goerendt to the "Hilfskasse der NSDAP," Gelnhausen, 21 August 1939, BDC.

8. Confrontation in the Conference: November–December, 1933

1. "Protokoll der 27 November 1933 Konferenz," unpub. transcript of faculty meeting, EDH. The transcript is heavily edited to enhance the narrative.
2. Geheeb-Ferrière conversation, 3 April 1934. The use of "Heil Hitler!" as a greeting had become compulsory for most civil servants in the course of the summer. See the "Einführung des Hitler-Grüsse," *Zentralblatt für die gesamte Unterrichts-Verwaltung in Preussen*, vol. 75, no. 5, 5 August 1933, pp. 203–204.
3. Max Cassirer to Paul Geheeb, Berlin, 17 April 1934; Philipp Wilhelm Jung, for the Hessian State Ministry, to Max Cassirer, Darmstadt, 27 November 1933, EDH.
4. On the civil service, see Jane Caplan, *Government without Administration: State and Civil Service in Weimar and Nazi Germany* (New York: Oxford University Press, 1988), pp. 131–152.
5. Max Cassirer to Edith Geheeb, Berlin, 15 December 1933, EDH.
6. Paul Geheeb to Werner Meyer, Oberhambach, 20 December 1933, OSO.
7. Geheeb-Ferrière conversation, 23 December 1933.

9. The Splintering of the School: January–March, 1934

1. Max Cassirer to Reinhold Geheeb, Berlin, 2 January 1934, EDH.
2. Max Cassirer to Werner Meyer, Berlin, 6 January 1934; Max Cassirer to Edith Geheeb, Berlin, 6 January 1934; Max Cassirer to Edith Geheeb, Berlin, 13 January 1934, EDH.
3. Interview with Marina Jakimow, Wallersdorf, 31 January 1986; Edith Geheeb to Paul Geheeb, Oberhambach, 16 January 1934, EDH.
4. Paul Geheeb to Edith Geheeb, Berlin, 18 January 1934, EDH.
5. An archival search for information on Niessen's deliberations on the Odenwaldschule case was fruitless. Searches were conducted in the Bundesarchiv at Koblenz, the Berlin Document Center, the Geheimes Preussisches Staatsarchiv in Berlin, the Hessisches Staatsarchiv at Darmstadt, the Institut für Zeitgeschichte in Munich and the Bundesarchive in Potsdam and Merseburg while they were still under the supervision of the German Democratic Republic. The extensive files on Nazis discovered in East Berlin in May 1991 were found too late for integration into this research.
6. Adolf Messer-Bicker to Max Cassirer, Frankfurt, 28 January 1934; Adolf Messer-Bicker to Max Cassirer, Frankfurt, 29 January 1934, EDH.

7. Max Cassirer to Edith Geheeb, Berlin, 12 February 1934, EDH.
8. Quote from Alwine von Keller, "Eindrücke aus der Ecole d'Humanité," in Cassirer et al., *Die Idee einer Schule*, p. 107.
9. Elisabeth Sachs to Dennis Shirley, Ringwood, Britain, 14 November 1985.
10. Geheeb, *Briefe*, p. 170; Geheeb-Ferrière conversation, 3 April 1934, EDH.
11. Quote from Marina Jakimow, Wallersdorf, 24 January 1986; enrollment figures taken from Geheeb-Schäfer interview, p. 38, and the editors of *DNW*, "An unsere Freunde und Abonnenten!" *DNW*, January–March 1934, p. 1.
12. Geheeb, "Grundlagen," p. 158; Adolf Messer-Bicker, "Ansprache des Führers der Gemeinschaft der Odenwaldschule bei der Gründungs-versammlung am 17.3.34," unpub. ms., OSO.
13. Geheeb-Ferrière conversation, 3 April 1934.
14. Geheeb-Schäfer interview, p. 37; Paul Geheeb to Adolphe Ferrière, Oberhambach, 25 March 1934, EDH.

10. The Ecole d'Humanité, 1934–1945

1. Controversies regarding the dominance of the French or German lan-guage began even before the Geheebs left Oberhambach. See Geheeb's *Briefe*, pp. 174–180.
2. Geheeb-Ferrière conversation, 4 April 1934; Paul Geheeb, "Ansprache von Paul Geheeb an seine Mitarbeiter und Zöglinge anlässlich der Auf-nahme seiner erzieherischen Arbeit in Versoix am 17. April 1934," *Schweizerische Erziehungsrundschau*, vol. 7, June 1934, pp. 69–70.
3. Paul Geheeb, "Idee einer 'Schule der Menscheit,'" in Cassirer et al., *Die Idee einer Schule*, p. 102.
4. Ibid., pp. 102–106.
5. Group discussion, Dennis Shirley with twenty-four *Mitarbeiter* and alumni from the Institut Monnier, Goldern, 11 November 1985, tape recorded.
6. Max Cassirer to Paul Geheeb, Berlin, 17 April 1934, EDH.
7. Dr. Krauel to the Foreign Office (Auswärtige Amt), Geneva, 29 June 1934, HSAD.
8. Geheeb-Ferrière conversation, 13 and 14 January 1935.
9. Paul Geheeb to Adolphe Ferrière, Pont-Céard, 15 February 1935, EDH; Theda O. Henle, "Paul Geheeb—Versoix 1935," in Cassirer et al., *Erzie-hung zur Humanität*, pp. 30–31.
10. Huguenin, *Odenwaldschule*.
11. On Geheeb's choice and interpretation of this name for the school, see his *Briefe*, pp. 54–55; Max Cassirer to Paul Geheeb, Berlin, 29 December 1936, EDH.
12. Edith quoted from memory by Esra Steinitz to Dennis Shirley, 1 January 1986. Paul Geheeb described the Association as a "band of criminals" and an "enemy of culture." Paul Geheeb to Adolphe Ferrière, Fionnay sur Martigny, 30 July 1937, EDH.

13. Max Cassirer to Paul Geheeb, Berlin, 30 June 1937, EDH.
14. See Adolphe Ferrière, "A l'Ecole d'Humanité," *L'Essor,* 29 October 1937, p. 3. Ferrière used the address to define the two meanings of "humanité" in French. The first meaning is that of the human race, and the second is that of compassion. Part of Ferrière's messianic address appealed to students "to prepare the humanity of tomorrow, in which the social structure will be based on scientific techniques and the well-being of the community of nations, with neither impoverished proletarians nor victims of the unjust actions of the powerful, and where nations will sign legal and economic treaties which will be respected with neither one-sided renegations nor exploited and victimized peoples." Quote on Trouchet from Adolphe Ferrière to Paul Geheeb, La Sallaz, 26 October 1937, EDH.
15. Geheeb-Ferrière conversation, 20 December 1938.
16. Geheeb, *Briefe,* pp. 184–185; Paul Geheeb reports on anti-Semitic criticisms of the Ecole in a letter to André Golay, Les Pléiades, 4 March 1939, EDH.
17. Paul Geheeb to Adolphe Ferrière, Schloss Greng, 9 October 1939, EDH; for the quote from Spranger, see Eduard Spranger, *Briefe, 1901–1963,* vol. 7 of his *Gesammelte Schriften,* Hans Walter Bähr, ed. (Tübingen: Max Niemeyer Verlag, 1978), p. 190.
18. Interview with Wolfgang Haas, Goldern, 24 November 1985; Paul Geheeb to Adolphe Ferrière, Schwarzsee, 29 June 1940, EDH.
19. Geheeb, *Briefe,* pp. 185–186; Paul Geheeb to Adolphe Ferrière, Schwarzsee, 13 July 1940, EDH.
20. Paul Geheeb to Adolphe Ferrière, Schwarzsee, 12 August 1940, EDH; Adolphe Ferrière to Paul Geheeb, Geneva, 22 August 1940, EDH.
21. Büchinger for the Geheime Staatspolizei (Gestapo) to the Reichssicherheitsamt in Berlin, Darmstadt, 2 May 1941 L. R. Rodemacher of the Reich Ministry of the Interior approved the expatriation on 2 July 1941. From files in the Political Archives of the Foreign Office, Department Inland A/B, volume 224/1, nos. 76–83, Bonn; Paul Geheeb to Adolphe Ferrière, Schwarzsee, 27 January 1943, EDH.
22. Alwine von Keller, "Eindrücke aus der Ecole d'Humanité," in Cassirer et al., *Die Idee einer Schule,* p. 109; Edith Geheeb to Kurt Cassirer, Schwarzsee, 12 June 1943, OSO.
23. Sabine Löwy to "Rosalind," Schwarzsee, 18 November 1943, EDH. The letter was written in English and is printed here without grammatical corrections to convey its original tone.
24. von Keller, "Eindrücke," pp. 108–109.
25. Klaus Mann, "Portrait of a Pedagogue," *Tomorrow,* vol. 7, no. 1, September 1947, p. 37; the anecdote on the cherry pits was related in a discussion with Armin Lüthi, Goldern, 5 November 1986.

11. The Gemeinschaft der Odenwaldschule, 1933–1945

1. Friedburg Lorenz, in "Uebergänge," pp. 49–50.
2. Maria Funk-Rüstow, "Meine guten OSO-Jahre," *OSO-Hefte,* vol. 10, 1986,

p. 217; Dankwart Rüstow, "Die Verwandlung der alten Schule," in Cassirer et al., *Die Idee einer Schule,* pp. 100–102, quote from p. 101; Clewie Kroeker, "Podiumsdiskussion," pp. 45–47. The Rüstows' recollections are particularly interesting because of the political background of their family. Their father, Alexander Rüstow, was a high Social Democratic official in the Ministry of Finance of the late Weimar Republic. Their mother had a strong communist and pacifist orientation, and experienced difficulties at the University of Heidelberg during the First World War because of her convictions. She decided that she must leave Heidelberg, and she moved to the Odenwaldschule, where Geheeb gave her a position as a "helping guest" before she traveled to Berlin, participated in the revolutionary postwar events, and met her future husband. After suffering harrassment from the Nazis in the spring of 1933 Alexander Rüstow decided to emigrate to Turkey, but he wanted his children to continue to receive their education in Germany. Believing that the Geheebs' Odenwaldschule would provide a safe haven for the children, he sent Dankwart and Maria Rüstow to the school in April 1933, after Ringshausen's purge of the old faculty. When the Geheebs emigrated, Alexander Rüstow decided that his children should continue in the new Gemeinschaft der Odenwaldschule.

3. Interview with Hedwig and Alexander Schlimmer, Darmstadt, 20 September 1985; Heinrich Sachs to the Landesverkehrsverband in Breslau, Oberhambach, 22 December 1936, OSO.
4. Funk-Rüstow, "OSO-Jahren," p. 217; telephone interview with Hanno Klassen, 15 January 1990.
5. n.a., "Gemeinschaft der Odenwaldschule" (Oberhambach: Druckerei der Gemeinschaft der Odenwaldschule, 1936).
6. Telephone interview with Thomas Cassirer, 31 May 1989.
7. The author's name is illegible. The report is written on the stationery of the Hessian Regional Office, or *Kreisamt,* in Heppenheim, with the title "Betreffend Anna Carstens Stiftung der Odenwaldschule," Heppenheim, 22 May 1934, Hessisches Staatsarchiv at Darmstadt (henceforth, HSAD).
8. For Sachs's individualistic approach to education see his "Vom Leben und Bilden einiger Kinder," unpub. ms., 1925, OSO, partially printed in *OSO-Hefte,* vol. 9, 1985, pp. 43–54; Marina Jakimow to Dennis Shirley, Wallersdorf, 11 February 1986; Geheeb, *Briefe,* p. 162. "My husband gave himself the name of Erasmus and I also used it, because I felt the essence of my husband more therein than in Heinrich. And then everyone called him Erasmus." Elisabeth Sachs to Dennis Shirley, Ringwood, 14 November 1985.
9. Heinrich Sachs to Paul Geheeb, Oberhambach, 17 November 1934 and 3 March 1936, EDH.
10. Paul Geheeb to Werner Meyer, Pont-Céard, 12 April 1935, OSO; Werner Meyer to Paul Geheeb, Oberhambach, 25 December 1935, EDH.
11. Dr. Walter Mann, untitled, unpub. ms., Oberhambach, 21 February 1938, OSO.

12. Quote from Bernhard Rust, "An die Unterrichtsverwaltungen der Länder" (form letter), Berlin, 4 April 1936, OSO. Sachs's letter is from Oberhambach, 25 May 1936, OSO. The letter of approval is from Hans Leip of the Hessian Ministry of Culture, Auerbach, 20 December 1936, OSO. On Sachs's delicate negotiations with the authorities, see Hans Leip to Paul Geheeb, Bensheim, 26 September 1951, EDH.
13. Viktor Dahm and Hedi Schlimmer, "Podiumsdiskussion," pp. 52–53.
14. Dankwart Rüstow, "Erinnerungen an die Odenwaldschule, 1933–1939," *OSO-Hefte*, vol. 8, 1984, p. 34; Ingeborg Helm to Dennis Shirley, Marburg, 11 April 1986.
15. The student population numbers given here are taken from the "Erhebungsbogen zur Statistik der höheren Lehranstalten" for the "Schuljahr 1933/1934 und Stand vom 15. Mai 1934"; from the "Fragebogen für höheren Schulen," dated 15 May for 1935 and 1936, 25 May for 1937 to 1940, and 15 October for 1941 and 1942; and from the "Statistik der höheren Lehranstalten," dated 15 October for 1943 and 1944. All documents are from the file on "Behörden, S-Z, 1934–1946" in the school records of the Odenwaldschule in Paul Geheeb Haus.
16. There is a major difference between definitions of Jewry in the historical data from the Odenwaldschule and in that from the Gemeinschaft der Odenwaldschule. In the first case, Jewry is a religious confession; in the second, it is a race. According to the documents, the new school never enrolled more than four Jewish students in any given year. The decline in Jewish enrollment was simply one small reflection of the gradual exclusion of Jews from schools in the Third Reich. From 1933 to 1937, Jews were subject to numerous petty harrassments and restricted from participating in school events, but their legal access to schooling remained codified. Following Crystal Night in November 1938, Jews were forbidden to attend public schools with Aryans. In April 1941 private instruction to Jews was forbidden, and in June 1942 all Jewish schools were closed. On Nazi educational policy and the Jews, see Eilers, *Schulpolitik*, pp. 98–103.
17. Funk-Rüstow, "OSO-Jahren," p. 219; Traute Probst to Rose Schröder, Oberhambach, 2 May 1940, OSO; Heinrich Sachs to Karl and Fritz Weiss, Oberhambach, 6 March 1943, OSO.
18. Girls made up roughly thirty-six percent of the student body in the Geheebs' Odenwaldschule and thirty-three percent in the Gemeinschaft der Odenwaldschule. These figures were compiled by adding all of the male and female students recorded for Geheeb's school from 1910 to 1925 and Sachs's school from 1934 to 1944 and taking the average percent of girls. The fluctuation of male and female enrollments in the Gemeinschaft der Odenwaldschule bears no relationship to the increasing regimentation of society in the Third Reich and varied considerably on a yearly basis. On coeducation in this period in general, see Stephenson, *Women in Nazi Society*, pp. 116–129.
19. For examples of Meyer's appropriation of Nazi rituals, see Joachim Boeckh, *Chronik der Odenwaldschule, 18 Januar 1938–20 April 1943*, unpub. ms., OSO; and Rüstow, "Erinnerungen," p. 36. On the changes

in the course system, see the unpub. mss., Heinrich Sachs, "Mitteilung der Odenwaldschule," 20 December 1939; and Werner Schmitz, circulatory letter, Oberhambach, July 1942, reprinted in *OSO-Hefte*, vol. 9, 1985, p. 60; quote from Rüstow, "Die Verwandlung der alten Schule," p. 102. According to Schäfer, Sachs stalled the construction of the shooting range so that it never was completed. See his *Odenwaldschule*, p. 52.

20. n.a., "Die Odenwaldschule" (Oberhambach: Druckerei-Werkstatt der Odenwaldschule, 1939).

21. The correspondence between Sachs and Meyer during the war is preserved in the Archives of the Odenwaldschule. Materials on Wickersdorf in the Third Reich are located in Wyneken's files in the Archives of the German Youth Movement.

22. On Cassirer's expatriation, see the unsigned letter from the Gestapo in Darmstadt to the Reichsstatthalter in Hesse, Landesregierung, Abteilung 7, 6 October 1941, OSO. On the prospect of nationalization, see Schmitz, circulatory letter, p. 60; Heinrich Sachs, in *Der Lindenstein*, no. 4, July 1944, p. 2, OSO; Heinrich Sachs, circulatory letter to parents, Oberhambach, 25 July 1944, OSO. For background information on Heissmeyer, see Eilers, *Schulpolitik*, pp. 92–98. Much interesting material on *Landerziehungsheime* was collected by Otto Seydel of the Pädagogische Arbeitsstelle der Vereinigung Deutscher Landerziehungsheime for a conference on "*Landerziehungsheime* under National Socialism" held in the Odenwaldschule from 27 February to 2 March 1986 and photocopied in a collection entitled "Materialen für die von der Pädagogischen Arbeitsstelle der Vereinigung Deutscher Landerziehungsheime veranstalteten Tagung mit dem Thema 'Geschichte der Landerziehungsheime.'" This material is currently being reworked for publication.

23. Heinrich Sachs to the Reichsstatthalter in Hesse, Landesregierung, Abteilung 7, Oberhambach, 27 October 1944, OSO; Dr. Malzan to Heinrich Sachs, Bensheim, 30 October 1944; Marina Jakimow, untitled article, *Der Lindenstein*, no. 5, 28 December 1944.

24. Interview with Marina Jakimow, Wallersdorf, 31 January 1986.

25. Marina Jakimow, "Odenwaldschule 1945," in Cassirer et al., *Die Idee einer Schule*, p. 111.

12. Postwar Developments and Geheeb's Legacy

1. Elisabeth and Heinrich Sachs to Paul Geheeb, Oberhambach, 4 February 1946; Elisabeth and Heinrich Sachs to Paul and Edith Geheeb, Oberhambach, 1 August 1945, OSO.

2. Edith Geheeb to Kurt and Eva Cassirer, Schwarzsee, 21 August 1945, EDH.

3. Thomas Mann, Harry J. Carman, and Truda T. Weil to Eugene Anderson, 29 August 1945, EDH.

4. Heinrich Sachs to Paul Geheeb, Oberhambach, 16 September 1945, EDH; Paul Geheeb, "Ein Dank," *Neue Zürcher Zeitung*, 7 July 1946.

5. Minna Specht, *Gesinnungswandel* (Welwyn Garden City, Herts, England: Renaissance, 1943).
6. Klaus Fuchs-Kittowski is identified only as "ein weiterer Gesprächsteilnehmer" in the "Podiumsdiskussion," p. 40; Marina Jakimow to Paul and Edith Geheeb, Heidelberg, 10 January 1946, EDH. On denazification, see James F. Trent, *Mission on the Rhine* (Chicago: University of Chicago Press, 1982), pp. 50–57.
7. Fuchs, *Mein Leben*, vol. 2, pp. 217–268. Heinrich Sachs gathered letters of support in a dossier entitled "Rechtfertigung." See the letters therein from Emil Fuchs, Frankfurt, 13 April 1946; Rudi Vogel, Redwitz, 28 February 1946; Philipp Harth, Offenhausen, 26 February 1946; Herr Schwedes (first name illegible), Marburg, 22 February 1946, all unpub. mss., OSO; Liselotte Vogel, "Podiumsdiskussion," p. 65.
8. Eduard Zuckmayer, Ankara, Turkey, 30 August 1946; Lilli Feit, Hersfeld, 17 February 1946; Käte Lidemann, Osthavelland, 16 March 1946; Konstantin Balaszeskul, Berlin, 2 January 1946, all in Sachs's "Rechtfertigung," OSO; Michael Balaszeskul, in "Uebergänge," pp. 53–54.
9. Ewa Liesegang, "Alte Kameraden versuchen zu helfen," in Cassirer et al., *Die Idee einer Schule*, p. 114; interview with Marina Jakimow, 26 January 1986, Wallersdorf.
10. Elisabeth and Heinrich Sachs to Paul Geheeb, Oberhambach, 4 February 1946, EDH; Edith Geheeb, "Aus meinem Leben," pp. 34–36.
11. "Humanity School," *Life*, vol. 20, no. 18, 6 May 1946, pp. 51–54.
12. Paul Geheeb to Heinrich Sachs, Goldern, 20 August 1946, EDH.
13. Interview with Marina Jakimow, 26 January 1986, Wallersdorf. The tensions among alumni and old *Mitarbeiter* were most clearly expressed in a special workshop on the history of the Odenwaldschule at its seventy-fifth anniversary in 1985. For a transcript, see "Uebergänge," pp. 44–96.
14. Werner Meyer to Paul Geheeb, Altenbürg (Thuringia), 1 October 1947, EDH; Dankwart Rüstow, "Podiumsdiskussion," pp. 9–10.
15. Minna Specht, "Bericht," p. 69.
16. Peter Conradi in "Uebergänge," p. 23; interview with Wolfgang Edelstein, Berlin, 4 October 1985; interview with Ernest Jouhy, Bad Soden, 12 August 1985; Klaus Fuchs-Kittowski, identified only as "ein weiterer Gesprächsteilnehmer," "Podiumsdiskussion," p. 41.
17. Trude Emmerich, "Feier des achtzigsten Geburtstags Paul Geheebs und des vierzigjährigen Bestehens der Odenwaldschule, 26–29 Juli 1950: Bericht über die offiziellen Festtage für alle unsere Freunde," *OSO-Hefte*, vol. 10, 1986, pp. 69–77.
18. A. S. Neill quoted in *Erziehung zur Humanität*, p. 12; on Zoe Neill in the Ecole d'Humanité, see Jonathan Croall, *Neill of Summerhill* (New York: Pantheon, 1983), pp. 309–312.

Conclusion

1. Hannah Arendt presented the classic formulation of totalitarianism in her *Origins of Totalitarianism* (New York: Harcourt, Brace, Jovanovich,

1973); for examples of polycratic interpretations, see Kershaw, *Popular Opinion;* Peukert, *Inside Nazi Germany;* Broszat et al., *Bayern in der NS-Zeit.*

2. Kershaw, *Popular Opinion,* pp. 143–148; Broszat et al., *Bayern in der NS-Zeit,* vol. 1, pp. 528–529; Jarausch, *Unfree Professions,* pp. 102–107, 164–165, 255.

3. Richard Bessel, "Political Violence and the Nazi Seizure of Power," in Bessel, ed., *Life in the Third Reich,* pp. 1–16, quote from p. 5.

4. Heinz-Elmar Tenorth, "Deutsche Erziehungswissenschaft 1930 bis 1945," *Zeitschrift für Pädagogik,* vol. 32, no. 3, June 1986, pp. 299–321; Wolfgang Keim, "Einführung," in Keim, ed., *Pädagogen und Pädagogik,* pp. 7–14; Geheeb, *Briefe,* pp. 128–131; Nohl, *Die pädagogische Bewegung,* p. 1. There were, of course, major differences in the Nazi synchronization of Nohl's Pedagogical Institute at the University of Göttingen and in the Odenwaldschule. For a recent review of primary sources and secondary interpretations of Nohl's conduct, see Erwin Ratzke, "Das Pädagogische Institut der Universität Göttingen. Ein Überblick über seine Entwicklung in den Jahren 1923–1949," in Heinrich Becker, Hans-Joachim Dahms, and Cornelia Wegeler, eds., *Die Universität Göttingen unter dem Nationalsozialismus: Das verdrängte Kapitel ihrer 250 jährigen Geschichte* (Munich: K. G. Sauer, 1987), pp. 200–218.

5. For the forms of opposition in these other schools, see the relevant passages in Feidel-Merz, *Schulen im Exil;* Hochmuth and de Lorent, eds., *Hamburg: Schule unterm Hakenkreuz;* Arbeitsgruppe Pädagogische Museum, eds., *Heil Hitler, Herr Lehrer;* Köhler, *Die Volksschule Harsum;* van Dick, *Oppositionelles Lehrerverhalten.*

6. On the *Sonderweg* thesis, see David Blackbourn and Geoff Eley, *The Peculiarities of German History* (New York: Oxford University Press, 1984); on "illiberalism," see Konrad H. Jarausch, "Illiberalism and Beyond: German History in Search of a Paradigm," *Journal of Modern History,* vol. 55, no. 2, June 1983, pp. 268–284; on foreign analogues to the German youth movement, see John R. Gillis, "Conformity and Rebellion: Contrasting Styles of English and German Youth, 1900–1933," *History of Education Quarterly,* vol. 13, no. 3, Fall 1973, pp. 249–260; on the influence of Rousseau and Pestalozzi on the idealists, see Paulsen, *Geschichte des Gelehrten Unterrichts,* vol. 2, pp. 191–194, Flitner, *Goethes Pädagogische Ideen,* pp. 127–132, and Hugh Pollard, *Pioneers of Popular Education* (Cambridge: Harvard University Press, 1957), pp. 12–51; on the "German movement," see Nohl, *Die pädagogische Bewegung,* pp. 15–16.

7. Ward, *Reddie,* pp. 111–138.

8. Feidel-Merz, *Schulen im Exil,* pp. 70–103, 107–148.

9. See *Leben und Arbeit,* vol. 26, no. 3, 1933–34; Bohrer and Renner, "Historisch-kritische Untersuchung"; Gustav Wyneken, "Grundsätzliches aus dem Gedankengut der Schulgemeinde Wickersdorf" (n.p.: n.p., n.d.), which replaced the earlier "Grundsätze der freien Schulgemeinde Wickersdorf" (n.p.: n.p., n.d.), ADJ. A forthcoming anthology to be edited by Hartmut Alphei, Gerold Becker, and Otto Seydel will present brief histories of the different schools in the period of national socialism.

10. On Nelson and Lietz, see Minna Specht, "Gedächtnisrede auf Hermann Lietz," in Kutzer, ed., *Hermann Lietz,* pp. 121–134. Petersen's legacy is particularly complex. See Peter Kassner and Hans Scheuerl, "Peter Petersen, sein pädagogisches Denken und Handeln," *Zeitschrift für Pädagogik,* vol. 30, no. 5, October 1984, pp. 647–661; Peter Kassner, "Peter Petersen—die Negierung der Vernunft?" *Die Deutsche Schule,* vol. 81, no. 1, 1989, pp. 117–132; and Wolfgang Keim, "Peter Petersens Rolle im Nationalsozialismus und die bundesdeutsche Erziehungswissenschaft," *Ibid.,* pp. 133–145; Hans-Werner Johannsen, "Peter Peterson und der Nationalsozialismus," *Die Deutsche Schule,* vol. 81, no. 3, 1989, pp. 362–365; Ulrich Hermann, "Geschichtsdentung als Disziplinpolitik?," ibid., pp. 366–372; Wolfgang Keim, "Noch einmal: Worum es eigenlichgeht," ibid., pp. 373–376. The best comparisons of different "new education" movements to date have been presented by Jürgen Helmchen in "Die Internationalität der Reformpädagogik: Vom Schlagwort zur historisch-vergleichenden Forschung" (Oldenburg: Oldenburger Universitätsreden, 1987) and "Le Relacion du Bureau International de l'Education avec la Reformpädagogik," *Journal of International and Comparative Education,* vol. 9, March 1991, pp. 520–550.

11. For criticisms of the idealist legacy, see Mosse, *German Ideology,* pp. 8–10; Stern, *Cultural Despair,* pp. xxiii–xxx and 267–298; Kunert, *Reformpädagogik und Faschismus;* Schonig, *Irrationalismus;* Kupffer, *Der Faschismus und das Menschenbild,* pp. 124–155. Not one of these works examines individuals who used the idealist tradition in a politically progressive fashion.

Index